THE USE OF PRESIDENTIAL POWER

THE USE OF PRESIDENTIAL POWER
1789–1943

By

GEORGE FORT MILTON

1965
OCTAGON BOOKS, INC.
NEW YORK

Copyright 1944, by George Fort Milton

Reprinted 1965
by special arrangement with Little, Brown and Company (Inc.)

OCTAGON BOOKS, INC.
175 FIFTH AVENUE
NEW YORK, N. Y. 10010

353.03
M642m

LIBRARY OF CONGRESS CATALOG CARD NUMBER: 65-16778

Printed in U.S.A. by
NOBLE OFFSET PRINTERS, INC.
NEW YORK 3, N. Y.

For
HELEN

Introduction

The reader will wish to know how this book came to be written, and it is proper that he should, for books are seldom born by accident.

For some twenty years, I have tried to relate our American past to the present and future, because history is the best teacher in the school of experience, and have deemed the use of presidential power both important and interesting in the study.

Developments after Pearl Harbor have convinced me that, grave as have been war's impacts on our society and economy, the coming transition from war to peace will bring with it even more possibilities of national disaster. The tragic failures after Lincoln and Wilson are fire bells in the night.

Such consequences of lack of presidential leadership when the country is in high crisis led me to examine the office and powers of the President from George Washington's time to the present, in the hope that past performance might throw light on the emerging future. Never have I undertaken a more stimulating historical task. The faults of this volume arise neither from lack of importance in the theme nor from any scarcity of material bearing upon it. So far as I am aware at the moment, the book is free from errors of fact; yet personal experience assures me that this will soon be proved untrue. But I have sought to avoid them, and those that exist are not there by any deliberate design.

Any misconception in the generalizations are my own, and flow out of the picture I have come to have of the presidents as a major factor in our equation of national change.

As I read the record, since Washington took the oath there has been a continuing increase in the power of the President, growing out of the general readjustment of executive and legislative importance in governments in a world undergoing great functional change. But there has been no orderly growth of presidential power in this country — rather, an ebb and flow which often obscured the main current of increasing strength. Doubtless both characteristics will continue. What is important is that the history of the office is rich with examples of the way great leaders, confronted with great crises, can keep the nation whole.

Many have helped me in this book, and I am most grateful. The entire manuscript has been read critically by several in whose knowledge and judgment I have great confidence. My appreciation is due to Professors E. Pendleton Herring, of Harvard; Quincy Wright, of the University of Chicago; Hemphill M. Hosford, of the University of Arkansas; Judge Karl Greenhaw, of Fayetteville, Arkansas; Congressman Estes Kefauver, of Tennessee; and Mr. Roger L. Scaife, of Boston. Professor William F. Ogburn made pertinent suggestions on the influence of crises on presidential fame. Miss Jim Matthews, of Fayetteville, Arkansas, made useful suggestions on style. Great, too, is my debt to able scholars and men of affairs who aided on particular chapters. But for them, many errors of facts and faults of judgment would have gone uncorrected, while material of importance would have escaped my attention.

Professor Edward S. Corwin, of Princeton, made valuable criticism of the chapter on the Constitutional Convention, as did the late Dean Julian S. Waterman, of the School of Law, University of Arkansas. Burton A. Konkle, of Swarthmore, Pennsylvania, generously shared his knowledge of James Wilson's career and influence. The chapters on Washington and Jefferson benefited from the scrutiny of Dr. Arthur P. Whitaker, of the University of Pennsylvania. Samuel Flagg Bemis, the well-known diplomatic historian of Yale, and Dumas Malone read the Jefferson chapter critically. My research on Jackson and Van Buren was guided by Marquis

James, both through correspondence, and by his criticism of Chapters IV–V. Edward Eyre Hunt, of Washington, D. C. furnished useful suggestions.

Dr. James G. Randall, of the University of Illinois, the recognized authority on constitutional problems under Lincoln, read my two Lincoln chapters, and gave me invaluable support and suggestion. Professor Clarence E. Berdahl, of that same school, made useful criticisms, as did Professor Roy P. Basler, of the University of Arkansas. The Grover Cleveland chapter benefited from suggestions by Allan Nevins, that President's understanding biographer. Robert Lincoln O'Brien, Executive Clerk to Cleveland in the second term, illuminated many questions on Cleveland's personality and presidential action. Professor Austin Venable, of the University of Arkansas, made useful comment.

Mark Sullivan has been of assistance in my appraisal of Theodore Roosevelt, while James Grafton Rogers furnished some revealing recollections. Professor Charles E. Merriam, of the University of Chicago, and the late William Allen White, of the *Emporia Gazette,* helped to guide my judgment on Theodore Roosevelt, Woodrow Wilson, and Franklin D. Roosevelt.

In treating President Wilson, I am under obligation to Professor Lindsay Rogers, of Columbia University. Morris Llewellyn Cook, of Philadelphia, contributed some useful data on the early 1918 War Department reorganization. Louis Brownlow, of Chicago, and Huston Thompson furnished interesting reminiscences on the Common Council Club. Walter S. Rogers, of New York, told me important details of the President's 1913 approach to relations with Washington correspondents, and the origin and operation of the 1918 world-wide news-distributing organization. Barnet Nover made interesting suggestions concerning the treaty negotiation and fight.

The gathering of material for the three chapters on Franklin D. Roosevelt's Presidency, and the formation of opinion upon the kaleidoscope of these eleven years, have been aided by information, suggestion and points of view from many men. Homer S. Cummings gave me invaluable information and suggestion as to the bank holiday, Court fight and other episodes. Others who helped in the account of the present President include Will W. Alexander, Solon J. Buck, Will Clayton; the late Brigadier Vivian Dykes, of the British Military Mission; Clark Eichelberger, of New York; Harry Hawkins; Cordell Hull; Theodore Kreps; Ernest K. Lindley; Major William McChesney Martin; the late Marvin H. McIntyre; Archibald MacLeish; Eugene Meyer, Jr.; Samuel I. Rosenman; Harold D. Smith; Sumner Slichter; George W. Taylor; the late William Allen White, and Sumner Welles.

I am indebted to many for aid in procuring relevant books and literature, particularly Dr. Thomas P. Martin, of the Manuscript Division and Miss Florence Hellman, bibliographer of the Library of Congress; Mr. Karl Trever, Librarian, Miss Elizabeth Drewry and Miss Mary Christopher, of the National Archives; Miss Ruth Fine, of the Bureau of the Budget Library, Edwin A. Miller, Librarian of the University of Arkansas Library, and Miss Grace Upchurch and Miss Minnie Davidson, of the staff of that institution.

The manuscript itself was prepared chiefly by the attentive industry of Mrs. Henry Eyssell, III, of Fayetteville, Ark., final additions and revisions have been competently made by Mrs. Marie Hevenor of Arlington, Virginia, and Mrs. Pauline Rothfeld of Washington, D. C. To them I testify my appreciation of their thoughtful service. Mr. Joseph Greenbaum, of New York, has prepared the index with customary skill.

But for the thoughtful care with which Miss Helen Slentz has encouraged the writing and appraised the manuscript, it would never have made its way into print. To her belongs much of the credit for this volume.

GEORGE FORT MILTON

WASHINGTON, D. C.
January 8, 1944

Contents

Introduction — vii

I. Birth of the Presidency — 3
II. "First in Peace ..." — 23
III. Philosopher in Power — 50
IV. The People's Leader — 73
V. The Presidency at Low Ebb — 95
VI. Commander in Chief — 107
VII. Also Poet and Prophet — 123
VIII. White House under Fire — 137
IX. Trustee of All the People — 154
X. Direct Action in the White House — 173
XI. Spokesman of the People — 197
XII. But There Was No Peace — 224
XIII. Recovery by Proclamation — 251
XIV. Recessional — 273
XV. World Strategist — 288
XVI. Retrospect and Prospect — 311

Bibliographical Note — 323
Index — 329

The Constitution on the President

ARTICLE II

Section 1.

1. The executive Power shall be vested in a President of the United States of America. He shall hold his Office during the Term of four years, and together with the Vice-President, chosen for the same term, be elected as follows: . . . [A description of the electoral college method, later amended by Article XII.]

5. No person except a natural born Citizen, or a Citizen of the United States, at the time of the Adoption of this Constitution, shall be eligible to the Office of President; neither shall any Person be eligible to that Office who shall not have attained to the Age of thirty-five Years, and have been fourteen Years a Resident within the United States.

6. In Case of the Removal of the President from Office, or his Death, Resignation, or Inability to discharge the Powers and Duties of the said Office, the same shall devolve on the Vice President, and the Congress may by Law provide for the Case of Removal, Death, Resignation or Inability, both of the President and Vice President, declaring what Officer shall then act as President, and such Officer shall act accordingly, until the Disability be removed or a President shall be elected.

7. The President shall, at stated Times, receive for his Services, a Compensation, which shall neither be Increased nor diminished during the Period for which he shall have been elected, and he shall not receive within that Period any other Emolument from the United States or any of them.

8. Before he enter on the Execution of his Office, he shall take the following Oath or Affirmation: — "I do solemnly swear (or affirm) that I will faithfully execute the Office of President of the United States, and will, to the best of my Ability, preserve, protect and defend the Constitution of the United States."

Section 2.

1. The President shall be Commander in Chief of the Army and Navy of the United States, and of the Militia of the several States, when called into the actual Service of the United States; he may require the Opinion in writing, of the principal Officer in each of the executive Departments, upon any subject relating to the Duties of their respective Offices, and he shall have Power to Grant Reprieves and pardons against the United States except in Cases of Impeachment.

2. He shall have Power by and with the Advice and Consent of the Senate, to make Treaties, provided two-thirds of the Senators present

concur; and he shall nominate, and by and with the Advice and Consent of the Senate, shall appoint Ambassadors, other public Ministers and Consuls, Judges of the supreme Court, and all other Officers of the United States, whose Appointments are not herein otherwise provided for, and which shall be established by Law: but the Congress may by Law vest the Appointment of such inferior Officers, as they think proper, in the President alone, in the Courts of Law, or in the Heads of Departments.

3. The President shall have Power to fill up all Vacancies that may happen during the Recess of the Senate, by granting Commissions, which shall expire at the End of their next Session.

Section 3.

He shall from time to time give to the Congress Information on the State of the Union, and recommend to their Consideration such Measures as he shall judge necessary and expedient; he may, on extraordinary Occasions, convene both Houses, or either of them, and in Case of Disagreement between them, with Respect to the Time of Adjournment, he may adjourn them to such Time as he shall think proper; he shall receive Ambassadors and other public Ministers; he shall take Care that the Laws be faithfully executed, and shall Commission all the Officers of the United States.

Section 4.

The President, Vice President, and all civil Officers of the United States, shall be removed from Office on Impeachment for, and Conviction of, Treason, Bribery, or other high Crimes and Misdemeanors.

ARTICLE I

Section 7.

2. Every Bill which shall have passed the House of Representatives and the Senate, shall, before it becomes a Law, be presented to the President of the United States; If he approve he shall sign it, but if not he shall return it, with his Objections to that House in which it shall have originated, who shall enter the Objections at large on their Journal, and proceed to reconsider it. If after such Reconsideration two thirds of that House shall agree to pass the Bill, it shall be sent, together with the Objections, to the other House, by which it shall likewise be reconsidered; and if approved by two thirds of that House, it shall become a Law. . . . If any Bill shall not be returned by the President within ten Days (Sundays excepted) after it shall have been presented to him, the Same shall be a Law, in like Manner as if he had signed it, unless the Congress by their Adjournment prevent its Return, in which Case it shall not be a Law.

THE USE OF PRESIDENTIAL POWER

CHAPTER I

Birth of the Presidency

In the one hundred and fifty-five years since George Washington took the oath to "preserve, protect and defend the Constitution," the President of the United States of America has become the principal representative of the will of the people of the most powerful democracy in the world. It was not so in 1789, but Constitution, crisis, and custom, the great architects of our political institutions, have joined to confide immense power to the holder of that office.

This they have done, in the main, by imposing on him six types of public service, which he is expected to perform jointly and severally as the nation's Number One Man. As our Chief of State, and as such the embodiment of the people's elective will, the President is clad with the prerogative of the office, and possesses more actual sovereign power than any British king since George III. In his role as Chief of Foreign Relations, from the beginning he has been the sole organ of the nation in its external relations, and its sole representative with foreign nations. While the Senate must advise and consent to any treaty, the President has exclusive initiative in their negotiation.

As Commander in Chief of the Army and Navy of the United States, he has an almost untrammeled power in time of war, rebellion or other high crisis. General Washington, according to legend, had this duty embedded in the Constitution, and Lincoln found in it the new sources of executive strength required to save the Union.

The fourth role of Chief of Government reposes directly upon the President through his constitutional duty to "take care that the laws be faithfully executed." In consequence, he bears upon his shoulders the direct responsibility for the nation's enormous executive government.

In addition to these four major grants of power in the national charter, two further roles, both of an extra-constitutional character, have become inseparable from the person of the President. One is his position as Chief of Party. While parties were not in the Founding Fathers' scheme of general government, from 1800 the political party has provided the unofficial electoral college. The candidate's primary appeal to the voter is that he has become the chief of a great national party. If he is elected, the iron compulsion of facts compels him to employ the party's machinery to carry out its platform commitments and his own presidential aims. Even in times of national emergency Jefferson, Wilson and Franklin Roosevelt carried their programs forward as much through party leadership as through being Chief of State.

Finally, the President must lead public opinion. As Wilson said and showed, with the people the President is everything, without them nothing. To a much greater degree than we realize, ours is a government of public opinion, and we look to our chosen leader to sense our doubts, fears, hopes and aspirations and be the nation's spokesman.

Since 1789, thirty-two men have taken the presidential oath, and more than half held the office in time of war abroad, rebellion at home, political upheaval, or economic crisis. One can find certain common denominators among this group of strangely different men, but the analogies are often more apparent than real. Each of six, for example, was Commander in Chief in a major war — Madison, Polk, Lincoln, McKinley, Wilson, and Franklin Roosevelt. But it is difficult to discover a resemblance between Madison's miserable conduct of our worst-planned war and Polk's excellent direction of the campaigns against Mexico; or between Lincoln's fumbles in strategy and command until he found Grant and Sherman, and Franklin Roosevelt's veritable genius in planning combined operations in the planetary war. Four Presidents directed bloodless revolutions under the forms of law — but few men ever lived more different in spirit and manner than Jefferson and Jackson, or Wilson and Franklin Roosevelt.

The fact remains that the splendors and miseries of the office brought growth to almost every man who held it. Some underwent a great organic growth of character — as Lincoln changed from pettifogging Illinois politician to nation-saving statesman, while Grant and Harding sought to redeem their earlier mistakes. The very office, it would seem, widens the vision and deepens the devotion to duty of those who hold it.

In turn, men have built the Presidency. Each occupant left some impress upon the office. Some, like Coolidge, did not choose to make major use of powers but kept them in a napkin; some, like Buchanan, let them drain out until they were helpless, as he was in the matter of secession. But these were exceptions; many more built than slumbered or threw their powers away. Several asserted some particular power theretofore unused, and enlarged the scope and strengthened the foundations for the power and prestige of their successors.

In this volume, we propose to take a look at the way the chief among these men won their place and used their powers. The emergencies they confronted, how they discovered authority for action, and what these did to the institution of the Presidency will be our field. Our focus, in the main, will be not so much on constitutional debates or judicial opinions as upon the conduct of the men who developed the office: we can best study how they did so in the school of experience, with history in the chair.

In the beginning, the Constitutional Convention created the office of President of the United States of America. No trailing clouds of glory attended its entry upon the American scene; rather, doubts and misgivings among many of the Convention delegates — the physicians who attended its birth.

The place was Pennsylvania's State House in Philadelphia; the time September 17, 1787, when the delegates concluded their sessions of some sixteen weeks by adopting the Constitution for submission to the American States.

The Convention, it should be said, had not come together to debate ideal forms of government in abstract terms. Instead, it represented the determination of despair. The Colonies had won their Revolution, but independence was strong drink to them and led to a maudlin debauch of localism. Since the revolted States had signed the Articles of Confederation and Perpetual Union, confusion had grown worse confounded. Maryland and Virginia could not agree on common use of the Potomac River and Chesapeake Bay; Connecticut and New Jersey threatened New York with a commercial embargo; and Massachusetts had to suppress a civil war.

The Congress of the Confederation proved impotent to check this chaos. States neglected or rejected its drafts for proportionate contribution to general expense; its currency was worthless, the service of the foreign debt badly behind. Britain ignored her peace treaty obligations to withdraw frontier garrisons; Spain defied us at the Mississippi's mouth.

Congress lacked neither patriots nor statesmen, but it had no power, and persuasion had proved a rope of sand. Under the Articles of Confederation, not the people but the individual States were the high contracting parties, and the Articles could be amended only with the consent of all the States. The powers they confided to the Congress were explicitly described and jealously delimited. States sent delegates — virtually ambassadors — to the Congress, and votes were by States, not by individual delegates. The Congress annually elected a President, but he was no more than presiding officer. The executive power remained in the body of the Congress, which clung to the hope that a plural executive could function. "Departments" would be set up, to handle important fractions of continuing administrative concern, and to meet emergencies. But their Secretaries were not ministers, in the British sense, for they had no collective responsibility.

These faults were plain as pikestaffs. James Wilson, of Pennsylvania, saw in the disorder of the unfunded debt, the chaos of currency, the empty Treasury dependent for revenue on the unwilling and belated grants from the States, the principal disease of the new nation. In 1783 he proposed an amendment to give Congress a small financial power over the States. Congress submitted it with trepidation. By 1787, eleven States had agreed, but the refusal of two blocked the proposal.

Such instances of the hopelessness of attempting reform through the existing system stimulated James Madison, of Virginia, and other leaders in the commercial States to other lines of approach. In 1786 Virginia persuaded Maryland to join in an invitation to the other States to send commissioners to Annapolis, to concert uniform commercial regulations. Only five States responded, but Madison was there, as was young Alexander Hamilton, who had procured his own appointment on the New York delegation. All the group could do was to summon a new Convention, and Hamilton wrote the invitations for a gathering at Philadelphia on Monday, May 14, 1787. These went to the States; at the same time Congress was asked to join in the call.

Twelve State Legislatures formally chose delegates to the Convention, Rhode Island being the only abstainer. Of the sixty-five selected, all but ten attended some of the sessions. Twenty-nine had graduated from colleges in America or England, over half were lawyers, many had served in the Revolutionary Army, and there were eight signers of the Declaration of Independence.

These men varied in age and nature all the way from Alexander Hamilton — able, imperious and just turned thirty — to Benjamin Franklin, so frail in his early eighties that others must read his prepared speeches to the Convention. His amazing life had developed in him that intellectual humility which is one mark of greatness. "The older I grow," Franklin told his fellow delegates, "the more apt I am to doubt my own judgment, and to pay more respect to the judgment of others."

Weeks earlier, and by common consent, George Washington had been solicited to become president of the Convention. The delegates knew that, but for him, independence probably would not have been won; and that a new government could best be founded on the rock of his character. Now fifty-five and improved in health, he reached the City of Brotherly Love before the day appointed for the meeting. Others were tardy, and it was not until May 24 that a quorum of States was obtained. Franklin had asked permission to nominate General Washington, but was ill that day. Robert Morris did it on his behalf, and the election was unanimous.

A great many delegates affected the final Constitution, but only a few had major parts in the shaping of Article II, which vested the executive power in the President of the United States of America. Perhaps the most influential was James Wilson, whose amendment efforts have been remarked; others of great weight were Gouverneur Morris, Charles Pinckney, Alexander Hamilton, Roger Sherman, Edmund Randolph and James Madison.

Scottish by birth, son of a mathematical philosopher and student at three great universities, James Wilson brought with him to America in 1765 the belief that all power resides in the people, and that kings should be upheld only as long as they contribute to the people's good. He studied law under John Dickinson and then practised in Reading, Carlisle and Philadelphia.

But his big practice — 346 cases in five years — could not keep this energetic, ambitious Scot from public affairs. One of his pamphlets, as Lord Mansfield told the House of Lords, showed conclusively that "the supremacy of the British Legislature must be complete, entire and unconditional; or, on the other hand, the Colonies must be free and independent." In June 1776, he proposed that the people of the Colonies declare their independence of the British Crown. Later he became Agent General of the King of France, in the United States, and for some years handled France's commercial relations with us. William Pierce, a Georgia delegate, wrote that Wilson "has joined to a fine genius all that can set him off and show him to advantage. He is well acquainted with man, and understands all the passions which influence him. Government seems to have been his peculiar study; all the political institutions of the World he knows in detail." While Franklin was titular head of the Pennsylvania delegation, and Robert Morris a respected member,

Wilson chiefly formed its policies and gave them weight with the delegates.

Gouverneur Morris, too, was an extraordinary figure. With a background of family and wealth, his service in the Continental Congress brought him praise. The loss of his left leg in 1781, in an accident, neither checked his career as a man of fashion nor dimmed his eye for the fair; his diary of his years abroad as Washington's Minister to France notes his boudoir victories. Morris took a most active part in the Convention, and addressed the Chair more than any other delegate; his 174 speeches topped Wilson's 168 and Madison's 161. Morris was as oratorical in his form of persuasion as he was practical in his purposes. "No man has more wit," wrote a colleague, "he winds through all the mazes of rhetoric and throws around him such a glare that he charms, captivates, and leads away the senses of all who hear him."

Charles Pinckney, an aristocratic planter-lawyer-politician from South Carolina, was a vastly vain young man of thirty, whose abilities and accomplishments at times almost measured up to his claims for them. A soldier in the Revolution, he was in Congress in 1784–1787, and brought to Philadelphia with him in his saddlebags the Pinckney draft of the Constitution. Some thirty of its propositions were finally accepted by the delegates. One able historian has concluded that he "had a larger share than any other individual in the determination of the form and content of the finished Constitution." Undoubtedly he did constructive work on the Office of President. Handsome and something of a roué, Pinckney saw his own achievements in heroic proportions and resented the general acclaim of Madison as Father of the Constitution.

Hamilton's great services to the Constitution were persuasive writing in the *Federalist* and astute floorwork in the New York Ratifying Convention. In his thirtieth year when the Constitution was made, this precocious genius from the West Indies never quite divested himself of a rather uncritical admiration for the British King and central control. Service as confidential Aide to General Washington gave him an intimate acquaintance with the weakness of the Union among the States. In 1782 New York's Legislature made Hamilton a delegate to Congress, but he could stomach only a year of its wrangles. Not a native of any one State, but a National man, the delegates' contentions about State's Rights seemed to him cheap pettifogging, and their jealousy of an effective general government almost suicidal. The free government in which he believed was that of "the wise, the rich and the good," not that of the common people, whom on occasion he termed "a great beast."

After he drafted the invitation to the 1787 Convention, Hamilton determined that New York should be represented there, spent months getting elected to the New York Assembly and then maneuvering so that it would send a delegation to Philadelphia. But Governor George Clinton had no interest in strengthening the Union, and saw no point in changing his status as the number one wielder of power in the sovereign State of New York.

The result was a drawn battle. Thanks chiefly to his own ability to persuade others against their will, Hamilton managed to pass a resolution for New York to send a delegation, and got himself named one of the delegates. But the two other delegates, John Lansing and Robert Yates, were determined opponents of Federalism; the Clintonians stubbornly refused to increase the size of the delegation, and Hamilton went to Philadelphia knowing that New York's vote would be cast consistently against his views. He salvaged what he could from such a situation.

During sixty-six years (of the delegates, only Franklin was older) Roger Sherman of Connecticut had tried his hand at a multitude of trades: cordwainer, cobbler, surveyor, lawyer, merchant, justice of the peace, delegate to the Continental Congress from 1774 to 1781. He came to Philadelphia "disposed to patch up the old scheme of Government."

Edmund Randolph, Virginia's able, unstable Governor, had named a distinguished Virginia delegation, including George Mason and George Wythe in addition to Washington and Madison. To add official status, he became its chairman and took an active part in the Convention's proceedings.

The foresighted Madison had induced Governor Randolph to gather the Virginia delegates for a comparison of views before going to Philadelphia, and had submitted a draft for a new national government. With some changes, this became the Virginia Plan, which Randolph laid before the Convention four days after it had been organized.

James Madison's massive reputation rests almost entirely upon these labors at Philadelphia in forming and backing this Virginia Plan. His achievements in the First Congress, where he drafted many acts which thereafter determined national policy, were an epilogue to the constitutional creation.

His reading was encyclopedic, his memory excellent in detail, his industry prodigious. Madison's colleagues said that he was both profound politician and careful scholar, and hailed him as "the best informed man on any point in debate." Thirty-six years old at the assembly of the Convention, he was six years older than Hamilton, eight years younger than Jefferson. Unlike the tall, gangling author of the Declaration, who was sturdy and pink-cheeked until after he left the White House, Madison was small and wizened; continued mental effort made him sick, and he struggled constantly against ill health. Jefferson had a poor voice, could not make himself heard and therefore hated public speaking, but Madison was an extraordinarily powerful parliamentary debater. His was not the gift of oratory, his style lacked verbal embroidery, his delivery involved no pyrotechnics, and there was neither eloquence nor personal magnetism in his speaking. Rather, he depended on the power of pure intelligence; seldom at a loss to draw the needed facts from his vast knowledge, his ideas were clear-cut; he perceived the situation of the argument and never had to plead surprise.

The commission given the delegates was to "devise such provisions as shall appear necessary to render the Constitution of the Federal Government adequate to the exigencies of the Union, and to report to Congress such an act as, when agreed to by them and confirmed by the legislature of every state, would effectually provide for the same." This meant amendments to the Articles, which had already proved virtually unamendable. One of the Founding Fathers' first great decisions was to go beyond the initial frame of reference, and draft an entirely new plan of general government.

Virginia, New Jersey, South Carolina and other delegations laid their ideas before the Convention. New York had no plan but opposition; for all this, Hamilton presented his personal views in a speech of five hours' length, which Gouverneur Morris later described as the most impressive he had heard in his life. Many others praised it, but no one took it seriously, and Hamilton soon found pressing business at home. Presently the two other delegates washed their hands of the Federalist mess and went home too.

The Confederation's ills, according to Madison's diagnosis, arose from its being a league of States — sovereignties represented in the Congress by ambassadors — and his plan proposed to transform Congress into a parliament chosen by and directly responsible to the people. Coming from the ultimate source of power, it would have as much authority over them as Britain's Parliament had over British subjects. Inasmuch as it would represent the people, it could tax them directly, and adopt laws for their government. To collect these taxes and enforce these laws the plan proposed a Federal Executive and a Federal Judiciary. This whole structure would be superimposed upon the existing system of States, without destroying them.

Thus it is Madison who deserved full credit for this formula of political physics, by which two governmental systems could occupy the same space at the same time.

The Convention immediately began an active examination of the plans before it. Virginia's had several counters, such as William Paterson's New Jersey Plan and the influential Pinckney proposal. The Constitution eventually was hammered out on the anvil of compromise, and was chiefly notable for its new principles of "Dual Federalism" (to use Professor Corwin's phrase) and "Separation of Powers." The former, which undertook to divide governmental power over the people between the new Federal Union and the States, was the great compromise which assured the Constitution.

The doctrine of Separation of Powers much more directly concerns the subject matter of the present volume, because out of it stemmed our independent executive, recently termed "one of the very greatest contributions made by our Nation to the development of modern democracy."

Supposedly this idea came from the philosophic loins of Aristotle, who suggested that government involves three separate categories of force and action. After John Locke had alluded to this enigmatic hint, his French disciple Montesquieu made it the basis for the thesis that a distributed government is the ideal form for a free people.

Although the delegates at Philadelphia were more practical politicians than philosophers — Bryce remarks shrewdly that they "included nearly all the best intellect and the ripest political experience that the United States then contained" — they were eagerly seeking precedent for a form of government which would establish an independent executive as counterweight to a legislature that might turn tyrant. It included many who had experience in State government.

Too, educated Americans were intimately familiar with Montesquieu's writings, which had been especially influential on the early State Constitutions. Like Blackstone's *Commentaries* and Locke's political essays, they had been required reading for two generations. Not all accepted Montesquieu's theses unreservedly. Jefferson felt that this author had "common-placed all his reading," and that, as a result, his *Spirit of the Laws* contained "so much of paradox, of false principle and misapplied fact as to render its value equivocal." But the delegates found one of Montesquieu's passages made to order: —

> In every government there are three sorts of powers: The legislative; the executive in respect of things dependent on the law of nations; and the executive in regard to matters that depend on the civil law. . . .
>
> When the legislative and executive powers are united in the

same person, or in the same body of magistrates, there can be no liberty; because apprehensions may arise, lest the same monarch or senate should enact tyrannical laws, and execute them in a tyrannical manner.

Again, there is no liberty, if the judiciary power be not separated from the legislative and the executive. Were it joined with the legislative, the life and liberty of the subject would be exposed to arbitrary control; for the judge would then be the legislator. Were it joined to the Executive power, the judge might behave with violence and oppression. There would be an end of everything, were the same man or the same body, whether of the nobles or of the people, to exercise these three powers, that of enacting laws, that of executing the public resolutions, and of trying the causes of individuals.

Likewise the members found ready at hand Lord Bolingbroke's famous essay, *The Idea of a Patriot King,* a cogent and persuasive plea for a strong, independent "National Executive." The British King was the only chief of state with whose record they had close acquaintance, the "Glorious Revolution of 1688" was part of the American heritage, and they wanted an executive modeled on George III, without Lord North. Bolingbroke deemed a patriot king the direct representative of the people, deriving his prerogative and power from them, and being their agent.

These themes of familiar political philosophers played their part in the birth and growth of the American Presidency.

Four problems as to the National Executive aroused prolonged debate: The number of persons to constitute it; the method of its choice; the tenure of the office; and the nature of its powers.

The seventh of the resolutions through which Randolph had submitted the Virginia Plan proposed: "That a National Executive be instituted; to be chosen by the National Legislature for the term of ―― years; to receive punctually at stated time a fixed compensation for the services rendered, in which no increase or diminution shall be made so as to affect the Magistracy, existing at the time of increase or diminution, and to be ineligible a second time; and that besides a general authority to execute the National laws, it ought to enjoy the Executive rights vested in the Congress by the Confederation."

On June 1, James Wilson moved and Charles Pinckney seconded that the National Executive "consist of a single person." This touched off a heated debate, in which Roger Sherman of Connecticut expressed the anti-Federal, weak-executive feeling of most of the small State delegations.

Sherman told the delegates that he considered "the executive magistracy as nothing more than an institution for carrying the will of the legislature into effect, and that the person or persons ought to be appointed by and accountable to the legislature only, which was the depository of the supreme will of the Society. They were the best judges of the business which ought to be done by the executive department, and consequently of the number necessary from time to time for doing it. He wishes that the number might not be fixed, but that the legislature should be at liberty to appoint one or more, as experience might dictate."

To Wilson this was heresy; he "much preferred a single magistrate, as giving most energy, dispatch and responsibility to the office. He did not consider the prerogatives of the British Monarch as a proper guide in defining the executive powers." Some were legislative, such as declaring war, or peace; "the only powers he conceived strictly executive were those of executing the laws, and appointing the officers not appertaining to and appointed by the legislature."

Governor Randolph denounced a single executive as "the fœtus of monarchy," and could not see why the great requisites for the Executive Department — vigor, dispatch and responsibility — "could not be found in three men, as well as in one man. The Executive ought to be independent. It ought therefore (in order to support its independence) to consist of more than one." The exact reverse was the case, rejoined Wilson; unity in the National Executive "would be the best safeguard against tyranny," but a plural system would probably produce a tyranny as bad as the thirty tyrants of Athens. Madison interjected that, before deciding on the number of the National Executive, it would be proper to fix the extent of its authority. It was then agreed that the office be clothed with power to carry into effect the national laws, and to appoint to office in cases not otherwise provided for.

Wilson urged the Executive's choice by the people, and for a three-year term, with re-eligibility; the experience of New York and Massachusetts had shown "an election of the first magistrate by the people at large was both a convenient and successful mode." But Sherman again insisted on election by a legislature, and on making the Executive absolutely dependent on that body, as the legislature's will was that which was to be executed. "Any dependence of the Executive on the Supreme Legislature," in Wilson's view, was "the very essence of tyranny." Mason proposed a seven-year term, with no reappointment; and, by a vote of five States to four, this was decided on.

The next day Wilson brought forward the germ of the idea of choice by electors secured by the people. Elbridge Gerry, of Massachusetts, warned that a legislature should not choose; "there would be a constant intrigue kept up for the appointment, the legislature and the candidates would bargain and play into one another's hands."

Franklin urged that the Executive should not be made an office of profit; that, while its necessary expenses should be paid out of the Treasury, its members were to "receive no salary, stipend or reward whatsoever for their services." Two passions have a powerful influence on the affairs of men, he argued, "the love of power, and the love of money. Separately each of these has great force in prompting men to action; but when united in view of the same object, they have in many minds the most violent effects." Those who would strive for "this profitable preëminence" would not be the wise and moderate, the men fittest for the trust, but "the bold and the violent, the men of strong passions and indefatigable activity in their selfish pursuits. These will thrust themselves into your government and be your rulers."

The number of men to compose the Executive pressed on the delegates' minds, and on June 4, Pinckney brought it up again and Wilson argued it, asking why no State had installed three governors. A plural system would not produce tranquillity, but "uncontrolled, continued and violent animosities, which would not only interrupt the public administration; but diffuse their poison through the other branches of government, through the States, and at length through the people at large." The motion for a single executive then carried, with only New York, Delaware and Maryland in the negative.

During the next six weeks the Convention did little more on the problem of the National Executive, because of its travail over the critical issue of whether the United States should continue as a league of States or become a consolidated republic. Both Washington in the chair and Franklin at his elbow were frightened at the impending schism. The General wrote Hamilton, on July 10: "I almost despair of seeing a favorable issue to the proceedings of our Convention and do therefore repent having had any agency in the business." Perturbed by one bitter debate on the floor, Franklin proposed that they summon a minister to pray for God's grace, which stilled the anger of the moment. In a few days the compromise was made, on Sherman's earlier proposal of the "Connecticut Compromise," which cut the Gordian knot by having the House selected on the population basis, the Senate on that of the States.

This out of the way, the nature of the Executive came to the fore again. The Convention had appointed a "Committee on Detail," to bring forth the detailed articles of a constitution. Much of the language it used in its draft of Article II came from the New York State Constitution, and Wilson, who became its chairman, took care that it proposed a single executive.

The delegates on July 17 again debated the method of selecting this chief officer, and would have neither choice by the people nor the electoral scheme, but election by Congress. This aroused the conservative leaders, who thought a powerful, reasonably independent executive indispensable to the new government. "The Executives of the States," said Madison, "are in general little more than cyphers; the Legislatures omnipotent. If no effectual check be devised for restraining the instability and encroachments of the latter, a revolution of some kind or other would be inevitable."

Gouverneur Morris charged that such an executive would be the mere creature of the legislature. It has been a maxim in political science, he argued, "that republican government is not adapted to a large extent of country, because the energy of the executive magistracy cannot reach the extreme parts of it. Our country is an extensive one. We must either then renounce the blessings of the Union, or provide an executive with sufficient vigor to pervade every part of it . . .

"One great object of the executive is to control the legislature. The legislature will continually seek to aggrandize and perpetuate themselves; and will seize those critical moments produced by war, invasion or convulsion for that purpose. It is necessary then that the Executive Magistrate should be the guardian of the people, even of the lower classes, against legislative tyranny, against the great and the wealthy who in the course of things will necessarily compose the legislative body. Wealth tends to corrupt the mind and to nourish its love of power, and to stimulate it to oppression. . . . The Executive therefore ought to be so constituted as to be the great protector of the people.

"If he were to be the guardian of the people let him be appointed by the people, because an election by the people at large throughout so great an extent of country could not be influenced by those little combinations and those momentary lies which often decide popular elections within a narrow sphere." He knew no alternative for making the Executive independent of the Legislature, "but either to give him his office for life, or make him eligible by the people."

Although the Convention now created three special committees to process the mass of details that had to be pressed together before there could be a completed constitution, several proposals about the National Executive were slow to get any sort of Convention action. One of these concerned the Council of State which Gouverneur Morris and others wished to wrap around the Executive. On July 21, the Committee of the Whole gave him a limited veto, but postponed action on the Council.

After several unavailing efforts, on August 20, Morris sought to make a major issue of the need for a Council of State to "assist the President in conducting the Public affairs." He would have had it consist of the Chief Justice of the Supreme Court; the Secretary of Domestic Affairs; the Secretary of Commerce and Finance; the Secretary for Foreign Affairs; the Secretary of War and the Secretary of the Marine. Under his proposal, the President could ask the advice of these councilors upon matters of state; they would be required to submit their opinions in writing, but the Chief Magistrate would not be bound by the Council's advice. The Convention finally turned it down, Maryland, Georgia and South Carolina alone voting aye.

On September 1, a new Committee of Eleven was set up, to which the Convention referred "such parts of the Constitution as have been postponed, and such parts of reports as have not been acted on."

Three days later it reported several recommendations as to the National Executive, now termed "the President," chief of which were that: "He shall hold his office during the term of four years, and together with the Vice President, chosen for the same term, be elected in the following manner: Each State shall appoint in such manner as its Legislature may direct, a number of electors equal" to the number of Senators and Representatives from that State. The person who should receive a majority of the votes cast by electors would be President, the second person Vice President. In the event no one had a majority, the names of the five having the highest votes would be submitted to the Senate, which would select the President and then the Vice President.

Sherman, for the Committee, explained that the object was "to get rid of the ineligibility which was attached to the mode of election by the legislature, and to render the Executive independent of the legislature." This touched off the last of the Convention's great debates about the Presidency. Randolph and Charles Pinckney asked why, after the delegates had repeatedly referred to the legislature as the body to elect the President, the Committee had put it in other hands.

Gouverneur Morris, who had finessed the Committee action, gave six reasons: "Danger of intrigue and faction" controlling the outcome, if the legislature elected; the inconvenience of the ineligibility of the President to a second term, which would be required if the legislature were to elect him, in order to lessen the evils of the mode; the difficulty of finding another court than the Senate to try the President on impeachment, which must be done if the Senate were to elect him in the first place; the fact that nobody had appeared to be satisfied with appointment by the legislature; the fact that many delegates had even wanted direct election of the President by the people; and the indispensable necessity of making the President independent of the legislature.

Pinckney put his finger on the flaw in the proposal: the Senate's right of choice among the five leading candidates if none had electoral majority. The difficulty would not pertain to the first President — all hoped and expected General Washington would be that man. But most of the delegates thought that after him would come the deluge. Therefore Pinckney's apparently prescient objections that this electoral college scheme would throw all appointments in fact to the Senate; the electors would be strangers to the candidates and couldn't judge their comparative merits; the Executive's re-eligibility would endanger the public liberty; and the same Senators who in fact elected a President would judge him on impeachment.

"This subject has greatly divided the House," Wilson admitted, "and will also divide people out of doors. It is in truth the most difficult of all which we have had to decide." But despite its imperfections, it was a valuable improvement, and would get rid of the first great evil to be feared, "cabal and corruption." Nor did he think the electors would long be strangers to the men seeking the position; "Continental Candidates will multiply as we more and more coalesce, so as to enable the electors in every great part of the Union to know and judge of them." He agreed with the South Carolinian's objections to the Senate's selecting, if no candidate had an electoral majority, but would cure this by letting the House choose the President.

Two days later, Wilson found it dangerous to entrust the choice of the President, lacking electoral majority, to the Senators, because "they will have in fact the appointment of the President, and through his dependence on them, the virtual appointment to offices; among others, the officers of the Judiciary Department. They are to make treaties and they are to try all impeachments . . .

"According to the plan as it now stands, the President will not be the man of the people, as he ought to be, but the Minion of the Senate. He cannot even appoint a tide-waiter without the Senate."

While the election plan was better than the old one, Wilson would not agree to purchase it at the price of Senate rule. Sherman now moved Wilson's earlier suggestion, that the House rather than the Senate elect the President when no candidate had an electoral majority. This was adopted by a vote of ten to one.

The Constitution was now almost completed. On September 8, a "Committee on Stile" was appointed by ballot, consisting of Gouverneur Morris, Madison, King, Hamilton and Johnson. Morris employed it to do more than proofread the syntax and vocabulary of the rough draft, and by choice of language it considerably broadened the presidential powers. The Committee on Detail had reported: "The executive power shall be vested in a single person. His style shall be 'the President of the United States' and his title shall be 'His Excellency.'" Morris simplified this to "the executive power shall be vested in a President of the United States of America . . ."

When the final draft of the document was read to the delegates September 15, the Convention did not pass separately on the restatement of the first sentence of Article II. After hearing it, Charles

Pinckney objected to "the contemptible weakness and dependence of the Executive." Yet "broad constructionists" soon regarded Morris' simple declaratory sentence as a broad grant of Executive power. The holdings of the Court and the practices of great Presidents have combined to make it one of the two great pillars of power for the President.

The second of these pillars is the power as Commander in Chief. There is some reason to suppose that General Washington was himself responsible for the extent of this grant, the broadness of which was at the time doubted, but later apparent. As President of the Convention, he scrupulously refrained from taking part in the public debates but did not hesitate to press his views informally. He had a lively apprehension that domestic tumults and disorders would require the Federal Government to employ armed force to make good its guaranty of republican form of government for the States.

The commitment of this power had little attack during the sessions, although near the end, Sherman had watered down the President's right to command the militia by the addition of the phrase, "when called into the active service of the United States." Lincoln later found in it the independent source of authority to do things Congress was forbidden to do, and thereby to save the Union. Washington's sage prevision made this possible.

The delegates voted, September 15, for the draft of the "Committee on Stile" to be engrossed for signature, and then submitted to the States for their action. On September 17, 1787, it was ready for final action. Benjamin Franklin was too feeble to talk, but wrote out this message, which Wilson read for him: —

"I agree to this Constitution with all its faults, if they are such. It astonishes me to find this system approaching so near to perfection . . . The opinions I have had of its errors I sacrifice to the common good."

Thereupon he moved its adoption and signature. All but three of the forty-two delegates present subscribed their names, the Constitution went to the States, and the office of President was born.

CHAPTER II

"First in Peace..."

For nine months after the adjournment of the Convention, the ratification of the new Constitution trembled in the balance. Anti-Federalists fought hard in many States, not only because they feared that central power would destroy individual freedom, but also because they doubted that the new National Executive officer would prove a check to a tyrannous Senate.

It had been generally expected that George Washington would consent to become the first President of the United States. All groups held him in affectionate respect, but even the prospect of the personally disinterested First Citizen did not still the doubts of many in the ratifying conventions that the new chief officer would become either puppet or tyrant. In Pennsylvania, the first large State to consider the Constitution, an active minority argued that the "contemptible weakness" of the office of President constituted a chief reason why the people should reject the new charter. They predicted that the President "would be a mere pageant of state, unless he coincides with the Senate." They saw in him a mere ceremonial officer who could be of little help in the quest for a more perfect union.

"Is it probable," they asked, "that the President of the United States, limited as he is in power, and dependent on the will of the Senate in appointments to office, will have either the firmness or the inclination to exercise his prerogative . . .?" Such rhetorical questions they answered mainly in the negative, in order to emphasize the prediction that, were the new government set up this way, the proposed Chief of State would become either "the head of the aristocratic junto" in the Senate, or "its minion."

James Wilson took a leading part in the persuasion of the Pennsylvanians, in December 1787. "We have a responsibility in the person of our President," he argued. "He cannot act improperly, and hide either his negligence or inattention; he cannot roll upon any other person the weight of his criminality. No appointment can take place without his nomination; and he is responsible for every nomination he makes. . . .

"That officer is placed high, and is possessed of power far from being contemptible, yet not a *single privilege* is annexed to his character; far from being *above the laws,* he is amenable to them in his private character as a *citizen,* and in his public character by impeachment."

Arguments of this sort, together with the general expectation about Washington, persuaded favorable action in Pennsylvania. They were also of great weight in Massachusetts, and in Virginia, where convention letters from Mount Vernon offset Patrick Henry's golden voice. By July 1788, one more than the indispensable nine States had ratified; a little later Hamilton persuaded a reluctant New York adhesion; then North Carolina reversed her rejection — and only Rhode Island remained out of the Federal fold. The Congress of the Confederation took the necessary measures to end its own existence through the establishment of the new government.

Fears now arose among Federalist leaders that some of the enemies of a strong central government might try to thwart the choice of Washington for President. "We all feel," Hamilton wrote Wilson, in January 1789, "how much moment it is that Washington should be the man; and I aver I cannot think there is material room to doubt that this will be the unanimous sense." But he was frightened by "the defect in the Constitution" over the choice of President and Vice President. Should the electors be unanimous for John Adams for the second place, "a few votes insidiously withheld" from Washington might put Adams in as President. Therefore he wished the vote for Adams diminished by a few electors, asked his Federalist friends in Connecticut and New Jersey to "waste" two, and wanted Wilson to arrange similar subtractions in Pennsylvania and Maryland. It turned out that Hamilton's apprehensions were unfounded, every electoral vote being cast for Washington — but twelve years later "the defect in the Constitution" almost made Burr President in place of Jefferson.

What manner of man was George Washington? How did his personality and character shape the office and develop the powers of the Presidency? Upon the man himself, there could be no better witness than Thomas Jefferson, who knew him well, served in his first Cabinet and then felt the force of his opposition. In 1812 Jefferson had an inquiry from one Walter Jones, who was writing a book about political parties, and deemed Washington a "monarchist."

The sage of Monticello replied that he thought he knew General Washington "intimately and thoroughly": he was no monarchist, but held "correct views of the rights of man." Furthermore, Washington had been determined that the experiment of the new republican government "should have a fair trial, and would lose the last drop of his blood in support of it." Then this great practical philosopher described Washington's traits, in terms so carefully weighed that we can be sure they represent his judgment after careful reflection: —

> His mind was great and powerful, without being of the very first order; his penetration strong; though not so acute as that of a Newton, Bacon or Locke; and as far as he saw, no judgment was ever sounder. It was slow in operation, being little aided by invention or imagination, but sure in conclusion . . .
> He was incapable of fear, meeting personal dangers with the calmest unconcern. Perhaps the strongest feature in his character was prudence, never acting until every circumstance, every consideration, was maturely weighed; refraining, if he saw a

doubt; but, when once decided, going through with his purpose, whatever obstacles opposed.

His integrity was the most pure, his justice the most inflexible I have ever known; no motives of interest or consanguinity, or friendship or hatred, being able to bias his decision. He was, indeed, in every sense of the words, a wise, a good, and a great man.

His temper was naturally irritable and high-toned; but reflection and resolution had obtained a firm and habitual ascendancy over it. If ever, however, it broke its bonds, he was most tremendous in his wrath.

His heart was not warm in its affections; but he exactly calculated every man's value, and gave him a solid esteem proportioned to it . . .

Washington took a "free share in conversation," but "his colloquial talents were not above mediocrity, possessing neither copiousness of ideas nor fluency in words. In public, when called upon for a sudden opinion, he was unready, short and embarrassed. Yet he wrote readily, rather diffusely, in an easy and correct style. . . ."

His character was, in its mass, perfect, in nothing bad, in few points indifferent; . . . never did nature and fortune combine more perfectly to make a man great . . .

In addition, Jefferson emphasized Washington's role in the new independent nation, and wrote of his "conducting its councils through the birth of a government, new in its form and principles, until it had settled down into a quiet and orderly train; and of scrupulously obeying the laws through the whole of his career, civil and military, of which the history of the world furnishes no other example."

The First Congress of the new United States of America was supposed to assemble in New York, the seat of government of the old Confederation, on March 4, 1789. But travel was slow-paced in those days, and its two Houses had no quorums until six weeks after the day announced for the beginning of the new government. The discarded Congress kept functioning during the interregnum; indeed, at Washington's request, portions of its administrative machinery continued to operate until the new Congress set up the necessary departments to take over. It was late in April, however, before enough members were on hand for House and Senate to organize and for the President to be inaugurated.

Problems of title and ceremonial occupied some of the time of waiting. Washington asked the advice of several friends upon his personal etiquette. Vice President Adams, who had been our Minister to The Hague and much under the influence of Dutch forms, was anxious for Washington to have a lordly title, and Richard Henry Lee proposed "Elective Highness."

A Committee of the Senate actually reported the title of "His Highness the President of the United States of America and Protector of the Rights of the Same." Senator Maclay, snob-hating Republican from western Pennsylvania, insisted that the Constitution itself had named him simply "the President of the United States of America." Adams replied wrathfully that "If people outside hear only George Washington, President of the United States, they will despise him *to all eternity*."

Adams likewise furnished the comic relief for the ceremonial of the President's inauguration. On April 25, he read the Senate a committee report about the plan of procedure, and then asked how the President and he were to sit. Should both be seated in "the wide chair"? "Gentlemen," Adams went on, "I feel great difficulty how to act. I am possessed of two separate powers; the one in *esse* and the other in *posse*. I am Vice President. In this I am nothing, but I may be everything. But I am President also of the Senate. When the President comes into the Senate, what shall I be? I cannot be [President] then. No, gentlemen, I can not, I can not."

At this point, as if oppressed with a sense of his distress, he threw himself back in his chair. A solemn silence followed. Senator Ellsworth, of Connecticut, thumbed the sheets of the Constitution and then said gravely: "Mr. President, I have looked over the Constitution (*Pause*) and I find, sir, it is evident and clear, sir, that wherever the Senate are to be, sir, there, sir, you must be at the head of them. (*Pause*.) But further, sir, I shall not pretend to say."

On April 30, the day of the Inauguration, the Senators gathered, the Representatives entered, and Washington then advanced between the two bodies, bowing to each. He was dressed in deep brown, with metal buttons decorated with eagles, white stockings — and a sword. After he took the oath, all returned to the Senate chamber, and he began his address, quite agitated and embarrassed. One who heard him expressed the wish that all set ceremony were in the hands of the dancing masters, and was hurt that Washington . . . "this first of men . . . was not the first in everything."

Washington went into office determined to be "the President of all the people"; by this, in all likelihood, he meant the people in their collective personality — as the Romans did in *Senatus Populusque Romanus* — and not the downtrodden masses. He had lost much of his faith in the lowly, soon after peace; as had the great majority of the foremost men of 1783. Certainly most of the possessors of property and position came to doubt not only the good sense but also the sound heart of the multitude which manifested its will in selfish, violent, capricious and dangerous ways. But the acceptance of the Constitution led the First Citizen to revise his views, and he entered the Presidency determined to represent the entirety of the nation. Like the Constitution, he ignored the possible emergence of political factions or parties.

In a sense, he clutched an illusion. Party, faction, schism, bitter division, lawlessness and rebellion had marked the years between Cornwallis' surrender and the adoption of the Constitution. While parties had not yet consolidated into two almost equal opposing masses, events moved in that direction. Through all this the President had lived, of much of it he was a part, and the wish to ban party spoke well for his integrity of purpose, but not for his usual awareness of realities.

Washington's formula for a nonpartisan government was a Cabinet of all the talents. He proceeded in the expectation that men with such polar differences as Thomas Jefferson, whose enduring trust through life was in the soundness of the common people, and Alexander Hamilton, who thought the people "a great beast," could be brought to pull together on fundamental issues.

Undoubtedly the way Washington handled the Cabinet played a great part in its concert of policy for the first three years. After his own Presidency, Jefferson emphasized this trait of Washington as a great initial force in the establishment of the new government. That first Cabinet had been divided two and two "by as marked an opposition of principle as Monarchism and Republicanism could bring into conflict. . . . But the President heard with calmness the opinions and reasons of each, decided the course to be pursued and kept the Government steadily in it, unaffected by the agitation. The public knew well the dissensions of the Cabinet, but never had an uneasy thought on their account, because they knew also they had provided [in Washington] a regulating power which would keep the machine in steady movement."

President Washington's most conspicuous achievements were as Chief of Government, particularly in selecting his agents to enforce the laws, and supervising their faithful administration of the tasks. He was born, apparently, with a passion for detail. This was well, for his duties as Commander in Chief of the Continental Army had confronted him with practically every problem of executive action in a civil government. He had to maintain relations with a Congress which was jealous of him, many of whose leaders hated him and sought to set up rival generals. He kept on trying to squeeze money out of States which paid no heed to requisitions from Congress, with the result that soldiers went for months on end without a shilling. He was forced to master the problem of supplies, which

Congress refused to simplify through establishing any single agency of overhead control.

As Commander, Washington's correspondence was enormous, and he sought to give personal attention to every letter that came in, every report received. When he had made a decision, it stayed decided. He generally rose at the crack of dawn, and did not go to bed until the guttering candles had done service late into the night. In consequence, he knew his Army in detail. He knew his principal lieutenants — though sometimes a little belatedly, as in the cases of Charles Lee and Benedict Arnold. He knew the condition of supplies, and did not hesitate to send out parties to seize food and clothes to reduce the misery at Valley Forge. He had to be a diplomat, to handle Rochambeau and de Grasse, and he had to be stiff in his demands that the French send cash as well as ships and soldiers. From Bunker Hill to Yorktown, George Washington did postgraduate work in the school of the commander. As a by-product he learned the job of Chief of Government.

The Constitution made the President the fountainhead of all appointing power. Washington's mail between ratification and inauguration teemed with applications from Army officers and civilians for offices under the new government. These he filed away and, in due course, filled the bulk of the offices from among those who had applied for them, but in no instance gave even the shadow of advance commitment. "I will go to the chair," he wrote, "under no pre-engagement of any kind or nature whatsoever." In particular, he was determined not "to suffer connections of blood or friendship" to sway his choice.

Washington made up his mind on principal officers well in advance of taking the oath. To John Jay, but for whose patient persistence the Confederation probably would not have achieved the little it did, he offered the choice between the two principal posts of Chief Justice and Secretary of State. Jay preferred the judicial position, and his nomination was promptly confirmed.

The President shrewdly refrained from pressing Congress to pass the acts enabling him to establish "the great departments" of

State, Treasury and War. After a considerable struggle in Congress, involving jealousy between the two Houses, the bills passed.

Washington's most urgent need was a Treasury Department, and he summoned Alexander Hamilton to head it. Regarding the judicial system "as the chief pillar upon which our national government must rest," and believing that the Attorney General must have talents equal to those of the new justices, he asked Edmund Randolph to undertake that task. He had no hesitation about the new War Department: General Henry Knox, of Massachusetts, was a mountain of a man in industry as well as flesh, Washington had found him useful and dependable in the Revolution; the Confederation had made him Secretary of its War Department, and the President nominated him to continue his work. Similarly, Samuel Osgood continued as Postmaster General, although he did not gain Cabinet place until 1794.

The first executive department created, in point of time, was the Department of Foreign Affairs, in the bill Washington signed July 27, 1789, a name which came from the Confederation's agency; two months later Congress gave it power to administer some domestic affairs and retitled it "Department of State," and Washington asked Thomas Jefferson to take charge.

In his invitation, the President testified that he had been determined both by motives of private regard and by "a conviction of public propriety" to make the nomination. He pointed out that, as the government was organized, State "involves many of the most interesting objects of the Executive authority." He knew Jefferson's delight in his service as Minister to France, and therefore had considerably forborne to nominate a successor at the Court of Versailles until informed of his friend's determination.

The latter, who was visiting Monticello, replied that he preferred his present position and had come to America expecting to return, "but it is not for an individual to choose his post, you are to marshal us as may be best for the public good." Let the President determine, and "if it should be to remain at New York, my chief comfort will be to work under your eye, my only shelter the authority of your name and the wisdom of measures to be dictated by you and implicitly executed by me." Washington did indicate his definite preference, and Jefferson accepted the appointment.

His initial reluctance had not proceeded from any hostility to the new government; the term "anti-Federalist," as first applied to those who opposed ratification, did not fit Jefferson, whose complaint, like Sam Adams', had been the lack of a bill of rights. He saw the need for central authority and was not far from being a Federalist when he entered the first Cabinet.

Washington established and maintained good relations with his department heads, who responded productively to his clear-cut delegations of adequate authority to get a job done. Regarding it a "government of accommodation" as well as of laws, he instituted the cabinet system, and in the first few years seemed to vest the three senior members of the Cabinet with a sort of collective authority and responsibility. In the spring of 1791, when he was about to depart on a state journey through the South, he made Jefferson, Hamilton and Knox almost a Council of State to act in his absence; Chief Justice Jay and Vice President Adams were to meet with them, if in town. Several meetings were held, but no important actions occurred.

Aside from erecting and staffing the governmental structure, and getting it going, the Administration's chief problems were domestic: the establishment and maintenance of the public revenue and credit; the creation of a national military establishment; the provision of a permanent national capital; the encouragement of commerce and manufactures as the handmaiden of agriculture, and so on. By the end of Washington's first term, however, the French Revolution became explosively violent, and France declared war on Britain. Each had virulent partisans in America, whose passions threatened the new nation with civil commotion as well as foreign war.

Although the two problems overlap in time, they need separate treatment. The President's first concern was the public finance; unless it be secure, how could domestic tranquillity, the common defense and the general welfare — the purposes in the preamble to the Constitution — be secured? In Hamilton he had a man of genius as well as talent, one interested in public purpose as well as class benefit. His plan involved more than the mere reputation of the new Federal Union. The new government was successor of the Confederation, with all its debts and defaults; and likewise was concerned with the financial problems of the thirteen States. Hamilton, in a masterly report on the public credit, January 14, 1790, recommended that the new government pay the Confederation's foreign and domestic debt; and that in addition it assume and gradually pay all State debts contracted during the Revolutionary War.

Only a few opposed payment of the foreign debt, but the other items aroused bitter attack. Confederation paper had sunk almost to no value in the dark days of the Revolution, and speculators bought large quantities of it. Just before the assumption, many members of Congress and their relatives and friends picked up what they could of the old securities, for the profit from the public Treasury.

The opponents of such plunder argued that these speculators did not deserve these unearned gains; let them be reimbursed only for their actual purchase price perhaps with compound interest. Hamilton contended that "confidence" was the supreme need of the hour for the new government, and that the quickest and surest way to create it was by paying every penny of this inherited debt. He insisted that the government's promise must be as sacredly kept as the Eighth Commandment, and that its bonds were negotiable instruments, and should always bring par.

But Hamilton's private and much more powerful reason for redemption was that he felt it necessary to create a class of Americans who would have a money profit in the new government. He hoped to attach the predatory rich to the support of the Administration. In the event, "the wise, the rich and the good" responded.

With some help from Washington, who had believed in sound money since the French and Indian Wars, Hamilton finally got Congress to pass the redemption plan. But State debt assumption fared badly, and after bitter dissensions, Congress rejected it. Hamilton now resorted to political intrigue to get it through. No site had yet been chosen for the new National Capital, New York wanted to cling on, Pennsylvania hungered for the prize, and the Southerners wanted it on the Potomac, a desire in which Jefferson joined. Hamilton and his associates talked to the Secretary of State about it, and proposed State assumption as *quid pro quo* for Capital on the Potomac. Jefferson agreed, and the deal was carried through.

Spurred by these triumphs, Hamilton boldly proposed a National Bank, to be privately owned, like the Bank of England, but also to be the official depository of Federal funds and the government's agent in selling United States bonds. In addition, its notes would be backed by the public credit. Jefferson opposed the bank plan, both on its merits, and because he felt that Hamilton had taken advantage of him in the Capital deal, which quickened his distrust of the public ethics and intellectual integrity of the head of the Treasury.

The issue broadened from one of public policy to that of the government's power under the Constitution. Was that instrument's silence on the subject of a bank of such a nature a prohibition of the powers to form one, or were these to be implied out of the general powers conferred on the National Government? Jefferson held Hamilton's bill unconstitutional as well as unwise, but the New Yorker pressed the doctrine of implied powers, and at length the President signed the measure.

This was the first major battle between Jefferson and Hamilton. It took the form of constitutional interpretation; but the fact of difference was over who should rule, the few or the many. The seat of power, the fact of control, the distribution of the fruits of our human and material resources — these were then, as ever after, the principal objects of the political battles in America.

Stripped of all trappings, the issue was relatively simple. As Henry

Adams puts it, "to crush democracy by force was the ultimate resource of Hamilton. To crush that force was the determined intention of Jefferson." Hamilton saw a strong central government as a mighty engine making for control by the rich and well-born. Jefferson believed that if the National Government were weak in domestic affairs, the common people were less likely to be made to pay tribute to the powerful. The battle over national debt and the National Bank caused a schism in the Cabinet, because Jefferson smarted over the way Hamilton had overreached him. The President tried to compose the growing antagonism, but its causes were too deep for compromise.

Washington's general handling of the appointing power deserves description. While President, exclusive of members of the Supreme Court or his Cabinet, he named three hundred and fifty-one civil officers. His principles for selection were suitable qualifications, personal merit and former services. Many of the applications or recommendations for appointments were indorsed in his own hand, and most of them asserted fitness for office; many made incidental reference to military service, and a few mentioned this alone; several came from functionaries of the Confederation, who sought to continue in their old offices; a large number appealed to his benevolent consideration of personal distress, several of which he heeded.

There were others of a frankly political nature, to which Washington gave a good deal of attention. In the beginning, his appointments were designed to give the new government a better flavor in States which had been reluctant to enter the new Union. He was particularly careful about North Carolina appointments, because it had at first rejected the Constitution. His Rhode Island selections were frankly political, to build up, through self-interest there, support for the Federal Government.

The Senate rejected one of his first nominations, that of Benjamin Fishbourne to be Naval Officer of the Port of Savannah, without asking the President for any information about the nominee. Nettled at the absence of consultation, Washington immediately sent a message reciting Fishbourne's public record, to show that he "must have enjoyed the confidence" of a wide variety of groups, to gain the positions he had held. The lecture must have made a passing impression on the Senators, for they did not reject other Washington nominations for some time.

As party skirmishes grew into battles in his second term, he became quite determined that stanch Federalists alone should go on the payroll. "I shall not, whilst I have the honor to administer the government," he wrote in 1795, "bring a man into any office of consequence knowingly, whose political tenets are adverse to the measures which the general government are pursuing; for this in my opinion would be a sort of political suicide." The policy had quite practical application, faithful Federalists preceded deserving Democrats.

The first President made earnest efforts to persuade the Senate to team up with him, in those parts of the executive power which the Constitution had placed in the joint charge of the President and the Senate. Probably he suspected that this body would be jealous of any apparent presidential encroachment upon the executive powers the Constitution had reposed in it, and might insist on acting as an independent institution. While he acted on the other assumption, and took the initiative in team play, his experiences that first summer snuffed out his hopes that the Senate would become his partner in treaty-making and appointments.

Senator Maclay took careful note of the Senate's developing acerbity. The initial occasion for its displeasure was the way the House's bills for the organization of "the great departments" of the executive government seemed "to exalt the President above the Constitution, and depress the Senate below it." First point at issue was who had the power of removal of executive officers. Because the Constitution joined the Senate and the President in the process of appointment, the Senate inferred that it possessed an equal right in discharge. The House's first departmental bills explicitly fixed the removal right in the President, which the Senators resented as a move to deprive them of a veto upon removal, putting the President "beyond the power of responsibility."

When Washington's lieutenants sought to convince stubborn Senators that he deserved the right to remove all officers, Maclay told the Senate: "If the virtues of the present Chief Executive are brought forward as a reason for vesting him with extraordinary powers, no nation ever trod more dangerous ground. His virtues will depart with him, but the powers which you give him will remain, and if not properly guarded will be abused by future Presidents — if they are men."

But Ellsworth, of Connecticut, countered that if Washington were denied the right to discharge, they might as well lay his head on the block "and strike it off with one blow."

The issue quieted when Madison, the great government constructor of the lower House, concluded he had made a mistake in agreeing that the removal power must be legislatively delegated to the President. A re-examination of the constitutional issue convinced him that the President's right of removal was a clear implication of that document. In this case Congress could not confer a right which existed independently, and so the House dropped its bill to this end. (This interpretation continued virtually unchallenged until 1867, when the power-bent Radicals of Reconstruction passed the Tenure of Office Act, to emasculate Andrew Johnson's work.)

The Senate's first real chance to put the President in his place came in August. Washington paid it a visit, to ask "advice" on a treaty then in course of negotiation with the Creek Indians. After laying the proposed treaty before the members, he read them several written questions which could not be answered yes or no. After an uncomfortable silence, Gouverneur Morris moved that the papers be referred to a committee, and Maclay supported the mode of doing business by committees, arguing that they were used in all public deliberative bodies. This determination to act at arm's length angered the President, who started up "in a violent fret" and said: "This defeats every purpose of my coming here." But, as Maclay noted, "he cooled off by degrees; we waited for him to withdraw," and finally he did so.

In this fashion the Senate served notice on the President that it was no consultative body, no Council of State whose informal advice he could secure. The framers of the Constitution may have intended such friendly comparisons of view when they joined the President and the Senate in the executive power concerning both appointments and treaties. But in its very first term the Senate showed its determination to come to its conclusions quite independently of the President.

Washington now realized this, and on returning to the Senate a few days later, for further talk on the Creek treaty, he was "placid and serene, and manifested a spirit of accommodation." Doubtless he was already planning less direct modes of handling the Senate.

During this first two years the process of communication between the executive and legislative branches was fashioned by trial and error into enduring routine. Later, John Adams said that Washington's authority had been weak throughout his Presidency, and especially in the Senate, which was "equally divided in all great constitutional questions, and in all great questions of foreign relations." But the Republicans felt quite differently about it. "It is believed," Maclay recorded, "that any measure that can be fairly fixed on the President will be submitted to by the people."

One method he adopted early, to influence Congress, was his annual message on the state of the Union, carrying out his constitutional duty to recommend such measures as he should judge necessary and expedient. His messages were full, explicit, and often quite persuasive.

Washington sensed the fact that the President must be Chief of Public Opinion, and in the first three years made four trips of State, to carry the dignity and the personality of their Chief Magistrate to the people themselves. In the fall of 1789 he visited each of the New England States except turbulent Rhode Island, which still had not ratified. The people saw him "as he really is" — the words are

Maclay's: an impressive figure, "in stature about six feet, with an unexceptionable make, but lax appearance. His frame would seem to want filling up. His motions rather slow than lively, though he showed no signs of having suffered by gout or rheumatism. His complexion pale, nay, almost cadaverous. His voice hollow and indistinct, owing, as I believe, to artificial teeth before his upper jaw." Almost a schoolboy out on a holiday, he enjoyed the hospitality of the humble more than the plaudits of the great. He was well received everywhere. Even vain John Hancock, Governor of Massachusetts, finally bent the knee to him. The next spring he toured Long Island for five days, and in August spent a week in Rhode Island, which had finally ratified.

An almost nineteen-hundred-mile coach trip to the South, which took from early April to late June, 1791, carried Washington to the Savannah River and back. Its itinerary was planned with care, he was able to keep his published schedule, and was greeted all along the way with extraordinary enthusiasm. One purpose had been "to acquire knowledge of the face of the Country, the growth and agriculture thereof — and the temper and disposition of the inhabitants towards the new government." A good observer, as he went along he learned at first hand what problems pressed upon the gentry and commoners, their hopes and fears, needs and interests. He saw the face of the people, and was aided in the conduct of his duties. They saw that the President was no distant abstraction, unconcerned with their trials and distresses, but the careful custodian of their interests. He pioneered in this important presidential duty, to lead the people. More than a century before the age of "mikes" and nation-wide hookups, he made the coach-and-four his channel for communication.

Washington gave the closest attention to his duties as Commander in Chief. He showed great concern over the lack of men and matériel for the common defense, strove to persuade Congress to provide a less flimsy military establishment, and sought to make the most efficient use of the slender forces he had.

In August 1789 he advised Congress of the Army inherited from the Confederation, and asked that it "be conformed by law to the Constitution of the United States." Congress rejected Knox's appeal for five thousand troops to campaign against the troublesome Creek Indians, as just an excuse of Washington's to get a standing army, instead of militia. But the President used Hamilton and others of his official family to bring Congress around, and made repeated efforts to establish effective Federal supervision over State Militia. By the end of his second term this management was bringing substantial results.

The anti-Administration Republicans gained control of the House in 1792, and tried to halt this trend to a strong standing Army, ostensibly because the War Department was costing twice as much as all other departments. But a confidential communication from the President checked their efforts. A little later he asked for an expanded military program, used patronage to get Republican votes, and finally secured it. "The influence of the Executive on events," wrote Jefferson, "the use made of them, and the public confidence in the President are an overmatch for all efforts Republicanism can make."

The Republicans viewed a professional Navy as a danger to the people's liberty, and fought off Washington's requests for one until Barbary State depredations on our Mediterranean commerce grew unendurable. Late in 1793, the President declared the protection of a naval force indispensable to an active external commerce; even the most sincere neutrality "is not a sufficient guard against the depredations of nations at war," and the House passed a bill appropriating $600,000 for building six ships.

Washington's chief duties as Commander in Chief arose out of Indian troubles. While he hoped for peace, he knew the white settler could not be restrained, that the red man was doomed to be uprooted, and the most he could do was to cushion the change. While the Creek treaty eased things in the South, British instigation and natural indignation at white seizure of tribal lands provoked Indian troubles in the Northwest. The first generals he sent to the seat of war did badly, but at length Washington sent "Mad Anthony" Wayne, who prepared carefully, then attacked with crushing force, and the Indians sued for peace.

But the most extraordinary employment of this power came in the Whisky Rebellion in western Pennsylvania in 1793, which he made a test of the ability of the National Government to collect the revenue taxes and enforce the laws.

On Hamilton's bidding, the first Congress had levied an excise tax or duty on whisky made in the United States. To enforce it, the President was authorized to divide the States into excise tax collection districts, with surveyors of the revenue and deputies galore. Western Pennsylvania farmers would not obey this law. It was a region of hunting caps, squirrel guns and "butcher-knife boys," with the adventurous lawlessness of the frontier. For years they had violently resisted a Pennsylvania State tax, and the State Legislature had winked at their evasion. Most of the Pennsylvania delegation in the second Congress opposed the tax, and Maclay warned that "it could not be enforced by collectors or civil officers of any kind, be they ever so numerous; and that nothing short of a permanent military force could effect it."

And so it proved, for Federal collectors were thwarted by stealth or by riot; many feared for their lives and quit the service. Then the opposition organized, and made open threats of defiance. President Washington accepted the challenge, and on August 7, 1794, issued a proclamation against the rebels. "If the laws are to be so trampled upon with impunity," he declared, "and a minority (a small one, too) is to dictate to the majority, there is an end put, at one stroke, to republican government; and nothing but anarchy and confusion is to be expected hereafter."

When the Proclamation did not end the resistance, he summoned the State Militia of Pennsylvania, New Jersey, Maryland and Virginia into Federal service. The Governor of each State took the command of his troops, who together made a force of fifteen thousand — more than Washington had ever commanded at any one time during the struggle with Britain — and the President personally accompanied them to field headquarters at Carlisle. This aroused bitter complaints from the Republicans that the office of Commander in Chief did not authorize him to command in the field.

On October 23, 1794, he ordered the Army to cross the mountains and defeat the rebels. The march proved almost a triumphal procession, leading citizens greeted the columns, and particularly the President, with words of loyalty, while the Militia showed enthusiasm, not sullenness. Word came from the neighborhood of Pittsburgh that the rebels were greatly alarmed. Armed resistance seemed less and less likely, and Washington announced that he would return to Philadelphia. But not, he added indignantly, because of the impertinent Republican claims that he could not, "constitutionally, command the Army whilst Congress is in session." The Army occupied the insurgent regions almost without resistance, the rebels laid down their arms and besought clemency. Some were tried for treason but not convicted. The Whisky Rebellion ended without the shedding of blood, and the supremacy of the nation's laws had been maintained.

Yet even in the latter part of his first term, Washington had not been happy in the office of President. The increasing bitterness between Jefferson and Hamilton foreshadowed a contest between parties for control of the government. The President, tired of the turmoil, longed to spend the remainder of his days "in ease and tranquillity" at Mount Vernon, and believed that the time had come for him to surrender the reins.

Accordingly, in February 1792, he broached the subject to Jefferson, later talking it over with Hamilton, Knox and Randolph. In May, he asked Madison, whose draftsmanship he greatly admired, "to think of the proper time, and the best mode of announcing the intention," and outlined the subjects he wished worked into "a valedictory address from me to the public." Those he consulted urged against retirement. "The confidence of the whole nation," declared Jefferson, "is centered in you. Your being at the helm will be more than an answer to every argument which can be used to alarm and lead the people in any quarter into violence or secession." Madison also wrote in urgent tones, but the President remained reluctant.

Later that summer Washington did make another effort to reconcile Jefferson and Hamilton, writing each that while differences in political opinion were unavoidable, the dissensions caused him grief. Unless there were more harmonious relations, it would be "difficult, if not impracticable, to manage the reins of government, or to keep the parts of it together." Therefore he pleaded for "liberal allowances, mutual forbearances, and temporizing yieldings *on all sides*."

Each responded with accusations of his opponent. Hamilton attacked the Virginia Republican's conduct, but made the equivocal promise "that if you shall hereafter form a plan to reunite the members of your Administration upon some steady principle of co-operation, I will faithfully concur in executing it during my continuance in office." Jefferson renewed his request that his proffered resignation be accepted, and added that he would not suffer his retirement "to be clouded by the slanders of a man whose history, from the moment at which history can stoop to notice him, is a tissue of machinations against the liberty of the country which has not only received and given him bread, but heaped its honors on his head." But so long as Jefferson continued in office, he promised not to provide "aliment" for further feuds.

These slight evidences of hope for peace between the giants, together with the general wish for him to continue, and the impact of the foreign war, caused him to abandon his insistence on serving only a single term. There never was any question of his re-election. The opposition was not to Washington but to Hamilton and the Federalist Party. Every one of the 132 electoral votes went for Washington, but Federalist John Adams continued as Vice President with only 77.

Jefferson reluctantly consented to stay with Washington through 1793. The latter so appreciated his talents and integrity, particularly during the French perplexity, that late in the fall he again asked Jefferson to change his mind, but without avail.

Foreign relations proved the most important problem of the

Washington Administration, for the new nation's future was imperiled by both France and Britain, while Spain's control of the mouth of the Mississippi provoked threats of the secession of the frontier communities across the mountains.

The French gave the first trouble. Jefferson had been there during the best period of the Revolution, the time of enlightened patriotism and true devotion to the rights of man, which intensified his theoretical attachment to the rule of the people. Gouverneur Morris, his successor as American Minister, had a diametrically opposed public attitude, joined with "levity and imprudence of conversation and conduct." Jefferson, who did not trust his discretion, gave the most detailed instructions; as well he might, for while the nomination was being debated, Morris was up to his neck in a plot to smuggle King Louis XVI out of Paris.

The month after Washington's re-election, the French National Assembly selected Edmond Charles Genet to represent the new republic in the United States. Morris soon reported Genet "a Man of good Parts and very good Education," who had more of genius than of ability, and "the Manner and Look of an Upstart." After Genet had sailed, Morris learned that the Executive Council had given him three hundred blank commissions for privateers.

A French frigate bore the new Minister to Charleston, South Carolina, where he landed April 8, 1793, was received with acclaim, and began passing out the privateering commissions to almost anyone who could sail a sloop. Then he made a leisurely but triumphal march up the Atlantic coast, being met with favor everywhere, and he acted as though the United States were a province of revolutionary France.

In the meanwhile France's declaration of war against Britain confronted the President with a concrete problem. The United States had two treaties in force, one of qualified alliance with France, the other the treaty of peace with Britain. But it was to the immediate interest of the United States to stay at peace, because to be involved as ally of either belligerent would probably destroy the young Republic. While Jefferson wanted this country to be neutral in fact, he was reluctant to draft the document, so Attorney General

Randolph drew the Proclamation, which was issued April 22, 1793.

Although it cleverly avoided the use of the word "neutrality," the Proclamation brought instant attack on the President and his Administration. Many Republicans regretted the disregard of obligations to France and were bitter because of "the seeming indifference to the cause of liberty." Some assailed the action as a usurpation of authority by the Executive. Hamilton argued, in letters signed "Pacificus," that the Constitution's enumeration of particular authorities belonging to the President intended "merely to specify the principal articles implied in the definition of executive power, leaving the rest to flow from the general grant of that power. . . . The executive power of the nation is vested in the President."

The President received Genet officially, and the latter complained over his lack of cordiality. Jefferson presently found the French hotspur plotting against every major foreign doctrine of the government. Moreover, he would pay no heed to the government's injunctions against sending out privateers, which the case of the *Little Sarah* brought to a head. Against direct orders of Jefferson, the French envoy planned to send her to sea. The Secretary reported the facts to the President, who fired up: "Is the Minister of the French Republic to set the acts of this Government at defiance *with impunity?* And then threaten the Executive with an appeal to the people?"

The Secretary of State, who at length saw through Genet, sought in June "to destroy the dangerous opinion that has been excited in him, that the people of the U. S. will disavow the acts of their government, and that he has an appeal from the Executive to Congress, and from both to the people." Then when Genet published an appeal to the people, Jefferson was realist enough to say that the Republican Party should "approve unequivocally of a state of neutrality." Madison was in full agreement.

The Cabinet, in August, unanimously decided to demand that the French Government recall Genet. Some sought to expel him at once, but Jefferson preferred first to make representations to Paris, which he did in a letter of consummate art, which let Genet condemn himself by his own words and actions, while it reaffirmed

America's love for the French people. The revolutionary government in Paris unequivocally reprehended the Minister's conduct, recalled him and sent a more seemly successor. It asked also that Morris be brought back to America.

At the same time the Administration must give heed to the looming threat of a British war. The British had neither evacuated the border-region forts awarded to the United States in the Treaty of Paris, in 1783, nor made reparation for slaves, ships, money and property seized during the war. She treated the new nation with studied contempt. The French demands, though outrageous, involved little actual invasion danger; while Britain's did, for she had built a new Navy since the Revolution, and was now as at no other time the Mistress of the Seas. She used this power to the full against revolutionary France, and in doing so dealt the United States many grievous blows.

Jefferson had sought for a live-and-let-live treaty with the British, before leaving the State Department; but Pitt, the Prime Minister, had not seen its advantages. Early in 1794, Washington concluded that war was ahead, unless we could find some basis of peace, even at large temporary sacrifice. Having made up his mind "to seek peace and pursue it," he sent John Jay to London as an envoy extraordinary, to bring back the best possible treaty.

The Chief Justice came close, as Professor Bemis shows, to making the worst of a rather promising situation in London, and Hamilton meddled in State Department affairs and helped mess things up. At length, on November 19, 1794, the Chief Justice put his name to the resultant treaty. Should it fail of ratification, he wrote the President, he despaired of another. When the treaty reached Washington's hands the next March, he realized the passionate protest it would evoke. To the people west of the mountains, Jay was already suspect for his projected treaty with Spain in Confederation days, under which she could close the mouth of the Mississippi to American trade; and the terms of the new British instrument relit these still smoldering fires. It brought little redress to American grievances. Neither impressment of American seamen, indemnity for slaves seized in the Revolutionary War, nor relaxation of Orders in Council against American trade with France was mentioned, though it did provide for clearing up boundary questions, and for paying old American debts to the British.

The Republicans raised immediate protest, and Washington wrote that "at present the cry against the Treaty is like that against a mad-dog." The back-country rage over a Mississippi navigation clause was immense. In 1796, in her first State Constitution, Tennessee insisted that the rights of navigation of the Mississippi should not be alienated "to any prince, potentate or power whatsoever."

Undoubtedly the Jay Treaty occasioned the greatest convulsion of popular feeling of the Republic's early life, but the United States did get peace in place of war. Washington and his close followers thought that this supremely necessary maintenance of peace justified the sacrifice. He summoned the Senate, which ratified after an acrimonious struggle and without a vote to spare over the required two thirds, hooking on a reservation as it did so.

The passions evoked by this humiliating treaty quickened the growth of organized political parties. Jefferson took active charge of the drilling of the Republicans, and developed party press, political pamphlet and private letters into effective instruments.

Circumstances compelled Washington to head the Federalist Party in his second term, although Hamilton and others handled its machinery. His office did not protect him from the blows of party battle, criticism of his motives cut to the quick, and he would hear no argument for a further continuation in office. During 1796 he dug out of his files the draft Madison had made, four years before, of a valedictory address to the people. Hamilton and others refurbished it, with Washington's careful correction. Early in the fall it was published as the Farewell Address.

It seems to be generally accepted now that Washington declined a third term only because of his desire to establish the important precedent that eight years was long enough for any man to hold the nation's principal office. This may be true in large part, but undoubtedly his decision was also influenced by the decline of his popularity and prestige during the second term. He looked around for a successor, and had some of his friends, including John Marshall, sound out Patrick Henry. But with Henry, as most men, emotions softened as arteries hardened with the years: he looked on the scene with no relish, and was "unwilling to embark in the business." Washington was not enamored of John Adams, a good but not wise man; but the Federalists could find no other with whom they felt they could beat Jefferson.

During the fall of 1796, some of Washington's close personal friends sought to surround his departure from the President's chair with expressions of public esteem. They knew there would be many public resolutions taking note of it, but feared some might be cold and tepid praise. A frigid resolution in the lower House of Virginia provoked Marshall to offer a substitute, which referred to Washington's "wisdom, valor and patriotism." By a majority of three votes, the House of Delegates refused to admit that Washington had shown "wisdom." Then the Federalist leaders proposed the statement that Washington's life had been "strongly marked by wisdom in the Cabinet, by valor in the field, and by the purest patriotism in both." This too failed to pass, and the address that came to him from the Legislature of his native State was a dagger of ice.

When the first President went out of office, March 5, 1797, the nation's leading Republican journal, the *Aurora* of Philadelphia, insisted that "when a retrospect is taken of the Washingtonian Administration for eight years . . . this day ought to be a JUBILEE in the United States." No wonder Washington wrote Jefferson that he had never conceived it possible that the parties would or even could go to such lengths; "that every act of my administration could be tortured . . . in such exaggerated and indecent terms as could scarcely be applied to a Nero — or even to a common pickpocket!"

During those eight years he had founded the office of President of the United States, discovered the chief of its powers, and fashioned them into ready tools for those who would follow. He entered office with the honor of having been "first in war." His accomplishments as President made him "first in peace." But such were the passions of those stormy years that it was almost a generation before he became "first in the hearts of his countrymen."

CHAPTER III

Philosopher in Power

Near noon on March 4, 1801, Thomas Jefferson walked from his boarding house to the unfinished Capitol in Washington, and took oath as the third President of the United States. His First Inaugural, read without elocution, remains one of the finest expressions of a statesman's hopes for a democratic people. It contains phrases which have reverberated down the corridors of time: "Honest friendship with all nations, entangling alliances with none . . . Government must not take from the mouth of labor the bread it has earned . . . Honest payment of our debts and sacred preservation of the public faith . . . Encouragement of agriculture, and of commerce as its handmaiden."

Also it made another statement whose high importance was not sufficiently marked at the moment: "We are all Republicans, we are all Federalists." This served notice on any who would look beneath the surface of words that Jefferson the agitator had not entered the White House; Jefferson the conservator had.

Jefferson became President after four years of intense political warfare, in which he commanded the Republican Party in the first "people's revolution." His fight was not so much against John Adams, who in 1797 had nosed him out of the first office by only three electoral votes; it was against the power-hungry Federalist leaders who had tried to use the Adams Administration for their own ends.

Adams' relations with his successor as Vice President had continued cordial until after the latter entered the White House. As President of the Senate, Jefferson kept at arm's length from the partisan debates on the floor, but amused himself and instructed the Senate by compiling a manual which continues to this day the foundation for the rules of order of that body. In 1797, Adams considered dispatching him to France to compose the breach between the two Republics, but Jefferson thought it an unwise step, the leading Federalists frothed at the mouth and the idea was dropped.

As President, Adams had done some things which affected the office of President. In 1798, when it looked as though France was about to attack us, he wrote Washington that he wished he could turn the Presidency over to him the better to meet the crisis. A little later, he wrote Washington appointing him Commander in Chief of the Army and Navy of the United States, and transmitted the nomination to the Senate, which unanimously confirmed it. This had the nature not of a delegation of part of the President's power, but of a self-divestment of a duty expressly vested in him by the Constitution. Yet there is little evidence of contemporary challenge to this action. Washington acted under it, and styled himself Commander in Chief.

Then again, after the failure of Adams' first negotiating commission to France, he had announced that he would never dispatch another Minister to that country until he had unequivocal official evidence in advance that the envoy would be received as the representative of a free, great and powerful Republic. This had seemed to close the door to peace, but in time Talleyrand changed his tune, gave the needed assurances, and Adams forced a rebellious Senate to authorize the dispatch of new commissioners to negotiate peace. Such Federalist leaders as Hamilton knew, all too well, that theirs was now the war party, and that a peace with France probably would result in a Republican victory at the 1800 election. Hamilton and his cabal denounced Adams bitterly, but the President put peace above party, the commissioners went, and peace was the result. This high-principled course of the President as Chief of Foreign Relations comports oddly with the way William McKinley weakly yielded to the war party a hundred years later.

* * *

It had been Jefferson's habit, at Monticello, to withdraw to his study after breakfast and to read, reflect or write, without benefit of family small-talk, until dinner in the mid-afternoon. Yet in public life little pleased him better than the easy general conversation of dinner table or drawing room, in which he charmed both men and women; he was perhaps America's greatest master of making public policy over the coffee cups. He could listen as well as talk; he had a sharp wit, which he generally restrained; informality was his rule, he ignored protocol, and he upset stiff-necked ministers from abroad by banishing seating by rank at his White House dinners, in favor of what he called *"pêle-mêle."*

But Jefferson could mix his study of scientific agriculture with the most effective composition of diplomatic letters. He would turn from letters on the rights of man to the efficient but autocratic dispatch of the public business. After he had trained himself to administer the office of President, he handled it seemingly without much effort.

It must have been hard for this scholar of the closet to school himself in the arts of the practical politician, so that he could take the raw materials for a new party and fashion them into a force which unseated the Federalist hierarchy.

Consider the obstacles: The Federalists sat in the seats of the mighty. The wealth and wisdom of the country supported them. Federalists filled the government offices, exerted the power, and lived off the payrolls. They took every advantage of the prestige of General Washington. These assets they offset by an autocratic manner of command: "It has been decided . . ." — almost a voice from Hamilton's throne.

To this day it remains a mystery exactly how Jefferson functioned politically. He developed an uncanny ability to keep his right hand from knowing what his left hand did. He knew the walls had ears, and Federalist postmasters eyes for the contents of every writing that passed through the mails. So he spent his years as Vice President writing with both hands and talking out of both corners of his mouth. He saw the need for a party press, had Republican papers established at key posts over the country, and took care that his views on current political controversies came to them from the pens of others. Madison served as Chief of Staff in this general propaganda work. Political pamphlets proved effective, and so did centrally arranged but seemingly spontaneous resolutions from State Legislatures.

Thomas Jefferson made himself into the master politician of his day and generation. Perhaps he remains to this day America's most consummate practitioner of that art.

Seldom have the feelings of our people been so inflamed as during the 1800 election campaign. Federalist clergymen portrayed Jefferson as a French atheist. John Fiske recounts a story told him by his grandmother: when word came of this impious profligate's election, old ladies in Connecticut hid their family Bibles to keep them from being seized and burned by his order! Republican suspicions of the "monarchial plans" of the Federalists were no less sharp. The 1800 presidential canvass was probably more bitter than even that of 1860.

The willingness of many leading Federalist politicians to take advantage of the flaw of the Constitution's electoral college provision, in order to put the unprincipled Burr in as President over Jefferson, measured the sweep of partisan fury. It failed only because Hamilton hated Burr more than Jefferson; one can only imagine the stormy battle in his bitter soul in having to make such a choice between Beelzebub and Satan!

The campaign and its aftermath greatly changed Jefferson. He saw the necessity for a major move to end the party war, so that counter-revolution would not follow Republican victory, accepted the election with a full understanding of the factors in it, and with a determined purpose to banish the civil war between the parties. The Federalists were astounded when he resolutely refrained from any effort to mark the new day of democracy by seeking to put the bottom rail on top. The fact of power changed him; the danger of civil conflict in 1800 sobered him; and he administered the government so quietly and efficiently that in a short while its success became an accepted fact among the masses.

Moreover, the people took Jefferson to their hearts — not only the Republicans he had commanded in the five years of the political offensive before his first election, but most of the Federalists, whose hates and fears subsided until embargo time. His White House successors — Madison, Monroe, even John Quincy Adams — awaited advices from Monticello, the truest attest of his statesmanship.

Jefferson neither remade the Constitution nor set aside the governmental construction Washington, Hamilton and Madison had built upon it. He soon perceived the practical merit of many Federalist bureaucratic devices, and did not disturb them.

Nor did he remove Federalists en masse from the public payroll. He thought that attracting Federalists of the milder school would serve to abate hot partisan passions, and make his election triumph permanent. While the "incurables" — the leading bitter-enders — should have no favors, and the scores of appointments Adams had nominated and the Senate confirmed after the election should be treated as nullities, he set his face against removals on the ground of party alone, because it "would revolt our new converts and give a body to leaders who now stand alone." Therefore he sought a course to "conciliate the honest part" of the Federalists by retaining many in office.

"Of all the duties imposed on the executive head of a government," he wrote, "appointment to office is the most difficult and the most irksome." He read personally all applications for jobs, marked each one, and considered it from the double standpoint of the influence the appointment would have on party welfare, and its effect on the proper conduct of public business. The Republicans, excluded from the patronage for almost ten years, were famished for the loaves and fishes, and expected a mass exodus of their enemies. When they found new jobs a trickle, not a flood, they pressed him mightily. Even so, in July 1803 Federalists still held 130 out of a total of 316 appointive offices.

Because of policies of this sort, despite the very real change in political control the government went along without disturbance. The leader of the revolution took care that the laws were faithfully executed. This capacity to change under the compulsion of facts suggests Jefferson's organic growth of character.

His principles of administration were few. Professor L. K. Caldwell finds five major ones: Harmony was the first; Jefferson deemed the fact that his Presidency "was conducted with cordiality and harmony among all the members" one of its most fortunate circumstances. Again he emphasized simplicity — "we have more machinery of government than is necessary." Good administration should heed the necessity for constant change, for "laws and institutions must go hand in hand with the progress of the human mind." Also it should be decentralized, because "it is not by the consolidation or concentration of powers but by their distribution that good government is effected. . . . It is by division and subdivision of duties alone that all matters great or small can be managed to perfection." He felt it equally indispensable for responsibility to be exacted from administrators, although those who accepted great charges must "risk themselves on great occasions, when the safety of the nation or some of its very high interests are at stake."

Jefferson's first Cabinet contained two men of mental greatness, James Madison and Albert Gallatin; and his relations with them were so informal and intimate that each today would be thought of as an Assistant President.

Madison's duties as Secretary of State did not become unbearable until the renewal of the war in Europe, in May 1803. Thenceforward, the problems were terrific, his dry, tortuous logic not any too well adapted to their handling, and the President often stepped in to handle diplomatic crises.

With Gallatin it was different. A Genevese by birth, he left Switzerland to aid in the Revolutionary War, and finally wound up a bad farmer and worse merchant in western Pennsylvania. He sympathized with the economic woes of the natives in the Whisky Rebellion, and came to Congress in 1795. Jefferson had been delighted with his operation as floor leader of the Republicans, and knew that his skill in handling people equaled the cold, fast, sure action of his mind. He put Gallatin in charge of the Treasury, to supervise the central item on his program.

Economy was the magic word with Jefferson, but Gallatin went him one better. They inherited a Treasury well stocked with specie while receipts were running a little over $10,000,000 a year. Gallatin thought this income would continue for the next eight years, that $3,500,000 would meet operating expenses, and that the national debt could be extinguished in fifteen years. He tightened up the spending system, urged specific item appropriations and direct accountability. In consequence, Congress expanded its use of the committee system, until they put detailed controls on the actions of the department heads, and prescribed the items of expenditure to the last gaiter-button.

The President promised cuts in the cost of every spending agency — and made good on them, the chief sufferers being the military services, which starved through both of his terms, and the first three years of Madison's. Jefferson could never overcome his fear of a standing Army or a large professional Navy. As Governor of Virginia in the Revolution, he knew the weakness of the militia system; but such was his fear that a standing Army would rob the people of their liberties that he said it would hurt less to lose a war to a foreign power than to win it with a military dictatorship. He rationalized his dislike of a large Navy, saying building and maintaining one would "pull on our own heads that load of military expense which makes the European laborer go supperless to bed."

He preferred that the nation's whole energies be put on developing the continent; his interest in national planning, as pointed out by Charles E. Merriam and Frank Bourgin, stemmed out of the continually bettering government income. In his Second Inaugural he referred to the expectation that the liberated revenues might, after constitutional amendment, be distributed among the States to be applied "in time of peace, to rivers, canals, roads, arts, manufactures, education and other great objects within each state." In his annual message in 1806, he urged the maintenance of the tariff on luxuries, and the application of its proceeds "to the great purposes of the public education, roads, rivers, canals and such other objects of public improvement as it may be thought proper to add to the constitutional enumeration of Federal powers."

Two years later, with Jefferson's approval, Gallatin made his famous report proposing the accumulation out of surplus of twenty million dollars to build roads and canals. One recommendation was for great canals along the Atlantic coast, to join New England and the South; a second for communications between the Atlantic and Western waters; another for connections between the Atlantic, the St. Lawrence River and the Great Lakes; and a series of interior canals and roads. Not only would these aid peace time commerce but they would enable the easier mobilization of our military forces at any point of danger.

For the first few years the people applauded the short rations for the Federal departments, expenditure was kept under appropriations, and revenue ran so much ahead of Gallatin's cautious estimates that, by 1810, the national debt had been cut over $27,000,000, and in addition France had received $15,000,000 for Louisiana. The money came from the tariff for revenue only. Over Gallatin's protest, the excise tax on whisky had been repealed and the Federal Government had no internal revenue during these years.

This epoch of economical efficiency held the public attention for most of the first term. The struggle between the Republicans, controlling the executive and legislative branches, and the Federalist Supreme Court had no such contemporary importance as it has grown to have through the interpreters of succeeding generations.

Jefferson went into the White House firmly persuaded that, as President, he had the right and the power to interpret his duty under the Constitution independently of whatever view might be taken by Congress or Court. He insisted that "our country has thought proper to distribute the powers of its government among three equal and independent authorities constituting each a check on one or both of the others in all attempts to impair its Constitution." Each therefore must have a right, in matters within its proper functions, "to act in the last resort and without appeal, to decide on the validity of an act according to its own judgment, and uncontrolled by the opinions of any other department."

He had received appeals from many persons prosecuted under the Sedition Act, and felt "called on by the position in which the nation had placed me, to exercise in their behalf my free and independent judgment. . . . On mature deliberation, and under the tie of the solemn oath which binds me to them and to my duty, I do declare that I hold that act to be in palpable and unqualified contradiction to the Constitution. Considering it then as a nullity, I have relieved from oppression under it those of my fellow citizens who were within the reach of the functions confided to me."

Jefferson and his party had a sense of outrage at the way Adams and the Federalists, in the time between their defeat and end of office, had created sixteen new judgeships, with attorneys, marshals, clerks, and other aids, and filled them with tried Federalists. The Congress got rid of these "midnight judges" by the repeal of the new judiciary act. Then one Marbury, a Federalist whose commission as Justice of the Peace for the District of Columbia had been kept from him, brought a mandamus proceeding to force the Secretary of State to deliver it.

The Supreme Court which passed on it had a new Chief Justice, who saw in it the chance to harm the Jefferson Administration at the same time that he proclaimed the supremacy of the Court. This was John Marshall, a cousin and bitter foe of Jefferson, whom Adams had nominated after John Jay refused a reappointment. Some Federalist Senators felt the selection showed Adams' "debility or derangement of intellect," and confirmed it with reluctance. Years later, Adams said, "My gift of John Marshall to the people of the United States was the proudest act of my life."

The new Chief Justice, in his opinion in *Marbury* vs. *Madison*, handed down in 1803, held that Marbury had a property right in the office to which he had been appointed: the commission should have been delivered to him and he had the right to sue. Marshall thus affixed on Jefferson the commission of a public wrong. Then he asked whether the Court possessed the constitutional right to assume jurisdiction in the Marbury case, which had been sought under its original jurisdiction rather than on appeal. He found that Congress had no constitutional right to confer such original jurisdiction on the Court, so Marbury's case was dismissed. He had contrived an opinion which technically sustained Jefferson, after a stump speech of *obiter dicta* about how wrong he had been.

To the public of 1803 (says Charles Warren, the great historian of the Supreme Court), "The case represented the determination of Marshall and his associates to interfere with the authority of the Executive, and it derived its chief importance then from that aspect.... Jefferson's antagonism to Marshall and the Court at that time was due more to his resentment at the alleged invasion of his Executive prerogative than to any so-called 'judicial usurpation' of the field of Congressional authority."

Jefferson's most interesting collision with Marshall occurred in the trial of Aaron Burr for treason, which came before the Chief Justice in the latter's circuit duty, at Richmond, Virginia, but never reached the Supreme Court. The President had never forgiven Burr's hand in the attempted thwarting of his election, the Vice President's retainers had not been able to get Federal jobs, and Jefferson had pushed Burr himself out of public life. The great Blennerhassett "conspiracy" had been about the last hope of a fascinating adventurer whose air-castles of foreign empire had collapsed. Many Federalist judges had embraced the doctrine of constructive treason. Marshall himself once verged near it, and his insistence at Richmond upon the strictest tracking of the letter of the Constitution on the crime of treason suggested an about-face.

The Federalists adopted Burr's cause, so much so that Washington Irving went to Richmond on an "informal" retainer in order to "be of service with his pen." Before the Grand Jury brought the indictments, Marshall remained the whole evening at a dinner where Burr was a guest. Before the end of the trial, the accused and the Government had almost changed positions through Burr's charge of "Presidential persecution" and through the attitude of the Court. Not without reason did William Wirt, for the Government, ask if defense counsel "flatter themselves that this Court feels political prejudices which will supply the place of argument and innocence on the part of the prisoner."

During the trial, Burr's counsel said they needed the correspondence between General James Wilkinson, principal Government witness as to the conspiracy, the President, the Attorney General and other Federal officials. After argument, the Chief Justice issued a *subpoena duces tecum,* for Jefferson to appear as a witness, together with the papers sought.

The President, astounded, wrote that he did not believe the district courts had the power "of commanding the Executive Government to abandon superior duties and attend on them, at whatever distance." He would not, by any notice of the subpoena, set a precedent "which might sanction a proceeding so preposterous." Moreover, he felt it necessary to safeguard "the necessary right of the President to decide, independently of all other authority, what papers coming to him as President the public interests permit to be communicated, and to whom." Otherwise he was ready voluntarily to furnish, on all occasions, whatever the purposes of justice might require. He sent a letter for presentation to the Court, together with a copy of General Wilkinson's letter, which omitted "some passages entirely confidential, given me for my information in the discharge of my executive functions, and which my duties and the public interest forbid me to make public."

This statement that the President's overriding duty as Chief Executive, to say nothing of his prerogative as Chief of State, exempted him from dancing attendance on the courts as a witness has never been successfully challenged. Grant wanted to testify in the Whisky Ring cases, but only because he was anxious to protect a bribe-taking private secretary, and this he did by deposition. Nor has the President's right to independent discretion in the disclosure of his correspondence ever been upset.

* * *

The most conspicuous event of Jefferson's Presidency was the Louisiana Purchase. It reshaped the United States into a continental nation marching toward world power. In his First Inaugural, he had spoken of America as a rising nation "advancing rapidly to destinies beyond the reach of mortal eye." By the end of three years, this extraordinary procurement had added an area equal in size to that of the then United States. The necessity for prompt action to consummate the bargain, and then the emergency need for quick absorption of the new lands into the Union, caused the downfall of the policy of strict construction of the Constitution. It can be argued, writes Frederick J. Turner, that the Louisiana Purchase doctrines "were farther reaching in their effect upon the Constitution than even the measures of Alexander Hamilton. All the decisions of later American history were either traceable to or in some measure shaped or determined by it."

An unusual train of circumstances led Napoleon to persuade Spain to retransfer the vast Louisiana region to the French flag; and Jefferson had a stroke of luck in Napoleon's immediate mood in the spring of 1803, and consequent willingness to sell. The juncture of irritations which caused that strange genius from Corsica to give away an empire for $15,000,000 was not of American creation, but stemmed out of the power politics of Europe and her colonies in the West Indies. So far as Americans are concerned, the credit was shared between Jefferson, Madison, Livingston, and Monroe.

The President was much concerned over finding the constitutional way to bring Louisiana under the ownership of the Government of the United States. His proposition had once concerned only the Island of Orleans. But here was the Treaty — conveying, for a paltry $15,000,000, an area of territory larger than the entire land area of the Federal Union. And here was the Constitution of the United States, which said nothing about the acquisition of land beyond the existing borders.

Hamilton had said, in the *Federalist,* that "It is impossible to foresee or define the extent and variety of national exigencies, or the correspondent extent and variety of the means which may be necessary to satisfy them." The Jeffersonian doctrine, as a spokesman told Congress earlier that year, was that "This government is to be administered according to defined objects and situations. It is a government of definition and not of trust and discretion." But if Jefferson were to insist on waiting until a constitutional amendment should authorize such acquisitions, Napoleon might change his mind; his moody irascibility made time of the essence in carrying out the obligations of the treaty of purchase.

Congress was not in session, and the President first thought of taking no action until it assembled the next December, at which time it could submit to the States another amendment to the Constitution, under which the Government of the United States would be authorized to acquire, through purchase or seizure, new territory, rather than be forced to have it acquired by an existing State. But the logic of his prior political position did not fit the reality of the situation. He wrote a few letters voicing it, drafted a possible amendment, then dropped the idea and called Congress in special session.

The New England Federalists were bitterly antagonistic to the bringing-in, as a future counterweight to their Northeast, of this huge region of future population, wealth and political influence to the far Southwest and West. To forestall defeat at their hands, the President instructed a Kentucky Senator to get the Western members there the first day of the extra session; they must cast metaphysical subtleties behind them, "ratify and pay for it." During the public discussion, Gouverneur Morris was asked what the 1787 Constitution framers thought about taking in new territory. "I knew as well then," he answered, "as I do now that all North America must at length be annexed to us . . . It would, therefore, have been perfectly Utopian to propose a paper restriction." The treaty was ratified by the vote of all but the New England Federalist Senators. Then the House initiated and both branches backed up the appropriations to pay for the purchase.

Jefferson's views on the form of government for the new territory went through the same sort of conversion under heat and pressure.

He first thought the organization pattern should be meticulously prescribed in a Constitutional amendment, and drafted one of about six hundred words in length. Gallatin thought it much too detailed — he had to collect the Louisiana revenue. By the assembling of Congress, the President had reached the point of saying: "With the wisdom of Congress it will rest to take those ulterior measures which may be necessary for the immediate occupation and temporary government of the country; for its incorporation in our Union . . ."

None the less, he himself actually sketched the bill which Congress passed. It put in the President's hands the appointment of all officers in Louisiana Territory, and thus made Jefferson the Executive, Legislature and Judiciary of Louisiana. Article III of the Treaty had provided that the inhabitants should be admitted "to the enjoyment of the rights, advantages and immunities of citizens of the United States." The people, however, had no voice whatsoever as to their government, and all rights had to be legislated into the Territory from outside. John Quincy Adams opposed on the ground that it was government for the people without their consent. Jefferson drafted and applied the act because circumstances demanded. Again he acted as a realist.

During his first term Jefferson had a record of almost uninterrupted success. His Inaugural promises of economy had been redeemed, Louisiana had been added, trade flourished — and his passion for peace had not been thwarted. In 1804 he was elected to a second term, winning all but two of the States and all but fourteen of the electoral votes. His Second Inaugural recorded high accomplishment, and even brighter future hopes.

He had no reason to expect trouble with Congress, which had been his loyal lieutenant since he entered the White House, despite the fact that, in contrast to his pre-presidential theory that "the Executive secures its instructions from the legislature," he had suggested what Congress needed to do. He used the party caucus to enforce discipline, through floor leaders of House and Senate, who were appointed by Jefferson and dismissed at his pleasure. He drilled them incessantly, deeming conferences with them about as important as Cabinet meetings. Throughout the first term — and, indeed, until 1808, the year of the Embargo — Congress adopted most of his policies. As Howard White puts it, "That body never became so unruly as to oblige Jefferson to use the veto."

But the second term brought troubles at home and abroad. John Randolph of Roanoke, a weird genius of rule or ruin, tilted against Jefferson's control chiefly because of dislike for Madison, and the President found it harder to direct Congress through table-talk or messages sent by aides. Dissensions broke out in the Cabinet between Gallatin and Smith, the Secretary of the Navy; while Madison grew jealous of Gallatin's accomplishments and influence.

Napoleon renewed the war with Britain within three months of the signing of the Louisiana Purchase Treaty. Almost at once the shipping of the United States became the target of both belligerents.

This was inevitable because, until the War of 1812, America was the most prosperous neutral carrier. When the British Navy and privateers stopped direct trade between France and Spain and their colonies, American shipowners stepped in to take the profits of this vast commerce. Then the British intensified their use of the Rule of the War of 1756 to destroy this lucrative new trade.

Jefferson and Madison were continuously searching for ways to avoid British prohibitions and French reprisals, and succeeded sufficiently for the Americans to build up a huge carrying trade, not only of Colonial produce but also of such American staples as cotton, tobacco and flour. In 1805, the British grew desperate over their own losses of trade, their sinews of war; and their courts of admiralty hardened their hearts. Jefferson undertook to force relaxation of the Orders in Council through a policy of commercial restriction. At his urging, in April 1806 Congress passed the Non-Importation Act, which was designed to be a club to enable American envoys to deal with the British. But the latter had their backs to the wall, and would not make terms acceptable to Jefferson.

In 1807, the British Government issued two new Orders in Council, one of which forbade neutral ships to trade between the ports of France, her allies and dependencies, while the other decreed a paper blockade of all ports under French control. Napoleon's Milan Decree answered that any ship which submitted to these Orders in Council became lawful French prize. This meant that no American ship could visit a French port unless it had first paid tribute to a British customhouse, while if the ship did so, or even if she had been stopped by a British warship, the French would condemn both ship and cargo.

The United States had the choice between fighting both the Mistress of the Seas and the foremost of land tyrants in a triangular duel, or submitting to outrages intolerable for a sovereign State, no matter how modest its position in the concert of nations. Deeming the first alternative quixotic and the second unthinkable, Jefferson brought forward the Embargo as a measure short of war, yet attaining some of its ends.

In doing so, he followed both the precedent of Colonial resistance to Britain, and the logic of his own career. As Secretary of State he had endeavored to bring commercial pressure on the British. American trade had grown many-fold since 1793. Neither Britain nor France recognized a neutral right she would respect; each had a bankrupt diplomacy which spurned American good will. When adopted, in December 1807, the Embargo was perhaps the best substitute for war so far devised.

To attain its ends, the Embargo must safeguard American shipping, at the same time that it awakened the consuming populations of Europe to the folly of the course of their governments, through cutting them off from needed overseas supplies. The Embargo was a positive policy to the extent that it accomplished these things, but was negative in its neglect to defend our rights. None the less, it was a tool ready at hand to assert our national dignity against injuries beyond our immediate military power to repel.

The more practically imaginative Gallatin accepted the policy reluctantly. From every point of view — privation, suffering, revenue, effect on the enemy, politics at home — he preferred war to a permanent embargo, because "government prohibitions do always more mischief than has been calculated." If adopted at all, it should be but for a short time, so that if it did not work it could be dropped without appearing to retreat.

Jefferson pressed his bill, and his party machine put it through Congress in short order. But it had been drawn too hastily, carried no penalties for violation, and the final amendments were not made until late in April 1808.

Under the plan, the Governors of the States were to work with the Secretary of the Treasury, his Collectors and other officials in its enforcement. The President issued a proclamation to the Governors authorizing them to detain all coasting vessels and their cargoes, on suspicion of intent to evade the Embargo, and designated flour, a large export item, as a suspect commodity. Governors were allowed to issue to trusted merchants warrants to import amounts of flour needed by their respective communities. Gallatin thought the Collectors would prove the best issuers of licenses, and that the Governors would issue warrants wholesale, but in the outcome, with one exception the Governors acted well.

The Embargo put Thomas Jefferson in a strange position. The author of the maxim that "that government governs best which governs least" had to transform himself into an autocrat, in order to direct the arbitrary enforcement of a highly inquisitorial statute, which could only succeed through trenching upon what many people regarded as their dearest rights. As long as enforcement was slipshod, there was no uprising. But after several months, thanks to Gallatin's administrative genius, the Embargo became surprisingly well enforced. The coastwise trade was brought under control; and then public irritation began to rise. Jefferson found that the fact of force could not be offset by tactful words.

One interesting effect of all this was that the President developed a new zeal for domestic manufacture. "There can be no question in a mind truly American," he said, "whether it be best to send our citizens and property into certain captivity and then wage war for their recovery, or to keep them at home, and to turn seriously to that policy which plants the manufacturer and the husbandman side by side, and so establish at the door of everyone that exchange of mutual labors and comforts which we have hitherto sought in distant regions, and under perpetual risk of broils with them." . . . Hamilton might as well have held the pen.

The French were less hurt by the Embargo than the British; their merchant fleet had already fled the ocean, and their survival in the grim world struggle did not rest, as Britain's did, on the import of raw materials, their manufacture and sale abroad. While Napoleon shabbily took advantage of every excuse or circumstance to confiscate other people's ships, goods and money, he had put his faith in the god of battles and not in that of trade.

As Jefferson had hoped, however, the Embargo dealt British industrial labor a grievous blow. Mills shut down, labor starved; the Poor Law was invoked more than it had been since Elizabeth's time — but the workers' suffering did not translate into political action; the "rotten boroughs" were still sending more men to the House of Commons than all the manufacturing towns.

The crowning blow came to Jefferson's foreign expectations with Napoleon's invasion of the Spanish peninsula at just about the time Jefferson's Embargo law was taking hold. The Portuguese House of Braganza promptly fled to Brazil. The Spanish Bourbons did not get away, their people revolted — and their American dominions opened their ports to the British, whose commerce revived overnight.

All of which might have been good for the world, but proved very bad for the American Embargo. Britain's 1807 exports to the United States were nearly twelve million pounds; those in the Embargo years only five million, two hundred and fifty thousand. But the increase in her exports to the Americas, exclusive of the United States, was a little over six million pounds. In total world exports, her drop was under seven per cent. This was one of the two principal reasons the Embargo did not work. The tremendous resources of a new continent did not give the United States a monopoly power against Britain, whose flag sailed every sea.

Castlereagh, the British Foreign Minister, had been clearly aware of the distress of the laboring class. One of the Cabinet in Britain had proposed that the British guarantee the safety of every merchant ship, neutral or belligerent, on a voyage to or from a British port — a seemingly friendly act toward America. But Castlereagh preferred that the Jefferson party stew in their own juice; "the continuance of the embargo for some time is the best chance of their being destroyed *as a party;* and I should prefer exposing them to the disgrace of rescinding their own measures at the demand of their own people than furnish them any creditable pretext for doing so." These expectations came close to being realized. In September, Madison admitted that there was no further hope of Napoleon's changing his policy — "We must therefore look to England alone for the chances of disembarrassment."

The Embargo created its own opposition in the United States, and this really caused its doom. From the start it hurt American morale. From a psychological standpoint, it lacked the customary incentives to patriotism. It required a passive rather than active course, and would achieve its ends through endurance rather than fighting, a psychology alien to the American tradition. Added to that, it hurt the economic life of all Americans.

Late in the summer of 1808, Jefferson gathered the impressions of trusted observers. Mississippi was in distress because of the loss of market for her cotton but seemed a little philosophic about it. South Carolina still backed the Administration, and said it deserved well of the country. North Carolina was against the Embargo; around New Bern "the majority of our citizens are as loyal subjects to John Bull, in their hearts, as any about St. James's Palace." Virginia was a little better, but Wilson Cary Nichols termed it a poor measure, and the planter distress was growing acute.

The Middle States suffered more from the impact on shipping than on agriculture. Philadelphia lamented that the ruined carrying trade was even less hurtful than the stagnation of trade. But native manufactures started up vigorously, Philadelphia was in a boom;

and a new paper, the *Price Current,* advertised the change. The 1808 Pennsylvania election went Republican.

Undoubtedly New England was the worst injured section in trade. Vermont, an agricultural State, had low prices, no markets, and her debtors crammed the jails. Massachusetts went violently against the law; much of her shipping was tied up, though some was kept in service through the connivance of the British Navy. To stimulate New England secession it deliberately did not blockade that part of the coast, which helped the Federalists sweep the fall elections. Timothy Pickering kept up a treasonable correspondence with the British Government, and the Hartford Convention laid the basis for a New England revolution under the claim of constitutional right. Smuggling over the Canadian border got so bad that Collectors of Customs resigned to avoid the odium of disapproving neighbors, or a shot in the night. New England produce and goods moved by Lake Champlain, the St. Lawrence and Passamaquoddy Bay; at times insurgent bands guarded its transit; the people's sympathies were with neighbors, not the distant government.

The President asked the Governor of New York to furnish militia to help the Collector of the Oswego district enforce the law. Governor Tompkins demurred that he could do this only if insurrection were proclaimed. Jefferson answered, "This may not be an insurrection in the popular sense of the word; but being arrayed in warlike manner, actually committing acts of war, and persevering systematically in defiance of the public authority, brings it so fully within the legal definition of an insurrection that I should not have hesitated to issue a proclamation except for public opinion and morale reasons."

Gallatin reported that "we must depend entirely on force" until Congress met again in December 1808. Then that body "must either invest the Executive with the most arbitrary powers and sufficient force to carry the Embargo into effect, or give it up altogether." To this he saw no alternative but war.

Jefferson was the last to admit the failure. Until late in the year, he discounted the partisan Federalist attacks and thought public opinion at the worst was not against him, because he misinterpreted passive submission, under threats of force, for active support. Nor would he change until trusted friends warned that there were limits beyond which his own party would not sustain him. In January 1809 he wrote despairingly, "There never has been a situation of the world before, in which such endeavors as we have made would not have secured the peace."

Jefferson had reluctantly summoned Congress in November 1808, right after the national election in which James Madison, his closest friend, had been elected to succeed him, the first of the once-famous "Secretarial succession" which lasted until 1828. Jefferson had been pressed to serve a third term, but had announced months before the election that he would follow Washington's example. As was later clear, he could have gone out of office at no juncture more harmful to his reputation as a statesman. Had he served a third term, he might have redeemed the Embargo and avoided the needless war with Britain. Instead, he left the White House with failure stamped on his statecraft.

During the months between the assembly of Congress and Madison's inauguration, Jefferson tried to divorce himself of any major role in the determination of policy. "It is fair," he wrote, "to leave to these who are to act on them the decisions they prefer, being myself but a spectator. I should not feel justified in directing measures which those who are to execute them would disapprove." He described himself as "chiefly an unmeddling listener to what others say." Federalists sneered that fear of responsibility and love of popularity had become his master-passions.

Gallatin did not like this, insisted that the President act, and President-elect Madison concurred: "You must decide the question absolutely so that we may point a decisive way." But Jefferson would not shoulder the burden of decision. His heart and hope had been so bound up in the measure short of war that he would not desert his child. He felt, as did the Federalists, that the Administration would be disgraced by repeal.

Jefferson intimated he would like the Embargo repeal not to take effect until some time after he left office, but Congress was in a panic and would not wait. In substitution it put through a non-intercourse measure, which proved more workable than the Embargo. Jefferson signed the repealer his last day in office, saying: "Never did a person released from his chains feel such relief as I feel on casting off the shackles of power."

In retrospect, Jefferson chiefly influenced the Presidency through establishing the importance of party leadership. Inasmuch as parties were to choose the person who would become Chief Executive, and thus make the Electoral College a surplus number with mere accountancy effect, the President must dominate the party which he represented, and employ it in the other branches of the government, to effectuate his policies and programs. He was perhaps the most skillful Chief of Party among all the Presidents.

During the first term, the same was true of his direction of public opinion. It was only in his last two years that he lost his mastery over molding the public mood. Nor did he then lose out to the degree that Wilson did, after the 1918 by-election, in the fight with the Senate isolationists.

Jefferson was especially successful as Chief of Government. An experienced administrator, he went into office more interested in planning for the morrow than in handling momentary details, but overcame much of this feeling during his first two years. His insistence on economical expenditure as well as efficient operation was no pretense, and it paid large dividends. Perhaps there never was a better team than Jefferson and Gallatin for getting much more than value received for every dollar of public funds expended: any comparison of Coolidge and Mellon with them is absurd.

He had been in the White House only a few months when he informed his Cabinet that he would return to Washington's method of keeping control of executive business, and that his department heads were to report all policy matters to him, orally or in writing. He saw such visitors every day while in the Capital, and when at Monticello had an efficient courier service to keep him advised. He did not follow Washington's idea of the Cabinet as a collective body, he said, because of constitutional objections, but he maintained quite intimate relations with most of his advisers. Madison and Gallatin frequently dined at the White House, and the President used them as an informal planning board.

The position of Commander in Chief aroused little interest in him, doubtless because of his aversion to a standing Army. He neglected the Navy until he had need of it in Embargo days, and then it was too weak to perform. The nation was to pay bitterly for this phase of his policy, during the War of 1812.

To his service as Chief of Foreign Relations he brought an extraordinary diplomatic experience, and he worked at it all the time. His mind possessed intuitive powers far above Madison's industrious but irritatingly argumentative logic. To a large extent he was his own Secretary of State, and he did manage to avoid war.

His dislike for pomp caused him to slur deliberately the ceremonial dignity incident to service as Chief of State. But his personal preference for carpet-slipper informality in receiving ministers of foreign nations meant no surrender of the presidential prerogative. He guarded it as jealously as he did the Chief Executive's unqualified discretion.

Despite all these things, the chief effect he had upon the presidential operation was in his role as Chief of Party. He exercised his powerful control of the Republicans in Congress through persuasive and informal methods, but through his first term most of the party leaders in both Houses did his bidding without undue contention or delay. In consequence, Jefferson was enabled to maintain the form that Congress framed the national policies and he enforced them, although in reality Congress made most of its laws on Jefferson's initiative, and often on his unamended drafts.

His leadership of the party was translated, through its majority in the National Legislature, into the fact of control of the National Government. It was his example of the employment of this power which Woodrow Wilson and Franklin Roosevelt studied and put to good use.

CHAPTER IV

The People's Leader

When Andrew Jackson entered the White House on March 4, 1829, immense new strength came to the office of President. This "hempen homespun of the backwoods," this "swashbuckling desperado" — to use but two of the sneering terms employed by his rivals — commanded the confidence of the common people perhaps better than any President of the century.

He came to the office by virtue of a political revolution. As President, not only did he keep faith with the people by driving the patricians from power but, even more importantly, he found new piers for the authority of the Chief of State, as the protector of the people. Not without reason was he given the sobriquet "Old Hickory," for Jackson's will was the most inflexible, his courage the most consistent, of any among the Presidents.

Interestingly enough, he was neither ill-mannered nor inexperienced when he took office. His personal charm and gracious conduct while visiting Harvard, among Whig ill-wishers, almost persuaded them to become Jacksonians. His spelling was bad, because of lack of schooling during the Revolution, but his vocabulary was wide, his reading quite broad, and his correspondence prodigious. Jackson wrote a good letter, not enveloping the subject as did Jefferson, but going directly to its heart.

He was more than the soldier in politics. Unlike the first Harrison, Zach Taylor, and Grant, other traits as well as military laurels brought him to power, and his reputation did not suffer a White House collapse. Jackson had a varied experience in civil government. He was prosecutor, then judge, in Tennessee, before being

Militia general, conqueror of the Creeks in the Alabama country and the hero of the Battle of New Orleans. He served in the Senate when Jefferson presided, and in 1823 was elected again.

He made money farming on the Cumberland, and likewise in a Nashville bank. Prudent in business, scrupulous in meeting the obligations of honor, politics, or public service, his mood was imperious, his mind was his own, his trust in friends and retainers superb. He knew the west country intimately. Although he was considerable of an aristocrat — John Sevier made beaver hats but Jackson wore them — he heard the heartbeat of the masses and hearkened to it. They trusted him, and followed him to victory. He may have been "King Andrew" — but he was the people's king.

The years between Jefferson and Jackson, while full of matters of public concern, were not marked by many novel extensions or employments of presidential power. Of the three men who held the office in the interregnum, history has been kindest to James Madison, the least competent, and most critical of John Quincy Adams, probably the most deserving. Monroe is chiefly remembered as the author of the doctrine which bears his name.

"In politics," writes Francis Hirst, "Madison was Jefferson's brother; in scientific knowledge of politics he was Jefferson's equal. But he had no divine spark of genius, nor the personal magnetism which had ensured harmony and unity in Jefferson's Cabinet. Nor was he fitted either to resist a war party or to conduct a war."

In addition, it was Madison's lot to inherit the office when a new group was thrusting for power. Since the Republicans had come into office, in 1800, a great new country had grown up across the Appalachians, a mid-continent empire unexcited over the party contentions of the late 1790's and more interested in the war with the Indians than that in Europe. By 1810, the South and the West began sending new men, young men, to Congress, conspicuous among them Henry Clay of Kentucky, John C. Calhoun of South Carolina, and Felix Grundy of Tennessee. Neither these men nor the people who sent them shared Jefferson's passion for peace. They felt that the tortuous diplomatic intercourse with France and especially that with Britain had been somewhat shameful. These War Hawks made Clay Speaker of the House and Calhoun chairman of its most powerful committee.

The South Carolinian Calhoun, not yet thirty, took the lead in converting the Republican Party from its 1798 doctrines of peace to a new nationalism of war and expansion. He scored the "calculating avarice" of the Embargo and Non-Intercourse Acts; such a motive was only fit for shops and counting houses; "whenever it touches sovereign power, the nation is ruined." Johnson, of Kentucky, said that if we did not forcibly resist Britain's encroachments, we must "formally annul" the Declaration of Independence. Grundy, of Tennessee, urged that the British be driven from the continent, because, when we had fully peopled Canada, the Northern States would lose their power, and "be at the discretion of others."

These new pressures forced Madison's hand and he soon brought Monroe into the Cabinet as Secretary of State. The latter took office, John Randolph of Roanoke told the House, with the firm conviction that the American Government must resent unjust treatment not by arguments and protests merely, but by an appeal to arms; therefore his appointment was "the signal of war with Great Britain."

The Federalist leaders made no last-ditch fight against the war; the British Minister reported to London that they intended to vote for war, which "will turn out the Administration, and then they will have their own way, and make a solid peace with Great Britain." In February 1812 they asked him to urge his government not to revoke the Orders in Council; if Britain would not bend, the Republicans "must be lost, either by the disgrace of having nearly ruined the trade of the United States . . . or else by their incapacity to conduct the government during war."

But Britain had lost her zeal for a war with her former colonies, for in 1811–1812 she was close to economic ruin. Five years earlier she had paid seventy-eight shillings for a quarter of wheat, now it cost one hundred and twelve shillings. Her exports had dropped over a third, and the Tory government, for all its stolid incompetence, had been stirred to change its policy toward the United States. During the spring of 1812, her Ministry made up its mind to recall the offensive Orders in Council, and perhaps to abate the impressment of our seamen. But the assassination of their Prime Minister delayed their action. On June 18, 1812, Congress declared war, just two days before the British Parliament voted for peace.

When Madison proclaimed the war, as was noted by Richard Rush, he visited in person — a thing never known before — all the offices of the Departments of War and the Navy, stimulating everything in a manner worthy of a "little Commander in Chief, with his little round hat and huge cockade."

The declaration greatly enhanced Madison's status in the government. The sessions of Congress did not alter in character, but suddenly became unimportant in comparison with executive actions. No longer did it directly counteract the presidential will, or refuse the legislation he required. For the first time since he had been President, Congress carried out the requests of his annual message like orders. In November, he won a second term despite the loss of New England and New York to DeWitt Clinton.

From the start, however, Madison fumbled in war administration. In September 1812, Senator William H. Crawford, of Georgia, expressed the general "want of confidence in the leaders of our forces" — particularly in Secretary of War Eustis, "who consumes his time in reading advertisements of petty retailing merchants to find where he can purchase a hundred shoes or two hundred hats." Moreover, the custom of Secretary of the Navy Paul Hamilton of "instructing his naval officers to supply the heads of the departments with pineapples and other tropical fruits could not fail to bring disgrace upon them and the nation." Unless Madison would dismiss such incompetents, "his accountability to the nation will be great indeed."

Once in the war, the hopes of easy conquest of Canada were quickly ended. Two New England Governors refused militia for a Canadian expedition, our military forces performed miserably, and it was America's worst-fought war. Jefferson's fears of a strong military establishment had a part in our unpreparedness, but the chief trouble was Madison himself, our poorest Commander in Chief in time of war. It took two years of humiliating defeat on land to force him to try to improve the sorry administrative mess.

Madison and most of his Cabinet seemed to believe that military disasters would unify the country, but John Taylor of Caroline remarked truly that it was folly to go on with the war in the belief that "defeat has raised the spirit of the nation." The old Jeffersonian jealousy of the Navy vanished in the *Constitution's* first broadside against the *Guerrière,* but the smart of Detroit's surrender and other land disasters was hard to overcome. Madison's preparations to defend the National Capital from Admiral Cockburn's 1814 foray were too little and too late. While personally on the field at Bladensburg — at one juncture giving some military orders as Commander in Chief — he retired rapidly from the action, and the British seized Washington.

Jefferson had written his successor that two things had to be done to keep the war popular: Indian barbarities had to be stopped, and this could be done only by conquering Canada; and the government must furnish markets for American produce. Incompetent generals of ill-supplied armies in un-co-ordinated campaigns destroyed hope of the first. The fact that the United States, cutting the largest wheat crop then on record, was cut off from foreign and coasting trade by the British blockade caused much of the crop to rot in the barns. The farmers began to suffer from the war.

Had it not been for the extraordinarily fine single-ship actions on the Atlantic and Commodore Perry on Lake Erie, our naval story would have been naught more than that of being landlocked by the efficient British blockade. The American forces in the North fought one creditable major engagement — Lundy's Lane, where Jacob Brown and Winfield Scott covered themselves with honors. Andrew Jackson, the greatest hero of the war, fought the battle of New Orleans three weeks after the signature of the Peace of Ghent.

* * *

Madison got himself re-elected in the fall of 1812, chiefly because the opposition could not agree on the choice of a candidate. Peace swept away almost overnight the discredit of his nonadministration. Not long afterwards, as a penalty for its often treasonable opposition to the war, the Federalist Party suffered such loss of public esteem that, by 1820, it was no more.

His successor, James Monroe, was high in Jefferson's affection; their relations were almost those of teacher and disciple. Monroe had not the slightest Federalist tinge. Like Washington, he was re-elected without a single opposing electoral vote — although one elector deliberately refrained from voting, so that the Washington parallel would not be complete.

Monroe's famous Doctrine, which he announced in a message to Congress, represented a distinguished performance as Chief of Foreign Relations. When Czar Alexander I of Russia, a strange mystic, tried to use the Holy Alliance to help Spain reconquer her revolted colonies in the Americas, Britain would have nothing to do with the plan. George Canning, her Prime Minister, then proposed to Monroe a joint declaration between the Anglo-Saxon nations that they would not permit any such move from the Continent of Europe. There ensued a penetrating correspondence between Monroe, Jefferson at Monticello and Madison at Montpelier, all of whom favored it. But John Quincy Adams, our Secretary of State, argued against joint action, and it was declined. Soon thereafter, Monroe announced the doctrine for the United States alone. It seemed likely that he chose the unilateral declaration in order to please the prideful young Americans. Still those who concerted the plan knew that the United States must depend on British sea power to make good the pledge.

From a standpoint of domestic policy, the postwar period was marked by an increasing shift from the old strict-construction tenets of Jefferson and Madison. The new leadership claimed, and with considerable justification, that the war had brought many new problems of internal development, and that the Federal Government must provide the funds for meeting them with a national plan.

While Monroe vetoed the Cumberland Road bill, he approved some others, and Jefferson became partially converted to this program of public works, even though its execution required a government of implied powers.

There were three major parts of the program — a high tariff, to protect our "infant industries"; large Federal appropriations for a system of post roads, pikes and canals, to get the produce west of the mountains to market; and finally, the establishment of a new Bank of the United States, to provide loans for the expanding manufacture, commerce — and land speculation. Before he had left the White House, Madison had persuaded a clever youngster named Nicholas Biddle to become a government director in the second Bank of the United States. In a few years he was its head, and had made it the most powerful economic institution in the country. Within ten years it was called "the Octopus," and he was "Emperor Nick."

In 1820, the Republicans were a very different party from that which had gone in power in 1800 under the banner of the Kentucky-Virginia Resolutions. They now called themselves the National Republicans, and had embarked on an expansionist doctrine; they demanded a strong money-spending, central government to build a new America quick.

By 1822 the presidential campaign to pick Monroe's successor was actively under way, and at least five hats were in the political ring: Henry Clay, John C. Calhoun, William H. Crawford, Andrew Jackson and John Quincy Adams. In the beginning, the struggle was personal rather than political, but before long they divided into two groups. Clay, Crawford and Adams represented the "pork barrel" point of view, while Jackson and Calhoun sought to take Uncle Sam out of the contracting business, although they were not unwilling to have him continue buying stock or other grants in aid. When Monroe disapproved the Cumberland Road bill, in 1822, Jackson wrote his warm approval. Within a few years differences over public works split the Republicans into Democrats and Whigs.

Crawford, Monroe's Secretary of the Treasury, had been the choice of the Virginia-New York team which had picked the tickets since Jefferson's first term, and ratified their choice through the Congressional Caucus. All the other aspirants combined against Crawford in the best battle-royal style, and a stroke of paralysis aided them in knocking him out of the race.

Jackson's nomination by the Tennessee General Assembly caught on like wildfire everywhere west of the mountains. After he pushed Calhoun out as Pennsylvania's favorite, the latter was agreed on and elected Vice President. While Jackson had the most electors for President, his vote was short of a majority, and the choice went to the House, where John Quincy Adams was chosen by a majority of the State delegations. The claimed understanding, or "corrupt bargain," between Adams and Clay has never been proved, and the likelihood is that there wasn't any. But Clay promptly became Adams' Secretary of State and Jackson went to his deathbed believing that charge.

The 1828 campaign began even before Adams took the oath of office. The common people who had backed Jackson thought they had been cheated, and Old Hickory thought so too. Before this campaign, aspirants for the nation's first office had looked to the members of Congress, the local politicians, the merchants and bankers, for support. The struggle had been for this thin layer of a politically powerful elite. Jackson's principal support had been the "Popular Sovereigns," as the prideful many called themselves. He made up his mind to organize them into a political machine, to take charge of the National Government.

In just four years Jackson built such a party. He was not a party organizer, as Jefferson had been, but a party leader. He was not at his best in writing newspaper articles, preparing argumentative resolutions, securing his ends by massaging Congressmen's backs. He was a determined man, direct in his words and stern in his purpose. The masses followed him blindly, as shrewd politicians soon perceived. Martin Van Buren, the Talleyrand of New York politics, joined the General's banner and became his Chief of Staff. In 1828, it was Jackson by a landslide. He went into office as the people's President.

Jackson's inauguration opened a new chapter of American history. The General changed the whole course of our political philosophy, purpose and technique.

There was hardly a phase of the Presidency he did not vitally affect. His role as Chief of Foreign Relations perhaps occupied his attention the least, but even in it he forced the French to pay an old debt to us, and he recognized the independence of the new Republic of Texas. His duties as Commander in Chief did not press heavily; our army's chief employment was in the war against the Seminole Indians in Florida, and as an army of observation on the Texas border.

Jackson as Chief of Government disregarded practically every precedent. He had no use for a cabinet, in the collective sense that his predecessors had used it. He called few cabinet meetings, and customarily dealt directly with each department head.

He trusted Martin Van Buren implicitly, made him Secretary of State, and sought his counsel on practically every issue that arose. The New Yorker's personality and traits contrasted sharply with Old Hickory's. "The Little Magician" abhorred abrupt decisions or sudden enthusiasms, always planned his course far in the future, and with the exception of a place on the Supreme Court, secured every public position he sought. For all his caution against too positive commitment, Van Buren's counsel, both in friendly opposition and upon ways and means, helped Jackson greatly.

The General placed no such trust in any other man of his first Cabinet, but in 1831 the mind and courage of Roger Brooke Taney, of Maryland, whom he had made Attorney General in the reshuffle of the Cabinet, attracted Jackson greatly and led to Taney's elevation to the Treasury in the Bank fight, and then to his sublimation as Chief Justice.

Jackson made John H. Eaton, of Nashville, his Secretary of War, hoping to have an intimate personal friend in the Cabinet. But

Eaton became a horrible embarrassment, because of the scandals about his new wife, the charming Peggy O'Neale, and the refusal of the high-toned mesdames of official society to attend any White House function where this lush lady might be expected. Jackson's bitter memories of the way Whig malice had slandered his own beloved Rachel through the 1828 campaign — he thought it had caused her to die of a broken heart — made him Peggy's champion. He seems to have believed her tearful protestation of virtue, but he could not check the snubs of the embattled aristocratic dowagers captained by Mrs. Calhoun.

The bachelors and widowers of the Cabinet and diplomatic set helped Jackson in the social struggle by showing Peggy attention; but he could not win this petticoat war. Van Buren found the formula for easing out the Eatons. The President then changed his entire Cabinet, thus ending the quarrel.

His famous "Kitchen Cabinet" arose out of his habits of decision. As a soldier he had shied away from councils of war, and as President he made up his own mind but, legend to the contrary notwithstanding, he usually discussed pending matters with trusted subordinates. Once his decision was made, it was inflexible, but until then he eagerly sought information and, to a lesser extent, advice.

Andrew Jackson Donelson, Mrs. Jackson's nephew and the President's private secretary, personally disinterested and able, was probably as influential as any of the group. Others in the Kitchen Cabinet were William B. Lewis, a Tennessee intimate, Amos Kendall, a Kentucky editor who had worked wonders in the campaign; Isaac Hill, who had performed similar service in New Hampshire; and Van Buren and Eaton until the Cabinet change. At the outset Duff Green, Calhoun's chief Washington editor and public-opinion adviser, had been of the number, but he was eased out and Francis P. Blair came from Kentucky to take his place. All but two of these backstairs advisers came from west of the mountains, and had an intimate understanding of the mood of the West.

These masters of public opinion chiefly concerned themselves with so shaping Jackson's actions, either as President or as Chief of Party, that he could depend on the support of the people. Their skill was superb, and they seldom made a false step. The skillful handling of the patronage, in which they played a large part, had considerable consequence. But much greater was the way they took issues straight to the voters and enlisted them in the fight.

One of the charges customarily brought against Jackson is that he instituted the "spoils system" in the Federal Government. The fact is that anti-Jackson propaganda then and later has given it a prominence in political history out of keeping with its actual effect on the public service at the time. When he entered the White House, there were 612 presidential nominees on the payroll, and during his eight years in office, only 252 of these were removed. It is worthy of note that Grover Cleveland, who practised the doctrine that public office is a public trust, made more removals than Jackson. During the latter's Presidency, of some 8000 postmasters he ousted only 600, while deputy postmasters were not made presidential appointments until his last year in office. On the other hand, Old Hickory made several bad misappointments, being too greatly swayed by friendship and sympathy. Conspicuous among these was the selection for the Collector of Customs of the Port of New York of Samuel Swartwout, an engaging rascal who embezzled over a million dollars before he fled abroad.

Another major error of the Jackson patronage policy was his belief in "rotation in office." At one time he urged a measure that no person should have a permanent appointment, but at the most should serve only a four-year term. This might have been in keeping with the simplicity of most of the current clerical and administrative routines, but it gave no heed to the emerging need for technical and professional skills in governmental tasks.

In his years as President, Jackson faced two continuing oppositions: The part of the National Republican Party which after 1831 called itself Whig; and the Bank of the United States, which had substantial control over the country's financial, commercial and manufacturing interests. For a short time he was confronted with the overwhelming crisis of nullification. Most of the time he had to contend with an adverse Congress, and on occasion he acted directly against the decisions of John Marshall's Court.

He opposed the Whig pleas for an "adequate" tariff wall "indispensable to the prosperity of the country," and a "uniform system of internal improvements." Because of this, many writers place him as a "strict constructionist," although actually Jackson's nationalism was quite as determined as that of either Adams, or Webster, or Clay. His was a nationalism of the people. He believed the Union must be preserved, and that the nation was infinitely more important than the States.

The only areas of government in which he opposed the Federalist-Whig doctrine of broad powers were those which concerned the Congress and the courts. There was no more determined creator of power for the Executive than Andrew Jackson; not even Lincoln or Franklin Roosevelt surpassed him.

Jackson went into office confronted with a central government policy in which a legislature appropriated money almost at will for what were then regarded as social purposes. The revenues from tariff had grown so great that each year produced a large Treasury surplus. Jackson, who did not subscribe to the theory that the public debt is a public blessing, wished to use this surplus in clearing off the national debt. But the National Republicans wanted to continue to spend it on harbors, lighthouses, canals, turnpikes and myriad other Federally financed internal improvements.

He had to be cautious in the language with which he justified his disapproval. In 1822 he had written President Monroe to commend a veto of an appropriation for a road of only local consequence, remarking that his opinion had always been that the Federal Government did not possess the constitutional right to make such expenditures, because this right was "retained to the States." But when Tennessee sent him to the Senate, early in 1823, he had voted for a large number of road bills, chiefly because he believed there was a great military need for roads across the country, the lack of which had hampered the movement and supply of his troops in the War of 1812, and in his recent services in Florida. The expressions in his own first draft for the 1829 Inaugural leaned the same way, although it was pruned down to say only that internal improvements, "so far as they can be promoted by the constitutional act of the Federal Government," were of high importance.

Van Buren had never liked the Clay program, from fear of its financial effects as much as of its political benefits to the opposition. For several months he worked on the old General, until the latter was almost persuaded of the danger of a torrent of reckless legislation. At length Jackson asked his Secretary of State to select from a group of bills awaiting presidential action one so surely local that a good veto case could be made. The Little Magician found the Maysville road bill made to order.

The proposed pike crossed no State line, but began at Maysville and ended at Henry Clay's home town of Lexington, the region it traversed being the strongest Jackson district in Kentucky. Van Buren prepared a statement on its unconstitutionality, Jackson kept the document five days and then gave orders to have the veto prepared.

During the drafting of the message, rumors floated about Congress, and Richard Mentor Johnson, the Representative of the Maysville District, rushed to the White House to protest that a veto would destroy all support in Kentucky. On return to Capitol Hill, he told anxious colleagues that he did not think even a voice from Heaven could keep Jackson from sending a veto.

The significant ideas in the message were Jackson's, the literary style that of his aides. It was aimed at the masses, to persuade them that such measures did violence to their true interests. It recited the earlier vetoes by Madison and Monroe of public works appropriations not clearly related to a national benefit, and spoke of "a scramble for appropriations that have no relation to any general system of improvement." The House heard the message in severe silence, but the veto stood.

Jackson manifested a similar basic realism in his policy about the removal of the Indians from the Southeastern States. Here he went directly in the face of long-standing treaties with the Cherokee Nation and more recent decisions of the United States Supreme Court. Since Washington's Administration, these ill-fated Indians had had clear treaty rights to the undisturbed occupation of a large area in north Georgia. But Jackson sensed that the Indian was bound to lose out in the contest with the white settler, and that treaties could not save him. When the Court upheld the rights of the Cherokees, and reprehended the violent conduct of the State of Georgia, Jackson took the practical step of withdrawing the United States troops, so that they would not impede the State's application of force. Even so, there was mercy in Jackson's harshness, high-handed though it might be.

The story that he said "John Marshall has made his decision; now let him enforce it!" is of doubtful authenticity. His plainest utterance, in a letter to a Tennessee friend, was "The decision of the Supreme Court has fell still born, and they find it cannot coerce Georgia to yield." When the humanitarians and missionaries protested, the President asked how the people of the State of New York would like a foreign nation of tribal savages settled in their midst. A Whig organ remarked on the way he had made himself "supreme — the final arbiter — the very Celestial Majesty!"

"We are in the midst of a revolution," wrote Henry Clay, "hitherto bloodless, but rapidly leading towards a total change of the pure republican character of the government and to the concentration of all power in the hands of one man. The powers of Congress are paralyzed except when exerted in conformity with his will."

Jackson greatly expanded the powers of the President in his two greatest battles: one against the Bank of the United States and its directing genius, Nicholas Biddle; the other to defeat South Carolina's nullification effort.

Of all the men who opposed him, Biddle proved Jackson's toughest foe.

This son of a Philadelphia banker had graduated from Princeton at the age of fifteen, and then became Livingston's secretary at Paris during the Louisiana Purchase negotiations. In 1814 he helped Monroe straighten out the War Department. As has been noted, Madison put him in as a government director in the second Bank of the United States, and in 1823 he became its president.

Under the Bank charter, the government with $7,000,000 investment held a fifth of its stock, and appointed five of the twenty-five directors. It was legal depository for all the Federal funds, though the Secretary of the Treasury could deposit elsewhere if he would notify Congress of his reasons. No interest was paid on government deposits, and bank notes could be issued against them. Both sound and wildcat State banks hated "the Monopoly Monster of Chestnut Street," and actively supported all efforts to trim its claws. The Bank, in turn, would not recognize notes of State banks which on presentation would not redeem them in specie, a hostile policy which had helped clear up a currency chaos.

By the time Jackson became President, "Emperor Nick" was about the most powerful man in America. Able, determined, without scruple as to method and concerned only with the end result, he ran the Bank of the United States with an iron hand and had established it as the actual king of money and finance throughout the country. Probably no other than Jackson could have ended Biddle's reign, and it looked for much of the time as though Old Hickory would be defeated.

Biddle had with him able leaders and large majorities in both Houses of Congress. Through his control of loans he could reward or bankrupt men throughout the country. He made useful loans to the Bank's friends in Congress, and financed several newspapers — the New York *Courier and Inquirer,* after turning to his support, borrowed over $50,000 it never repaid. Several of Jackson's Cabinet were for Biddle, and the wonder is he did not win.

While the Bank's charter did not expire until 1836, Clay and the National Republicans believed the effort to renew it would make a first-rate issue for the 1832 campaign. At first Biddle had thought so, but the President had not stirred the issue and the Bank was willing to let it wait. Clay insisted on forcing the fight. In December 1831 the National Republicans nominated Clay for President on a platform which urged the people not to destroy "one of their most valuable establishments to gratify the caprice of a chief magistrate . . . in direct contradiction to the opinion of his own official counsellors." In February 1832, the Bank presented a memorial, and it met little opposition until the Jackson forces got a special House committee of investigation, whose majority report made a good campaign document against the Bank. It had, however, no effect in Congress, the Senate voting recharter 28 to 20, and the House 107 to 85.

Jackson promptly vetoed the recharter. Much of his message was really addressed to the voters, and had its intended effect at the polls. The part that concerns the powers of the President dealt with his relations to the Supreme Court, which already had upheld the Bank's constitutional validity. Roger Brooke Taney, the new Attorney General, wrote this part of the veto, which, in concise language, denied that the Executive, in acts in its own province, was controlled by "the co-ordinate authorities," because each public officer who takes oath to support the Constitution "swears that he will support it as he understands it, and not as it is understood by others." Therefore the opinion of the Court had no more authority over Congress than that of Congress over the Court, "and on that point the President is independent of both," except in so far as the force of their reasoning might deserve.

The Bank lobby thought this veto had destroyed Old Hickory. Biddle had it reprinted to circulate over the country, because "it has all the fury of a chained panther, biting the bars of his cage. It is really a manifesto of anarchy." He could not muster the votes to repass it, over Jackson's veto, but he confidently expected the veto's repudiation at the polls.

Never was a man more mistaken. Whatever the rich may have thought, the common people distrusted and feared the Bank. This was chief among the issues taken to the hustings. Jackson received 219 electoral votes to Clay's 49; and the House went Democratic.

Re-elected, the President hoped Biddle would accept the voters' mandate and plan a slow and orderly liquidation. But this would have been out of character. The suspicion soon arose that the Bank planned to precipitate a panic, and out of the distress to force the White House to permit a recharter. Jackson determined to destroy the Octopus by the removal of the government's deposits.

Before he could launch this preventive offensive, Jackson had to get a Secretary of the Treasury who would take the step. In September 1833 he removed Duane; Taney took charge, and promptly directed that government funds thenceforth be put in State banks. As soon as Congress assembled, its fury burst forth, and Clay offered resolutions of condemnation.

As passed by the Senate, one resolution charged that the President "has assumed upon himself authority and power not conferred by the Constitution and the laws, but in derogation of both." This passed, in March 1834, by a vote of 26 to 20. A companion charge against Taney also passed. Jackson sent a formal protest, terming the resolution unconstitutional, which the Senate refused to receive or enter on its records. But the now Democratic House voted, 118 to 103, that the deposits should not be restored to the Bank.

Both sides now went to the people, in the mid-term election of 1834. Biddle tried to pave the way for Whig recovery through producing a sharp constriction of credit. He said that "this worthy President thinks that because he has scalped Indians and imprisoned judges, he is to have his way with the Bank. He is mistaken." But the election went heavily against Bank candidates. The people had approved the removal.

As epilogue, Senator Benton moved to expunge from the Senate journal the resolution against Jackson. Legislatures throughout the land instructed their Senators to vote to expunge, to redress the wrong against the President. On January 16, 1837, the Senate so voted, 24 to 19, and a black line was drawn around the resolution, the page being marked: "Expunged by order of the Senate." Jackson's triumph over the Bank was complete.

* * *

The nullification doctrine was not the invention of John Caldwell Calhoun. As a matter of fact, he went to Congress a nationalist, not a State's Rights man; he favored internal improvements, a protective tariff and the second Bank of the United States. But South Carolina still had a low-order colonial economy, the tariff began to hurt, the State's Rights faction agitated the issue and began to undermine Calhoun at home. To save himself, he moved to the other side as fast as his reputation for consistency would permit. In the late twenties he began to toy with the doctrine of nullification, which the other South Carolina faction had evolved from Jefferson's Kentucky-Virginia Resolutions, and in 1828 became its high priest. Its great and leading principle, he wrote, is that the general government emanates from the States, not from all the people, wherefore the Constitution is "a compact to which each State is a party." It follows that the States "have a right to judge of its infractions, and in case of a deliberate, palpable and dangerous exercise of power not delegated, they have the right, in the last resort . . . to interpose for arresting the progress of the evil, and for maintaining, within their respective limits, the authorities, rights and liberties appertaining to them."

Calhoun and Carolina deemed the 1828 "Tariff of Abominations" just such an offense, and there would seem little question that it did injure the particularistic economic interests of the State's economy, which was geared to Europe rather than the United States. Then, as often afterwards, South Carolina was more state of mind than State of the Union, and so it resorted to this logical though unrealistic theory. But Calhoun did not go the limit on this new doctrine immediately Jackson went into office. It was not until he lost hopes of presidential succession that he put nullification in high gear.

There was a prelude to the test of Calhoun's claim that the State could veto the will of the nation. At a dinner in celebration of Jefferson's birthday, April 15, 1830, Jackson proposed the toast:—

"Our Union, it must be preserved!"

This stunned the State's Rights contingent, who now knew where

Jackson stood. The Vice President sought to offset it by offering: "The Union, next to our liberty most dear. May we all remember that it can only be preserved by respecting the rights of the States and distributing equally the benefit and the burthen of the Union." This was far from as moving a battle-cry as Old Hickory's terse toast.

When nullification threats were first bandied about, Jackson sent this word to Senator Hayne: "Tell them from me that they can talk and write resolutions and print threats to their hearts' content. But if one drop of blood be shed there in defiance of the laws of the United States, I will hang the first man of them I can get my hands on to the first tree I can find." Benton heard Hayne doubt this, and told him: "When Jackson begins to talk about hanging, they can begin to look for the rope."

A new tariff bill, passed in July 1832, did not pacify the hotspurs. South Carolina's Legislature ordered an election for a convention, whose members quickly passed an Ordinance of Nullification. This declared the Federal tariff acts of 1828 and 1832 unconstitutional, prohibited South Carolina citizens from obeying them after February 1, 1833, and threatened secession if the National Government sought to oppose these edicts. The Legislature then implemented the Ordinance with bristling punitive laws aimed at any who sought to pay or collect customs duties.

Jackson made note in his personal journal: "South Carolina has passed her ordinance of nullification and secession. As soon as it can be had in authentic form, meet it with a proclamation. . . . It must be arrested by the good sense of the people, and by a full appeal to them by proclamation, the absurdity of nullification strongly repudiated as a constitutional and peaceful measure, and the principles of our govt. fully set forth, as a government based on the Confederation of perpetual union made more perfect by the present constitution, which is the act of the people. . . ."

His task of enforcement would not be easy. Technically, the President might send troops into a State only if the Governor called for help to suppress an insurrection, which would not occur in this instance; or to see to it that the laws enacted by Congress were faithfully executed. But these laws aimed at the individual citizen, and provided no enforcement machinery against violation by a State. The President prepared to ask Congress for a force bill, to fill this void; until then he must depend on the *posse comitatus* theory. He urged the vigorous Union minority in the State, led by sturdy old Joel Poinsett, to be ready; gathered arms in readiness for them; sent a warship and several revenue cutters to Charleston, where he put Winfield Scott in command.

The message to the December Congress was deceptively mild; John Quincy Adams termed it "a complete surrender to the nullifiers." But Jackson bided his time. The Proclamation which was issued December 10, 1832 is the greatest state paper of the Jackson era. It combined Jackson's spirit and Livingston's admirable style.

The President gave the essence in a letter to a Tennessee friend. "Can any one of common sense believe the absurdity," he asks, "that a faction of any State, or a State, has a right to secede and destroy this Union and the liberty of our country with it, or nullify the laws of the Union? Then indeed is our Constitution a rope of sand; under such I would not live ... When a faction in a State attempts to nullify a constitutional law of Congress, or to destroy the Union, the balance of the people composing this Union have a perfect right to coerce them to obedience. This is my creed ... The Union must be preserved, and it will now be tested by the support I get by the people. I will die for the Union."

This was not mere rhetoric — the old hero felt just that way. In the final passages of the Proclamation itself, he called upon the "fellow citizens of my native State" to realize that there could be no peaceable interference with the execution of the laws, "disunion by armed force is *treason*. Are you ready to incur its guilt?"

Adams and Webster exulted at this call to union. Clay was silent. The Proclamation frightened nullifiers, non-nullifiers and tight-rope walkers like Van Buren. Soon State Legislatures began to adopt resolutions of agreement, and the President sent word to Poinsett that the national voice from Maine to Louisiana had declared nullification and secession "confined to contempt and infamy."

Jackson made his plans. "The moment they are in hostile array in opposition to the execution of the laws," he wrote Poinsett, "let it be certified to me ... and I will forthwith order the leaders prosecuted and arrested. If the Marshal is resisted by twelve thousand bayonets, I will have a posse of twenty-four thousand." Offers of volunteers came from every State in the Union, and he could have put two hundred thousand in the field in six weeks' time. Should he be informed of the illegal assembly of an armed force, to set the laws aside, "I will forthwith call into the field such a force as will overawe resistance, put treason and rebellion down without blood, and hand over to the judiciary for trial and punishment the leaders, exciters and promoters of this rebellion and treason."

He waited for evidence of hostile action, but the nullifiers had informally agreed not to enforce the ordinance on its effective date. At length the President asked Congress for special powers to enforce the revenue laws. A "force bill" was introduced, but the anti-Jackson politicians held it back while they sought to deprive Jackson of the credit for checking nullification by themselves lowering the tariff. Henry Clay was in the Senate, Calhoun resigned as Vice President to take a seat there, and they made a deal. Clay's compromise tariff passed March 2, 1833, a few hours before the force bill, which they had delayed to deprive the President of credit for the success of his course. South Carolina's Convention gathered again, repealed the tariff nullification, and claimed complete victory.

This was by long odds Jackson's finest battle. The steps he took involved every role of the office of President but that of Chief of Foreign Relations. He acted because of his oath, as Chief of State, to preserve, protect and defend the Constitution. His duty as Chief of Government, to see to it that the laws were faithfully executed, was directly challenged by the Ordinance forbidding the payment of Federal customs duties. As Commander in Chief, he made explicit plans for armed force from the regulars, the militia and volunteers, and would have taken command of the forces in the field. As Chief of Party, he made use of the Democratic hosts of North and West. In the notable Proclamation, the Chief of Public Opinion appealed to the nation's conscience.

Few men have ever had more moral courage than Old Hickory. He feared no man. He spoke forth boldly and bluntly, to the dismay of his friends but the delight of the people. In his conduct of office, he was altogether indifferent to his private and personal interest — he left the White House as poor as he entered it. His public concern was the nation's welfare as he conceived it: its authority, interests and honor. Jefferson might have been a philosopher in power, but Jackson was will incarnate.

CHAPTER V

The Presidency at Low Ebb

Presidentially considered, the years between Jackson and Lincoln are depressing. The Presidency does not fill itself, its powers are not self-executing, a man must hold and employ them, and it was America's bad luck in this quarter-century that, with the exception of Polk, none of the eight who sat in the White House measured up to the task.

As a result, the Presidency grew flabby from the nonuse of the hard muscles Washington, Jefferson and Jackson had built on its body. This was the low ebb of the nation's first office: not even the harassed procession from Johnson to Cleveland was so bad. Amazingly enough, the office itself did not lose its vitality but continued an Aladdin's Lamp, whose powers could still move mountains, if only its possessor had the magic touch.

Though Martin Van Buren, heir apparent to Old Hickory, lacked the latter's inflexible will and much else, he was, in reality, a casualty of the 1837 depression. The fight with Biddle was partly responsible for this financial catastrophe, though less so than the decade's mania for land speculation which had swept like a cyclone through the Prairie States. The sufferers now pled for Federal assistance, but Van Buren believed the people should support the government, not the government the people. His annual message in December 1837 proposed no use of Federal credit to fend off foreclosures; rather the crash must run its course. But he did administer the executive government efficiently, and after eighteen months of misery, recovery began.

But the depression temporarily unsettled the Democrats' hold on the man of the voters, and the Whigs began to smell the scent of victory. Clay's enemies pushed him aside, furbished up William Henry Harrison, the down-at-the-heels hero of Tippecanoe, and elected him after the Log Cabin and Hard Cider campaign. His running mate was John Tyler, not a Whig at all, but a narrow-minded, high-willed, strict-constructionist Jeffersonian Democrat.

The old General died three weeks after his inauguration, and Tyler moved into the White House. Henry Clay promptly took steps to put this unintended President in his place.

Tyler's troubles arose chiefly because of his inability to become either Chief of Party or Chief of Public Opinion. They illustrate the types of difficulties which seem particularly the lot of a Vice President who succeeds to the Presidency because of the death of the elected President.

Only three Vice Presidents became President by election after they had served a full term as Vice President — John Adams, Jefferson and Van Buren. In the first two instances, each was the leader of his party in his own right, and in the third, Van Buren was party leader by Jackson's command. In all three, the Vice President became President in such a way that he had no difficulty in acting as Chief of Party and in commanding appropriate public response.

But it was distinctly different in most of the other successions of the theoretically second men in the Executive Government. Tyler took over Harrison's office but not Harrison's position as head of the Whigs — instead, Henry Clay stepped into Harrison's shoes as party leader. During the first summer of Tyler's service, the magnetic, power-hungry Kentuckian found an excuse to read him out of the party. There was a mass resignation from the inherited Cabinet, and he had to depend on reluctant Democrats for what little support he got. But Tyler had both will and temper, did not retreat from a hopeless political battle, and dealt many wounds as well as receiving many.

Millard Fillmore, the next President by death, was a suave Buffalo lawyer and local political figure whom the Whigs put on the ticket with Zachary Taylor for geographical reasons. Fillmore entered the White House on Taylor's death in the summer of 1850, at the height of the Congressional struggle over the admission of California, with no sympathy for the vigorous nationalism of "Old Rough and Ready," and helped Clay, Webster and Douglas effectuate the Compromise of 1850. While not quite a pigmy in statesmanship, Fillmore had little strength in his own right, and neither the Whig Party nor public opinion accepted his leadership.

The most conspicuous disaster of deathbed succession was Andrew Johnson, who had no claim whatsoever to succeed Abraham Lincoln as the Chief of Party. It was because Johnson was a Democrat, a deliberate plebeian, that Lincoln had made him Military Governor of Tennessee. It was because Lincoln determined to seek re-election, not as a Republican, but as a National Union man, that he contrived to have Johnson nominated as his 1864 running mate by not the Republican but the National Union Convention. As a result, the Johnson who stepped into the shoes of the assassinated Lincoln had no Republican Party status at all. For the same reason, Johnson had no real chance to exert a major influence upon the formation of public opinion. As soon as he challenged the Radical Republican revolution, his support withered away.

Chester A. Arthur, who succeeded Garfield, resembled Fillmore in being a New York politician who was put on the tail of the ticket to pacify Senator Conkling, the State boss. Arthur surprised many by being a reform President, but the Republican leadership shunned him, and he could not impress his leadership on the masses of the people.

The story of Theodore Roosevelt, which stands out in sharp contrast to those described above, is treated in Chapter X. Calvin Coolidge came the closest to party leadership of any of the Vice Presidents who moved up, except "T. R." His personal qualities shone by contrast with those of Harding. But his contemporary success was a symbol of stock-market prosperity. He did not choose to lead the people, and left little lasting impression on party or public opinion. Senator Reed Smoot, the powerful Mormon Elder, was virtually the dominant executive instrument. In terms of party leadership, except for "Teddy" none of the Vice Presidents who succeeded through the death of the incumbent were men of strength. They lacked stature in their own parties, could not control them, and so were even less effective in their conduct of the office of President.

John Tyler's decisive deed as President was the annexation of Texas. Old Hickory, from his retirement at the Hermitage, had a hand in its initiation. He had liked the way Tyler stood up to Clay, urged close friends in Washington to lend him a hand, and did not sheer off when his foeman Calhoun took Webster's place as Secretary of State.

Jackson became an ardent Texas annexationist in the early Forties. The Republic had twice offered to join the Union, only to be repulsed. Now Sam Houston, its President, offered to take the initiative a last time, if he could be assured of a two-thirds Senate vote. The ex-President wrote to Washington that the golden moment to obtain Texas must not be lost. Tyler presented a treaty in April, 1844.

The outraged Mexican Government began gathering troops to punish Texas, which Tyler countered by placing the American ships and soldiers where they could sustain the Lone Star Republic against attack. This provoked Senate opponents, and that body adopted a resolution of inquiry. The President responded: —

"It is due to myself that I should declare it as my opinion that the United States, having by treaty of annexation acquired a title to Texas which requires only the action of the Senate to perfect it, no other power could be permitted to invade and by force of arms to possess itself of any portion of the territory of Texas pending your deliberations upon the treaty without placing itself in a hostile attitude to the United States and justifying the employment of any military means at our disposal to drive back the invasion." Tyler did not withdraw the United States forces, but abolitionist and antislavery opposition in the Senate, together with Whig dislike of Tyler, caused the rejection of the treaty by a strict party vote.

The President then backed a plan to annex, not by treaty, needing a two-thirds Senate majority, but by a joint resolution of both Houses, which could be passed by a simple majority in each. Some Senators denounced this as a trick play against the constitutional intendment, but Tyler stuck by his guns, both bodies passed the resolution, and on March 1, 1845, he signed it. Tyler pioneered in this method of adding Congress to the Senate as a recognized legislative organ of foreign relations. The two-thirds vote requirement for Senate consent is a flaw in the Constitution, its practical effect that of a one-third veto, which plays into the hands of pressure groups.

Because one of Old Hickory's devices for controlling the Democratic Party worked in reverse, James Knox Polk became President in 1844, rather than Van Buren. This was the so-called two-thirds rule, which Jackson had imposed upon the 1832 Democratic National Convention to show that an overwhelming majority of the party's delegates demanded "Little Van's" choice as his running mate. Twelve years later, Van Buren's equivocation on Texas annexation alienated the Deep South, his majority on early ballots could not be built to two-thirds, and Polk became the nominee.

The Tennessean who succeeded Tyler strengthened the Presidency. During the campaign the Whigs called him "a blighted burr that has fallen from the mane of the War Horse of the Hermitage," but he was a man of courage and Presbyterian conscience and made a strong President, although lack of personal magnetism kept him from being a great one. His diary affords an invaluable inside view of the problems which beset a President in time of war.

Texas had been smuggled into the Union just before Polk took oath, but there was every prospect of hostilities over the ill-defined boundary. Although he had been elected on the slogan "Fifty-four forty or fight," he knew the United States could not fight both Britain and Mexico, and so negotiated a compromise Oregon boundary. Early in 1846 he persuaded the Senate to agree in advance that it would consent to the convention he planned to propose to the British — a sharing of the Executive's initiative in the process of treaty negotiation which under the circumstances proved wise.

Mexico rejected all of Polk's peace suggestions, there was a border clash and the Mexican War was on. Although John Quincy Adams and the Northern Whigs termed it an "illegal, unrighteous and damnable war," waged so that the slavocracy could get new territory for shackles and lash, the weight of the evidence is that Polk had sincerely tried to keep peace.

His problem in conducting the war was of extreme difficulty. It was a Democratic war, but Zachary Taylor and Winfield Scott, the principal field commanders, were both Whigs; if victories were won, theirs was the credit; if lost, the Administration would be blamed. Taylor took terrible chances, deliberately disobeyed orders; Buena Vista gave him visions of the White House; Polk thought he acted with folly and deserved no higher command than a regiment. Scott, whom the President sent to march from Vera Cruz to Mexico City, planned, marched and fought very well. But he was vain, jealous, full of contention and deserved his sobriquet "Old Fuss and Feathers."

The President asked Congress to authorize a new lieutenant-generalship for Thomas H. Benton, to take charge of the Army in the field. He patiently argued "the impossibility of conducting the war successfully when the General-in-chief of the army did not sympathize with the government and co-operate with it in the prosecution of the war."

But he got nowhere; Calhoun's Southern Fire-eaters opposed Benton because of his Jackson record, the Whigs because of conscience — and the next year's presidential campaign. The President noted his embarrassment: "I am held responsible for the War, and I am required to entrust the chief command of the army to a general in whom I have no confidence." Polk's experience, like Lincoln's, shows the high importance of trust between the President as Commander in Chief and his military agents.

Through the war, contentions in Congress plagued Polk, who followed Old Hickory in placing the Union above all else. He reprehended the Wilmot Proviso and the so-called Conscience Whigs, but was even more bitter against Calhoun for stirring up the slavery question. He felt that both factions desired to mount slavery as a hobby, and that Calhoun himself was wholly selfish and without patriotism. Polk would not yield to the extreme sectional view.

Entering office with four great measures on his mind — tariff reduction, an independent Treasury, settlement of the Oregon boundary dispute, and the acquisition of California — he accomplished them all. In addition to adding half a million square miles to the area of the country, Polk administered the executive establishment firmly and soundly. George Bancroft, both from experience in the Cabinet and later study of his papers, judged him "one of the very foremost of our public men, and one of the very best and most honest and successful Presidents the country ever had."

Polk resolutely refused to seek a second term — in which only Hayes and Arthur resembled him. Exhausted by the labors of the office, he died three months after Zachary Taylor took his place.

In nominating Old Rough and Ready, the Whigs deliberately abstained from adopting a platform, while the General in accepting said he was unwilling to be the exclusive candidate of any party. But the struggle over whether California would come into the Union slave or free State forced declaration of his purpose. In his Inaugural, he emphasized his oath to "preserve, protect and defend the Constitution," and warned that his Administration would not support any section or merely local interest. His annual message of December 1849 proclaimed the dissolution of the Union the greatest of calamities: "Whatever dangers may threaten it, I shall stand by and maintain it in its integrity, to the full extent of the obligations imposed and the power conferred upon me by the Constitution."

Early in 1850, some Southern extremists asked Taylor if he were ready to maintain the Union at any cost. He replied that in case of armed resistance, he would blockade every Southern port, call for volunteers from the Northern and Western States, put himself at their head, and execute the leaders of the secession. Many Southerners said he should be impeached. But in July, cholera morbus cut short his career, and the controversy was temporarily stilled under Fillmore, who aided the Compromise of 1850.

The ensuing ten years represent the low ebb of the office of President. Fillmore did nothing to increase the powers or better the administrative methods of the Executive. Franklin Pierce, who followed him, while hailed as a "Young Hickory," made a miserable failure. The conduct of the office by his successor, James Buchanan, had tragic national consequences.

"Old Buck" gave the appearance of a statesman — large frame, good head, polished manners, always well-tailored, but he was both weak and stubborn. If personal responsibility for secession and civil war could be affixed on any one public figure of the Fifties, not John Brown but Buchanan would be the man. Democratic rivals called him "Old Obliquity." His battle with Stephen A. Douglas over "Popular Sovereignty," and his tricky course in the Kansas controversy led to the break-up of the Democratic Party in 1860, Lincoln's election as a minority President, and then the secession parade. At times Buchanan showed a positive genius for pulling down the pillars of the temple of Union. To his credit, after the election he attempted a conciliation policy, but it had little restorative effect.

The secession-bound Southern States did not wait for the formality of the balloting. In October 1860, Governor Gist, of South Carolina, wrote each Slave State Executive urging concert of action. With the election, the Palmetto State's Legislature met and he recommended quitting an unendurable Union. The Federal Grand Jury refused to function, the Federal Judge dramatically resigned, the two United States Senators surrendered their commissions. A Constitutional Convention was elected, and in six weeks Calhoun's State proclaimed its freedom from the Union. By mid-February, 1861, eight States had formally withdrawn and a provisional government had been organized, at a Montgomery convention, under the title of the Confederate States of America.

This onrushing revolution distressed President Buchanan and his Northern supporters, who had admitted the North's wrong in the sectional struggle and now were caught in the net of their own emotional fixations. Late in October, Winfield Scott, General-in-Chief of the Army, sent the President his "Views" of the situation. There were nine important Federal fortresses in the South, six with no garrisons, the others with skeleton forces: let them be manned at once. The Commander in Chief paid no attention to this advice, but played with fanciful schemes for compromise; should the North decline to kneel, the South "would stand justified before the whole world for refusing longer to remain in a confederacy where her rights were so shamefully violated."

Early in November, 1860, Buchanan prepared an elaborate document, which urged "submission" to Lincoln's election and hinted possible Federal force. The Southerners in the Cabinet dissented violently, and the President backed down. On November 17, he asked the Attorney General, Jeremiah Sullivan Black, for an opinion on his powers in the emergency. The latter answered shortly that the Constitution contained neither the sanction for a State to secede, nor the powers by which the National Government could coerce it. But he also pointed out that there was no shadow of a doubt that the President had complete constitutional power to see to it that the laws were faithfully executed.

In his annual message to Congress, in December 1860, Buchanan played both sides against the middle. He emphasized the North's wrongs to the South, and urged a national convention to redress them. But the founders of the government had not been, "at its creation, guilty of the absurdity of providing for its own dissolution . . . Secession is neither more nor less than revolution." The Federal Government's property right to her forts, magazines and arsenals in South Carolina was unquestioned, he had ordered the commanding officer there to act on the defensive; if attacked, "the responsibility for the consequences would rightfully rest upon the assailants."

But the succeeding sections made faces at those just cited. He seemed to think the President, "wisely limited and restrained as is his power under our Constitution," able to do little to meet the crisis. His province was not to make but to execute the laws. In the instant case, the responsibility and true position of the Executive was to execute the laws. He must rely on the acts of February 28, 1795 and March 3, 1807 to do so. These required a summons from a Federal District judge before the President could act. He reported that all such in South Carolina had resigned, and so his hands were tied.

But what could Congress do: "Has the Constitution delegated to Congress the power to coerce a State into submission . . . ?"

"After much serious reflection," Buchanan responded, "I have arrived at the conclusion that no such power has been delegated to Congress or to any other department of the Federal Government. . . . The power to make war against a State is at variance with the whole spirit and intent of the Constitution. . . . Our Union rests upon public opinion, and can never be cemented by the blood of its citizens shed in civil war . . . Congress possesses many means of preserving it by conciliation, but the sword was not placed in their hand to preserve it by force."

With justice, Seward remarked that the message shows conclusively that it is the duty of the President to execute the laws — unless somebody opposes them; and that no State has a right to go out of the Union — unless it wants to.

Buchanan toyed with the idea of sending a Federal warship to Charleston. Then the South Carolina authorities, who sought to breach the Constitution in a most constitutional way, pledged they would not attack the forts if the government would not reinforce them, and the Chief Executive agreed. But he did determine on a token resistance, and sent orders to Major Anderson, commanding at Charleston, that if attacked, he must defend the forts "to the last extremity." The resignation of Lewis Cass, the Secretary of State, on Buchanan's refusal to strengthen the garrisons, roused him a little to the danger of his blind affection for the Southern Ultras. He reorganized the Cabinet, and his policy thenceforth was not quite so supine.

South Carolina seceded, December 20, 1860, and immediately dispatched three Commissioners to Washington, to negotiate with the President for the transfer of the Federal property to the claimed independent State. Douglas and the National Democrats of the West did not think Buchanan would so demean the dignity of the government as to receive them. But receive them he did, and promised to transmit to Congress their truculent demands, which included Sumter's surrender. A little later the President submitted his proposed reply for the views of his reorganized Cabinet. He repeated the government's lack of authority to coerce, disavowed Anderson's concentration of forces in Sumter, and regretted that the South Carolina Commissioners had suspended negotiations! Three Northern members listened in amazement, but Buchanan stubbornly persisted until they sent word they would resign. On this he crumpled. The answer to the South Carolinians, though apologetic, did proclaim the President's duty "to defend Fort Sumter as a portion of the public property of the United States against hostile attacks from whatever quarter they may come."

Then he wabbled again, sent the Commissioners word that if they rephrased their demand to accord the President a proper respect, he might accede. They did so, but now the President faced more Cabinet opposition, together with fears of impeachment. He returned the note, with an unsigned indorsement that the President declined to receive it. The Commissioners denounced his duplicity and departed for Charleston.

The Cotton States Senators and Congressmen took charge of the situation in December 1860, organized themselves into an unofficial general staff for secession, with a three-phase plan of campaign: Each State should sever its ties with the Union as soon as it could go through the forms; a convention should be held at Montgomery, by mid-February, to organize a Southern Confederacy; the section's members of Congress should remain in Washington until March 4, 1861, to "keep the hands of Mr. Buchanan tied." They abandoned the third point, because secessionists back home objected to members lingering in Washington after the Federal tie had been cut; but the rest of the program went through according to plan.

From beginning to end, Buchanan took no effective step to nip the revolution. He liked the Crittenden compromise, but disliked Douglas' support of it, and would not throw his weight to persuade the Cotton States to give it a chance. He was ceremonially courteous to the February Peace Convention, which sent commissioners to him, and to the Governors of the seceded States, asking both to abstain from any acts "calculated to produce a collision of arms." He replied he had no constitutional right to make such a pledge. He got rid of Floyd, Secretary of War, not because of the latter's secession sympathies but because of the disclosure of a shocking irregularity in accounts. Then he agreed to the plan of Holt, Floyd's successor, to send help to Sumter. The *Star of the West* left on the mission, but did not try to enter the port.

Washington was filled with rumors that Lincoln's inauguration would be prevented by force. No evidence of any such plot has been found, but General Scott moved to protect the Capital, forty cars of Federal troops arrived, and artillery was properly emplaced. The initiative was that of the brave old Virginia general, not that of the outgoing President. No incident marred the inauguration ceremonies. At last a man of will and action held the office of President.

Buchanan, theoretically, possessed all the powers that Lincoln later used to save the Union. He too was Commander in Chief, and as such able to employ the immense strength of that office. But no man of withered will can meet a crisis. Had Old Hickory rather than Old Obliquity been in the White House, the story might have been quite otherwise.

CHAPTER VI

Commander in Chief

No other of our Presidents entered office faced with problems so formidable, nor under such personal and political handicaps, as Abraham Lincoln. Neither has any other found so many new sources of executive power, nor so expanded and perfected those others already had used.

He found a rich mine of new power in the simple sentence in the Constitution making him Commander in Chief — and thus furnished Wilson and Franklin Roosevelt abundant precedent for executive wartime control of great areas of civilian life. As Chief of Foreign Relations, he prevented British and French recognition of the Confederacy. His intuition of the limits of public support enabled him to keep a majority of the people of the Loyal States behind the Union cause up to the final day at Appomattox Court House.

As Chief of State, Lincoln did not hesitate to embrace the Jackson concept of his independent power and duty, under the oath, directly to represent and protect the people, irrespective of States, Congress, or Courts. But neither his frame, the way he corkscrewed his feet on the mantel, nor his salty stories comported with the traditional dignity of the office. Uninterested in routines, he was an indifferent Chief of Government; the able, humorless Chase thought the government sure to fail if he were not displaced. His reign as Chief of Party was soon challenged, a group of Radical Republicans secured the control of both houses of Congress, and after 1862 Lincoln's policies for restoring reoccupied Southern States were riding for a fall.

* * *

A chief problem at the start of his Presidency was where to get the power to fight the Civil War. To a degree this arose because he was a minority President. If all the votes actually cast for other than Lincoln had been concentrated on one candidate, Lincoln still would have had a comfortable majority in the Electoral College; none the less, it is not likely that the number voting against him would have been so low had only one man opposed him, since many voters have a horror of "wasting" their vote. Professor J. G. Randall points out correctly that Lincoln's victory came out of "advantageous distribution of his votes among populous States," but has been puzzled by the effects. Lincoln came to Washington confronted with the possibility that Congress might refuse to follow his leadership.

His next handicap was the legacy of the Buchanan policy. Lincoln felt that his predecessor had frittered away the conventionally recognized presidential powers, and that he would be forced to find a new reservoir of strength, a situation not altogether unlike that which faced Franklin Roosevelt in 1933.

Buchanan was the target for Radical Republicans, who set a traditional pattern for criticism of his conduct. As has been said, he had harmed the country more by his war on Douglas than by his conciliation course after Lincoln's choice. In Jackson's 1837 Farewell Address, which had deplored coercion and said that the Union rested on "the affections of the people," he found a certain justification for his own feeble efforts at preserving the Union through conciliation rather than force. His tergiversations are generally examined against a South Carolina-Cotton States background, but he regarded the situation also from the background of Washington, where Congressional emphasis was still on a peaceable solution.

This, doubtless, was the psychological frame of reference for Buchanan's course, but his manner of executing it had created an extraordinarily serious situation for Lincoln. In his last annual message the President had mined the road his successor must tread, by holding the North responsible for the South's fears, and urging that, inasmuch as Lincoln had been constitutionally elected, "reason, justice, a regard for the Constitution all require that we shall wait for some overt and dangerous act on the part of the President-elect before resorting to such a remedy" as revolution.

These among other reasons led Lincoln to seek some source of executive power not fouled by misuse or wrecked by sabotage. He believed the President's power broad, that of Congress explicit and restricted. Even before Sumter, he seized upon the President's designation as Commander in Chief, coupled it to the first sentence of Article II of the Constitution — "the executive power shall be vested in a President of the United States" — and joined them as "the war power" which authorized him to do many things beyond the competence of Congress.

In his Message of July 4, 1861, Lincoln declared that "the Executive found the duty of employing the war power in defense of the Government forced upon him. He could but perform this duty or surrender the existence of the Government. . . . He felt that he had no moral right to shrink nor even to count the chances of his own life, in what might follow."

This concept began as a transition device, to be validated by Congress when it assembled. In less than two years it grew into an independent power under which he felt authorized to suspend the execution of the writ of habeas corpus, issue the Emancipation Proclamation, and restore reoccupied States.

His proclamation of April 15, 1861, called for 75,000 troops. Their first service "probably" would be to repossess the forts, places and property; but they would take the utmost care "to avoid any devastation, any destruction of or interference with property, or any disturbance of peaceful citizens in any part of the country." The same proclamation also summoned a special session of Congress, but not to meet until July 4. The delay was, of course, deliberate; Lincoln intended to take the first steps himself.

"In the interval between April 12 and July 4, 1861," declares Professor Dunning, "a new principle thus appeared in the Constitutional system of the United States, namely, that of a temporary dictatorship. All the powers of Government were virtually concentrated in a single department, and that the department whose energies were directed by the will of a single man."

Lincoln ranged wide under the war power. He first called for troops under the Act of 1795, to use them as a *posse comitatus,* "to enforce the faithful execution of the laws of the United States." Within a few days he asked for 42,034 volunteers; increased the regular Army strength 22,714 and directed the enlistment of 18,000 seamen; proclaimed a blockade of Southern ports; and authorized the Commanding General or his subordinates to suspend the writ of habeas corpus. He had the Treasury pay out several millions for war costs, without the prior authorization or appropriation of Congress.

The Supreme Court, early in 1863, approved his right to use the war powers without benefit of Congress. The decision was upon the Prize Cases, suits attacking his right legally to institute a blockade. Although his Proclamation, issued April 19, 1861, had been validated by Congress on August 6, claimants contended that, under the Law of Nations, a blockade could be instituted only as a measure of war under the sovereign power of the State. The Constitution empowered Congress exclusively to declare war, therefore only Congress could declare a blockade, and all prizes seized before the legislative declaration were illegal. Counsel for the claimants denounced the assumption "that the Constitution contemplated and tacitly provided that the President should be dictator, and all constitutional government be at an end, whenever he should think that 'the life of the nation' is in danger." He had no power and right to use all the forces at his command to save it.

The Court, 5-4, upheld Lincoln's right to act as he had. It was a narrow squeak, and he was sustained by judges three of whom — Swayne, Miller and Davis — he himself had appointed. The greatest of civil wars, said Justice Grier, however long its previous conception, "sprung forth suddenly from the parent brain, a Minerva in full panoply of war. The President was bound to meet it in the shape it presented itself, without waiting for Congress to baptize it with a name, and no name given to it by him or them could change the fact."

If the President, in executing his duties as Commander in Chief in an insurrection, found the conflict of such size that the rebels must be accorded the character of belligerents, the decision was his, "and this Court must be governed by the decisions and acts of the political department to which this power was entrusted." It did not approve his increase of the Army and Navy, but Congress had already cured that unauthorized action.

Lincoln seems to have been assured by this decision that his war powers needed no Congressional support. In 1864, when Senator Zach Chandler protested his pocket-veto of the Radical reconstruction bill, Lincoln said: "I conceive that I may in an emergency do things on military grounds which cannot constitutionally be done by the Congress." Professor Randall, the recognized authority on constitutional problems under Lincoln, is positive that he acted under the belief that "as President he had extraordinary legal resources which Congress lacked."

Moreover, he did not long lack legal buttresses for his belief in plenary powers. In 1862, William Whiting, the Solicitor of the War Department, brought out a volume, *War Powers under the Constitution,* which sought to furnish legal support. The old Latin maxim, *inter arma silent leges* — among arms, the laws remain silent — became a justification for ignoring the Bill of Rights. While Whiting's chief concern was its use in military arrest cases, he gave it the broadest sweep: "The sovereign and almost dictatorial military powers existing only in actual war ... are, while they last, as constitutional, as sacred, as the administration of justice by judicial courts in time of peace." Also the Constitution "requires" the President as Commander in Chief in time of war to see that the laws of war are executed. The Supreme Court did not challenge Lincoln's employment of war powers until more than a year after his death.

The President's use of his war powers fell in two generally separate fields: the actual overall direction of military operations; and the curbing of civilian resistance to the war effort in areas outside the actual theaters of war.

Although the new Commander in Chief lacked military education, no overweening pride of opinion closed his mind to instruction. In politics and public opinion he moved craftily, and with a shrewd estimate of probable consequences. In military matters he was eager to learn, and almost never repeated the identical mistake. He knew he must find generals he could trust and must have trust in return and, after repeated failures, he found the right men.

In a democracy at war, the technique of command ranks among the hardest problems. The right relation between civil chief and military agent is hard to achieve on either side. The supremacy of the civil executive must go unquestioned, for the military is the servant of the government just as war is an instrument of national policy. The reverse of the shield is that the civil chief is on dangerous ground when he personally directs tactics as well as grand strategy of military action. His duty is to discern the purposes of a war, provide men and matériel for its prosecution, and fit strategy to resources.

Both civil chief and military agents need statesmanship to develop this sensitive balance between civil supremacy and military effectiveness. There must be real confidence between the senior and the junior partner. Each needs to understand the way the other's mind works, and his infirmities of will and temperament. When a President loses confidence in a commander, the latter should resign or be dismissed. For a President to refuse his confidence to his general, or intrigue against him, is intolerable. But also, the commander's unwillingness to disclose to his chief the broad nature of his military purpose warrants his discharge. Commander in Chief Lincoln made mistakes in all these matters — but learned from his errors. His Richmond opposite number made them too, and profited less from experiences.

The McClellan episode was full of error. This "Little Napoleon of the West," though an excellent supplier, organizer and trainer, was psychologically naïve and unable to comprehend the public necessity for at least apparent activity by the new Army. Though his war plans were much better conceived than Lincoln's, he had delusions of grandeur, and pettishly refused to confide them to his Chief. The latter's ensuing blunder of withholding promised reinforcements probably saved Richmond and added three years to the war. But McClellan had not hesitated to take time out from the Peninsular Campaign to talk to a New York Democratic politician about the 1864 presidential nomination. He was the chief architect of his own removal from command.

Halleck's story displays another side of Lincoln. That General, who had not left his headquarters in St. Louis, took credit for Grant's capture of Donelson. The President, straining to find a strategist to plan a unified war, sent to the Congressional Library for Halleck's translation of Jomini's *The Art of War*. After reading it, and consulting Scott, he brought Halleck to Washington as General in Chief. But the latter's learning did not translate into good campaign plans; Lincoln saw through him and ceased to give his advice much weight.

He made another try with "Fighting Joe" Hooker, excellent with troops in thick of battle but intriguer for power and, after Burnside's tragedy of Fredericksburg, the Radical candidate for command. In appointing him, Lincoln sent Hooker a wise letter: "I have heard it said in such a way as to believe it of your recently saying that both the Army and the Government needed a dictator. Of course, it was not for this, but in spite of it, that I have given you the command. Only those generals who gain success can set up as dictators. What I now ask of you is military success, and I will risk the dictatorship. The Government will support you to the utmost of its ability." Even after the Chancellorsville muddle he did not remove Hooker, but replenished his shattered formations and advised him shrewdly when Lee crossed the Potomac. But when Hooker, in a fit of temper, asked to be relieved of command, the President complied at once.

At length the trusted commander came out of the West. After Shiloh, Lincoln had stood by Grant: "I can't spare that man — he fights!" The capture of Vicksburg after many failures, then the redemption of Chickamauga at Missionary Ridge, gave Lincoln full confidence that at long last he had found his man. Grant learned the hard way that Lee, Longstreet and the Hills were a different breed from Pemberton and Bragg. His army lost 55,000 men between the Rapidan and the James, but he would not disengage, and his chief applauded: "I have seen your dispatch expressing your unwillingness to break your hold where you are. Neither am I willing. Hold on with a bulldog grip, and chew and choke as much as possible."

After Atlanta's fall, Grant as well as Lincoln was slow to acquiesce in Sherman's march to the sea — there was strategic novelty in the shift of mission from Hood's army to Georgia's economy. But after Savannah's capture, the President confided fully in that general and conferred with him, in March 1865, on terms for Joe Johnston's soldiers. No longer was he a tyro as Commander in Chief of military operations.

Lincoln's employment of his war powers outside the theaters of war evoked determined opposition, echoes of which are still heard; "dictator" was mild among the epithets of abuse. Indeed, the class and party hatred of him was even more bitter than that against Washington or Franklin Roosevelt.

Of these acts, the suspension of the writ of habeas corpus came first in time, perhaps in importance. It was soon obvious that at the same time he must use the armed forces to suppress open resistance from the Potomac to the Rio Grande the President had also to cope with a fifth column in the Loyal States, as the Baltimore riots quickly showed. On April 27, 1861, he instructed the Commanding General of the Army that if "you find resistance which renders it necessary to suspend the writ of habeas corpus for the public safety, you personally, or through the officer in command where resistance occurs, are authorized to suspend that writ."

The military arrested and confined one Merryman for drilling a company of secession sympathizers. Chief Justice Taney, on circuit duty in Baltimore, granted his application for a writ, but on instruction of the Executive Department the writ was ignored. Thereupon

Taney filed a stern protest against what he termed a type of usurpation. Those suspected of treason should be dealt with judicially, otherwise the people "are no longer living under a government of laws; but every citizen holds life, liberty and property at the will and pleasure" of the military. He put the burden squarely on the President, whose duty it was, "in fulfillment of his Constitutional obligation . . . to determine what measures he will take to cause the civil process of the United States to be respected and enforced."

Lincoln made no public reply until his message to the special session of Congress, July 4, 1861. In an early draft he replied directly to the Chief Justice's strictures, but in the one sent he treated only the issue. "It was considered a duty," he argued, "to authorize the Commanding General in proper cases . . . to arrest and detain without resort to the ordinary processes and forms of law such individuals as he might deem dangerous to the public safety. This authority has been exercised but very sparingly."

Nevertheless the country's attention had been called "to the proposition that one who is sworn to 'take care that the laws be faithfully executed' should not himself violate them. Of course, some consideration was given to the questions of power and propriety before this matter was acted upon . . . Are all the laws but one to go unexecuted, and the Government itself to go to pieces lest that one be violated? Even in such a case, would not the official oath be broken if the Government should be overthrown, when it was believed that disregarding the single law would tend to preserve it?"

But on constitutional authority no such question had been presented; the Constitution in effect declared that the writ could be suspended "when, in cases of rebellion or invasion, the public safety may require it." It had been asserted that Congress, not the President, had the power to suspend, "but the Constitution itself is silent as to which or who is to exercise the power; and as the provision was plainly made for a dangerous emergency, it cannot be believed that the framers of the instrument intended that in every case the danger should run its course until Congress could be called together." Elsewhere in the message, he remarked of this, as of other executive actions, "it is believed that nothing has been done beyond the constitutional competence of Congress." That body finally passed a suspension of the writ, but deferred to the President's view by employing ambiguous language which left undetermined the locus of the power to suspend.

In the light of the incandescent passions of the day, the government would seem to have employed these powers with restraint. There were many frivolous or careless arrests, but most persons so confined had been enemy agents, spies, suppliers, saboteurs or inciters of desertion. The most famous instance was the exiling of Clement L. Vallandigham.

This brilliant, bitter Ohio Copperhead was arrested in May 1863, for violating an order of General Burnside, Commander of the Military Department of the Ohio. A military commission tried and convicted him for having said in a public speech that it was "a war for the freedom of the blacks and the enslavement of the whites," and similar antiwar expressions. The General then sentenced him to confinement at Fort Warren for the duration.

The President had not ordered the proceeding, and was greatly embarrassed. He must not weaken the General's authority by disapproving the finding, but approval would bring bitter attack from Northern conservatives. He changed the sentence from imprisonment to being passed through the lines to the Confederacy. But this essay in avoidance, with its comic twist, did not halt conservative protest. Seymour, New York's Democratic Governor who had sustained Lincoln with troops, wrote that "we pause to see what kind of government it is for which we are asked to pour out our blood and our treasure." Ohio's Democratic leaders challenged the assumption of "an indefinable kind of constructive treason . . . subject to the will of the President."

Lincoln's responses went to the heart of the practical problem: The constitutional guarantees had become the cloaks for aiders and abetters of secession and treason; civil courts had proved "utterly incompetent" to punish these transgressors; "a jury too frequently has at least one member more ready to hang the panel than hang the traitor. And yet he who dissuades one man from volunteering or induces one soldier to desert, weakens the Union cause as much as he who kills a Union soldier in battle . . .

"Must I shoot a simple-minded soldier boy who deserts while I must not touch a hair of a wily agitator who induces him to desert? . . . I think that, in such a case, to silence the agitator and save the boy is not only constitutional, but withal a great mercy."

The true form of the issue raised by the Ohio Democrats, he wrote, was "simply a question who shall decide, or an affirmation that nobody shall decide, what the public safety does require in cases of rebellion or invasions." The Constitution does contemplate the question "as likely to occur for decision, but it does not expressly declare who is to decide it. By necessary implication, when rebellion or invasion comes, the decision is to be made . . . I think the man whom, for the time, the people have, under the Constitution, made the Commander in Chief of their Army and Navy, bears the responsibility for making it." Here was a deep and penetrating judgment upon the practical location of the fount of power in this no man's land of the Constitution.

Lincoln's subordinates showed hair-trigger zeal to elide the constitutional guaranty of the freedom of the press. When conservative or Copperhead papers attacked Burnside's course in the Vallandigham case, that General issued an order which declared the *New York World* a "pernicious and treasonable influence," and forbade its distribution in his Military Department. The *Chicago Times,* being published within his immediate command, he ordered "suppressed," and his soldiers forcibly stopped its publication; but Lincoln soon overruled the bombastic order.

In May 1864 Stanton inveigled Lincoln into signing an Executive Order to suppress two New York papers, the *World* and the *Journal of Commerce,* which had been tricked into printing a bogus presidential proclamation calling for a day of national humiliation and prayer, and also for a new draft of 400,000 men. The War Secretary charged them with inciting treason, and prepared a Military Order directing the Commanding General at New York to stop their publication. Lincoln and Seward signed it and for three days soldiers held their plants. When Lincoln was convinced the papers had been the victim of a hoax, he let them resume.

This summary procedure outraged Governor Seymour, who took process to cause the Department Commander, John A. Dix, to be arrested and tried in a New York State Court for kidnaping and inciting to riot. The General pleaded the order from the President, and the authority of the Indemnity Act of March 3, 1863. The Court held this statute unconstitutional, and ordered Dix held for Grand Jury action. No true bill was returned, so the illegality of the suppressions received no final court test.

Lincoln proclaimed emancipation as Commander in Chief — a war measure for military ends. The President determined upon it principally as a diplomatic weapon abroad and a psychological one at home. In the beginning, he deemed the social gains incidental to the war purpose.

The 1862 campaign had opened badly, and McClellan's procrastination upset the President, who felt increasing need for some secret weapon, some untried menace to the Confederates, to bring the war to a swift close. Abolitionists plagued him with petitions, exhortations and demands for freedom for "God's image in ebony," but their hysteria left him cold. When Greeley thundered in the *Tribune* a "Prayer of Twenty Million People" for immediate emancipation, the President answered calmly: —

"My paramount purpose in this struggle is to save the Union, and is not either to save or destroy slavery. If I could save the Union without freeing any slave, I would do it; and if I could save it by freeing all the slaves I would do it; and if I could save it by freeing some and leaving others alone, I would also do that. What I do about slavery and the colored race I do because it helps to save the Union; and what I forbear, I forbear because I do not believe it would help to save the Union."

When the madcap Frémont ruled Missouri like a Robespierre, in the fall of 1861, and issued a military order freeing the slaves of that

State, Lincoln overruled and removed him. David Hunter, another Radical general, then commanding a narrow strip on the South Carolina coast, declared martial law in Georgia, Florida and South Carolina, and followed it with this General Order: "Slavery and martial law in a free country are incompatible; the persons in these three States . . . heretofore held as slaves are therefore declared forever free." Lincoln promptly disavowed and voided it in a proclamation, May 19, 1862, which added that "whether it be competent for me, as Commander in Chief of the Army and Navy, to declare the slaves of any State or States free, and whether at any time, in any case, it shall have become a necessity indispensable to the maintenance of the Government to exercise such supposed powers, are questions which, under my responsibility, I reserve to myself . . ."

This reservation almost gave away the decision which at last he had made. McClellan's failure to capture Richmond, together with his political demands on the Administration, catalyzed the President's determination. He wrote the first draft of the Emancipation Proclamation on the steamer bringing him back from McClellan's headquarters. Then he told Seward and Welles of his conclusion "that it was a military necessity absolutely essential for the salvation of the Union, that we must free the slaves or be ourselves subdued. We have about played our last card, and must change our tactics or lose the game."

A few days later, he laid the draft before the Cabinet, remarking that he had already decided that it was expedient and sought comment only on style. Seward shrewdly suggested that he not make it public after a defeat, but only after a victory, otherwise it might be regarded "as the last measure of an exhausted Government . . . a shriek on the retreat." The President therefore bided his time until after Antietam, and then issued the now famous document.

The Emancipation Proclamation itself was a warning that unless resistance ceased, the Southerners would be deprived of their slaves. After the first of January, 1863, all slaves "within a State or designated part of a State the people whereof shall then be in rebellion against the United States shall be then, thenceforward and forever free . . ."

The next New Year's Day the President issued the definitive Proclamation, which recited that he based his action on "the power in me vested as Commander in Chief of the Army and Navy of the United States in time of actual armed rebellion against the authority and Government of the United States, and as a fit and necessary war measure for suppressing said rebellion." The Proclamation, after enumerating the States and parts of States wherein the people were then in rebellion, declared the slaves therein free. He also pledged that the executive government, including the military and naval authorities, would "recognize and maintain the freedom" of these slaves. He described the act as one of justice, "warranted by the Constitution and by military necessity."

After the September jubilation a faction of the Republican Party called "the Radicals" had not been too keen about the breadth or depth of the presidential emancipation. Some derided it for excepting from its operation those areas controlled by the Union Army, and offering freedom only where the Confederates ruled. But Lincoln believed it would greatly weaken the Confederate economic output (in which he proved mistaken) and that it could only be sustained constitutionally as a war weapon directed against slaves working for enemy citizens (in this he was altogether correct). Neither President nor Congress could free slaves in unseceded Border States. It took the Thirteenth Amendment to abolish involuntary servitude.

Another area of national policy in which Lincoln intervened through his war powers was the government of reoccupied secession territory. From his experiences in the control of portions of Tennessee, Louisiana and Arkansas, through military governors of his appointment, Lincoln developed the doctrine of presidential restoration of States to the Union. Congress challenged his assertion of this power, through such defiances as the Wade-Davis reconstruction bill of 1864, which Lincoln pocket-vetoed. The struggle between the two ends of Pennsylvania Avenue went on after his assassination, and led to the impeachment of his ill-fated successor, Andrew Johnson.

Following the Donelson capture, the President appointed Johnson, then a Senator without a State, Military Governor of Tennessee, "the furnace of treason." Johnson's courage and energy reestablished some civil government and the State took part in the 1864 presidential election. It was Lincoln's guinea pig for his restoration program. The Louisiana scheme was somewhat different, that for Arkansas also cut to fit the cloth of local circumstance.

He presented his policy December 8, 1863, in the Proclamation which offered presidential pardon to Southerners who wished to resume their allegiance to the United States, and would take and keep a prescribed oath. Whenever a tenth of the qualified voters in any State, as measured by the 1860 presidential election, had thus purged themselves, they could move to bring the State back into the Union. He stipulated that the new State government must be republican in form, and must recognize emancipation. He added that the admission of members to Congress "constitutionally rests exclusively with the respective Houses, and not to any extent with the Executive."

In his annual message the same day, Lincoln transmitted the Proclamation to Congress, and stated that under it, nothing would be attempted "beyond what is amply justified by the Constitution." No man would be coerced to take the prescribed oath, and "the Constitution authorizes the Executive to grant or withhold the pardon at his own absolute discretion, and this includes the power to grant on terms, as is fully established by judicial and other authorities." There must be a test; to let unrepentant rebels dominate a revived State government would be simply absurd; the opposing elements must be separated, "so as to build only from the sound." The oath tested the individual's soundness by the sworn recantation. In view of the ends sought, it was "sufficiently liberal."

The President concluded with a justification of his having taken the initiative: "We must not lose sight of the fact that the war power [of the Executive] is still our main reliance." This bold seizure of control of restoration touched off the Radical Republicans. Henry Winter Davis, a Radical Republican Congressman from Maryland, insisted on the reference to a special committee of that part of the message which treated restoration. By legislative custom, as maker of the motion he became chairman of the special committee, and a little later brought in a measure for Congressional reconstruction which cut the heart out of the Lincoln plan. After elaborate debate, it was passed in July 1864, just before Congress adjourned.

The President was at the Capitol July 4, signing bills, when this one appeared and he set it aside. Senator Zach Chandler of Michigan vainly demanded action, but it died with a pocket veto. A little later Lincoln issued a proclamation to explain that he allowed this to happen because he was "unprepared by a formal approval of this bill to be inflexibly committed to any single plan of restoration," or to set aside "the free State Constitutions already adopted and installed in Arkansas and Louisiana . . . or to declare a constitutional competency in Congress to abolish slavery in States."

This enraged the Radicals. Davis and Senator Wade soon drafted and published a manifesto which assailed the President in the bitterest terms. His pocket veto was "a rank and fatal act," which had proceeded from the lowest personal motives. If he expected any aid from the Radicals, he must begin "to obey and execute, not make the laws — to suppress by arms armed rebellion, and leave political reorganization to Congress." This was the most powerful challenge to Lincoln's war powers, but it checked his use of them not at all.

CHAPTER VII

Also Poet and Prophet

While President, the lonely spirit from Springfield was much more than man of war. Among the problems of his first month was to demonstrate that he was, in fact, President, and not mannikin to be manipulated by another's will. The challenge came from William H. Seward, who assumed the rights of Premier as well as of Secretary of State.

In the feverish weeks before Sumter, Seward emitted all sorts of orders to military commanders and civil officials without consulting or informing the affected Cabinet member, often not even the President himself. The climax was on April 1, 1861, when he submitted a paper entitled "Some Thoughts for the President's Consideration." After a month in office, it stated, the Administration was "yet without a policy, either domestic or foreign," and the time had come to adopt and prosecute policies. On the home front, "we must change the question before the public from one upon slavery, or about slavery, for a question upon Union or Disunion." Inasmuch as Sumter was now deemed a party question, the Administration should drop any plans to provision or reinforce it, but at the same time must take steps to "defend and reinforce all the forts in the Gulf, and have the Navy recalled for a blockade," because this would raise the issue of Union against Disunion.

A foreign war would be even better, and current Caribbean and Mexican affairs could be made the occasion. The President should demand, "categorically, at once," explanations from Spain, France, Britain, and Russia, and at the same time send agents into Canada,

Mexico and Central America "to arouse a vigorous continental spirit of independence" against European intervention. Should Spain and France not answer satisfactorily, Lincoln must "convene Congress and declare war against them."

To this proposal of foreign war as purgative for domestic revolution, he added: "Whatever policy we adopt, there must be an energetic prosecution of it. For this purpose it must be somebody's business to pursue and direct it incessantly. Either the President must do it himself, and be all the time active in it, or devolve it on some member of his Cabinet. Once adopted, debates on it must end, and all agree and abide. It is not my especial province. But I neither seek to evade nor assume responsibility."

Here was a clear proposal that the President turn over to his principal constitutional adviser both the formation of policy and the executive administration of a combined civil and foreign war. Whatever his inner anxieties, Lincoln did not hesitate to make his point of view clear to Seward, answering that same day that his Inaugural pledge to "hold, occupy, and possess the property and places belonging to the Government" had guided his instructions to the Commanding General. He ignored the proposal for a foreign war, but as to "energetic prosecution" replied curtly that "if this must be done, I must do it." Furthermore, on all such issues, "I wish, and suppose I am entitled to have, the advice of all the Cabinet." This sharp rebuke meant that Lincoln would not devolve the actuality of the Presidency upon Seward or any other, and become a mere museum piece. Nor would he have all advice funneled to him through Seward. Abraham Lincoln would be Chief of State in fact as well as name.

Others occasionally ignored his status as Number One Man, but found that he had good memory and long reach. When McClellan tried this, although the President made a pleasantry about being willing to hold the General's horse if only he would win victories, before long he demoted him from General in Chief to the command of only the Army of the Potomac, and after Antietam retired him from active service. Hooker's bubble, too, burst quickly.

The man he found hardest to handle was Stanton, his Secretary of War.

This man was a strange combination of genius, conspirator and madman. He has been termed "the Carnot of the Civil War," because of his feverish, resultful energy in the administration of the business of war. The North's conversion from civil commerce to war production in 1861–1862 presented problems of improvisation even more difficult than those which faced us in our soft war before Pearl Harbor.

Yet Stanton procured the Army's ordnance, quartermaster and subsistence requirements admirably. His prosecution of contractors who mulcted the government through short measures or shoddy goods had some effect, though corruption by no means ceased under him. Military transport was continually improved, the Iron Horse was harnessed to war by skilled railroaders, the military telegraph knit the War Office to Grant at City Point, Sherman at Rome, Thomas at Nashville. But politically, Stanton was a treacherous intriguer. When still a Buchanan man, he had likened Lincoln to Paul du Chaillu's ape, and after he galvanized into Republicanism he acquired little more respect for his chief.

The Secretary of War worked hand in glove with the cabal which ran Congress's Joint Committee on the Conduct of the War, a group which almost succeeded in bludgeoning the choice of commanders and control of campaigns out of the hands of the Commander in Chief. In 1917, an antagonistic group in Congress made moves toward setting up a similar committee to handcuff President Wilson. The latter protested vigorously and successfully that such a committee would "render my task of conducting the war practically impossible," and called attention to the "very ominous precedent in our history," the Civil War committee, which had been responsible for "constant and distressing harassment, and rendered Mr. Lincoln's task all but impossible." Lincoln was well aware of Stanton's connivance with this effort to trench on his power, but said he did not know where to find another man to run the War Office so well. To gain Dr. Jekyll, he endured Mr. Hyde.

As Chief of Government, Lincoln was a misfortune. Like Andrew Jackson, he played by ear, and, administratively speaking, was even more tone-deaf than Old Hickory. His informality and casualness in conducting the President's business was the despair of Nicolay, Hay and other secretaries, who came to love him deeply but never knew what to expect. His was a disordered genius which would not be cribbed, cabined and confined.

Certainly the President had little use for the Cabinet system. Welles lamented that Cabinet meetings were infrequent, irregular and without system. Each department managed its own affairs and informed Lincoln only to the extent it wished. Stanton did not attend half the meetings. Chase, who felt no responsibility beyond the Treasury and public finance, complained: "Had there been an Administration in the true sense of the word — a President conferring with his Cabinet and their united judgments, and with their aid enforcing activity, economy, energy, in all departments of the public service — we could have spoken boldly and defied the world."

Lincoln handled patronage with an amused disregard if not disrespect for administrative efficiency. Needy applicants for department clerkships played on the same warm heart that the relatives of court-martialed soldier boys found so tender. The right Congressman could make post offices sprout like cabbages from his lean cheeks. The rush of officeseekers his first month in the White House kept him so busy that he couldn't take time out to be President.

Success crowned Lincoln's endeavors as Chief of Foreign Relations. In one sense this resulted from his own often uncanny sense of the diplomatically possible; thus far he would go but no farther. Such able aides as Seward in Washington and Charles Francis Adams, his Minister to Great Britain, contributed largely to the success. Although he did not like "the god-like" Sumner, Chairman of the Senate's Foreign Relations Committee, Lincoln procured the latter's co-operation.

Seward accepted Lincoln's early rebuke, readjusted his expectations and loyally and ably carried out the President's instructions in foreign affairs. The Secretary's intimate friendship with Lord Lyons, the British Minister in Washington, cushioned the shock of stiff notes. Also he selected Adams for the London post, Lincoln acquiesced, and Adams proved worth several Army corps.

The principal foreign issues were the *Trent* affair, late in 1861; the danger of British and French recognition of Confederate independence from the summer of 1862 until after Gettysburg and Vicksburg; and the British Government's strange blindness to her neutral duty not to permit Confederate men-of-war to be built in her yards. Lincoln handled the first in a competent manner, in the second his genius in molding the public mood did good service in Britain; Adams deserves principal credit for the third.

Captain Wilkes's act in removing from a British packet James M. Mason and John Slidell, Confederate diplomats assigned respectively to Britain and France, produced a general Northern enthusiasm which made it doubly difficult to accept the harsh but justified British demand for their release. Seward had no formula for response save pettifogging or flag-waving. But Thomas Ewing, wise elder statesman from Ohio, led Lincoln to yield the prisoners because their capture had followed British 1812 naval doctrine, which we fought then and still disapproved. With this sugar-coating, the pill of their return proved not too unpalatable at home.

The recognition menace grew more slowly and took patience and skillful handling of British public opinion. The Federal blockade had cut off Europe's principal cotton supply; and after 1862 tens of thousands of British and French textile workers starved. Additionally, Emperor Louis Napoleon's Mexican adventure with Maximilian caused him to desire Confederate success, but he would not recognize its independence without simultaneous British action. The President skillfully sought to offset the political consequences of this economic distress by measures which would arouse Britain's moral sentiment against slavery. This was one motive for the Emancipation Proclamation, which softened Britain's disappointment at Congress's first statement of the war purpose: "The Union as it was and the Constitution as it is." He sent many able speakers, and propagandists, such as Robert J. Walker, across the ocean to preach the Emancipation gospel, while Sumner touched the Duke of Argyll and his group. By 1863, even the starving textile workers of Lancashire lauded the land that caused their unemployment. This great campaign of public persuasion, rather than diplomatic notes, led the British Government to dismiss its ideas of recognition and raising the blockade, and Napoleon III would not go it alone. This was foreign policy direction of a high order.

"The Master Politician of the Ages" — so another genius in that art whispered as the martyred President was being laid to rest in Springfield. And yet Lincoln was not a great success as Chief of Party. As the war went on, he could do less and less with his party's chiefs in Congress. By the summer of 1864, most of these were disaffected, and such powerful leaders as Zach Chandler, Ben Wade, Thad Stevens and Lyman Trumbull bitterly assailed his course. Nor was he in much better odor with such Republican war Governors as Andrew of Massachusetts, Morton of Indiana, or Curtin of Pennsylvania.

A principal explanation for this was that many Republicans on the Hill felt left out of any real part in the conduct of the war. Frustration made them bitter, and girded them to fight against the President. Similar reactions developed against Wilson in World War I, and Franklin Roosevelt today. The basic reason for such Congressional heartburnings is the inescapable nature of the direction of war — an executive act no debating society can successfully perform. It calls for central and not centrifugal control, so Governors must subordinate themselves to the dictates of Washington. It necessitates some lessening of log-rolling, and a relaxation of the party test for admission to public service. Few war emergency changes go well with power-hungry party leaders or patronage-seeking party hacks.

But Lincoln compounded the felony by exhibiting his belief that he did not depend chiefly on Congress — that is to say, the Republican majority in Congress — for the powers with which to win the war. While he did not assail it so bluntly as Jackson did in his

Bank fight, he bypassed Congress again and again, going direct to the people. This would seem a chief reason for the organization, at the turn of the year 1861, of the Joint Committee on the Conduct of the War, and later for the Radical Congress's determination to take over the reconstruction of the Southern States. Congress wanted to sit in the driver's seat.

Then too, Lincoln was an antislavery man, not an abolitionist. He had no great zeal for sudden creation, but preferred some cushion for change; witness the patient efforts he made through 1864 to persuade Border States to take the half-loaf of compensated emancipation. Such economic wisdom ran counter both to the social inertia of the Borderers and to the Radicals' unwillingness to pay master for slave. Congress, with more than the customary quota of expert employers of emotion-moving phrases, did not relish the President's progressive or "Moderate" rather than "Radical" position. To maintain any important influence on the party in Congress, he must appeal to the Republican rank and file back home. His moves to this end helped offset the resistances on Capitol Hill.

Lincoln cannot have thus designed his course for the 1862 midterm election campaign. The war purpose, not domestic politics, animated the series of disturbing actions culminating in emancipation, which made 1862's balloting a Republican disaster.

It was different when he sought the second term. During 1863 disaffection ran rife through the party. When Chase and his Radical friends catapulted Hooker into command of the Army of the Potomac, the General understood that his military success would be used to promote the Secretary's candidacy for President. Lincoln knew of Chase's maneuvers, but said: "He is like a bluebottle fly and lays his eggs in every rotten spot, but I cannot spare him from my Cabinet. Wall Street believes in him." That fall, the Treasury head became an active under-cover candidate, lamenting the President's administrative incompetence far and wide. But Senator Pomeroy, Chase's campaign manager, wrote a stupid letter, the Republicans of his own State of Ohio indorsed a second term for Lincoln, and the Secretary was forced out of the race.

Lincoln likewise mastered a rival nomination of General Frémont by the Republican "lunatic fringe." Some four hundred attended their convention at Cleveland, wherefore Lincoln quoted the Scripture on the gathering in Adullam's Cave: "And every one that was in distress, and every one that was in debt, and every one that was discontented, gathered themselves under him, and he became a captain over them: and there were with him about four hundred men." Four months later he bought them off by easing the conservative Montgomery Blair out of the Cabinet.

Lincoln's major re-election concern was not the internal war in his own party, but how to get the Union vote outside. The old-line Democrats seemed to be making headway with their dictatorship charges. Through Kentucky, Missouri, Ohio, Indiana and Illinois, the Sons of Liberty menaced ballot box as well as military prisons. Lincoln must find the way to bring War Democrats and independents to vote for him. The plan he devised, nomination by the advocates of national union rather than Republican partisans, worked like a charm.

Delegates were chosen to a "National Union" (not a "Republican") Convention. The President dropped Hamlin for running mate, and substituted War Democrat Andrew Johnson, who had proved his courageous patriotism as Military Governor of Tennessee. This shrewd as well as statesmanlike broadening of the base of campaign purpose did essential service. The Union thesis, energized by Sherman's capture of Atlanta, brought triumph at the ballot box.

This vindication at the polls restored Lincoln's strength with the party organization through the Loyal States. He had not been the only victor; Republican candidates from Congressmen to constable clung to his coattails and got into office. He had demonstrated that he could carry a whole organization along with him to victory. His credit as Chief of Party rose high among the rank and file.

To be sure, it was different among the Radical leaders in Congress who wanted their part of the power and the prestige he kept out of their hands. Had he lived, the struggle with the new Congress would have been terrific. But Lincoln had armed himself with his triumphant re-election.

None have surpassed Lincoln, and few have equaled him as Chief of Public Opinion, a role as unknown to the Constitution as the equally unofficial headship of the party which nominates him for President. Powers are abstractions until given content through being exercised and having effect. There are few more illusory maxims than "Ours is a government of laws, not of men." Physical force can imprison an individual, or end his life, but there are limits to the efficiency of force against the will of the people. Some measure of consent is necessary to the direction of any type of government. In a democracy, consent generally comes out of understanding. None sensed this better than Lincoln.

From inauguration until assassination, he always tried to inform the people of some among the controlling reasons for his policies and acts. While he paid some heed to the sanctity of military secrets, he declined to worship at that shrine. He knew that the people had ears, whether the walls had them or not, and took advantage of every appropriate occasion to tell them his innermost thoughts.

It is hard to realize the rudimentary nature of the apparatus for measuring and molding public opinion in the Sixties. There was no systematic sampling of public opinion by such sure-fire system as Gallup polls. Those who felt the public pulse did not debate among themselves how to pick the sample and weight the average. They learned their interview techniques "by guess or by God," and practised them while riding the circuits or gathered about the cracker barrel in the country store. While there was an Associated Press, there were not nearly so many customary channels for getting stories to the people. No President had yet thought of a regular White House press conference, to "plant" his views as "background material not for direct quotation" in the papers over the land. This did not come until after Theodore Roosevelt. Wilson made good use of it until we entered World War I; then he found it a two-edged sword and abandoned it.

Lincoln gave many stories to favorite correspondents. He wrote deeply human letters, as that to Mrs. Bixby, many of which eventually found their way to print. But he had no brigade of press agents such as Seward or Stanton had, perhaps because he placed little confidence in purchased puffs. Being a good politician, he cultivated friendly editors; then and until the turn of the century the editor determined the paper's policy, instead of some business manager who sought cold cash rather than public credit. Many, like Medill of the *Chicago Tribune,* he influenced to their mutual advantage; a few, like Henry J. Raymond, of the *New York Times,* came among his small circle of intimate advisers.

In the main, this moody, occasionally morose poet, prophet and seer moved the public opinion by the things that he did, rather than through the gadgetry of public relations experts, or massaging editors' backs. He seldom made a move without explaining its purpose, and often outlining the whole background of events which had forced the action. He frequently used a particular power right to the limit, but never without letting the people know why circumstances had forced this to be done for the public good. And he found, as his intuition had told him he would, that the people in the middle of the road between the fringes of unwavering friends and undying enemies always relished the truth, and eventually understood and sustained him.

Lincoln's dependence on public opinion was shown most clearly in his exercise of the powers of Commander in Chief. Considered narrowly in a technical, legal and constitutional sense, his power here was more plenary, here he was more in reality a dictator or tyrant, than in any other major function. Yet even in his control of the actual military operations, the "C in C" had out his antennae for public reaction.

He ordered "On to Richmond," in July 1861, for no other reason than the general public outcry for action. His General Order Number One, directing a simultaneous advance by all Union forces, to begin February 22, 1862, was more prop to civilian morale than spur to McClellan's "slows." Militarily, little new happened that

Washington's Birthday; but psychically, the people knew that the President was just as eager to get on with the war as they were. This patient following of opinion was even more apparent in the care with which he justified his use of the war power outside the theater of operations: his suspension of the writ of habeas corpus; his trying of fifth columnists under military law, as in the Vallandigham and Indiana treason trials; sustaining the oppressive machinery of the draft; emancipation as a military necessity.

The President cleverly availed himself of the public's sense of fair play, to thwart a palace revolution promoted by Radicals at both ends of the Avenue. Its immediate objective was to purge the Executive Department of its conservative element by forcing Seward out. The Conservative swing in the 1862 election doubled their attack on the "envious, ambitious" Secretary of State, who finally handed the President his resignation. But Lincoln would not act on it until Chase, too, wrote out one — and then he kept both men! This announcement that the "Unseen Hand" would stay in the Cabinet angered the Radicals, but independent opinion throughout the North relished the smooth way Lincoln continued to ride two horses at once. Public opinion sustained him in his balanced Cabinet, and the victory was important to his power as Chief of Government.

Perhaps Lincoln's most masterly performance as Chief of Public Opinion was the way he checkmated the 1864 peace offensive. While Gettysburg, Vicksburg and then Missionary Ridge had made it clear that the Confederacy would not win the war through military victory, her leaders clung to the hope that the North might tire of the toll of casualties and drop the contest. From the fall of 1863, Davis pinned his hopes for independence upon the collapse of Northern morale, which he sought to precipitate by close support of the Knights of the Golden Circle and its successor "fifth column" societies; secret agents and saboteurs to cripple Federal war production; and the dispatch to Canada of diplomatic agents to spread the word that, with Richmond ready to reach peace by negotiation, further slaughter was positively criminal.

This whisper found willing ears, as casualties mounted on Grant's bloody march on Richmond. Lincoln had no illusions — he knew the Confederate President would take no peace which involved return to the Union, the one thing the United States Government must have. He knew, too, that large parts of the Northern people were not convinced of this, and that he could not afford to alienate the trust and support of the uninformed by refusing to explore every avenue to peace and Union. There were four major efforts, each of which he handled skillfully, and in the issue, by so doing he helped the prosecution of the war.

The first involved Horace Greeley. In the early summer of 1864 the editor of the *Tribune* was advised that two ambassadors of Davis were in Canada "with full and complete powers for a peace." The editor, with his instant enthusiasm, demanded that Lincoln negotiate at once, because "a frank offer by you to the insurgents of terms which the impartial will say ought to be accepted, will, at the worst, prove an immense and sorely needed advantage to the National cause. It may save us from a Northern insurrection."

The President promptly threw the petard back to Greeley by naming him the agent to conduct the negotiations. The latter sought to evade, but Lincoln insisted: "I not only intend a sincere effort for peace, but I intend that you shall be a personal witness that it is made." Greeley proceeded to Niagara Falls.

Lincoln sent him a letter addressed "To Whom It May Concern." This stated that any proposal which included peace, reunion and freedom, "and which comes by and with an authority that controls the armies now at war against the United States, will be received and considered by the Executive Government of the United States," which would meet them with "liberal terms on other substantial and collateral points." It soon became clear that the Confederate "Commissioners" had no real authority to negotiate. Greeley tried to shift the onus of failure to the President, but in vain.

About this same time Lincoln reluctantly permitted two peace zealots, Jaquess and Gilmore, to cross the lines to Richmond, where they had two hours with Davis, who rejected out of hand, as "altogether impractical," their vague plan for a reunion referendum in the Confederacy. "Say to Mr. Lincoln," Davis concluded, "that I shall at any time be pleased to receive proposals for peace on the basis of our independence. It will be useless to approach me with any other."

Earnest concern marked the third effort, made by Francis Preston Blair. This Union war-horse of Jackson's days believed that, because of the collapse of the Southern capacity to resist, Davis would negotiate. Lincoln furnished safe-conduct through the lines, but no letter. Blair suggested to Davis domestic peace, with a combined North-South military attack on Maximilian and his French troops; apparently Confederate independence was not discussed. Davis leaped at the idea: He would name a commission to confer with one from Washington. Blair's report left Lincoln cold; he would go no further than to say that he stood ready to do the best he could to obtain "peace between the people of our common country."

The sequel was the fruitless conference on the *River Queen* in Hampton Roads, February 3, 1865. Davis sent three commissioners; Lincoln came in person, along with Seward. The Southerners sang the theme of the joint war on Mexico, but the President promptly ended that dream: He had not authorized Blair's suggestion, and could countenance no peace except the complete restoration of the Union. His description of the pending Thirteenth Amendment threw more cold water on Southern hopes. Lincoln hinted that, if there were a prompt end to resistance, some payment might be made for slaves, but there was no meeting of minds and the conference adjourned *sine die*. Within three months the Confederacy was no more.

In appraising Lincoln's performance of the demanding duties that press upon a President in time of crisis, he would seem to have reached his heights in the way he handled public opinion. His almost intuitive understanding of the tangled moods of the people is his best title to greatness. In an ideal world, each man who became

President of the United States would be endowed with each of the great qualities so important for him to meet the multiple problems of our democracy in crisis, whether peace or war. But inscrutable Providence seems reluctant to entrust all the traits and talents to any one man, and much dross must accompany the gold.

Lincoln's faults almost obscured his virtues for his contemporaries. He had no talent for or interest in the efficient administration of the public business. His War Government was never collective, the virtually independent departments resisted his sporadic efforts at co-ordination. He did not learn by experience, as had Jefferson, to pull things together. Neither did he gain the latter's finesse in managing a refractory party in Congress. A child about public finance, he let Chase make blunder after blunder, until gold soared to the danger point.

Yet as we look back, we can see that on Lincoln the President, as on Lincoln the man, these facts were no more than the warts on Cromwell. They need to be painted, that the portrait may show the true strength of the man. As Commander in Chief, he found and used the powers without whose employment his Presidency might have been almost as flabby as Buchanan's. Militarily, he earned a postgraduate degree in the school of command. As Chief of Foreign Relations, he avoided wars abroad. His success in both these roles stemmed out of his genius as Chief of Public Opinion.

Lincoln's example might indicate that, in a time of crisis, it is more important that the President be a master of this public opinion leadership than of the other tasks of the office; Lincoln succeeded chiefly because he was poet and prophet and seer.

CHAPTER VIII

White House under Fire

The twenty years after Lincoln were marked by the heaviest political attacks ever made on either the person, the office or the powers of the President. Not until Grover Cleveland's first term did the position of Chief of State really recover from the Radicals' blows.

In the epoch between Jackson and Lincoln, the chief cause for the Presidency's down-curve was the heat of the sectional contention, for which the inevitable forums were the halls of Congress and the hustings of the countryside. In such a time, no President could lead a people who were making up their wills to disagree. But Johnson's effort to carry on Lincoln's restoration policy led to a bitter attack on him individually, and on the Presidency as a national institution, by a Congress which was determined to destroy its competitor's power and prestige.

The Radicals came within a vote of convicting the plebeian President on articles of impeachment which today seem quite strained. His immediate successors in the office lived under the shadow of the terror. Grant became the master of the palace for the Radical oligarchy of Congress. Hayes, despite the taint on his title, sought to turn government and country from a dead war to a live peace. His turn to honest, well-administered government evoked the wrath of the Republican plunderbund. With his exception, each of the Presidents between Lincoln and Cleveland lived in terror of the oligarchy; and not without reason, for seldom have such men ruled Congress or the Republican Party as Zach Chandler, Oliver P. Morton, Roscoe Conkling, Ben Wade, James G. Blaine, Henry Wilson and their counterparts.

Able, tough, ruthless, they knew what they wanted and would stop at nothing to get it. They fashioned a firm working alliance with the speculators and exploiters, and the resulting marriage of High Tariff and Bloody Shirt ruled our national politics into Theodore Roosevelt's term. They wanted weak Presidents, and generally nominated and elected them. Anyone who bit the hand that fed him was rushed to the political guillotine.

No one's offense equaled Andrew Johnson's, and for none was the headsman's axe so sharp. Oddly enough, on his succession leading Radicals rejoiced that here was a man of their own kidney, sure to be a great improvement over the compromising Lincoln. But before long the new President adopted the policies of his predecessor, and the concentrated hate of the Radicals descended on his head.

On May 9, 1865, Johnson issued a proclamation for the restoration of North Carolina to the Union. This set out the steps the people must take to purge themselves of the crime of treason and disaffection and appointed a Provisional Governor to guide their course. In essence, he adapted Lincoln's Louisiana-Arkansas scheme to the immediate postwar situation, and based his program on two powers Lincoln had consistently employed: that of the Commander in Chief, and the pardoning power.

During his tenure, the Supreme Court as well as Congress operated upon his powers as Commander in Chief. The Court in 1866 performed its chief surgery through its decision in *ex parte Milligan,* a hang-over from the Indiana treason trials of late 1864.

Milligan, an Indiana fifth columnist, had been tried and convicted by a Military Commission, deriving its authority from Lincoln's Commander in Chief and other war powers. When the case reached the Court on petition for a writ of habeas corpus, it unanimously held his conviction contrary to the Constitution. While the justices took pains to reprehend treason, the nature of his trial court controlled the decision. The Supreme Court solemnly declared: "The Constitution of the United States is a law for rulers and people, equally in war and in peace, and covers with the shield of its protection all classes of men, at all times and under all circumstances. *No doctrine involving more pernicious consequences was ever invented by the wit of man than that any of its provisions can be suspended during any of the great exigencies of the Government."*

It followed that martial law, to be valid, must be instituted to cope with "actual and present" necessity, and not a threatened invasion. No such situation had existed in Indiana at the time of the trial, "therefore one of the plainest constitutional provisions was infringed when Milligan was tried by a court not ordained and established by Congress and not composed of judges appointed during good behavior."

On the illegality the Court was unanimous. It divided mainly on the moot point whether Congress by legislative action could have clothed the Commission with powers. By a bare majority vote the Court said that would not meet the constitutional test. Lincoln's friend and appointee, Justice David Davis, wrote the majority view containing the sentence italicized above. In regard to its strictures, Professor Corwin has remarked that "among judicial records it would be difficult to uncover a more evident piece of arrant hypocrisy . . . According to the decision then and there being handed down, the Constitution had been 'suspended' in this very case, which was but one of many!" In 1863 this Court had refused even to grant a writ of certiorari to Vallandigham to hear his counsel's protest against the constitutionality of Burnside's commission. But *ex parte Milligan* was decided a year after Appomattox!

In general, the Court took to the dugout of delay or avoidance during the Radical Congress's total war on Johnson. In *ex parte McArdle* it deliberately delayed passing on the constitutionality of the Reconstruction Acts, until Congress could convene and amend the Judiciary Act so as to deprive it of jurisdiction over the suit. In other cases it shunned like poison any attribution of implied power to the President. This was not malice against the incumbent, but the Court's own instinct of self-preservation.

Congress attacked the Commander in Chief power much more

directly, through the creation of statutory obstructions to Johnson's ability to issue a military order and have it obeyed. By the fiat of Congress, the General of the Army was to presume that any order which came to him from the Secretary of War — the treacherous Stanton — was by direction of the President! The Military Reconstruction Acts sought to deprive Johnson of effective command of the Army of Occupation of the conquered provinces, and largely attained that objective. But he was impeached over the right of removal or suspension of civil officers, not his efforts to maintain some reality of army authority as Commander in Chief.

The pardoning power Johnson had used to implement his North Carolina proclamation, and the similar ones for other Southern States, was never successfully attacked. Its form was broad, "a full pardon for all offenses committed by his participation, direct or implied, in the Rebellion." In 1865 Congress had decreed that any person who could not take oath that he had never voluntarily borne arms against the Union, or given aid or comfort to its enemies, would not be allowed to practise in a Federal Court. One Garland challenged this, and in 1867 a divided Court declared: "A pardon reaches both the punishment prescribed for the offense and the guilt of the offender; and when the pardon is full, it releases the punishment and blots out the existence of guilt, so that in the eye of the law the offender is as innocent as if he had never committed the offense." Its effect, therefore, if granted before conviction, was to prevent the penalties and disabilities which flow from guilt; if after conviction, to make him a new man and give him "a new credit and capacity." Johnson used his pardoning power to the full, including a general amnesty near the close of his term. The Radicals writhed, but could not stop this clemency which, to a degree, lessened the harm of bayonet rule in the South.

The question is often raised: Had Lincoln lived, would the nation have escaped Reconstruction and its tragic aftermath? This is one of the most fascinating Ifs of History. Probably not — the Wade-Davis 1864 Manifesto evidenced the Radical rage at Lincoln. Had he lived, and persisted in seeking a compassionate peace, undoubtedly the relentless leaders of this Age of Hate would have made war on him as they did on Johnson. But there was this difference: Within limits, Lincoln was supple; he had a backbone of steel, and could bend, then spring back close to original position. His course was straight, with tolerances for readjustment to necessities. Johnson had no such zone of accommodation. His spine was cast-iron; he could not bend but had to break.

Johnson was a better administrator of public business than Lincoln, and gave great heed to the Cabinet as an executive implement. Had he been other than a prisoner in the White House, Johnson might have made a reputation as an efficient Chief of Government. Neither ignorant nor vain, he sought no pomp of power. Courage he had in embarrassing measure, and devotion to his concept of the Constitution. But his brittle spirit never learned how to get along; its few yieldings were too little and too late.

Even more important than the personality of Johnson, the Radicals were under the imperative necessity of putting the Executive in irons. They had a majority in Congress only because the Southern States were not represented, so the South's continued exclusion was a matter of life and death, and Congressional Reconstruction the obvious delaying device. After the Radicals should have transformed their minority into majority, it would not matter if "unreconstructed Rebels" took the empty seats.

Subsidiary motives, too, played their part in the struggle: The sincere concern of the humanitarians and "For God's sakers" for the welfare of the hapless freedmen; the belief of the social reconstructors that the Negroes deserved the lands and chattels of their ex-masters; the carpetbaggers and scalawags, who saw their opportunity for plunder and gold-plated spittoons.

The Radicals in Congress made no bones about their ultimate purpose. Thad Stevens, who took command of the House in December 1865, was the most powerful Congressional dictator in our annals. This Caliban of Reconstruction proclaimed boldly the inferior status of the President; he was not the direct servant of the people, as claimed by Jackson and Lincoln; he was their servant only as they spoke through Congress. Johnson must learn "that as Congress shall order he must obey. There is no escape from it. God forbid that he should have one tittle of power except what he derives through Congress and the Constitution."

But Johnson could not be coerced so long as he could maintain his veto on new legislation. After Stevens had organized the House, the President could persuade no further legislation to implement his plans, but this did not cripple him unduly; his course was founded on executive rather than legislative authority. The Radicals could not work their will until they built up a two-thirds majority in each House, to ride roughshod over White House vetoes.

This majority came, at the 1866 election. Race riots at New Orleans and Memphis furnished needed Radical propaganda, which the President himself cubed in intensity by a foolish "swing around the circle," when questioners goaded him into expressions of spleen. The Democrats regarded him as a deserter, the Republicans treated him as a traitor, and he could found no party of his own.

Now the Radicals sat in the seats of the mighty. Bill after bill rolled through their legislative mill, came back from the White House disapproved, and was promptly repassed by the constitutionally required two-thirds majority to make it a law just the same. The First Reconstruction Act, then a second to draw tighter the strait-jacket on ex-Confederates; the 1867 Army Reorganization Act, and finally the Tenure of Office Act, undermined his power. His veto messages were strong, soundly reasoned, today read most persuasively, but seldom shifted a vote.

It was a revolution in the character of the government. Its most serious aspect, from the President's standpoint, was the fact that he had a traitor in his Cabinet, in the person of the Secretary of War. Stanton's retention exampled Johnson's worst trait as administrator, his unwillingness to get rid of men he had reason to distrust.

The Tenure of Office Act, passed over the President's veto, March 2, 1867, ordained that every person holding any civil office to which he has been appointed with the advice and consent of the Senate, or thereafter so nominated and confirmed, "shall be entitled to hold such office until a successor shall have been in like manner appointed and duly qualified." The aim was to preserve Radical payrollers from discharge by the President. It added the grievous proviso that the seven heads of executive departments "shall hold their offices respectively for and during the term of the President by whom they may have been appointed and for one month thereafter, subject to removal by and with the advice and consent of the Senate." The principal purpose of this clause was to maintain Stanton against the President's will.

Every member of Johnson's Cabinet, including the Secretary of War, advised him the bill was unconstitutional, because the right of removal was constitutionally vested in the President. Stanton's condemnation of the law was "the most elaborate and emphatic" of the Cabinet members, and he advised Johnson it was his "duty to defend the power of the President from usurpation and to veto the law"!

During the next few months Stanton's double-dealing grew so patent that on August 5, 1867 the President sent him a curt note: "Public considerations of a high character constrain me to say that your resignation as Secretary of War will be accepted." Stanton replied that "public considerations of a high character, which alone have induced me to continue at the head of this Department, constrain me not to resign the office of Secretary of War before the next meeting of Congress."

The next week Johnson ordered that "by virtue of the power and authority vested in me as President by the Constitution and laws of the United States, you are hereby suspended from office as Secretary of War, and will cease to exercise any and all functions pertaining to the same." He named General Grant Secretary *ad interim*. Again Stanton denied his right to suspend "without the advice and consent of the Senate and without any legal cause," but physically left the office.

The President had more in his mind than hatred of Stanton. He was anxious to bring the question quickly before the Supreme

Court, for final authoritative decision. He knew the Senate, when it reassembled in December 1867, would not ratify Stanton's suspension, and that worthy would seek to reoccupy his office. If the interim Secretary would refuse to give it back, legal process could be instituted to get the issue before the Court.

But Grant was not willing to resist the Radicals, and broke his promise to notify Johnson in advance of quitting the War office. Stanton moved in almost the instant of Senate disapproval, barricaded himself against Lorenzo Thomas, the next interim choice, and Radical gunmen came down to defend him. The House now rushed through Articles of Impeachment, to remove Johnson as President for "high crimes and misdemeanors" against the peace and dignity of the United States, the principal one being the crime of desiring to get rid of a Secretary of War he could not trust.

Impeachment is a mighty engine. The House is both grand jury and prosecuting attorney, the Senate constitutes the Court. When President or Vice President is on trial, the Chief Justice presides over the Senators sitting as judges. A Court of Impeachment has no body of precedent except the slender record of earlier impeachment proceedings; these do not control, and often do not persuade. The Senate which tried Johnson made its own rules of procedure and evidence — in almost every instance tailor-made to convict "that monster in the White House."

The House had eleven counts in its indictment: ten were specific charges of illegal action, the other was a sort of catch-all. All these articles had been shaped so as to fit the mood of the doubtful Senators. The conduct of Chief Justice Chase as presiding officer was conspicuous in its devotion to justice, at some danger to his own political future. The certainty that, were Johnson expelled, "Bluff Ben" Wade, the violent Radical president of the Senate, would step into the White House probably kept at least one Republican from voting for conviction.

But whatever motives animated the doubtful members, the impeachers lacked one vote for the needed two thirds required for conviction. The President was not convicted and expelled. Then Stanton fled from his usurped office, and General Schofield became Secretary of War. The Senate's failure to remove the President served for the time being as a left-handed indorsement of the Chief Executive's removal power. But the memory of the nearness of Johnson's conviction hung like a Sword of Damocles over the heads of his immediate successors in office. In practical effect, the Radicals lost the battle but won the campaign.

The impeachment trial is chiefly important today in the light it throws on the President's right of removal. Few students of the subject would now disagree with the contention of Johnson's counsel that the Tenure of Office Act breached the rights of the President. The Constitution goes into considerable detail on the process of appointment but says not a word about removal. The location of the removal power was debated in the First Congress when it formed the State Department. In the earlier drafts, the bill had contained a provision vesting in the President the authority to remove the Secretary and other officers. Madison, on reflection, had had this stricken out; it was both redundant and *ultra vires,* for the Constitution clearly implied it as a part of the appointing power — without any implication of the Senate's being associated in its exercise.

Every President before Johnson had exercised this power. While their right to do so, without Senate concurrence, had been assailed in Congress, it had not been passed on by the Court. Its justification was "the Decision of 1789" by Congress, not the Court, and the succeeding precedents of unimpeded removals by the Executive.

The President's attorneys also joined issue with the prosecutors (or "Managers," as they are officially entitled) upon the course the President should take in regard to the enforcement of an Act of Congress he believed contrary to the Constitution. Evarts defended the President's efforts because they were designed to get the issue before the Courts. Groesbeck took the other branch, to answer in the negative the question: "Shall he execute all laws?"

"If a law be declared by the Supreme Court unconstitutional, he should not execute it," he declared. "If the law be upon its very face in flat contradiction to plain express provisions of the Constitution, or if a law should forbid the President to grant a pardon in any case, or if a law should declare that he should not be Commander in Chief, or if a law should declare that he should take no part in the making of a treaty, I say the President, without going to the Supreme Court ... is bound to execute no such legislation; and he is cowardly and untrue to the responsibilities of his position if he should execute it."

The Radical Managers contended that Congress could repeal an unconstitutional Act, or the Court hold it null, but the Executive could only execute it until the one or the other of these events occurred. Manager Boutwell insisted that the repeal was legislative, the Court's declaration judicial, "but the power to repeal, or annul, or set aside a law of the United States, is in no aspect of the case an executive power. It is made the duty of the Executive to take care that the laws be faithfully executed — an injunction wholly inconsistent with the theory that it is in the power of the Executive to repeal, or annul, or dispense with the laws of the land."

From this point, the Massachusetts Congressman advanced to this logical *reductio ad absurdum:* "To the President in the performance of his executive duties all laws are alike. He can enter into no inquiry as to their expediency or constitutionality. All laws are presumed to be constitutional." Whether in fact they were or not, "it is the duty of the Executive so to regard them while they have the form of law."

The Senate which tried Johnson settled neither of these great issues of constitutional intendment and public policy. The practice of succeeding Presidents repudiated the Boutwell thesis that the Executive had not even a qualified discretion in enforcement.

Grant had not been in office two weeks before he asked Congress to repeal the Tenure of Office Acts, and on April 5, 1869, it removed the most hateful of the restraints. But the remaining provisions still oppressed this General who had aided Johnson's impeachment. In his first annual message, Grant urged their total repeal, because surely "it could not have been the intention of the framers of the Constitution, when providing that appointments made by the President should receive the consent of the Senate, that the latter should have the power to retain in office persons placed there by Federal appointment against the will of the President. The law is inconsistent with a faithful and efficient administration of the Government. What faith can an Executive put in officials forced upon him, and those, too, whom he has suspended for reason? How will such officials be likely to serve an Administration which they know does not trust them?"

In 1876, the General's last year in the White House, Congress inserted in a post office appropriation bill the provision that "postmasters of the first, second and third classes shall be appointed and may be removed by the President with the advice and consent of the Senate. . . ." An even half century after enactment, this clause brought the first Court decision upon removal. The case was Myers *vs.* United States, the plaintiff being a postmaster at Portland, Oregon, whom President Wilson had removed. Chief Justice Taft wrote the majority opinion, which held the challenged provision unconstitutional. Article II, he held, conferred on the Chief Executive a right to remove executive and administrative officers of the United States nominated or appointed by him, without the least restraint or limitation by the National Legislature. The Constitution intended such officers to serve only at the President's pleasure.

Grant in war was heroic, Grant in the White House a humiliation. Only Harding's Administration vied in degree of corruption, and in the shadow it threw upon the person of the President. In both instances, the ill fame was not altogether undeserved. The Radical oligarchy nominated and elected Grant, and controlled him through the two terms, partly by corruption of his intimates and partly through his own fear. Stevens led it in the House till his death, and Morton in the Senate. Roscoe Conkling, of New York, who went from House to Senate, was their junior partner, and channeled their orders to the White House. Grant was not inherently bad or corrupt, and in quiet times, without grave problems or a group determined to run him, might have made an unexceptionable mediocre Chief Executive. But his inept trust of weak or evil associates and relatives left him without defenses against Reconstruction's storms.

The Radicals forced him to abandon the Appomattox policy of generous treatment for the South, until he became persecutor and oppressor rather than healer and guide. The Congressional dictatorship's thirst for power was unquenchable; there was no legislative infamy to which it would not resort. At times its lengths frightened Grant, who then would not fully execute the orders from Capitol Hill, though usually he yielded.

Grant as Commander in Chief directed the military rule of the South. He heeded Radical wishes in the choice of commanding generals over the desolated States. The Ku-Klux Klan counter-offensive of the Southern whites brought brutal repression, including especially high-handed bayonet rule over South Carolina. Grant in peace proved a torturer to the unreconstructed white South.

He was a poor Chief of Government. The administrative departments were loaded with incompetent or rascally political retainers, and the extravagance, inefficiency and corruption beggared description. His first choice for the Treasury, William A. Richardson of Illinois, proved unsatisfactory, and early in the second term was replaced by Benjamin H. Bristow, of Kentucky, who had a passion for reform. He abolished the scandal-surrounded Office of Supervising Architect, consolidated the Customs and Internal Revenue administrations, and tried to clean up the corruption and inefficiency in the collection of customs. This aroused Conkling, who for years had treated the New York Customs House as a private preserve, and handled it as Boss Tweed handled New York's city government.

In 1875, Bristow sprung a trap on the infamous Whisky Ring, which had been defrauding the Government of taxes on distilled spirits, with a trail of corruption leading into the White House itself: Babcock, Grant's private secretary, took its bribes in return for protection, while the President himself, doubtless without knowledge of the tainted source, accepted the present of a handsome team and equipage. After stalling off prosecution as long as possible, Grant sent a deposition to the trial at St. Louis asserting Babcock's "integrity," and soon removed the United States District Attorney who had pressed the charge. Bristow also felt the President's displeasure, and resigned in 1876.

Grant likewise picked a tartar in Akerman, his first Attorney General, who took his duties seriously. When the Interior Department asked his official opinion on railroad efforts to grab huge new tracts of public land, Akerman insisted that they be resisted. The greedy railroad manipulators pressed the President, who dismissed the Attorney General, so that a new man could give them their spoils. In doing so, Grant wrote Akerman a curious letter which said that "a change in the office you now hold is in the best interests of the Government," but then praised his "zeal, integrity and industry," and offered him any Federal district judgeship he might wish!

As Chief of Foreign Relations, Grant was more fortunate. Under Hamilton Fish, his able Secretary of State, that Department was extremely well run. The principal achievement was the arbitration at Geneva of the American claims against Britain for the Civil War losses due to the captures of our merchant vessels by the *Alabama, Florida* and other Confederate men-of-war built in British yards. The American claim was substantially upheld; in 1871 Britain paid damages of $15,500,000 and the basis was laid for better feeling between the Anglo-Saxon nations.

The effort to annex Santo Domingo failed completely. This strange episode stemmed out of actions of the President much more than out of those of Fish. Baez, the momentary dictator of that Caribbean republic, had vainly tried to interest Andrew Johnson in the idea, but the latter would not bother with it. The scheme set Grant on fire, he dispatched Babcock to the island soon after he took office, and the latter quickly negotiated a treaty of annexation. But the President had not taken the Chairman of the Senate Committee on Foreign Affairs, Sumner, into his confidence; he furiously opposed this expansionist venture, and the Senate debated the proposed treaty month after month. Enraged by Sumner's course, Grant sent a naval squadron and occupying troops to the island to give effect to the terms of the unratified treaty. Also he persuaded Congress to name a commission to investigate the project. In April 1871, Congress punctured his dream by tabling the commission's report. But Grant's employment of an executive agreement in lieu of a constitutionally ratified treaty did afford Theodore Roosevelt a precedent for similar action some thirty years later.

Rutherford B. Hayes came into the White House under the cloud of "the Crime of '76," but conducted the office in admirable contrast to Grant. For the ensuing four years the Presidency was redeemed both from partisan and corrupt administration and from subservience to the Radical oligarchy. Hayes had no hatred for the South, and no wish to continue bayonet rule over the three States still unreconstructed. Though he had been a Union Brigadier, and most of his Ohio political strength had come from veterans, his emotional interest focused on reform, not revenge. The Radicals, who had nominated Hayes to avoid Blaine, soon could not abide him because of his zeal for the sort of statesmanlike policies the Democratic Tilden had proclaimed.

While Hayes was physically slight and inconspicuous, and an indifferent speaker, he had purpose and courage. His deficiencies in the field of ceremonial — his W.C.T.U. wife made the White House a Sahara — have been remembered, but his merits as Chief Executive have been obscured. The experience of three terms as Governor of Ohio, together with native industry and attention to detail, made him a first-rate Chief of Government. Administratively, he sought a Cabinet of good executives rather than party war horses. Evarts, of Johnson's counsel in the impeachment trial, took the State Department. He placed John Sherman in the Treasury, and under the President's guiding hand that unstable statesman did a masterly job of financial recovery from the Panic of '73. Sherman proved his pithy epigram, "the way to resume is — to resume," when the government began to redeem greenbacks with gold.

Hayes recognized the Liberal Republicans by putting Carl Schurz at the head of the Interior Department, a choice which spoke the language of reform. He held out an olive branch to the Southern Conservatives by selecting David M. Key, a former Confederate officer, for Postmaster General.

His first important task was to carry out the deal his managers had made during the election contest, and remove the Federal troops from South Carolina, Louisiana and Florida, the three States the Southern Democrats had permitted to be counted for Hayes in return for the promise of home rule. He performed his side of the bargain; on April 10, 1877, on his order as Commander in Chief, the Federal troops marched out of the South Carolina State House. The new President held his nose but redeemed his managers' patronage promises to the Louisiana and Florida rascals who had thrown out enough votes to give him the wisp of title to those States' election certificates.

At the same time he showed a strange determination to keep on the statute books Federal election-control laws he himself had made a nullity. The 1878 election had given the Democrats control of the Senate, they already had the House, and soon tried to repeal the Radical Reconstruction Acts. The very Hayes who had withdrawn the troops, so as to make them a nullity, insisted that the veto remain on the statute books, vetoed the repealers, and noted in his diary: "No precedent shall be established with my consent to a measure which is tantamount to coercion of the Executive."

The condition of the public service alarmed him, particularly in the Conkling-ruled New York Customhouse, where some two hundred ward-heelers stayed on the payroll year after year without ever coming to the Customhouse! When the President undertook to correct this, Conkling declared open war. Finally Hayes removed the Collector — he was Conkling's first lieutenant, Chester A. Arthur. After his new nominee had been blocked by the Senate for many months, Hayes publicly exposed the rascality, which forced confirmation. This gave the first real impetus to Civil Service reform.

All of which indicates Hayes's bent of mind and stubbornness of purpose. Independents over the country began to applaud his honest courage. The Radicals spewed venom on him for his realistic decision that Reconstruction was a failure, and must be liquidated, but their day was well over the meridian, and Hayes would not bend the knee. Eckenrode, his latest biographer, terms him the first modern President.

Hayes's immediate successor, James A. Garfield, was another Ohio Republican general-politician who had the soldier vote in his pocket. In the 1880 National Convention, the Radical chiefs, Conkling, Cameron and "Black Jack" Logan, had insisted on a third term for Grant, but the delegates did not respond. Garfield, floor manager for Senator John Sherman of Ohio, attracted attention by his nominating speech, and was chosen on the thirty-sixth ballot by a stampede of the delegates.

On entering office, he continued his predecessor's fight on Conkling's private preserve of the New York Customhouse. The Senator denounced Garfield as a dictator, and then resigned dramatically from the Senate, that the New York Legislature might attest that State's support by re-electing him. This led Guiteau, a crazy lawyer, to shoot the President, and to proclaim his deed a "political crime," because he preferred Arthur in the White House!

That new President promptly disappointed his political friends by becoming an honest, courageous and independent Chief of Government. Six feet two in height, he looked the part of a great leader; though he revived the ceremonial and convivial tradition of the White House, he devoted himself to carrying out policies substantially identical with those of Hayes. He suffered the handicaps of Tyler and Johnson. His pre-presidential stature had not been great enough to enable him to be Chief of Party or the molder of public opinion.

The Radicals were incensed because Arthur insisted upon the merit system in governmental appointments. The corruptionists, who had expected the reopening of the gates to plunder, could not understand the attitude of the recent Conkling man. He maintained a tolerant policy toward the South, continued John Sherman's financial policies, and gave Civil Service reform quite as energetic backing as Hayes. By the time of the next presidential campaign, he wanted and deserved renomination, but the very qualities of his unexpected good service retired him to private life. Hayes and Arthur set the stage for Grover Cleveland.

CHAPTER IX

Trustee of All the People

"Sir, it is a solemn thing to be President of the United States!" These words, written by Grover Cleveland's heavy fist, reflect his conduct of the office. "I am President," he said, "of all the people — good, bad and indifferent," and he sought to maintain the public rights of all. Jackson alone equaled his positive courage; only Lincoln his independence of Congress; and none his unremitting attention to the details of executive government. He added cubits to the stature of the Presidency.

Cleveland fought neither for personal glory — though he relished praise from trusted friends — nor for his beloved Democratic Party, which he eschewed when he believed it wandering after heathen idols. This twenty-second Chief Executive practised the maxim that "Public office is a public trust."

Never had a President's rise been so rapid. In 1881, he became Mayor of Buffalo, two years later Governor of New York, and in 1884 was elected President! Chance rather than destiny presided over this sudden ascension. Like Wilson, he was Presbyterian by birth and Democrat by conviction; unlike him, Cleveland had no chance to become a scholar. On his way to the West, he tarried at Buffalo, read law on the side, sowed some wild oats, but advanced in his profession and in local Democratic politics. At the age of forty-four he was elected mayor, to clean up Buffalo's ring rule. Mayor Cleveland learned government the hard way of trial and error. The City Council submitted complicated ordinances for his approval, but he always turned over the rock to see what it concealed. He wrote detailed vetoes and the people backed him. His courageous course soon attracted statewide attention.

This came at the time New York Democrats were grooming for the 1882 campaign. The Republican Administration had done poorly, Tammany was in especial disrepute, and the Tilden reform wing of Empire State Democracy made this mayoral Lochinvar the Democratic candidate for Governor. He won the election by a good margin, and moved to Albany. As in Buffalo, Cleveland did not hesitate to tackle every duty as it came to hand. He toiled until midnight on mastering the papers that flowed over his desk; a friend once remarked that "he is the kind of man who would rather do something badly for himself than to have somebody else do it well" — which, in its way, was a compliment.

Tammany despised him, a compliment which he returned with works as well as words. Cleveland's challenge to this disreputable Democratic machine not only won State support, but brought him a national reputation as he showed both sides of the shield of courage: Both the negative courage to resist others' importunities, as Andrew Johnson, and the positive courage to step forward into the unknown.

Nationally, the Democratic Party saw a green light. In 1882 it captured the House of Representatives and made gains in the Senate. If it could maintain partisan enthusiasm and at the same time attract the independent voters or "Mugwumps," it could win the presidential election. Cleveland represented both Democracy and reform. The anti-machine elements in the party launched his candidacy for the 1884 nomination, Tammany gathered its own hosts, but Bragg of Wisconsin, a sturdy Union veteran, electrified the Democratic National Convention by saying of Cleveland: "We love him for the enemies he has made."

The nominee had to pass through perhaps the most abusive campaign since 1828. Tammany wielded the knife, his managers urged him to kneel, but Cleveland would not promise them even a fourth-class post office.

Democratic papers revived the Mulligan letters about James G.

Blaine, the Republican nominee, who had evaded frank explanation of the inference that he had taken railroad bonds for his official influence, and marked on one explanation: "Burn this letter." The Republicans got a Buffalo preacher to sermonize on one of Cleveland's follies at thirty-nine, which had issue in an illegitimate child, whom he supported. To his Buffalo friends' frantic appeal for instructions, the nominee telegraphed: "Whatever you do, tell the truth!" In the long run, this somewhat offset the effect of the scandal. In the closing days, Burchard, a preacher, speaking in a meeting with Blaine, called the opposition a compound of "Rum, Romanism and Rebellion," which further aided the Democratic cause, and Cleveland narrowly won the election.

He knew nothing about being President when he took office, and almost nothing about the great national issues. Urged to go after the tariff, he answered: "Yes, the tariff is a great issue, but I know so little about it." But he brought courage, energy and industry to the office, and grew with experience. The man's devotion to detail amazed his associates, as did the way he would give as much time to a pension veto as to the formation of a major policy.

He had no retinue of familiars who accompanied his progression from Buffalo to Albany to Washington. He named complete strangers in his Cabinet (in two instances men who had denounced him), but these soon came to hold him in affectionate respect. Nor did he cling to men who had outlived their usefulness; indeed, on his return to the White House in 1893, Cleveland let it be known that his Cabinet would be entirely new. He brought along young Robert Lincoln O'Brien, a Boston newspaperman who had helped in the 1892 campaign, and made him Executive Clerk. On the latter's resignation, two years later, the President replaced him with George B. Cortelyou, a Republican and stranger. When Cortelyou manfully disclosed the embarrassment his party tie might be to Cleveland, the latter waved it aside.

Furthermore, Cleveland had no inseparable confidential adviser. While Commodore E. C. Benedict, a rich New York broker, glowed with the social prestige of the President's friendship, and the latter used Benedict's brokerage services as well as his hospitable yacht, their relation resembled Coolidge's with Stearns rather than McKinley's with Hanna or Wilson's with House.

Cleveland believed in the maxim of General Robert E. Lee: "Duty is the noblest word in the English language." Entering the Presidency alarmingly unfamiliar with such great national problems as tariff, the gold standard and foreign relations, he worked at his job as no other President. Night after night he would spend in his study, and then be back at the desk early the next morning. He always made the first draft of correspondence or speeches with his own heavy hand. Cortelyou recalled but one letter he had composed for the President in two years' time. The latter referred to his longhand as "copperplate," said he had no style, but would "rummage the English language" to find better ways to say what he thought.

As President, Cleveland deemed himself the direct representative of the people; and every application for pardon gave him a sense of his deep duty to the individual concerned, for "I am the only man who can see that he is justly treated." Often he would send to the Department of Justice for the full trial record, read every line of it, sometimes write directly to the Judge, the United States Attorney, and the defendant's counsel for additional information and advice. Then he would dispose of the case with an explicit direction of three or four lines.

Cleveland vetoed more bills and resolutions from Congress than all the Presidents together before him. Most of his 250 messages of disapproval concerned private pension bills, which had become almost a racket. The President began reading these acts, sending for the case record, getting the facts and vetoing scores of them: John McBlair had died from epilepsy, not a war wound; Congress should not double Andrew Hill's present pension; another had been lamed as a boy, not in service; here was a man who had never served a day in the Army getting a gratuity . . . and so forth and so on. In June 1886, he exposed the machinations behind this mass of pension bills giving public money to individuals who had no claim. There had been no real Congressional sanction for these gratuities. In fact, most of these bills had never come before a majority of either House, but passed at "nominal sessions held for the express purpose of their consideration and attended by a small minority of the members." The rebuke had some effect.

Considerably more important was his handling of political patronage, the toughest first-term problem. Although Cleveland took more pride in his appointments to office than in his other executive functions, the "incessant pester about office" was irksome, he disliked visits from delegations, and after six months of officeseeker pressure issued a "Statement to the Public" that the public welfare imperatively demanded that the President's time be differently occupied. So loath was he to favor friends for office that many deemed cordial relations an impediment. The President denied this, but defended his refusal "to compensate friends by misappropriation from the trust funds of public duty." His Buffalo law partner and intimate friend Bissell hungered for the Consulate at London, with its $40,000 fees a year, but was turned down coldly.

It was the President's habit to seek all possible information about aspirants, to read files of recommendations, even for a fourth-class postmastership, and often to make a careful job analysis, to fit the man to the job. Needing a new chief for the Coast and Geodetic Survey, he studied that office's problems and then wrote Charles W. Eliot, of Harvard, that he wanted a man whom the scientific people of the country would deem suitable, "and yet I must have a good administrator"; could Eliot suggest such a man? Equally precise was his prescription for a chaplain to care for the West Point cadets; the man chosen should be able to adapt himself to the ways of the boys and gain their confidence and respect, should be a good preacher too — and, he hoped, a Presbyterian!

In his second term, Cleveland had the responsibility of filling the most important post of Chief Justice. When consulted, the Associate Justices urged that because of the badly clogged docket, the new Chief should possess efficiency as a business manager, as well as wisdom as a judge; he nominated Melville Fuller because the latter had both gifts. Some years later, when he needed a new Secretary of State, Cleveland asked Fuller to resign as Chief Justice to come in the Cabinet, and seemed surprised when the latter replied giving nineteen reasons why he should stay on the bench. He envied his successor Harrison's judgment in finding exceptional men for the Federal bench. "I cannot see how he does it," Cleveland remarked. "I thought I realized the importance of the Federal Courts, resisting mere party pressure, and giving my appointments the most jealous care. But I must confess that Harrison has beaten me."

Just such zeal gave him a gift for building up government service, rather than a personal political machine. In investigation of an official against whom charges or complaints had been brought, he spared no one. When a Treasury investigator who had been assigned such a task feared presidential displeasure because a Cabinet member had procured the questionable appointment, and took his dilemma direct to the President, the latter ordered him to pursue the matter "to its remotest consequences. If you find that summary dismissal is right and proper, I will stand by you to the end."

The new President gave earnest support to the Civil Service Commission and the merit principle for employee selection. A hundred thousand places were subject to his will when he entered the White House, but he had already given notice that efficiency, fitness and devotion to public duty would determine their continuance on the payroll. He intended no blanket proscription of Republicans, but any guilty of "offensive partisanship" were in danger of removal, just as were Democrats for "pernicious activity." All must learn that "the quiet and unobtrusive exercise of individual political rights is the reasonable measure of their party service."

Cleveland had no great belief in the strong-man theory of government. Personal experience had convinced him that usually the great are great because we kneel to them. He was persuaded by his own quick translation from mayor to President that the country was full of men who would make first-rate members of the Cabinet, or President. During a hunt for a new Attorney General, he remarked that, if precedent permitted, he could get a competent one in any county seat with which he was familiar. "So long as we can go out," he added, "and, by seeking, find almost anywhere men with the fundamental qualities for carrying out our ideas, there is little likelihood that any overmastering man will ever become either a necessity or be able to command sufficient power to make himself a danger to our institutions."

Like every strong President, Cleveland clashed with the Senate. The conflict was both personal, political and institutional. In the beginning, he had his way, but in the final struggle, over the Wilson tariff bill, he fell a victim to what he termed the perfidy and dishonor of some Democratic Senators. He wrote that he was feeling "the punishment of again occupying the office of President without the previous advice and consent of the United States Senate."

He did not accept the practice that the Federal offices in each State "belonged" to its Senators. A New Jersey nomination caused Senator McPherson to give notice that he would thereafter make no recommendations; Cleveland answered that he would get along without them. He deliberately submitted two Missouri nominations which outraged Vest and Cockrell, who thenceforward fought him. He had a real contempt for the Senate as an organ of popular government. "Of all things that can be imagined as absurd and inconsistent with the theory and proper operation of our Government," he remarked, "the Senate, as at present and for years past organized, reaches the extreme."

His first great battle was with the Senate over patronage. While the Democratic strength in the upper Chamber had been increasing, there were sufficient holdovers in 1885 to continue Republican Senate control. These moved at once to keep as many Republicans as possible in office.

At first the Senate did not dare directly to challenge the President's right to remove for cause, but whenever he suspended a Republican incumbent, and then nominated a Democratic successor, would ask the department head involved to submit all the reasons and papers concerning the official conduct of the suspended Republican. Cleveland instructed the concerned Cabinet member to reply that, by direction of the President, he declined furnishing the reasons and papers because the public interest would not be promoted, and because the reasons and papers related to a purely executive act.

The matter came to direct issue over the United States attorneyship for the Southern District of Alabama. This being a political office, Cleveland suspended the Republican who held it and nominated a Southern Democrat as successor, and when the Senate asked for the reasons and papers took direct charge of the fight to preserve "the unqualified executive discretion of the President."

He told the Senate in May 1886 that it had, in effect, assumed the right "to sit in judgment upon my exclusive discretion and executive functions, for which I am solely responsible to the people from whom I have so lately received the sacred trust of office. My oath to support and defend the Constitution, my duty to the people who have chosen me to execute the powers of their great office and my duty to the Chief Magistracy which I must preserve unimpaired and in all its dignity and vigor, compel me to refuse compliance."

The public offices of the United States "were created for the benefit of the people and to answer the general purposes of government under the Constitution. . . . They are unencumbered by any lien in favor of either branch of Congress growing out of their construction, and unembarrassed by any obligation to the Senate as the price of their creation." He challenged the right of the Senate "in any way save through the judicial process of trial on impeachment, to review or reverse" the suspension, because the power to remove or suspend is vested in the President alone.

The Senate Republicans waved the bloody shirt, but could do no more than rant. Finally, on December 17, 1886, the Senate joined in the repeal of the Tenure of Office Act, and Cleveland exulted that the President had once more become "the independent agent of the people."

Most of the liberal papers supported Cleveland in this fight against the Senate, and were with him on most of the issues of his first term — but not by virtue of his management of relations with the press. This was one of the President's major difficulties in handling public opinion, for he couldn't learn how to get along with the press.

He was urged to invite friendly editors and publishers to his dinner table, but did not feel that he should make himself "familiar with them" merely because they were personally agreeable, and was little more cordial to reporters and correspondents. Making a merit of this liability of temperament, he declared himself "thankful that the efforts to create an unconscious but effective censorship of the press never had encouragement from me at any point in my public career."

Cleveland's inability to manage, sometimes even to get along with, his legislative partners proved a serious impediment. He had no legislative experience whatever, on occasion lamented this omission from his political training, but it is doubtful if it would have altered his inner contours. Cleveland would neither court nor flatter, had neither ability nor desire to coax or wheedle Senators or Representatives, and it was out of character for him to use his presidential patronage to influence for congressional votes, just as he refused to employ the social influence of the White House to soften them.

Cleveland's first four years further trained him in the art of government and gave him a broader perspective. He became expert in the housekeeping of the executive departments, and took more and more hand in influencing public issues as contrasted with institutional and managerial concerns. Chief among these was the tariff. He took the unusual step of confining his annual message in December 1887 to the tariff, because of "the paramount importance of the subject."

Today Cleveland is regarded as a conservative, almost a tool of "the wise, the rich and the good," but this is not a just estimate. He believed the government's aim was "the improvement of the people in every station." He saw the growing evils of Big Business and predatory finance. His 1888 message called attention to "the existence of trusts, combinations and monopolies, while the citizen is struggling far in the rear or is trampled to death beneath an iron heel. Corporations, which should be the carefully restrained creatures of the law and the servants of the people, are fast becoming the people's masters." Manufacturers were now making fortunes, not on merit, but because of "undue exactions from the masses." Classes were rapidly forming, one the very rich and powerful, another the toiling poor.

Cleveland's remedies for such harms to the people were drawn from the dismal science of economics and looked to long-run readjustment, not immediate relief. After he became President, he was indoctrinated with the "law" of supply and demand, "the iron law of wages," and the mathematics of that abstraction, the economic man, and came to regard them with about as much reverence as the Constitution. His devotion to these argumentative theories, which even in his day were dishonored through constant breach, illustrates the chief blind spot in this otherwise immensely practical and realistic man. This deficiency in ability to understand the emotional pressures upon the people led to his major failures both in party leadership and in handling public opinion.

His initial successes had arisen from his courageous leadership of reform, both against the Republican Radicals who waved the bloody shirt, and the Democratic Tammany machines. These same qualities helped his return to the White House. But it was no answer to the 1893 panic for Cleveland to insist, as Van Buren had done in 1837, and Hoover was to hint in the trough of the Great Depression, that the power and duty of the National Government must not be "extended to the relief of individual suffering."

In times of crisis, when the people are hurt, they strike out blindly; in the Nineties, many demanded that the hard money formula be adjusted to the people's distresses. Neither then nor later did Cleveland perceive the great new duty upon the National Government affirmatively to undertake these economic and social policies which the public from time to time concludes essential to the general good.

The people were willing to follow him a considerable way against their own preconceptions, prejudices and inherited folk ways of politics and policy. But when he counseled a course sharply against their sense of overwhelming need, the independents as well as the party liberals went the other way. Cleveland's blindness — or stubbornness — enabled the understanding Bryan to wrest the control of the party from his hands. He knew a majority of his party had left him, but believed that "a cause worth fighting for is worth fighting for to the end."

Cleveland's faithful adherence to his principles regardless of party consequences, and city machine disaffection, contributed to Benjamin Harrison's Electoral College victory in the 1888 presidential election. Cleveland, who had received a small plurality in the popular vote, left office without any bitterness, and told friends that his public life had ended. Nevertheless, he began studying the public records of predecessors he admired: the words and deeds of Washington, Jefferson, Lincoln and especially Old Hickory expanded his concept of the powers of the President.

In his First Inaugural, Cleveland had expressed a "cautious appreciation of the functions" of the Executive, but in his last term he deleted the adjective. His final statement of the nature of the Presidency, made some years after he left, termed it "pre-eminently the people's office," because every citizen, "in the day or in the night, at home or abroad, is constantly within the protection and restraint of the Executive power." The take-care clause was "equivalent to a grant of all the power necessary to the performance of his duty in the faithful execution of the laws," while the oath "binds the conscience" of every President.

This developing view of the solemnity of the trust was reflected in Cleveland's refusal to regard the place as something to be won by active self-assertion. His few speeches and published letters the first three years out of office were directed to arousing the people on issues. But the Democratic rank and file responded to his presentations, and by late 1891 his renomination was being demanded in many quarters.

The popular drift to him moved to high gear when Tammany held a "snap convention" to instruct the New York delegation to the national convention for Governor David B. Hill. Again Cleveland was loved and nominated for the enemies he had made. During the ensuing canvass, his campaign manager insisted that the nominee do something to appease Tammany opposition. Cleveland did attend a conference with Boss Croker and his two principal lieutenants, and bluntly announced that if the Organization did not support the national ticket, he would resign as candidate and tell the reason why. The public's knowledge of this trait within the man was one reason why he won over Harrison by the handsome plurality of 400,000 votes.

Cleveland's delayed second term presented problems of such magnitude that he was forced to shift much of the time customarily given administrative detail to major policy matters. There were four outstanding developments: The panic and the free silver fight; the struggles for real tariff revision downward; the bold action in the Chicago railroad strike; and the victory over Britain in the Venezuela boundary dispute.

The lack of staff assistance in the White House executive office, to help him master such problems, gave him great concern. In those days, the executive establishment contained neither "brains trust" to feed ideas to a President and furnish him a friendly opposition, nor expert group of literary verbalizers to draft his ideas into form for inspection, nor assistants "with a passion for anonymity" to do important chores. "As the executive office is now organized," Cleveland complained, "it can deal, with a fair amount of efficiency, with the routine affairs of Government; but if the President has any great policy in mind or on hand, he has no one to help him work it out."

He believed that Professor William L. Wilson, a historian and political scientist who had been in both Cabinet and House, was the sort of man he needed to do research and planning for the Chief

Executive, and considered naming Wilson Assistant to the President, at a salary of $10,000 a year. When he could find no appropriation available or procurable, Cleveland reluctantly abandoned the idea, saying that "I have even half a notion to offer him the place anyhow and pay him out of my own pocket."

The panic broke soon after he re-entered office, the President felt that "sound money" must take precedence even over tariff reform, and summoned Congress in special session in 1893 to wrestle with it. Ten years later he wrote that he deemed decision his "most self-sacrificing and patriotic service."

The currency crisis was an unhappy incident in a long economic down-swing. As commodities declined in gold dollar value, the country had desperate need either to go off gold, as in 1933, devalue the dollar or in some other way enhance the domestic purchasing power of the producer's dollar. But this was over thirty years before the days of Home Owners' loans or support from R.F.C. or Federal Reserve. The advocates of currency devaluation had no practical mechanism to offer except its dilution through the "free coinage of silver." In 1890, twenty-one Democratic State Conventions indorsed this doctrine which would legislatively declare sixteen ounces of silver worth one ounce of gold.

Cleveland saw the immediate flaw in the distorted ratio, and in February 1891 published his famous "Silver Letter," warning of the "dangerous and reckless experiment." He knew no remedy for the distresses of the agricultural South and West except bankruptcy, foreclosure, and slow readjustment into the next generation. But tariff reduction and his other projects for recovery addressed themselves to the gradual rebuilding of the house of the nation. Those who were its immediate tenants wanted President, Congress or Free Silver to put out the fire on the roof. He had the defects of his qualities. He could not see that it is just as much the job of the government to sustain the people as of the latter to support the government.

* * *

Cleveland's drastic and effective action in the Pullman railroad strike of 1894 represented the farthest stretch of his powers. The union railroad workers, after vainly seeking redress of grievances from their employers, called a nation-wide strike, chiefly effective in the region of Chicago, the rail capital of the country. Train movement ceased, distress spread over the blockaded cities, and riots were reported in Chicago. The President received appeal after appeal from rail executives, shippers and business leaders to intervene.

His action under these pressures is deemed very unfortunate by some close students of Cleveland's career. As Allan Nevins points out, the great question was what constituted lawless or violent obstruction, and what constituted restraint of trade. Attorney General Richard Olney, a Boston lawyer, took an extreme view and persuaded the President to agree with him.

When the United States Attorney at Chicago telegraphed that the situation was so grave that troops must be sent to allow the mails to be moved, Olney informed his chief that the statutes on protection of the mail, and the new Interstate Commerce Act of 1887, gave the President ample power to deal with violent obstruction of the mails, or with organized action in restraint of interstate commerce. Thereupon Cleveland authorized application for an injunction, and Olney knew how to get the Chicago courts to issue it. On July 4, 1894, troops were ordered to the seat of the industrial war, and before long, trains began to move again. The injunction was so sweeping that the socialist leader Eugene Debs, who spoke in denunciation of the President's "usurpation," was arrested for contempt of court, and sent to prison.

Cleveland had not consulted John P. Altgeld, Democratic Governor of Illinois, before sending the troops. That able public servant and leader of social reforms telegraphed demanding the soldiers' immediate withdrawal. He insisted that Illinois was ready to take care of herself; to furnish the Federal Government any military assistance it might need elsewhere; and that no one in Cook County, official or private citizen, had intimated that State troops were desired or necessary. "To absolutely ignore a local government," the

Governor charged, "not only insults the people . . . but is in violation of a basic principle of our institutions."

The President answered that the troops had been sent "in strict accordance with the Constitution and laws of the United States, upon the demand of the Post Office Department that obstruction of the mails should be removed, and upon representations of the judicial officers of the United States that the process of the Federal Court could not be executed through the ordinary means, and upon competent proof that conspiracies existed against commerce between the States." There was no intention on the part of the Federal Government of "interfering with the plain duty of the local authorities to preserve the peace of the city."

Altgeld challenged several of these assumptions, particularly the one that the Executive had the legal right to order Federal troops into any community in the country where a disturbance occurred, irrespective of the community's readiness and ability to enforce the law itself. He pointed out that the troops sent to Chicago were not under its civil authorities, which violated the fundamental American principle that, except in times of war, the military should be subordinate to the civil authority. He persisted that Federal interference with industrial disturbances was "a new departure," from which it needed but a very little stretch of authority to "absorb to itself all the details of local government."

"While I am still persuaded," Cleveland replied, "that I have neither transcended my authority nor duty in the emergency that confronts us, it seems to me that in this hour of danger and public distress, discussion may well give way to active efforts on the part of all in authority to restore obedience to law and to protect life and property."

This angry exchange by telegraph — though followed by the quick collapse of the strike — did bring before the public some of the constitutional issues soon before the Supreme Court: By what authority of Constitution or statute had the President sent troops without request of the Governor of Illinois? The actual case before the Court was the person of Eugene Debs, still held in prison for contempt of court. If he had been committed for violating an invalid injunction, he would regain his freedom.

Government counsel offered the Court a number of precedents sustaining the President's actions. Attorney General Cushing had given several opinions to aid President Pierce in enforcing the Fugitive Slave Act. One derived the President's right to make investigations from his oath to "take care that the laws were faithfully executed"; another put it within his executive discretion to have official counsel defend marshals and other ministerial officers enforcing Federal law; still another voiced the *posse comitatus* theory later employed by Lincoln.

In the Act of April 20, 1871, aiming at more rigorous Reconstruction, Congress had decreed that, whenever unlawful combinations within a State interfered with the execution of State or Federal laws, so as to deny any class its constitutional rights, the President had the duty "to take such measures, by the employment of the militia or the land and naval forces of the United States . . . as he may deem necessary" to suppress the insurrection or domestic violence. Hayes's action in the railroad strike of 1877 had further paved the way for Cleveland. When governors made informal appeals, and without the customary assurances that their legislatures could not be assembled in time, Hayes supplied Federal arms to State forces, and moved United States troops to places where "the influence of their presence" would overawe the rioters.

The famous Neagle case, decided in 1890, added more support. Supreme Court Justice Stephen Field's life had been threatened by one Terry; by order of the Attorney General, Marshal Neagle was guarding the Justice on his circuit duties; when Terry attacked, the Marshal shot and killed him. California officers took Neagle in custody for murder, but the Federal authorities sought a writ of habeas corpus. The Court held that, though Neagle had not acted under any precise Federal law, the President's duty embraced not only the enforcement of the acts of Congress and treaties of the United States, but extended to "the rights, duties and obligations growing out of the Constitution itself, our international relations, and all the protection implied by the nature of the government under the Constitution." Moreover, "there is a peace of the United States." Wherefore a Federal marshal had as much right to protect this Federal peace as a State sheriff had to protect that of his State.

In the case styled *in re Debs,* the Court must decide whether the injunction the United States Circuit Court had issued against the strikers had been within that Court's jurisdiction to grant. In its opinion, handed down the year after the riots, the Court admitted the lack of statutory authority for the process, but held that, despite that lack, the government had the right to protect its property, the mails.

From the particular it proceeded to the larger issue. "Every government," declared the Court, "entrusted by the very terms of its being with powers and duties to be exercised and discharged for the general welfare, has a right to apply to its own courts for any proper assistance in the exercise of the one and the discharge of the other."

The Court agreed that it was not the government's province to mix in merely individual private controversies. Still, "whenever wrongs complained of are such as affect the public at large, and are in respect of matters which by the Constitution are entrusted to the care of the Nation and concerning which the Nation owes the duty to all the citizens of securing to them their common rights, then the mere fact that the Government has no pecuniary interest in the controversy is not sufficient to exclude it from the Courts, or prevent it from taking measures therein to fully discharge those constitutional duties." Cleveland's course had the Court's attest.

Next to his handling of the Chicago railroad riots, Cleveland was best pleased with his course in the Venezuela boundary controversy with Great Britain. More than fifty years before, Britain and the Caribbean republic had disagreed over the boundary in the jungle between British Guiana and Venezuela. In the early Nineties, British threats to occupy the region aroused President Cleveland to insist that arbitration, not force, must settle the dispute. His diplomacy was ill-tempered and somewhat bungling, but he felt that "there was nothing left for us to do consistently with national honor but to take the place of Venezuela in the controversy, to vindicate the Monroe Doctrine."

In June 1895 Secretary of State Gresham died and Cleveland moved Olney to that post. The latter soon wrote Lord Salisbury, the British Minister of Foreign Affairs, a letter which in the President's view had good taste, but was vigorous and "caught the national spirit perfectly." After reviewing the birth and historical development of the Monroe Doctrine, Olney declared that, as the United States was entitled to resent and resist any sequestration of Venezuela soil by Great Britain, it was necessarily entitled to know whether such sequestration had occurred or was then going on. Inasmuch as arbitration provided the best way to make that determination, would Britain "consent or decline to submit the Venezuelan boundary question in its entirety to impartial arbitration"?

To Ambassador Bayard's disturbed inquiries from London, Cleveland responded that the Monroe Doctrine was important, it did relate to the Venezuelan question, and he couldn't see "how a doctrine would have any life, or could do any good or harm, unless it was applicable to a condition of facts that might arise, and unless when applied all consequence must be appreciated and awaited." It should be maintained and defended for its value "to our government and welfare."

When the British Government replied that no Monroe Doctrine matter was involved, and refused to arbitrate, Cleveland took the cause to the American people, through a famous message to Congress. A confidential adviser remarked that "towards the end it is just a little bit tart." The President replied: "That is just what I intended." Just the same he called it a "peace message."

He informed Congress that the enforcement of the Doctrine "is important to our peace and safety as a nation, and is essential to the integrity of our free institutions and the tranquil maintenance of our distinctive form of government." The United States must determine the true boundary line, and then "resist by every means in its power, as a wilful aggression upon its rights and interests, the appropriation by Great Britain of any lands or the exercise of governmental jurisdiction" over any territory which by right belonged to Venezuela.

"There is," he emphasized, "no calamity which a great nation can invite which equals that which follows a supine submission to wrong and injustice, and the consequent loss of national self-respect and honor beneath which are shielded and defended a people's safety and greatness."

Congress responded promptly. On December 21, 1895, it established an arbitration commission, and the next month that body got on the job. The British immediately reopened negotiations, in November 1896, the United States and Great Britain agreed upon an arbitration arrangement, the treaty was soon ratified, and all danger of war between the great Anglo-Saxon nations was at an end. In Cleveland's view, his course had "established the Monroe Doctrine on lasting foundations before the powers of the world."

Cleveland's principal influence upon our philosophy of government was his establishment of "the right of the general government to overcome all obstructions to the exercise of its functions in every part of our national domain." His major contribution to the Presidency arose from his successful assertion of his independence from Congress. He established the exclusive discretion of the Chief Executive, to the benefit of many successors. But if Cleveland had left no other presidential record than his appointment methods and veto messages, his terms would still be memorable for these examples of careful executive government.

The record of Cleveland's conduct of office should be required reading for every man who becomes President of the United States. His use of presidential power has been the starting point for much of the authority exerted by Presidents since.

CHAPTER X

Direct Action in the White House

"Whatever is received," runs a maxim of Aristotle and Aquinas, "is conditioned by the recipient." Few men have conditioned the Presidency more than Theodore Roosevelt, and at the end of his seven-and-a-half years in the White House, the American people had a new concept of the office.

Walter Hines Page characterized T. R. as "a stimulating breeze which was blowing over the National Government." Senator Edward Ward Carmack, of Tennessee, remarked that "his natural gait is running away, like Old Joe's mare." Only forty-three when he took the oath, Theodore Roosevelt's quivering energy reached every nook and cranny of the executive establishment. Nothing was too large — or too small — to engage his enthusiasm: whether organizing a "Tennis Cabinet" for a more strenuous life, keeping meat in the refrigerator until it was "high" enough for his palate, starting a crusade for simplified spelling, nominating newspapermen to the "Ananias Club," or incubating a revolution at Panama.

Many are the superficial resemblances in the careers of this Roosevelt from Oyster Bay and his third cousin from Dutchess County. Both had critical struggles against disease, T. R. in his college years, F. D. R. in life's mid-channel. Both were consummate politicians who went direct to the people for support. With similar liking for glamour and gadgets, both habitually played by ear and occasionally governed by impulse — Mark Sullivan points out that both were showmen. There is considerable similarity of temperament between Theodore Roosevelt and Eleanor, his favorite niece, but the resemblance between the two men is much less. Roosevelt I was a direct-actionist, who saw himself in the role of Andrew Jackson as "the steward of the people." Roosevelt II occasionally, and unexpectedly, takes direct action; but he has certain traits of subtlety, of accomplishing things by indirection and in doing things the "smart" way, unlike T. R.

Save for the Spanish–American War, Theodore Roosevelt would not have become President at the time he did, perhaps never. But that conflict gave the young Rough Rider the chance to ride to glory up San Juan Hill and then to gallop into the New York governorship. McKinley had not wanted that war; Cleveland tells of the President-elect's visit to him the night before inauguration. He went over the details of Cleveland's efforts to avert war over Cuba, approved them, and said that, if he could prevent hostilities, he would be "the happiest man in the world." And McKinley had the chance to do so, because two weeks before Congress declared war, the Spanish Government cabled Washington a formal offer of immediate independence for Cuba. But the President concluded that he would be swept aside if he balked the war party, and let national emotions take their course.

After San Juan Hill, Roosevelt became Governor of New York by the choice of Tom Platt, the Republican boss who for years ran the Empire State through an "invisible government" which treated governors and legislatures as puppets. Because of some bad scandals, he needed a war hero as candidate, and Teddy's nomination and election ensued. The latter entered office determined to be his own boss. The result was that generally he would work with Platt and his machine, but often, when he didn't have his own way, would make "a fair fight in the open." Usually he tried to force the legislature to pass his measures, on the contention that, while in theory the Executive had nothing to do with legislation, in practice he was or should be "peculiarly representative of the people as a whole."

More than half of his work as Governor was forcing legislation. His success in his spectacular first term made him want a second. Platt had a bear by the tail, and feared that two more years of T. R. as Governor would complete the ruin of his well-oiled political machine. So the State Boss moved heaven and earth to get the Governor nominated for McKinley's second-term running mate. Roosevelt didn't like it, wrote Henry Cabot Lodge that he "would a great deal rather be anything — say a professor of history — than Vice President," which was merely a "show office." Mark Hanna, who thought Roosevelt erratic and "unsafe," disliked the idea quite as much. "Don't any of you realize," he asked, "that there's only one life between that madman and the Presidency?" Platt had to get down on his knees to McKinley's mentor before the latter would yield. T. R. went to the convention and, saying he'd ne'er consent, consented.

When Inauguration Day neared, Platt announced jubilantly that he was going down to Washington to see Roosevelt take the veil. The latter regarded his duty of presiding over the Senate as a cruel and inhuman punishment, and sought other outlets for his restless energy. He thought of enrolling in the Georgetown Law School, consulted Justice White as to propriety and usefulness, and was advised against it. On September 6, 1901, however, the anarchist Czolgosz shot President McKinley, who died a few days later, and Roosevelt took the oath. "Now, look," Hanna ejaculated, "that damned cowboy is President of the United States."

The battle between Roosevelt and Hanna was among the most important of the elements of the former's first term. Hanna, be it said, was very much of a man; Davenport's cartoons of him as a hog on two feet, with dollar marks all over his clothing, do him injustice. He made his money in the cutthroat competition of the iron and steel industry, but through will, judgment and drive rather than corruption. When he fell in love with the lovable McKinley, Hanna put his organizing genius into politics. In eighteen months he put $100,000 of his own money into the quest of the Republican presidential nomination for his friend. Then he ran the election campaign, in which he shook down Big Business and the banks for a more than four-million-dollar "expense" fund, and in addition fashioned an emotional counteroffensive to the Bryan Cross of Gold crusade which helped the Republican Saladin defeat the Democratic Cœur de Lion.

In 1899, Hanna came to the Senate. Full-vigored, he took national leadership, and was about as close to a national "boss" as we ever had, but exercised his power benignly. Hanna's fine speech against declaring war on Spain provoked Teddy into telling him: "We will have this war . . . in spite of the timidity of commercial interests." Roosevelt was right in the prediction — because, as he said, McKinley had "no more backbone than a chocolate éclair." Hanna wielded his power not only by virtue of President McKinley's favor, but even more in his own right. Soon after his translation to Capitol Hill, his public views began to grow, particularly in regard to the status of labor. Shortly before his death, early in 1904, he announced his championship of collective bargaining, peaceful picketing, and a virtual labor voice in industrial management.

Many regarded Hanna as the man with whom to replace Roosevelt, as the 1904 G. O. P. nominee. No wonder the new-made President had said to him, at the McKinley funeral: "I hope you will be to me all you have been to him." Apparently Teddy liked his formidable rival.

The relationship between the development of crisis situations and the growth of the President then in office is one of the most interesting aspects of the ebb and flow of presidential power. Almost without exception, those generally regarded as great Presidents had to handle some major national emergency, either an economic disaster, a social upset, a civil insurrection or a foreign war. Although Theodore Roosevelt occupied the White House in relatively quiet years, he developed a positive genius for creating issues which might be magnified into Armageddons where he could battle for the Lord.

Such struggles gave him outlets for his enormous fund of physical and nervous energy — an almost indispensable quality for a great President — and helped him win more success than some others who had better intellectual equipment.

He was politician to the finger tips. Grover Cleveland, who had known him since his days as assemblyman in Albany, considered him "the most perfectly equipped and the most effective politician thus far seen in the Presidency. Jackson, Jefferson and Van Buren were not for a moment comparable with him in this respect."

Roosevelt claimed he was "just an ordinary man without any special ability in any direction," and there is useful revelation in his self-analysis, as recorded by his intimate and thoroughly dependable friend, O. K. Davis. "In most things," he insisted, "I am just about the average; in some of them a little under, rather than over." He termed himself only an ordinary walker, neither "remarkably good" rider nor good shot. While he wrote voluminously — he turned out about 150,000 letters while in the White House — he did not regard himself as a brilliant writer: "I always have to work and slave over everything I write." The things he had done, in one office or another, were all "just such things as any ordinary man could have done."

His explanation of the motivation of his action was about as simple: "Whatever I think it is right for me to do, I do. . . . And when I make up my mind to do a thing, I act." Having made a decision, generally he would not reconsider it. He didn't contend that his decisions were always right, but "in the long run less damage is done through the mistakes resulting from sticking to decisions once made than would occur from getting into the habit of constantly worrying whether you had decided rightly or wrongly, and changing your mind all the time. No man can get ahead on two or more courses. You have to go one way at a time to get anywhere."

Theodore Roosevelt admitted that many friends termed him "impulsive and jumpy," but claimed that, "as a matter of fact, I have really given full consideration to whatever it is that is to be done. But because I act when I have made my decision, and usually as vigorously as I can, it may sometimes seem to others that there has not been as much deliberation as some of them would have taken. The accomplishments of my record, whatever they may be, are all such as might have been accomplished by any average man who had made up his mind to decide promptly and to act on his decisions."

He rationalized his energetic conduct of the office by fashioning his own personal theory of the place of the President in American government and life. Political scientists have labeled it "the stewardship theory," and it is elaborately set out in his *Autobiography,* published in 1913, a volume as interesting in its justifications for actions as in its principles of executive conduct.

T. R. termed himself "the steward of the people," in the sense in which the word was used by the Scottish Presbyterians. He felt that the executive power "was limited only by the specific restrictions and prohibitions appearing in the Constitution, or imposed by Congress under its constitutional powers," and rejected the contention "that what was imperatively necessary for the Nation could not be done by the President unless he could find some specific authorization to do it." He insisted that it was not only his right but his duty "to do anything that the needs of the Nation demanded — unless such action was forbidden by the Constitution or the laws."

Every executive officer in high position, in his belief, must actively and affirmatively do all he could for the people. Cleveland's insistence on his duty to transmit presidential powers undamaged to his successors provoked T. R.'s remark that the President must not "content himself with the negative merit of keeping his talents undamaged in a napkin."

"I did not usurp power," he stated, "but I did greatly broaden the use of executive power. I did and caused to be done many things not previously done by the President and heads of the departments. In other words, I acted for the public welfare, . . . for the common well-being of all our people, whenever and in whatever manner was necessary, unless prevented by direct constitutional or legislative prohibition. I did not care a rap for the mere form and show of power; I cared immensely for the use that could be made of the substance."

The most far-reaching extension of presidential power Theodore Roosevelt ever undertook to employ was his plan to occupy and operate Pennsylvania's anthracite coal mines, under his authority as Commander in Chief. In the issue, he found other means than force to end the 1902 hard-coal strike, but he had made detailed plans to use his power as Commander in Chief to wrest the mines from the stubborn operators, so that coal production would begin again. In view of his direct action in such matters as Panama, there seems little reason to doubt that he would have carried out his occupational plans.

This strike, covering the whole anthracite field, began early in the spring of 1902, and resulted in virtual paralysis of coal production. The ensuing coal famine became increasingly disastrous to the populous industrial States from Ohio east. As it went into the fall, the specter of great public disorder disturbed ordinarily conservative men; the Governor of Massachusetts, the Mayor of New York and other officials warned the President that if the famine continued, the consequences would be frightful. T. R. believed the situation before Pennsylvania, New York and New England, by October, "was quite as serious as if they had been threatened by the invasion of a hostile army of overwhelming force."

The President must act to prevent public calamity, but what could he do? Each side wanted him to proceed against the other, for impeding interstate commerce, but coal was not being mined at all, and invoking the commerce clause would have little effect. Neither was the strike, in a constitutional sense, a Federal question. The mines were all in Pennsylvania, that State's troops kept a modicum of order, and her public authorities had not asked for United States troops.

Roosevelt was not the man to admit for a moment that, as President, he was without power to take positive steps for the general welfare. He proposed arbitration, the miners, led by John Mitchell, a real labor statesman, promptly agreed, but the operators insisted that they would not have their property rights interfered with in the slightest. Finally, on October 3, 1902, the President got representatives of both sides to meet with him. Mitchell kept his temper, but the operators, in Roosevelt's view, "came down in a most insolent frame of mind, refused to talk of arbitration or other accommodation of any kind, and used language that was insulting to the miners and offensive to me." After the meeting they added insult to injury by telling the papers that they had "turned down" both the miners and the President.

These coal barons were singularly ignorant both of the general public temper, and of the character of Theodore Roosevelt. The former was soon evidenced by a flood of letters to the White House backing his arbitration demand. Ex-President Cleveland wrote an unsolicited letter expressing his indignation at the operators' conduct, and hoped the President could discover the path to direct action.

Roosevelt needed no urging. As Mark Sullivan wrote in *Our Times:* "Any implication that the Government of the United States was helpless before any set of circumstances was always a challenge to Roosevelt, and stirred his deepest determination. He could not endure to be dared." Before the operators' refusal, he had determined that "somehow or other" the coal famine would be broken, by Federal operation if no other way. Cleveland's letter now catalyzed his purpose into a plan of action. His Democratic predecessor agreed to take chief place on an arbitration commission to decide the rights of the case, whether or not the operators asked for it or agreed to abide by its decision.

Roosevelt's next step was to pick a general, to lead United States troops into Pennsylvania, "to dispossess the operators and run the mines as a receiver." He summoned sturdy John M. Schofield, hero of the Battle of Franklin, whom he told that the crisis was only less serious than the Civil War; if the General went into Pennsylvania, "he must act in a purely military capacity under me as Commander in Chief, paying no heed to any authority, judicial or otherwise, except mine." Schofield replied quietly that if the President gave the order, he would take possession of the mines, and would guarantee to open them and run them without permitting either owners or strikers or anybody else to interfere.

Next, Roosevelt told Senator Matt Quay, absolute boss of the Pennsylvania Republican machine, that he would make another effort to get operators and miners together, but intended to get coal mined in any event. Would Quay "arrange" that whenever he gave the word, the Governor of Pennsylvania would ask him to intervene? This the Senator promptly guaranteed.

About this time the operators agreed to the appointment of a Commission, although they vetoed Cleveland. The President must constitute it of one engineer officer, one man with mining experience, one "man of prominence . . . eminent as a sociologist," one Federal judge of the Eastern District of Pennsylvania, and one mining engineer. Labor wanted a member, but the operators would not have it. Finally it dawned on T. R. that the operators would not mind a labor man being on the Commission if he was not appointed *as a representative of labor*. So he accepted the condition, and named a railroad union man as the "man of prominence . . . eminent as a sociologist." The miners went back to work immediately, and the Commission eventually established the basis for contract relations covering the field. Roosevelt did not send troops, although he said later: "I was all ready to act, and would have done so without the slightest hesitation or a moment's delay if the negotiations had fallen through."

Another instance of a novel employment of his commander-in-chief power came in 1908, when he sent the United States fleet on its famous trip around the world. Eastern seaboard Senators had balked the passage of the appropriation needed for the entire circumnavigation. The statute declares: "All sums appropriated for the various branches of expenditure in the public service shall be applied solely to the objects for which they are respectively made, and for no others." There was enough money in the specific item to take the fleet across the Pacific to Japan. Roosevelt sent it off, virtually thumbing his nose at Congress, which of course made a supplementary appropriation to let the fleet steam home.

Roosevelt's conduct as Chief of Foreign Relations was impulsive, dangerous, but successful. Four episodes are illustrative: his seizure of the customhouses of the Dominican Republic; his brusque threat of war with Germany over Venezuela; his attitude in the Russo-Japanese War; and the "revolution" which established the puppet republic of Panama.

The Dominican action was preventive, not imperialistic. In 1903, the little Caribbean republic, in the throes of continual revolutions, had fallen so far behind in its foreign debt service that European powers' seizure of its customhouses was feared. So the President ordered the United States Naval Commander in those waters to take charge of the customhouses and prevent revolutionary forces from interfering. A little later, he negotiated a treaty with the government of the moment, under which the United States would collect the Dominican customs, turn forty-five per cent of the money over to the local government, and put the rest in a sinking fund in New York for the benefit of outside creditors. He put this into effect as an executive agreement while the Senate paltered the ratification debate. In practice, the scheme worked out all right, the creditors were paid off, the Dominican Government got more actual cash than it had ever had before.

Roosevelt paraded the fact that all this was done without the loss of a life, with the consent of all parties in interest and without cost to the United States. Sharply attacked in the Senate for having violated the Constitution, he answered that while it did not explicitly give him power to make these agreements, it "did not forbid me doing what I did. I put the agreement into effect, and I continued its execution for two years before the Senate acted; and I would have continued it until the end of my term if necessary, without any action by Congress."

The threat to Germany was late in 1901, shortly after Roosevelt entered the White House. Again the exciting occasion was indifferent foreign debt service by a Latin-American Republic. Venezuela had flouted her obligations to German bondholders and, in collaboration with Britain and Italy, Kaiser Wilhelm II, a direct-actionist to whom T. R. was often likened, dispatched a strong fleet to the Venezuelan coast to seize the principal ports.

When news of this reached Roosevelt, he sent for Holleben, the German Ambassador, told him bluntly that if the Germans took any customhouses, the United States fleet would take them back. Hearing nothing from Berlin, he informed the Ambassador that he had directed Admiral Dewey to take our main battle fleet to the Venezuelan coast. There was no punitive expedition, and this episode made Wilhelm Hohenzollern a warm Roosevelt admirer. The President returned it in part, saying: "I do admire him, very much as I do a grizzly bear. For several years he has been profuse in his expressions of admiration and friendship for me. It goes back to the time when I warned him I would fight. I never make a bluff either in public or in private life."

His true relations with the Russo-Japanese War were secret until Dr. Tyler Dennett discovered the records of them in Roosevelt's unpublished papers some years after his death. Teddy had an emotional enthusiasm for the poor little Jap attacked by the Russian bear, which led him to strange secret commitments. In 1903, when Admiral Togo attacked Port Arthur without warning, the President, to use his own words, "notified Germany and Japan in the most polite and discreet fashion that in the event of a combination against Japan to try to do to her what Russia, Germany and France did to her in 1894 [after the Sino-Japanese War], I should promptly side with Japan . . . to whatever length was necessary on her behalf."

Toward the end of the war, Roosevelt made a secret executive agreement with the Japanese, which is a unique document. He had sent William Howard Taft, his Secretary of War, to inspect the Philippines, and to negotiate with Japan. On July 29, 1905, there was an "exchange of opinion" between Taft and Count Katsura, the Japanese premier, put in the form of an "Agreed Memorandum" and duly approved later by the respective Chiefs of State. The

American representative remarked to the Japanese: "I suppose that you do not desire to take the Philippine Islands away from us." The answer was that Japan had no such desire or intention.

The Japanese representative then said in substance: "You realize how difficult it is to preserve the peace of the Far East. There is danger that following the conclusion of the Russo-Japanese War, Korea will lapse again into a condition of anarchy. We are aware of the provision of the American Constitution which makes alliances so difficult, but it seems to us as though it would be possible for the United States to enter into a secret agreement with Japan and England for the preservation of the peace of the Far East."

Taft replied that, under our Constitution, such a secret agreement would be impossible, but he could assure the Japanese Government that the American people would be glad to act with the Japanese and British people for the preservation of peace in the Far East. In response to an inquiry as to Korea, Taft said that, "in his judgment, Japan would be fully justified in establishing a military protectorate over Korea and in taking charge of her foreign relations."

The President approved this document only twelve days before formal publication by Britain and Japan of the terms of their second alliance; only two weeks before the opening, at Portsmouth, New Hampshire, of the Peace Conference between Russia and Japan. He won himself a Nobel Prize for promoting the peace treaty — but never announced the Taft–Katsura Agreement.

Theodore Roosevelt considered the Panama Canal by far his most important action in foreign affairs. Since the Manifest Destiny dreams of the Fifties, the American people had hungered for an interoceanic canal across the narrows of Central America. United States capital built a Panama railroad to speed the passage of recruits to the California gold rush. In 1852, in Fillmore's Administration, the Secretary of State negotiated the Clayton-Bulwer treaty with the British, under which the Queen's Government and ours agreed that any canal would be a joint enterprise, and neither nation would extend its rights in Central America. Six years later, Lewis Cass,

Secretary of State under Buchanan, officially declared the government's view that "sovereignty has its duties as well as its rights, and none of these local governments . . . would be permitted, in a spirit of Eastern isolation, to close the gates of intercourse of the great highways of the world."

Ferdinand de Lesseps' success in digging the Suez Canal spurred American emulation even in Reconstruction days, which was heightened when he organized a French company to build a canal at Panama, under an agreement with the Republic of New Granada, predecessor to the later Colombia. We looked with such disfavor upon any European domination of an American canal that in the late Seventies the French Government formally disavowed any purpose of exercising control at Panama. But the French constructors could cope with neither the engineering difficulties nor the ravages of tropical diseases, and the company went bankrupt.

Such sturdy fighters as Senator Morgan, of Alabama, crusaded for session after session for a canal, preferably across Nicaragua rather than Panama, but in any event a canal. Action was spurred, during the war with Spain, by the *Oregon's* long and hazardous voyage around Cape Horn to join our Caribbean fleet. The Senate passed a canal bill early in 1899, and the new Hay-Pauncefote treaty with Britain, ratified in 1901, provided that the United States should build, control, police and protect the canal and keep it open to the vessels of all nations on equal terms.

Roosevelt soon opened negotiations with Marroquin, the Colombian dictator, who greatly desired Panama chosen as site instead of Nicaragua, and therefore in January, 1903, agreed to the Hay-Herran treaty. But when Panama was actually selected, Marroquin determined to get another pound of flesh. Since 1900, he had dispensed with any meeting of the Colombian Congress; but late in the summer of 1903 he assembled it in special session; by a unanimous vote it rejected the Hay-Herran treaty, and then went home.

In August 1903 President Roosevelt concluded that the Colombian dictator would stick by this smelly repudiation of the treaty, and began to consider carefully what to do. The Marroquin Congress would not actually adjourn, under its call, until the end of October. The people at Panama, whose mouths had been watering for the loaves and fishes of canal money, might well revolt if the remote dictatorship destroyed their dream. But if Panama remained quiet, Roosevelt had made up his mind to send American ships and soldiers to the Isthmus, occupy it at once, and proceed to dig the canal. He drafted a message to Congress, charging that Colombia had delayed, in order "to make extortionate and improper terms with us." The interest of the United States "demands that the canal should be begun with no needless delay," and we could not consent to permit Colombia "to block the performance of the work which it is so greatly in our interest immediately to begin and carry through."

The message was never carried beyond a rough draft, for T. R. was soon advised that he could depend on a revolution, thanks to a dependable *deus ex machina*. A Wall Street lawyer, William Nelson Cromwell, had arranged the purchase by a syndicate of the assets of the French Panama Canal Company, for which Uncle Sam was to pay $40,000,000. Bunau-Varilla, successor to de Lesseps in the defunct company, came to Panama to arrange the revolt. In a technical sense, the United States Government did not directly mount the revolution, but in October, two American Army officers just back from the Isthmus told the President they were "confident" it would take place as soon as the Colombian Congress adjourned. The President immediately directed the Navy Department "to station various ships within easy reach of the Isthmus, to be ready to act in the event of need arising."

The "revolution" occurred November 3; the United States gunboat *Nashville* persuaded four hundred newly arrived Colombian troops to re-embark for Cartagena; there was no bloodshed, and the Republic of Panama had been born. The President claimed later that "no one connected with the American Government had any part in preparing, inciting, or encouraging the revolution." But forty million dollars of government gold can be a powerful inciter. The new Republic was promptly recognized by the United States Government, a treaty signed, and the building of the canal soon began.

Roosevelt was reproached with having acted in an "unconstitutional" manner, but brushed this aside with the remark that the charge could be upheld "only if Jefferson's action in acquiring Louisiana be also treated as unconstitutional." He might have had precedent in Jefferson's specific act of acquisition, but before the third President would act he had had to dispel self-doubts of his authority; and in addition the Senate advised and consented to the treaty with Napoleon before Jefferson completed its ratification. Roosevelt never asked the Senate to advise and consent on the Panama Revolution, nor is there ground to suppose he had the least doubt about going ahead, for he said that "when nobody else could or would exercise efficient authority, I exercised it."

There never was a strong President who, at one stage or another of his tenure, did not get at loggerheads with Congress, and in particular with the Senate. Roosevelt I had many spectacular tilts with such varied solons as "Pitchfork Ben" Tillman, of South Carolina, the conservative high-tariff Aldrich of Rhode Island, Foraker of Ohio, and "Uncle Joe" Cannon, uncrowned House Czar — none of which approached the magnitude of his battle with Mark Hanna for control of the party.

Solicitous friends warned him, before his 1904 re-election campaign, that he should restrain his impetuous impulses or they might lose the election; but he replied that he would rather be a real President for three-and-a-half years than a figurehead for seven-and-a-half. His Democratic opponent, Judge Alton B. Parker, might have been "the Sage of Esopus," but he had no skill as a vote-getter, and T. R. won by a landslide.

Now President in his own right, he took charge with such a personal hand that the Tories were almost paralyzed. He indorsed Bryanism to such an extent, and forced so much of it into law or administrative action, that "the Peerless Leader" later charged that his issues had been stolen. T. R. forced the Chicago packers to reform their slaughterhouse evils, compelled the anthracite roads to give up direct ownership of their coal mines, pushed conservation to the limit, and passed most of his measures through Congress by the aid of Democratic votes.

All of which made him Chief of Party not as the excitable *locum tenens* for McKinley and Hanna, but in his own elective right. The people liked him, and he could almost always arouse them to put pressure on Congress and bring it to time. Roosevelt exerted his influence on public opinion in an extraordinary variety of ways. To test public reaction to policies or appointments he was debating, he sent up trial balloons in profusion, giving considerable heed to the nature of the response. This habit, by the way, was responsible for his once-famous Ananias Club; he would talk freely to a newspaper correspondent, but should the ensuing story bring an adverse reaction, T. R. would not hesitate to claim that he had been misquoted, words put in his mouth, or the writer had deliberately lied. At length newspapermen began coming in pairs, so that there would be two witnesses to the President's words. This was the beginning of the White House press conference technique.

Most of the papers panned Teddy, but the latter had a gift of pungent phrase that made headlines regardless of editorial page disapproval. Thousands of his letters were written for newspaper publication — it was his method of having a Fireside Chat. He spiced them with such phrases as "malefactor of great wealth"; "undesirable citizen"; "tainted money"; "out-patient of Bedlam," which struck the public fancy. He would jut out his teeth at people, but they went long distances to hear his speeches, and almost always he made a hit.

Roosevelt had a further thing, a sort of New England interest in matters of minor morals and household items. Applying this sort of test to his public crusades helps explain such strangely assorted things as the drive for simplified spelling, the breakfast with Booker T. Washington, almost the attack on the Northern Securities Company. The country saw the use as well as the humor in making paunchy colonels prove their fitness for field service by riding forty miles in the saddle.

The people seemed to like these things, just as they did his zeal for new gadgets to play with, his photographic memory, his amazing variety of detailed knowledge, and his love for the great outdoors. He liked to have companions on nature walks through Rock Creek Park. One day he took Jim Rogers, a young newspaperman from Colorado, on such a walk through the park. John Burroughs, then America's greatest naturalist, joined them; every now and then Roosevelt would point to a bird, and say: "John, what's that?" and then remark: "Young man, that bird isn't known in our country, but we've got something very like it," which he would specify out of his seemingly encyclopedic knowledge of natural life.

Theodore Roosevelt's ability as Chief of Government was demonstrated by the actual building of the Canal by a public agency, an early example of efficient government performance of economic function. He had immense administrative power, and his energy discharged itself under continual high pressure in unpredictable directions. He administered in the small as in the large; his energies were not so continually put to such housekeeping detail as Cleveland's were in his pension vetoes. But he would become zealous for "simplified spelling" — a last-generation predecessor of the "Basic English" cult of the moment — order the Public Printer to employ it, and then tell the House that if it would pass a resolution, he would withdraw the order.

The public relished but did not necessarily accept him, while it paid great heed to the way he carried on the government. Roosevelt exhibited keen interest in the administrative agencies and gave full confidence to those subordinates he happened to like and trust. His Western sojourns gave him a warm desire to protect the interests of the Indians; he secured a good Indian Commissioner in Leupp and backed him to the limit. When Congress passed a bill to sell a large tract of Indian land in Oklahoma at a minimum of $1.50 an acre, the President would not sign it until after it had been redrawn by Congress, Indian rights safeguarded, and the acre price raised to $5.00. As a result, the Indians realized $3,250,000 more than they would have otherwise. The public domain was being continually encroached upon by land-grabbers who would go to court to undo adverse administrative decisions by the Secretary of the Interior. T. R. saw to it that the government vigorously opposed such suits. He deemed action in these matters proper service by the "steward of the whole people."

He had little interest, apparently, in government through channel. Before the fleet started round the world, the admirals had doubted that the torpedo destroyers were sufficiently seaworthy for the trip, but he was told by two young naval officers on a destroyer he visited that these ships were sturdy and ready, so he ordered the destroyer flotilla to go along.

To many of his department heads Roosevelt gave a seemingly complete confidence, notably Root, Knox, Cortelyou, Moody, and Taft, but he had as little use for the Cabinet as an executive instrument as had Jackson, Lincoln or F. D. R., and he did not consult the Cabinet either before he ordered the fleet around the world, or before he took Panama. In the *Autobiography* he referred to the traditional lack of value of a council of war to a commanding general, and added: "In a crisis the duty of a leader is to lead, and not to take refuge behind the timid wisdom of a multitude of councillors."

Perhaps his most interesting employment as Chief of Government arose out of his oath to take care that the laws were faithfully executed. This involved his whole attitude toward business. Governmentally, he believed in the Hamiltonian thesis of a full-powered central government, to be employed for Jeffersonian goals; but to do this the people "must definitely abandon the *laissez faire* theory of political economy, and fearlessly champion a system of increased Governmental controls." He insisted that liberals blundered in expecting Federal action to restore competition to cure the pressing business evils; their willingness "to trust for justice solely to this proposed restoration of competition is just as foolish as if we should go back to the flintlocks" of Washington's Revolutionary Army.

In treating the trusts, he distinguished between those whose sin was size, and those which were piratical. In the 1907 Panic, banks were being crushed like eggshells, depositors frenzied by wild rumors, and catastrophe was right around the corner. One trembling bank held the controlling stock of the Tennessee Coal and Iron Company, chief Southern steel producer; if the Steel Trust, which had the cash, could buy it, the bank would be saved and the panic checked. Judge E. H. Gary, chairman of its board, and H. C. Frick, its chief operating officer, visited the White House November 4, 1907, to tell the President that "as a mere business transaction" they did not care to take over T. C. I., but that it was in their interest to do it to try to prevent a panic and general industrial smash-up. The acquisition would not increase the Trust's proportion of the nation's steel properties to sixty per cent. They would not buy if Roosevelt stated it ought not to be done.

The latter answered that, while of course he could not advise them to take the action proposed, he felt it no public duty to interpose any objections. The panic was arrested, and praise was the immediate meed of the White House. The acquisition helped the Trust substantially, and in a year or so it began to be charged that Gary and Frick had "misled" the President. During the succeeding Taft Administration, suit was brought to dissolve the Steel Corporation, on this among other charges. In 1911 T. R. told a House investigating committee: "I wish it distinctly understood that I acted purely on my own initiative, and that the responsibility for the act was solely mine." The Steel Trust won the suit.

Very different was his course in the Northern Securities case, brought in 1901 under the Sherman Antitrust Act, a statute with an interesting background. President Benjamin Harrison, in his first annual message, December 3, 1889, said that trusts organized to crush healthy competition were "dangerous conspiracies against the public good," and should be prohibited and made the subject of penal legislation. The next year Senator Sherman introduced and

Congress passed a measure to prohibit and penalize conspiracies in restraint of trade in interstate commerce. Its first real test came in 1895, when the Sugar Trust, which already had sixty-five per cent of the nation's output of refined sugar, obtained control of three other companies through an exchange of its stock, giving it control of ninety-eight per cent. Cleveland's Administration sought to have the acquisition set aside, the test case being *United States* vs. *E. C. Knight*. The Supreme Court, by an eight to one vote, held against the government. It declared that, while the fact of monopoly had been admitted, yet the Constitution, in conferring on the Federal Government power to regulate and control interstate commerce, had neither expressly nor by implication included power to regulate or control the production or manufacture of a commodity within a State. Therefore nothing in the law prohibited a corporation from acquiring all the stock of other corporations through exchange of stock. Even though the result was the trust's control of a commodity which was a necessity of life, the Court did not deem the stock transaction "commerce" in the constitutional sense! This decision not only effectively nullified the Sherman Act, but just about wrote FINIS to any further effort of the National Government to pass an effective law to destroy or control such monopolies. Under the shield of the Knight case, a host of trusts, or holding companies, were organized.

The 1901 treaty of peace between the Hill and the Harriman railroad interests took the form of a consolidation of power through the organization of the Northern Securities Company, which would exchange stock and control all the northwestern transcontinentals. Philander C. Knox, then Attorney General, advised the President as to proceedings he instituted to dissolve the railroad trust. Knox was almost alone among the great lawyers of the day in believing the Court could be made to reverse itself, and Roosevelt was charged with disrespect to the Court because he had the suit brought. But Knox made a compelling presentation of the effect, in contrast to the form, of the control, and by five to four the Court decreed the dissolution of Northern Securities. Justice Oliver Wendell Holmes, whom T. R. had nominated for the bench, wrote one of the dissenting opinions — much to the President's pain, as he lamented in a letter to Lodge, and there is some evidence that he expressed his displeasure directly to Justice Holmes and undoubtedly it caused a strained relation for a while.

Still, Roosevelt deemed the decision a major victory, because the new holding gave the government power to deal with industrial monopoly. He had suits instituted against the American Tobacco Company and Standard Oil, both of which were adjudged criminal conspiracies and ordered dissolved. He claimed later that these suits "made the great masters of corporate capital in America fully realize that they were the servants and not the masters of the people."

Elated as he was at this victory, T. R. found that it bore Dead Sea fruit. Standard dissolved, but the limbs of the deceased monster bore close resemblance to the corpse, the Tobacco Trust liquidation had equally unsatisfactory results, and the President felt the Sherman Act far from adequate to cope with modern business conditions and vast corporate wealth. Having concluded that verbal castigation in a judicial opinion was no substitute for actual realistic regulation in the public interest, he made morals rather than mass his yardstick for reform, and sought affirmative control through administrative action. He desired agencies of the nature of the Interstate Commerce Commission and the Bureau of Corporations to supervise businesses in interstate commerce and "to exercise authoritative control." In the case of a trust which enforced "monopoly prices," he would even go so far as to have ceilings put on them by Federal regulatory agencies, just as railroad rates were fixed by the I. C. C. If bad business practices could be eliminated, competition would again return as a "healthy factor." It would not, however, be all-sufficient, and the Sherman Act should be relentlessly invoked against corporations which refused to mend their ways.

Roosevelt's thesis of affirmative administrative control over business took more definite form after his exit from office, and in 1913 he gives this definition of his distinction, as a Progressive, between a good and a bad corporation: "I hold that a corporation does ill if it seeks profit in restricting production and then by extorting high prices from the community," or by in any way "offending against the moral law" either in connection with the public, its competitors, or its employees; such a company conspires against the public welfare. But one which produces more at lower cost, and treats labor, competitor and public well, is an "instrumentality of civilization operating to promote abundance."

As early as 1907, Theodore Roosevelt faced the problem of picking his successor. Being President fascinated him, and undoubtedly he would have liked a third term but, like Jefferson, he had announced long in advance that he would retire after the second term. About the time of the 1908 Republican National Convention, he wrote the British historian Trevelyan that much could be said for the theory that "the public has a right to demand as long service from any man who is doing good service as it thinks will be useful." Although he had felt "obliged to insist on retiring and abandoning the leadership," he admitted great qualms as to whether he was not refusing to do what he ought to do, and "abandoning great work on a mere fantastic point of honor."

Having determined not to run, he sought philosophic calm in the precedent set by Washington; in Roosevelt's view, this implied that, as there inheres in the Presidency more power than in any other office in any modern democracy, it could only be saved from abuse by having the people accept as axiomatic the two-term limitation. He did not believe any harm came from concentrating power in one man's hands — if the holder did not keep it beyond a definite time. But many instances in modern history showed "that the strong man who is good may very readily subvert free institutions if he and the people at large grow to accept his continued possession of vast power as being necessary to good government." It was "very unhealthy" that any one man should be deemed necessary to the people as a whole.

This may have been Spartan stoicism, but the fact remains that T. R. repelled the overtures toward the 1908 nomination. At the same time he did not make up his own mind any too early on a successor. For some reason, he was not attracted by Governor Charles E. Hughes, of New York, and his preference was either Elihu Root or William Howard Taft. The former he regarded as having the finest mind he had ever known. When Secretary of War, Root had created a General Staff for the Army in a masterly fashion, and his work as Secretary of State was outstanding. Roosevelt knew that his corporation clients would make the public suspicious, but said that, if Root became President with the public as his client, they would have his undivided genius employed in their behalf. Still he felt that it would be hard to convince the people of this, and he turned to Taft, for whom his affection then was very great. His backing brought the Southern delegations to the heir-apparent; his appointees through the country began to warm up. Nomination and then election came without any upset.

Psychological explanations of the quick cooling of Roosevelt's enthusiasm, poor Taft's inability to understand the way departure from power twisted the inside of T. R.'s soul and led him to fix the guilt of that deprival on his self-selected successor, belong to the social psychiatrists, and will not be undertaken here. The English have a saying that no Prince of Wales ever loved his father. It might be said with equal truth that no abdicated monarch ever loved the Prince of Wales to whom he gave the throne. The letters of Archibald Butt, an aide to both Presidents, who loved them both, throw light on the collapse of their friendship.

When he left the White House, Theodore Roosevelt exulted in the way he had used the office. "While President I have *been* President emphatically" — so he wrote the preceding summer. "I have used every ounce of power there was in the office and I have not cared a rap for the criticisms of those who spoke of my 'usurpation of power'; for I know that the talk was all nonsense and there was no usurpation of power."

He came out of the White House firmly persuaded that the efficiency of the United States Government depends on its having a strong central executive. Wherever he could, T. R. deliberately established a precedent for strength in the National Executive. He declared as to such matters as sending the fleet around the world, Santo Domingo, Panama, the coal strike, and antitrust suits: "I have felt not merely that my action was right in itself, but that in showing the strength of, or in giving strength to, the executive, I was establishing a precedent of value." The keynote of his Presidency was the statement: "I believe in a strong executive — I believe in power."

CHAPTER XI

Spokesman of the People

Woodrow Wilson is often likened to Jefferson and Lincoln, both in the way he worked and in the greatness of his effect upon the nation's development. Each of the three seized the fact of power, and employed it in the way he saw the common good. Hostile critics have gibbeted the three as proof positive that power always corrupts, and absolute power corrupts absolutely. But the common denominator goes little further than this.

Jefferson was an Aristotelian philosopher; John Knox and his moral imperatives were as alien to his spirit as they were akin to Wilson's. They went the same path in governing through their leadership of the Democratic Party, but Jefferson knew how to charm men's hearts as well as convince their minds, while his twentieth-century successor found it hard to project his magnetism beyond his little group. In a sense, Jefferson was the true scholar in politics, for his research was more profound, his zeal for the application of principle to practice less immediate, his correction for error of fact or formula usually more ungrudging, than Wilson's. But the two had a tragic resemblance in the fact that each went into office when the world was at peace, with an essential program of domestic reform, only to have a world war destroy their edifice and wreck their presidential careers.

Although Wilson's study of our governmental operations gave him no such zeal for Jefferson as he had for Lincoln, yet in his Presidency he emulated the Jeffersonian practice of dominating government through party leadership, while the example of Lincoln's action against Court and Congress had little effect upon his course.

One wonders if he had any real understanding of that strange son of the Border who read men's hearts like an open book, and marshaled them to his needs. Often Wilson sought spiritual fellowship with Lincoln, as at the dedication September 4, 1916, of the cabin in Hodgenville, Kentucky, in which the Emancipator had first seen light of day. "It was a very lonely spirit," he said, "that looked out from underneath those shaggy brows and comprehended men without fully communing with them, as if, in spite of all its genial efforts at comradeship, it dwelt apart, saw its visions of duty where no man looked on. There is a very holy and very terrible isolation for the conscience of every man who seeks to read the destiny in affairs for others as well as for himself, for a nation as well as for individuals. That privacy no man can intrude upon. That lonely search of the spirit for the right perhaps no man can assist. This strange child of the cabin kept company with invisible things, was born into no intimacy but that of its own silently assembling and deploying thoughts."

Of all his predecessors, Wilson seemed more reverent of Lincoln than of any other, even Washington; but still one wonders how well the child of the manse understood the child of the cabin. The sentences quoted above may have reflected the brooding sorrow of the man who saved the Union, but unquestionably they portray the spiritual solitude in which Wilson sought guidance from afar.

Many have sneered at him as "scholar in politics," as if research knowledge should disqualify its possessor from taking part in the art of government. In fact Wilson was not scholar but professional expert; in 1910, when he became Governor of New Jersey, he was among the nation's most noted political scientists.

Wilson stemmed from Scottish Presbyterian preacher stock on both sides, and his boyhood in the South of Reconstruction intensified his indoctrination with his father's moral musts. His early college work was no more than average, and he graduated at Princeton in 1879 the forty-first in a class of over two hundred. After a law course at the University of Virginia, he practised a little law and much literature in Atlanta, then in 1882 took down his shingle and entered Johns Hopkins to master political science.

One of a brilliant group of graduate students, he worked zealously, became enamored of the pillars of the British Liberal tradition: Adam Smith, John Stuart Mill, Walter Bagehot, and Gladstone, "the Grand Old Man." The parliamentary system, with its consequence of accountable and responsible government, led him to examine the American structure, then as now neither flesh, fowl nor good red herring. *Congressional Government,* published in 1885, was a painstaking and disheartening analysis of the institutional imperfections of our nation's government, and brought him considerable acclaim.

Significant of the future, Wilson at twenty-eight defined statesmanship as "that resolute and vigorous advance towards the realization of high, definite and consistent aims, which issue from the unreserved devotion of a strong intellect to the service of the State." Writing when the Federal Government was at low ebb, he found neither responsible nor accountable government in the American practice. He held the committee system of the Congress chiefly to blame for the poor National Government and saw little hope for real reform save through a parliamentary method of the British type.

Wilson revised this view, first from Cleveland's strong use of the office, and then during the war with Spain. In the introduction to the fifteenth edition of that first book, in August 1900, he wrote, "When foreign affairs play a prominent part in the politics and policy of a nation, its Executive must of necessity be its guide; must utter every judgement, take every first step of action," and said the change might well "substitute statesmanship for government by mass meeting." But the student's growing belief in the Presidency as an organ of national leadership did not diminish the pertinence of his criticisms of Congress.

During these years at Hopkins, he engaged in the institution's debating activities with increasing zest, and we find him writing his fiancée, Ellen Axson, that he was much better able to dominate a group than to persuade individuals. He felt the qualities of public leadership developing, and lost whatever interest he had ever had in becoming a research historian. This went counter to the current — the German research cult, with its piling of fact on fact in never-ending train, had gotten lodgement in the American university world; but Wilson did not like it. He would rather take what others had found, draw the moral therefrom and then try to put it in words which would move multitudes. He considered himself a natural leader and tried to train himself to handle great tasks — even the Presidency.

The year his first book came from the press, Wilson won an associate professorship in history and political science at Bryn Mawr, and married Ellen Axson, who helped shape his life. In 1888 he shifted to Wesleyan University, in Connecticut, and two years later was called to Princeton to the Chair of Jurisprudence and Politics. During the ensuing twelve years he had active growth. He soon won the affection and respect of his students, and before long was in great demand for addresses throughout the East. These enabled him to perfect his style, so that it combined brevity of statement with felicity of phrase.

In these years as a teacher he wrote a great deal; all of it was readable, much of it good, some indifferent. His life of Washington was about as romantic as Parson Weems's, his five-volume *History of the American People,* confessedly written for self-improvement, went adrift on many national developments, but *The State* made a great success as a college text, with new editions year after year. In 1908 he published his last treatise on political science, *Constitutional Government,* in which he said that the office of Chief Executive is anything the holder has the sagacity and force to make it: —

"The President is at liberty, both in law and conscience, to be as big a man as he can. His capacity will set the limit; and if Congress be overborne by him, it will be no fault of the makers of the Constitution — it will be from no lack of constitutional powers on its part, but only because the President has the nation behind him and

Congress has not. He has no means of compelling Congress except through public opinion."

His views as to the President's party role had taken firm form: "He cannot escape being the leader of his party except by incapacity and lack of personal force, because he is at once the choice of the party and of the nation." But he was not greatly impressed with the need for administrative background; as it had been used and developed, the office "really does not demand actual experience in affairs so much as particular qualities of mind and character which we are at least as likely to find outside the ranks of our public men as within them." The reason was that "the President is becoming more and more a political and less and less an executive officer," his political powers being personal and inalienable. Therefore "there is no training school for presidents."

In 1902, when the President of Princeton resigned, Wilson was chosen to fill the vacancy at the special meeting at which his predecessor announced his retirement, and on the latter's nomination. Not long thereafter he was thrown into a battle for democratic principle as he conceived it, which ended only with his death. Princeton had been a college with a conscience — poor, proud, hard-working, set in the faith. But with the turn of the century, prosperous alumni built fine halls, their sons founded eating clubs like the Ivy and avoided the common herd. The new President felt that democracy in education demanded a caste-free student body, and proposed a preceptorial system something like the aristocratic democracies of Oxford and Cambridge.

This was not what some of the alumni had ordered; they approved the snobbish indolence of their offspring and undertook to make Wilson toe the mark. An important part of the faculty opposed him as an impractical theorist: surely those who paid the piper had the right to call the tune. Put on his mettle, Wilson took his side to the alumni, moderated the irritation in some quarters, and had about won the battle for the regeneration of the colleges of America. Then a huge bequest was made, contingent on the abandonment of his plan; he could not withstand three million dollars of gold from the grave. In a short while he turned from the bitter politics of the college to the comparative honesty of party politics.

This shift, under way for several years, came as a result of one of the most controverted chapters of his kaleidoscopic career. George Harvey, editor of *Harper's Weekly* and the *North American Review,* had been looking for a new national leader for the Democratic Party ever since Parker's effort, and picked Wilson for the job. After Bryan's third defeat, there was an open field and Harvey became energetic in grooming the Princeton president. As a first step, the editor began maneuvering for Wilson to be made Governor of New Jersey, a reactionary State run by a bi-partisan machine whose Democratic boss, Senator James Smith, was in working alliance with his Republican opposite number. Harvey sold Wilson to the Boss, who road-rollered his nomination for Governor. Smith, who had no promises from Wilson, should have known from the Princeton record that no political debt would affect his decision on things he deemed of a moral character. When a Republican leader addressed to Candidate Wilson certain searching questions, the latter answered that, if elected, he would deem himself forever disgraced if he "should in the slightest degree co-operate in any such system or any such transactions as the boss system describes."

Elected by 49,000 majority, he told the people in his inaugural address that he looked upon himself as their chosen leader and public spokesman, because representative and responsible government called for executive conduct transcending the conventional doctrines of compartmental powers. He declared himself in favor of the regulation of corporations, the establishment of a real public utilities commission and employers' liability law, the direct primary, equalization of taxes and a corrupt practices act.

This program, as pleasing as it was unfamiliar to New Jersey, he put into practice. It won him a national reputation as a real progressive, but brought the direct charge that he was an ingrate who betrayed the men to whom he owed his office. His method was illustrated by the way he took charge of a meeting of the Democratic whips which had been called to kill the reform program. Wilson asked permission to attend, and then argued his case so convincingly that the group indorsed his leadership, and the Legislature put most of his laws on the statute book. Thenceforward the Governor was New Jersey's unquestioned spokesman.

Was he an "ingrate"? In 1910, New Jersey held an advisory Democratic primary on the senatorial candidate to succeed Boss Smith, and James E. Martine, an anti-machine Democrat, won by a large vote. Smith had not entered that race, because the Legislature still elected the Senator and its members were not bound by the primary's "advice," but after the party's triumph in the 1910 election he later demanded another Senate term. Politically, the Governor could not "go along," because it would destroy his appeal to progressives for the Democratic presidential nomination; furthermore, his loyalties to ideas and duties overrode his sense of obligation to men. He insisted on Martine, and such was his marshaling of public opinion that Boss Smith received only four votes on the joint ballot. Then Croker, of Tammany Hall, sneered that "an ingrate is no good in politics."

Wilson's break with George Harvey added a count to the charge of lack of appreciation and disloyalty. This energetic editor's close connection with the House of Morgan began to embarrass the statesman shifting from the right to the left. After his gubernatorial election the two met with mutual friends, Wilson was asked directly if he felt Harvey's activities were hurtful, answered in the affirmative, and their relations and friendship ceased at once. Wilson exhibited no concern over the outcome. Men did not weigh against principles; "ideas live but men die."

No sooner had William Howard Taft succeeded Theodore Roosevelt than omens of political storm appeared. Taft's human sympathy had made him a magnificent Governor General of the troubled Philippines, as later his acute sense of comparative values made him a notable Chief Justice of the United States, but neither quality equipped him to contend with the unrest of the people during his unhappy White House years. The country did not know what changes it wanted, but was definitely dissatisfied. The President sensed this but did not know how to proceed. He sought to effect a tariff reduction, but the vested interests, operating through Czar Cannon and Senator Aldrich, procured the Payne-Aldrich tariff increase, in its day as deliberate a thwarting of presidential and popular wishes as was the Hawley-Smoot monstrosity of Hoover's term. The 1910 mid-term election returned a Democratic House majority, which went to work to turn the Republicans out. A little later T. R. returned from his big-game hunt in Africa and Europe; Taft vainly proffered the hand of friendship, but in a few months Roosevelt was busy wresting the party leadership from the President's hands. Taft was no good in the rough-and-tumble; governmentally regarding himself as Chief Magistrate more than people's leader, he had few resources in his role of Chief of Party save the reactionary organizations and Big Business, both animated by hatred of Teddy and his new program of reforms. It became plain that a Democrat would be the next President.

Wilson's nomination by the Democratic National Convention was but another of the miracles of his political career. Technically, he owed it to the two-thirds rule, for Champ Clark held a majority against him for many of the ballots preceding the Governor's victory on the forty-fourth. Actually, he owed it to William Jennings Bryan, who had magnanimously ignored Wilson's 1908 letter hoping that Bryan would be "knocked into a cocked hat." None who attended the gathering in the Baltimore Armory could forget the irresistible force with which that indomitable champion offered his resolution that the Convention should accept no aspirant backed by the Tammany-Wall Street combination of Murphy, Belmont and Ryan. The writer — in the press gallery, attending his first convention — recalls the pandemonium which broke out when Harry Flood of Virginia shouted that "the gentleman is no Democrat." Bryan stilled the tumult to answer that, on three separate occasions, more than six million Americans had attested his Democracy: "If the gentleman will send his name to the platform, I will have him recorded in the negative!" At length the machine delegates grew tired, and the ex-professor was nominated for President.

The Roosevelt delegates had walked out of the Republican Convention, and were organizing the Progressive Party, even before the Democrats began gathering at Baltimore. Wilson's election was never in question, only the amount of his vote. In the issue, he received about 6,200,000 votes to 4,100,000 for Roosevelt and 3,400,000 for Taft. But of the total popular vote he had only a plurality, about 42 per cent. His Electoral College strength was 435 votes, to 88 for Roosevelt and a pitiful 8 for Taft. The majority of the American electorate undoubtedly hoped for the dawn of a new day.

Could Wilson lead the people? The likelihood was that he would fail. Since 1866 the Republicans had constituted the majority party — the two Cleveland intrusions came largely in consequence of liberal Republican revolt against the rule of the oligarchy, a correction rather than a repudiation of "the party that saved the Union." The practical politicians, to whom control of government meant daily bread, did not believe the situation enough different from 1884 or 1892 for Wilson to have more than one term. They deemed him a political accident, and that "quick, bright things come to sudden confusion."

But Wilson regarded himself as the people's chosen leader for the fundamental reform of the policy and the government of the United States. He believed the people had elected him specifically to reintroduce morals into politics, and to provide responsible government under a personal leadership that could be held responsible if things went wrong.

This was a mighty charge, and a man less sure of his mission would have trembled both at the road ahead and over the sorts of lieutenants upon whom he must lean for support. He could not turn to "the wise, the rich and the good"; with notable exceptions these men were perfectly satisfied for a self-perpetuating elite to run the nation. He could not expect the Eastern Democracy to be of much help; it was made up of big and little Tammanys, together with tired Cleveland Liberals who had not escaped time's hardening of the mental arteries. For a Democratic Cabinet, he was forced to turn to the Bryanites; their zeal for free silver and similar unconventional issues had arisen primarily because of their interest in the common people, and Bryan had been the party's only great emotional force along progressive paths.

Not only must Wilson take Bryan, but he must fashion for himself a new personal party. The Southern Democrats, though they furnished the party's greatest remaining reservoir of electoral votes, were Democrats mainly by geography and tradition. Wilson must act as Chief of Party, but must also build a national personal following.

The thing Wilson could do best was convince the people of the rightness of what he thought. The nation never had a leader more supremely gifted to take a condition of baffling perplexity and describe and analyze it in such a way that those who heard or read him could grasp its essence and would demand the course he proposed. But he could not, like Jackson, command the confidence and trust of millions who never saw him; nor was he a human lodestone, like Clay, Blaine or Bryan, who were loved even for the errors they had made.

The most successful aspect of his Presidency was the way he handled Congress, until the 1918 Republican revolt. Writing in 1919 in a British quarterly, Professor Lindsay Rogers declared that Wilson, more than any of his predecessors, "has exerted an almost absolute authority over Congress." This was the case from the very start, and no member of Congress could plead surprise at the endeavor. The month before he entered the White House, in his letter refusing to be bound by the one-term plank in the Baltimore platform, he re-emphasized his belief that the President "is expected by the Nation to be the leader of his party as well as the chief executive officer of the Government, and the country will take no excuses from him. He must play the part and play it successfully, or lose the country's confidence. He must be Prime Minister, as much concerned with the guidance of legislation as with the just and orderly execution; and *he is the spokesman of the Nation in everything, even the most momentous and delicate dealings of the Government with foreign nations."*

In his Inaugural Address, March 5, 1913, the new President identified the major items to be altered: a tariff made for private profit and to the people's harm; a banking and currency system "perfectly adapted to concentrating cash and restricting credit"; and an industrial control "which holds capital in leading-strings, restricts the liberties and limits the opportunities of labor and exploits without renewing or conserving the natural resources of the country." Also he proposed Federal credit for farm lands, and the development of the nation's waterways and power resources in the public interest. "The firm basis of government," declared the champion of these new freedoms, "is justice, not pity. These are matters of justice."

Wilson promptly summoned Congress in special session and on April 18, 1913, appeared in person before the two Houses, to urge the measures he deemed imperative. This broke the precedent established by Jefferson, in 1801, when he sent his message to be read, rather than himself speaking it, as Washington and Adams had frequently done. The third President's reason was personal, not institutional: he spoke indifferently but talked well. The twenty-eighth Chief Executive's reasons were the reverse: he spoke with ease and persuasiveness, but he disliked Jefferson's method of using the hospitality of the White House as political or diplomatic tool. Gracious and charming in a small company of intimates, Wilson would not run a cafeteria for visiting firemen.

The opposition, in and out of Congress, pretended great alarm at the personal appearance, but phenomenal success attended his urging of the reform program. Our Federal annals afford no equal to the Wilson 1913 record for the speed and completeness with which a Congress followed executive initiative, except that during the first seventy-five days of Franklin Roosevelt's special session twenty years later, when he had to handle the desperate crisis of the bank collapse. Jefferson had set the precedent of the President forcing or persuading legislative action through his own ability as Chief of Party. But he generally worked by indirection, through intermediaries or party caucuses. The results, therefore, were more subject to emasculating amendment and longer delayed. Wilson confronted no country in a panic, he made no Jeffersonian disclaimer of determined leadership, and he ran Congress as it has never been run by another, before or since.

An interesting metamorphosis took place in his technique of leading Congress. He had come to the White House planning to work with the Liberals and Progressives on Capitol Hill, leaving the organization Democrats severely alone, as reactionaries opposed to his program. But by the late fall of 1913 he discovered that most of the Progressives were prima donnas, who would not work in chorus, so he began testing out the professional politicians. To Wilson's amazement, he found them ready to follow him because, as organization men, they knew they must yield their own views to the convictions of the party leaders. The conservative Simmons, of North Carolina, and Underwood, of Alabama, illustrated their acceptance of party discipline.

The President used Burleson as chief lieutenant at the other end of Pennsylvania Avenue. The Postmaster General proved a past-master at the combination of entreaty, cajolery and command required by the task. Some of the White House entourage did not like his insistence on "taking care of the boys in the trenches," but he got enough jobs, campaign contributions and other favors to keep them in the fight.

With Wilson's blessing, and perhaps instigation, a group of eager young liberals organized a "Common Council Club" to do special jobs for him. Composed of about thirty men of "Little Cabinet" rank, it met at the old University Club almost every Wednesday from late 1913 until we went to war with Germany in 1917. Prominent in its activities were Joe Davies, Robert Woolley, Oliver P. Newman, Henry Breckinridge, Huston Thompson, Louis Brownlow, Breckinridge Long, Joseph Folk, Louis F. Post and Franklin D.

Roosevelt. Three or four Senators and Congressmen came down every week.

In addition to active debates on governmental policies and methods, these men did many practical tasks. On suggestion from above or their own initiative, they would focus on some item of the President's program that was in rough waters in Congress, and select a group among them to go to the Hill to put on the heat. Wilson used them, too, for projecting his new ideas, as in the early months of 1917, when the Club arranged a large dinner to furnish him a sounding-board.

Though he considered leadership of Congress an imperative duty, Wilson did not like the contacts with the majority leaders of the two Houses. He preferred to send for the chairman of a committee which had control of a particular measure, and argue him into cooperation, or to appeal to the people back home to instruct the recalcitrants. He had genius in convincing the understanding but not in persuading an affection that would cause men to break with their beliefs and follow him. For all that, during his first three years in office, Wilson led his party more effectively than any who had preceded him, not excepting Jefferson. It is perhaps the best presidential example of the successful use of talents ill-adapted to the task.

For his first five years, Wilson had the fact of power and the essence of success. But he could not lead the nation, as Jackson did, against an adverse Congress. When the Republicans captured Congress in the 1918 election, Wilson had no substitute for control through party. The loss of Congress was a stroke of political paralysis which withered his strong right arm before he left to make the peace.

Among his earliest and sternest battles was that over the reduction of the duty on sugar, which he considered indispensable to the right sort of tariff reform. The attacks came from Louisiana cane-sugar, Colorado and other beet-sugar growers. But the President told Huston Thompson that he had learned what not to do in making a tariff, from poor Taft's experiences; the latter honestly wanted to redeem his 1908 platform pledge of general reduction, but after an initial compromise on sugar had to swallow a hundred others, and then to take the stump "to defend an altogether indefensible bill." Wilson made up his mind not to undot a single *i* or uncross a single *t*, for then "all the wolves would jump over the fence"; he was grimly unyielding and carried the bill through unchanged.

In addition, he forced the passage of major legislation fundamentally bettering the banking and currency evils by the creation of the Federal Reserve Banks and modernizing of the Sherman Antitrust Act through the Clayton, Federal Trade Commission and other bills. He consciously attempted to focus the country's attention on one proposal at a time. To this end, he would send a message or speak on the single subject, in order to arouse public opinion sufficiently to compel legislative action.

This quality was often present during the first Congress of his second term. "Perhaps the greatest triumph," wrote Lindsay Rogers, "that any American President has ever won in his relations with Congress was the passage of his Selective Service Act, when, at the time of the declaration of war, there was a clear majority in each House in favor of adhering to the voluntary principle." This measure showed the President's heed of the way Britain had been forced from volunteering to conscription. He had General Enoch Crowder dig out of the War Department files the analytical report of Provost Marshal General Fry, who handled those earlier efforts. The Civil War errors were not repeated, and the 1917–1919 draft methods bear deservedly high repute.

Wilson could not have led Congress as Chief of Party alone; he must drive the mighty engine of public opinion to stimulate the slothful and coerce the reluctant. This he did for the first four years with a skill unmatched until Franklin Roosevelt's. His speeches, messages and letters were clear, crisp and easy reading, because of the time he spent on condensation — once he apologized for a long letter because he "didn't have time to write a short one." Frequently he said too much in too few words, reversing the conventional fault of public utterance.

The Chief of Public Opinion perceived the difference between news columns and editorial page, and consistently "made news." Three days after inauguration, he set up an informal, unofficial committee of William G. McAdoo, Franklin K. Lane and Walter S. Rogers, a close friend of Charles R. Crane, to study the problem of presidential relations with the press. The Cabinet members could not spare much time, and so Rogers worked out the plan. The President wanted to avoid the correspondents' distrust of T. R., and their breaking of confidences with Taft. He himself distrusted the press, once saying, "If you see it in the paper, it's not so." But he drew the regularized White House press conference out of the Rogers report. At these he would explain, "off the record," the reasons for various policies and acts, and occasionally answer questions. Records were made of the sessions, a White House Correspondents' association came into being, and this phase of his direction of public opinion formation began being institutionalized. But he realized the dangers as well as the values of these catch-as-catch-can press relations. After we entered the war against Germany, the influence of White House news on the stock market, and other dangers of harm to morale, led him gradually to discontinue the conferences. It was a wise decision, for deliberate press twisting of words or tones of a President does not cease when the nation goes to war.

In part to pass public information to the people, but in larger part to soothe the feelings of Congress, which charged that he ignored it and went direct to the masses, Wilson went out of his way to keep Congress informed and to reveal his thinking to it. On many occasions, despite his possession of the power to do certain things, he would appear before the lawmakers to acquaint them with the situation, and to unburden his thoughts. Some believed that he went even beyond the necessary bounds in observing the place and powers of Congress. But he never wavered in his concept of leadership, as declared at Gettysburg, July 4, 1913: "I have been chosen the leader of the nation, I cannot justify the choice by any qualities of my own, but so it has come about, and here I stand."

Wilson had his own formula for efficiency in government, the major factor of which was the concentration of power, authority and responsibility in the hands of the President. This did not carry with it a determination personally to dot every *i* and cross every *t* of administration; indeed, he delegated detail as much as possible. Often the delegation involved major substantive actions, and almost always it was accompanied with power to act, and his continuing support to the agent. Power *qua* power was no indispensable vitamin to his emotional being; Wilson demanded powers to use them, not to work some to exhaustion and keep others unused "in a napkin."

There could be no better illustration of this than the way John J. Pershing was selected to become Commander in Chief of the American Expeditionary Force. Newton D. Baker, Wilson's Secretary of War, related the story to the writer in 1935, as proof positive of the President's reliance on trusted men. The Allies had appealed for the prompt dispatch to France of an American force, even if at first it would have no more than morale value for their weary people. After Wilson agreed, he directed Baker to make a careful study of the generals on the Army list, select the right man and report his name. Baker said he studied the records carefully, checked each of half a dozen men for the traits he deemed necessary in a good commanding general, and then called at the White House: He had made the analysis, would the President examine the comparative records? But Wilson answered, a trifle sternly, that he had delegated that task to the Secretary of War and desired only the latter's recommendation. Baker took another week, found Pershing's values outstanding and submitted his name and the reasons. The nomination went to the Senate the next day.

Once having chosen the General, Wilson backed him unreservedly, as was shown by the record of Pershing's insistence on keeping the A. E. F. a fighting Army, rather than mere reserves or replacements for British or French. Foch, Pétain, Haig, Lloyd George and Clemenceau tried to go over the General's head, but Wilson never let him down.

The President's personal habits with his constitutional advisers carried little flavor of martinet or dictator. "It is not true," wrote David F. Houston, after eight years as a department head, "that Wilson did not consult his Cabinet on new departures and policy, or on important matters." While he was quick and did not have to be "educated" on a new matter, "he was patient, very patient — patient even of dullness." His study of history caused him to view current matters in their perspective, in a systematic, orderly fashion. Slow in arriving at conclusions, Wilson would not be pushed into a snap action. Once decided, he was difficult to move, but "better reasons and sound reasoning would alter his views, and changed conditions would modify them."

Life with Wilson had its meed of the unexpected. At the time of the American occupation of Vera Cruz, noted Houston, "he startled the Cabinet by asking those who still believed in prayer to pray over the matter." With him, God was an immanent presence, and he believed that the wise heart never questions the dealings of Providence; "anyone is a fool who questions its ways." His own fear was only over being wrong, never of the consequences personal to himself of an act.

His thinking was hampered chiefly by the "single-track mind" to which he admitted with a sense of pride. Subordinates sensed his unwillingness or inability quickly to turn his thought and attention from one problem to another, or to see many things at the same instant or in quick succession. It was an unfortunate deficiency; one great need of the Presidency is the capacity to generalize out of the enormous mass of particulars which constitute the American present. This is not to deny that it is good administrative management for a chief to pick the right kind of lieutenants, and then to trust them with real delegations of fractions of his totality of executive power. But administrative talent of the first order demands, in addition, that he be alert to the problems of his aides, know the degree with which they handle them properly, and get rid of them if they fail at the job. Wilson was better at this than had been Lincoln, but still he was not an administrator of the first rank.

He was conscious of the need for better administrative organization of the White House, and appointed, in the summer of 1918, a committee to consider the nature of the President's office and how to organize administrative tasks. Charles Day, of Philadelphia, headed it, other members being Morris Llewellyn Cooke, George Norris the banker, and Vance McCormick. It was hard at work when the Armistice came, but made no report.

Houston remarked that "he took too little account of poor human nature, its weaknesses and foibles." Perhaps this was because he had no real familiars. While he admired many men, had affection for them and trust, he seemed at real ease with only a few, and these almost always men who had few angles, never took belligerent attitudes or stubbornly opposed him.

Wilson had gone into office with a great program of domestic reforms. His whole attention concentrated on them, and amazing success attended his efforts. While well aware of the immense importance of his position as Chief of Foreign Relations, he was determined that first things must come first — and these were the changes in the fundamental relationship between money and managements on the one hand, and labor and the consuming public on the other. It was with the utmost reluctance that he would permit the train of his thoughts to be stalled while he turned to emergency matters of foreign affairs.

As a matter of fact, these had never ranked high among his intellectual interests, and while his syllabus on comparative governmental methods, *The State,* had briefed the principal institutional forms and practices abroad, it had been derived, not original, work. He entered the White House a crusading leader for "the New Freedom," which was 99 44/100 per cent of, by and for the United States. Relations within the American hemisphere were within the outer penumbra of his attention, and a Mexican revolution was in process when he took the oath. This was led by General Huerta. President Porfirio Díaz fled to Paris, and Wilson, seven days after his inauguration, announced his Administration would not recognize any new foreign government which came into power through physical force or revolutionary intrigue. President Wilson appealed to Huerta to evacuate his office, a proposal the latter ignored. Many Latin-Americans spoke bitterly about new evidence of Yankee imperialism.

Wilson took occasion, in an address at Mobile, October 27, 1913, to declare the official Administration doctrine on inter-American relations. "Human rights, national integrity and opportunity," in his view, must become the yardstick for our action, and not material interest alone. He predicted that the United States would "never again seek one additional foot of territory by conquest." Shortly thereafter Carranza, one of Huerta's generals, raised the standard of revolt, and Wilson instituted a blockade against the entry of munitions and military stores into Mexico. When on shore leave, some sailors from our squadron off Vera Cruz were arrested by the local Mexican authorities, our Admiral demanded a salute to the United States flag, and on Huerta's refusal, by the order of the President Vera Cruz was captured and occupied. This action caused great uneasiness through the Latin-American nations, but in the following year Wilson invoked the good offices of the South American "big three," Argentina, Brazil and Chile, which resulted in a settlement satisfactory to all.

The Kaiser's declaration of war against Russia, August 1, 1914, took Wilson and America completely by surprise. The first reaction was gratitude for the Atlantic Ocean: the facts of geography would save us from the foreign holocaust. The President proclaimed neutrality, and urged the people to be neutral in thought as well as deed. Many leaders indorsed this insistence, soon to be made a reproach to Wilson; early that fall, ex-President Roosevelt told a delegation of Belgians that no other attitude could be contemplated. But the war soon clouded the American firmament. The New York Stock Exchange closed, the British blockade knocked the bottom out of the cotton and other export markets, the French recovery on the Marne set the stage for a war of exhaustion. However much the spokesman of reform might resent its intrusion, the World War was taking command.

The reluctance with which Wilson yielded, the way he kicked against the pricks, his efforts to persuade a peace without victory, then the reluctant resort to war, are an integral part of his slow self-transformation into the world leader, whose plan of peace was defeated at home — aspects which are treated in the next chapter. The present discussion deals with the matters of war and peace only in so far as they affected Wilson's domestic program or his institutional status as President.

Principal among these was his re-election, in 1916, to a second term; the first Democrat since Jackson who was continued in office for eight straight years. His opponent was Charles Evans Hughes, who resigned as Associate Justice to make the race. The Old Guard, which controlled the Republican National Convention, although it refused to take T. R. because he was a bolter, picked Hughes because he would have some appeal to the Progressives. Roosevelt had been nominated by the remnants of his Bull Moose Party, but hated Wilson so much that he refused to run.

The 1916 campaign amazed the political soothsayers, who had expected the exit of the Progressive Party to insure Hughes's election. Some students of public opinion suggest that if Roosevelt had been the G. O. P. nominee, he would have held the Far West. Wilson never referred to T. R. by name, but as "the articulate part of the Republican Party," as he termed Hughes and Taft "the inarticulate part." The ex-Justice made a poor impression on all but partisans determined to be pleased. Republican diatribes against the vagueness of Wilson's phrases fell flat as their nominee heeded the injunctions of the campaign managers not to offend the German-Americans, Irish-Americans or other hyphenated and pacifist groups. By nature thoughtful and candid, Hughes did not like being in wraps, and did not do well. In one city in which he spoke, in California, his Old Guard local managers did not let him know that Hiram Johnson, T. R.'s 1912 running mate, was in the same hotel, and the nominee did not call on the Senator. The latter resented the seeming snub; his powerful State machine ceased its efforts; and the Wilson groundswell carried the State.

In September, Wilson began a front-porch campaign, from Shadow Lawn, New Jersey, his acceptance speech pressing the theme that "we have in four years come very near to carrying out the platform of the Progressive Party as well as our own." Bryan set aside his sense of hurt over Wilson's changes in the 1915 *Lusitania* note to take to the hustings in the West. Vance McCormick, Democratic Chairman, followed a shrewd hunch of his Publicity Director, Robert Woolley, and spent several hundred thousand dollars on newspaper advertising in the Western States. The slogan "He kept us out of war" was the one argument that went home to the voters.

The chance for re-election grew more and more dubious. Labor did little for Wilson, despite the aid he had given them, culminating in the Adamson eight-hour law. Not only is it Labor's trait, politically, often to punish enemies more than to reward friends, but also much of its leadership then worshiped the Republican "full dinner pail" doctrine. The bankers and industrialists were almost a unit behind Hughes. The early results of the November 7 balloting indicated Hughes's election, because both New York and Illinois had gone for him. But later it turned out Wilson had captured New Hampshire, Ohio, and California, in addition to the expected South and West. His popular plurality was well over half a million.

Note must be taken of Wilson's intention, if Hughes won, to put him in office quickly. House suggested that Marshall and Lansing be gotten to resign, the President-elect made Secretary of State, and then Wilson himself would resign, so Hughes could succeed. The President said after the election that he would have done so, but left no such paper for posterity concerning it as Lincoln had in the summer of 1864.

Wilson had won the second term in a clean-cut victory over the reunited Republican Party. An ominous possibility now presented itself to the twentieth-century Hamiltonians: this successor of Jefferson might make the Democratic Party dominant again. The result was an intensification of the resistance to him. He felt the need for emergency powers to take over the railroads in the event of war; he asked for a corrupt practices bill with teeth in it; he wanted steeper income-tax rates; but Congress was indifferent to these efforts to set the house in order for the coming storm. Cordell Hull, a Tennessee Congressman, did energize the tax measure, but the Adamson law was not perfected for a long time.

When Germany's renewal of unrestricted U-boat warfare brought us into the conflict, except for the "hyphen groups" the entire country seemed eager to stand by the President — even in his phrase that this would be a war to make the world safe for democracy. The first threat to his executive control of the war came in the summer of 1917, when Congress considered the establishment of a Joint Committee on the Conduct of the War, of the type the Radical Republicans had saddled on Lincoln in December 1861. We have already indicated the nature of its conduct, and the use Wilson made of citing its example and the way it impeded his Civil War predecessor. This first effort to handcuff Wilson proceeded more from congressional anxiety to wield power than from any sudden increase in hatred of Wilson himself, and his earnest objection to the proposal put an end to it for the time being.

The early fall, however, was full of dissatisfaction with America's part in the war. Britain and France had not yet pleaded for the dispatch overseas of a huge American fighting force; twenty to thirty divisions, with supporting corps and army services and supply echelons, were all that Marshal Joffre initially sought, and the Allies expected the war to continue several years. America's industrial capacity was to be focused on new weapons, matériel, and supplies, for a knockout offensive in 1919.

The Army's General Staff, under Generals March and Bliss, planned the training and procurement programs on those assumptions. Many of the service branches, such as Ordnance, Quartermaster, Signals, handled their tasks bureaucratically or stupidly, particularly in providing heat, food, and blankets for the men in camp, while the airplane production failure became a public scandal. About this time, the Allied High Command became enormously apprehensive, over a coming German road-roller offensive, and almost trebled its call on American man power. The training program jumped from thirty to eighty divisions. The resulting confusion irritated the public, but the reasons for it had to be kept secret.

In consequence, by September the anti-Wilson elements renewed their attacks upon the executive handling of the war effort, their activities gaining weight because of revolutionary Russia's withdrawal from combat, the transfer of the released German divisions to the Western Front, and then the Italian debacle at Caporetto. Stories of bad conditions in the cantonments swept the country, together with "inside" information about contract scandals, lack of production of matériel of war, inefficiency in the War Department. The public mood resembled that of the summer of 1864, when Lincoln despaired of re-election until Sherman's capture of Atlanta.

The March 1917 Republican "truce" of party politics for the duration was more honored in the breach than in the observance. The industrial profiteers of East and Middle West had hated Wilson ever since the Clayton Antitrust Act; many mild-mannered Republicans could not accept a Democratic professor as lawful Chief of State. Theodore Roosevelt, his hatred of the President intensified by the latter's refusal to send him abroad at the head of a corps of volunteers, published a volume significantly entitled *Foes of Our Own Household,* which attacked the whole Administration, the worst "foe" being Wilson, and went on a speaking tour, to compare Wilson with the Kaiser. The Republicans in Congress, and some disaffected Democrats, began to call for a coalition government. The chief anti-Wilson Democratic Senators followed the lead of Chamberlain of Oregon, head of the important Military Affairs Committee, in asking for a drastic investigation of the War Department. Secretary Baker's testimony failed to satisfy them, and Senator Chamberlain told a New York meeting, January 19, 1918, that the nation's military establishment had failed "because of inefficiency in every bureau and department of the Government," a charge T. R. indorsed with great vehemence.

The claim is made by William E. Dodd, in his 1921 book on Wilson, that the events described above were part and parcel of a deep-laid plot to set up Theodore Roosevelt as a divider of the power of the Executive. Professor Dodd pictures the ex-President as expecting to become America's Minister of Munitions, on the Lloyd George model, and says that after the New York meeting he came to Washington "to hold court." Under the scheme, as Dodd envisaged it, Congress would pass a bill, over veto if need be, to establish such a position and designate the ex-President to its command.

Earnest efforts to check up on this have brought little confirmation. Dr. Charles E. Merriam, then close to the Roosevelt Progressive movement, feels sure Dodd badly misinterpreted the situation, and Walter S. Rogers agrees. William Allen White, who was then as close to "Teddy" as any man in the country, advised that it was a pipe dream; that while Roosevelt had "swallowed an awful lot of pride" when he went down to the White House to ask the President to send him to Europe at the head of a volunteer force, the thing he and all his friends were interested in just then was to see that he got the 1920 Republican presidential nomination.

Boies Penrose, the Pennsylvania G. O. P. boss, concluded that T. R. alone could win that year and sent word around. In 1918 the Rooseveltians expected to run the next national convention, and Will Hays set up a tentative platform committee under Ogden Mills, much like Spangler's group of 1943. This was the major trend of the Roosevelt people's thinking. Doubtless some hotheads of no great party influence did push the Munitions scheme; but, as the Sage of Emporia says, "Roosevelt was a practical man, and he would have known that to try any such scheme would queer him for 1920 even if it succeeded. . . . His ambition was tempered by craft."

It may have been that Wilson believed such a trick-play was to be tried, for during that month strenuous efforts were made to put a better face on War Department organization for over-all supply. Morris Llewellyn Cooke, a Baker aide, made a reorganization chart.

Soon Edward R. Stettinius was shifted from his post as Director General of Allied Purchasing in America to that of Surveyor General to co-ordinate the multiform procurement, warehousing and transport tasks. Lloyd George cabled congratulations and the press reported it as a great forward step. A little later he was made Assistant Secretary of War. But tough old Goethals did the real job of reforming the War Department, being successively Quartermaster General, Director of Storage and Traffic, and finally Director of Purchases, Storage and Traffic. Morris L. Cooke points out that Goethals functioned very effectively, Stettinius not at all, but the two moves stopped the Chamberlain offensive.

Late in January 1918, the President made a quick flank attack. He said that he had not been consulted about the new Munitions scheme, but that his difficulty was lack of power, and on February 6, 1918, a bill emanating from the White House was introduced. The provisions of this war power bill, while not as far-reaching as are those of the First and Second War Powers Acts of Congress for the present war, met strenuous opposition and many Democratic Senators fought it. But Wilson accepted a number of amendments, never let up his effort, and in May his dour persistence won.

The Act authorized him to make such redistribution of functions among the executive agencies as he should deem necessary; likewise to "utilize, co-ordinate, and consolidate" any executive or administrative commissions, bureaus and agencies then existing by law, and to transfer duties or powers or the personnel from one department to another. If he thought any agency should be abolished, he must report that conclusion to Congress, which would arrange for the transfer of appropriations in the reorganization.

This was an extraordinary commitment of powers by the National Legislature, the like of which Lincoln had never had. The power as well as responsibility was now the President's, and he did not hesitate to use it.

Seeing how Wilson had rehabilitated himself, the Republicans made a supreme effort to undo him in the approaching mid-term national election; if "the good, the rich and the wise" did not now destroy Wilson and "Wilsonism," their once great party might disintegrate like the Federalists or Whigs. Personal piques knelt before party necessities; T. R. and Taft met in a New York hotel and buried the hatchet; Hughes and Hiram Johnson blessed the reunion. The vested interests did not neglect the needed campaign fund, and Will Hays, an exceptionally shrewd political manager, was put at the campaign helm.

Wilson unwillingly shifted his single-track — from the preparatory moves toward peace to the imperative need to retain the Democrats in power. Joe Tumulty, Albert Burleson, Robert Woolley and some other party advisers asked for an appeal to the country for a Democratic Congress. This was in the best Republican tradition; in 1898, during the Spanish-American War, McKinley had pleaded that "this is no time for divided councils," while Theodore Roosevelt had warned that "a refusal to sustain the President" in his Spanish negotiations would be viewed by Europe as "a refusal to sustain the war and to sustain the efforts of the Peace Commission." While House claimed to have opposed, shortly before the election the President appealed to the people to "return a Democratic majority to both the Senate and House of Representatives," because otherwise he could not effectively represent the nation either in domestic or in foreign affairs. "The leaders of the minority," he wrote, "in the present Congress have unquestionably been pro-war, but they have been anti-Administration. The return of a Republican majority in either House of Congress would be interpreted on the other side of the water as a repudiation of my leadership."

This truth proved a tactical blunder: Republicans denounced it as a breach of the party truce. At the election the Republicans won enough new Senators to have a majority of two in that body, while they secured a lead of about thirty in the House.

In all probability, it was not Wilson's appeal, but the general irritation of a civil society unaccustomed to the strait jacket of war, which led to his repudiation. A myriad of regulations had grown irksome; people liked neither "meatless days" nor the emotional pressures of Liberty Loan drives; those with war contracts hated excess profits taxes, those without them blamed the President for the profiteering; the German hyphenates were determined to punish the man who had made war on the Fatherland; the Irish-Americans were bitter because we were associated with the hated Britons; as the Athenians had grown so weary of hearing Aristides called "the Just" that they banished him, the American people had tired of the preaching of morals as the basis of politics, and struck out blindly at Wilson.

It was not an especially novel situation for a President in his second term. As we have seen, Washington's prestige fell so low that the Virginia Legislature refused to pass a mild commendation. Jefferson's last year had been embittered by the repeal of the Embargo; when he reached Charlottesville, he asked ruefully whose ox there he had gored, and never once revisited the National Capital. But in Wilson's case more was at stake than merely his personal power, prestige or pride; more also than the immediate fate of the party he led: the issue at stake was the nature of the peace soon to come.

Two weeks before the German delegates entered Marshal Foch's palace-car to sign the Armistice, Wilson had possessed the ultimate of presidential power. During the half-year preceding, Congress had conferred additional executive authority which caused him to be hailed as "the most powerful ruler in the world." Now he had lost a critical election and his leadership of public opinion was dangerously crippled, at the very time that he most needed a united country behind him.

But it was still said that Woodrow Wilson possessed powers "greater for good or evil than those of any man living." So far, he had used his powers and his personal qualities wisely, decisively, to wage war. How would he use them to wage peace?

CHAPTER XII

But There Was No Peace

The worth of Wilson's qualities never showed more conspicuously than in his conduct of the war. After the Armistice the defect of these qualities was among the causes of the failure to procure a lasting peace. The school of experience could afford today's anxious generation, soon to make its own peace, no more moving lesson than the grandeurs and miseries of a quarter of a century ago. A defect in the Constitution allowing one over a third of the Senate to veto a treaty; personal malice and party bias against a Democratic President; Wilson's loss of leadership at home — these kept the United States out of the League of Nations, and sowed the seed of today's war. That tragic past must not be prologue to our repeating the identical mistakes.

Germany's declaration of war against Russia, August 1, 1914, was a stunning surprise to America. Wilson was little better advised than the intelligent man on the street that the murder of an Austrian archduke by a Serb conspirator would detonate a world conflict. Foreign affairs did not then occupy his single-track mind, he had grudged the attention he had to give the Mexican troubles, and personal attendance at the funeral services of the bluejackets killed at Vera Cruz strengthened the philosophical and moral pacifism at the core of his feeling.

Wilson's conduct during our World War I cannot be understood except in the light of his inner hatred of armed force as the governor of relations between men or States. When his friend Colonel Edward M. House wanted to go abroad, late in 1913, to sound out the top men of Germany, France and Britain on a peace scheme,

Wilson deemed it a good pacific exploration and urged him on. This interesting bit of amateur diplomacy, in the issue unimportant, illustrated Wilson's true passion for peace.

We must ponder the enigma of Mr. House of Texas, whose influence on the President was undoubtedly great — although how great, and how and why derived, are still debated. The casual reader of the declarations of those who assert House's greatness might conclude that, in the true sense of the word, he was the real President from March 5, 1913 until Wilson left Paris in June six years later. Some partisans of President Wilson give the impression that the will and the decision were always his; that House's chief role was that of a pleasant, industrious contact man and information specialist, a moon who delightedly reflected the sunlight of our Chief of State.

House, who had an independent fortune, relished a backstage importance in politics. Texans who didn't like him, like Senator Joe Bailey, termed him a "chinless wonder," and his most recent biographer, Arthur D. Howden Smith, states that "oddly enough, he had almost no chin — and yet no man ever lived who had a more iron will." Thomas B. Love, not House, introduced Wilson to the Texas Democracy; while House had had considerable part in the pre-convention campaign, he was not the undisputed father of the event; perhaps his chief service was with Bryan before Baltimore. The Colonel, who disliked the Governor's staff title, was en route to Europe during the convention struggle. He termed his relations with Wilson "the perfect friendship." Perhaps its principal foundations were a compatibility of intellectual interests and attitudes, and the even more important fact that he did not argue with the President, but expressed dissent by silence; the inference is that he expected any lack of comment upon a Wilsonian view to act as a dash of cold water upon the mind and mood of that self-confident man.

House's great talent was as a compromiser, a good Anglo-Saxon trait of give-and-take rather than fighting to the bitter end. Inasmuch as the Scots and the Scotch-Irish have less of this instinctive zeal for action by non-sequiturs, it may be wondered that Wilson put up with the way his lieutenant affixed wooden handle to pewter spoon. But the time was to come, after the President returned to France in March 1919, when he could endure it no longer. Mrs. Wilson, in *My Memoir,* quotes her husband's agonized remark that "House has given away everything I had won before we left Paris. He has compromised on every side, and so I have to start all over again. . . . He has yielded until there is nothing left."

Americans have difficulty in determining the influence of a presidential favorite. Doubtless Washington had one in Hamilton, but he was of the official family. Jackson had several, among whom Van Buren, "the Little Magician," was most important. Lincoln liked court jesters or retainers, but never gave his full confidence to any man. It is not until we get to McKinley and Hanna that we find any precedent for the relation of Wilson and House, or Franklin Roosevelt and Hopkins. Hanna made McKinley President, and often dominated that weak but lovable man's conduct of the office. But Hanna was of independent stature and power, while House, like Hopkins, was a treasured friend who seldom crossed his President. Without House, there is not much doubt that there still would have been a Wilson in the White House and an America in the World War. Without Wilson, perhaps House would have found another fount of satisfaction. It would seem a mistake to attribute to his influence every excellent course Wilson followed, and to its waning the Treaty's ill fate in the Senate.

A few days after the war broke out in Europe, the President issued a formal proclamation of neutrality, but went further in an appeal to the people to remain "neutral in thought as well as deed." This phrase raised no tumult at the time, but left a sour taste with the Allies, and later was to plague Wilson at home. Dodd advances the theory that Wilson, conscious of his difficulty as a minority President in carrying through his domestic reforms, did not wish to pronounce judgment upon the belligerents' motives lest this rouse new enmities at home. Some deem it evidence of lack of interest in foreign affairs, but probably it was one of many instances of his fatal felicity in phrase-making; later "watchful waiting," "too proud to fight," and "peace without victory" were to shift attention from his general proposition to attack upon the isolated phrase.

The President was soon confronted with the involvement of American interests, first because of the British blockade, not long later because of Germany's submarine campaign. Britain's greatest weapon was the blockade, which she employed ruthlessly, as Lincoln had in the Civil War — a precedent the British kept hurling in our face when we objected to their expansion of the contraband list, and their doctrine of continuous voyage and ultimate destination. The President insisted on "the freedom of the seas," in order to check interference with our trade to Holland and the Scandinavian neutrals, at the time virtual funnels to Germany. Secretary of State Bryan agreed completely with his chief in the vigor of protest, but the British Admiralty would not loose its clutch on supplies to the enemy, whatever the effect on our export of cotton and grain. Eventually the President found that our mid-Continent folk did not understand the implications of "freedom of the seas"; the appeal to make the world safe for democracy was his efficient substitute for the earlier and narrower appeal.

Germany undertook to "blockade" Britain and France through submarines, which seldom went through the formalities of warning, but sank merchantmen on sight. Scores of Americans were lost when the *Lusitania* went down, May 7, 1915, and a wave of anger swept over our people. In his insistent protest, Wilson differentiated sharply between human rights and property rights — so much so, in fact, that the peace-loving Bryan resigned over the language of an early draft of the first note. In an extraordinarily patient but unyielding series of notes, the President forced the German Government to pledge that ships would not be sunk without warning.

Ex-President Taft and others in the League to Enforce Peace won more and more support for their thesis. Wilson gave it indorsement May 27, 1916, in a speech which stressed the need for "an universal association of nations to maintain the inviolate security of the highways of the seas"; and to "prevent any war begun either contrary to treaty covenants, or without warning and full submission of the causes to the opinion of the world."

Nevertheless the course of the struggle during 1915-1916 made it plain that unless peace could be made, the United States almost surely would be forced into the war. As has been noted, never once during the 1916 re-election campaign did Wilson pledge to keep us out regardless of German injury to our national interests. From a surface standpoint, our relations with Berlin between June and December 1916 were good, but William Allen White and others came to the opinion that the President had made up his mind so to conduct our neutrality that, at the end, America would be on the side of the Allies.

His conscience, however, was concerned over the slogan "He kept us out of war," and he made a desperate effort to procure peace. Although the military stalemate in the west and the Rumanian overthrow late in 1916 favored the Central Powers, Wilson's concept of the machinery for an enduring peace involved a concert of strong powers to enforce it. But his overtures to von Bernstorff, the Kaiser's Ambassador at Washington, found no response, and Berlin rushed in with a peace offer through the Pope, actually a victor's peace, which the Allies refused.

Wilson then asked all belligerents for a public statement of their war aims. On January 22, 1917, he told Congress and the world that it must be a "peace without victory." He would extend the principles of the Monroe Doctrine to the whole world, "that no nation should seek to extend its policy over any other nation or people." He insisted that there was no "entangling alliance" in the keeping of peace through a concert of power; "when all unite in the same sense and with the same purpose, all act in the common interest and are free to live their lives under a common protection."

Allied opinion did not like the idea of peace without victory, but already it was a moot point; three days after Wilson's speech von Bernstorff told House that the struggle inside Germany between civil and military authority had been decided: "the military have complete control." On January 31, 1917, the Ambassador delivered formal notification that the 1916 pledge was withdrawn, and that unrestricted U-boat warfare would begin the next day. Wilson promptly ordered von Bernstorff's passports.

General von Ludendorff, General von Hindenburg and Admiral von Tirpitz had, indeed, determined on a fatal gamble to starve England into defeat. The decision was based on two grave errors. One of judgment: the Potsdam Crown Council expected the United States to declare war, but not to get into it efficiently, so that the Allies would be starved out in three months. The second was of ignorance: despite her amazing secret service, the German Government did not realize the imminence of the Russian Revolution, which broke out just six weeks later. Had Germany kept her *Sussex* pledge, such a determined pacifist as Wilson might not have brought America into the war. Without our millions on the Western Front, the Hohenzollern victory would have been assured. But Fate, Chance or Stupidity willed otherwise.

The President refused to go to war on the German note, and hoped no "overt act" would make war inescapable; but overt acts came, in abundant measure. Although he termed the Senate filibusterers "a little group of willful men" for stopping the passage of a bill to arm our merchantmen for defense, and as Commander in Chief put armed guards on the ships, at the same time he was wrestling with his hatred of war. At a Cabinet meeting, March 20, 1917, Burleson said that the people wanted the country to go into the war actively. Wilson replied that it did not make so much difference what the people wished as what was right. A few days later he asked, in anguish: "What else can I do? Is there anything else I can do?"

Nothing there was. On April 2, 1917, he appeared before a special session of the new Congress, to call for a war to make the world safe for democracy, a war in which the United States would "omit no word or deed" for victory. Four days later, Congress declared the existence of a state of war with Germany.

* * *

Wilson's war service was conspicuously successful. As Commander in Chief he did not follow the Lincoln example. Familiar as a historian with the latter's intervention in picking generals and planning campaigns, he avoided making identical mistakes. He would not yield to political pressure on top-flight Army appointments. Theodore Roosevelt was wild to lead a corps of volunteers in France, the Allies sent their blessing, but Pershing feared divided command and urged that he not be sent. When T. R. called at the White House, Wilson told him Pershing's attitude and refused to send him, and for the same reason he would not give Leonard Wood an A. E. F. command. Nor did he interfere in the details of Pershing's battle plans.

He pressed for unity of command even before the Italian debacle at Caporetto, sent House as his alternate on the Supreme War Council, and General Tasker H. Bliss, a truly wise mind, as military representative. After Germany's near break-through in March 1918, he backed Foch's selection as commander on the Western Front, though consistently sustaining Pershing in maintaining the integrity of the A. E. F.

Among the most interesting and timely of his employments of war powers was the taking over of the nation's railroads in December 1917. Our rail transportation had broken down under war loads; shop and other expert labor was being drained off to war industries which had better wage rates, bad-order car and motive-power situations grew appalling. But private management took no major steps to unsnarl the tangle, so the President had to act.

He asked the Attorney General whether he had power to take over the roads. Gregory said he had power to demand priorities but not to take full control. "What do you think I ought to do?" asked the President. Gregory answered that this was a question of policy as well as law. "Do you think the successful prosecution of the war depends upon taking over the railroads?" Wilson continued, and on affirmative answer declared: "Then I think I should do it, and then go to Congress for legislation." This he did: McAdoo became Director General of the United States Railroad Administration.

With his genius in picking good lieutenants and inspiring administrative accomplishment, things soon began to straighten out.

A second important co-ordinating action was the establishment of the War Industries Board. Bernard M. Baruch soon took it in hand, gathering good lieutenants, and it co-ordinated and quickened our war production. The President gave what guidance and direction he could to these enterprises, and to their counterparts in food, fuel, and other fields, though his principal role was in the selection of the head men for the new agencies. He was handed several "gold bricks," who eventually were gotten out; but in the main the dollar-a-year men handled their powers in the public interest. There is general testimony of the way he stood behind his men.

Even more resultful was Wilson's work in the field of public opinion — not only in the United States, where he campaigned over a familiar terrain, but even more so among the peoples of the enemy nations, with whom his methods have never been equaled. Not Wilson the President but Wilson the genius of persuasion did this job. He made words into weapons, and it is not too much to say that he did as much as, if not more than, Marshal Foch to bring Germany to her knees.

Walter S. Rogers, whose part in 1913 press relations has been noted, was in the Far East in the winter and spring of 1917, and on returning told Wilson that if he wished to appeal to the masses of the people of the world, he had failed to do so, because of the lack of machinery to disseminate the text of what he had to say. In Shanghai, for example, a paper had printed in parallel columns extracts from his January speech provided by British and German news sources, under the caption: "What Did the President Really Say?" If the President wished the actual texts sent throughout the world, they must be distributed quick enough to reach the newspaper offices before isolated extracts from news agencies and correspondents.

A few hours before Wilson was ready to make his speech on the Fourteen Points, in January 1918, he asked Rogers to arrange for the prompt world-wide distribution of its text, but no message was to start moving until he began to speak. By extraordinary exertion, this was done and the message of over four thousand words was published in extras in Tokyo as soon as in those of New York.

For the first time in history the world read a message simultaneously, and the President was one of the first to grasp the event's significance. Thereafter presidential and other American government statements of great moment were made textually available almost simultaneously to the press of the world.

Not without reason this pressure behind the Fourteen Point Speech, for this charter for a new world insisted on justice for small nations, self-determination for enslaved peoples, the freedom of the seas, arbitration before war, open covenants in place of secret treaties. It wreaked havoc on the German spirit. Airplanes scattered leaflets of his speeches over Germany, much more destructive to morale than high-explosive shell or mustard gas.

The effect of this crusade was indescribable. The minor Central Powers began plotting for peace. The Turks were ready to quit late in 1917, but the British wanted to punish rather than to bribe them. The Hapsburgs had had enough; Francis Joseph had died, Charles clung to the tottering throne, his Prime Minister went secretly to Switzerland to propose to George D. Herron, a special agent sent there for the purpose, the establishment of a federalized United States of Austria, but the plan was betrayed to Berlin. The British blockade, which planted famine through the Fatherland; the new legions at Château-Thierry and Saint-Mihiel; and Wilson, the soldier of the spirit — these three forces won the war.

The end came with startling swiftness. Bulgaria surrendered in September, Ludendorff concluded there was no hope, and on October 5, 1918, the Kaiser's government asked President Wilson for an armistice. Suspecting German good faith, the President asked the new Chancellor, Prince Max of Baden, whether his government accepted the Fourteen Points and his companion statements of the essentials of an enduring peace. Max agreed, and later declared that his plea for armistice and peace came from a government "which is free from any arbitrary and irresponsible influence, and is supported by the approval of an overwhelming majority of the German people." Then the President communicated the entire correspondence to the Allied governments, from whom he sought pledges that the Fourteen Points should be the foundation for the armistice.

During these many-angled negotiations with Berlin, London, Paris and Rome, he committed the fatal blunder of telling the American people the unvarnished truth: that he needed and wanted a new Congress that would support him in the peace so soon to be made. Aided by House, the President obtained the pledges of the Allies, except that Britain reserved and qualified "the freedom of the seas." Wilson in turn agreed to the doctrine that "compensation will be made by Germany for all damage done to the civilian population of the Allies and their property by the aggression of Germany by land, by sea and from the air." After these interchanges, "the Allied and Associated Governments" turned the making of military terms over to the generals and admirals.

"The Armistice," announced the President, November 11, 1918, "was signed this morning. Everything for which America fought has been accomplished. It will now be our fortunate duty to assist by example, by sober, friendly counsel and by material aid in the establishment of just democracy throughout the world."

A few days later, however, Theodore Roosevelt publicly warned that "our allies and our enemies and Mr. Wilson himself should all understand that Mr. Wilson has no authority whatever to speak for the American people at this time. His leadership has just been emphatically repudiated by them . . . and all his utterances every which way have ceased to have any shadow of right to be accepted as expressive of the will of the American people."

"Onward, Christian soldiers," or "Abide with Me"? — this was Wilson's first peacemaking problem. The Peace Conference was tentatively set to open in Paris December 17, 1918; should he attend it in person, or remain in Washington, influencing it as best he could from the end of a cable?

Had he done the latter, the delegation would have had to contain important public figures — such as ex-President Taft, Elihu Root, Nicholas Murray Butler or George W. Wickersham; he would be expected to send some Senators, as McKinley had; already there was pressure to choose his bitter personal enemy and political foe, Henry Cabot Lodge. The Massachusetts Senator, already slated for chairmanship of the Committee on Foreign Relations, had at one time favored a league. But two days after Wilson accepted the league principle in his address of January 22, 1917, Lodge recanted his support. Even more determinative of the President's decision were his suspicions, in which House joined, that the Allied chiefs had had their fingers crossed when they agreed to the Fourteen Points as armistice basis. Knowing that the principal European statesmen held him in slight regard, he determined to attend in person, to prevent a peace of revenge.

Was it a wise decision? Both Colonel House and Secretary Lansing, poles apart in purpose and policy, tried to prevent it; and, after the event, termed it a mistake. Birdsall, in his thoughtful *Versailles Twenty Years After,* suggests that probably "each man, in the assurance of his own superior wisdom, felt confident of exercising greater influence in Wilson's absence." William Allen White, himself in Paris, deemed the first trip definitely advantageous, the second one a mistake.

Examination of the details of the Conference reveals that, had he not gone both times, the Versailles Treaty would have been worse. He stepped off the pedestal, he made mistakes, but he remains the only man of real statesmanship at Paris, with General Smuts his nearest counterpart.

In addition to House and Bliss, already in Europe with the Supreme War Council, he put Robert Lansing and Henry White on the delegation. The former must have been chosen because of his office, for he had little emotional sympathy with the President and the latter paid him little heed in Paris. White was a Republican, a distinguished diplomat who knew the chancelleries of Europe intimately, although he had little political weight at home. The delegation was to be serviced by a body of experts in whom the President had real confidence. Set up by Wilson and House in 1917, under the mysterious title of "The Inquiry," it was completely dissociated from the State Department. The college faculties were searched for men with backgrounds of specific knowledge pertinent to the peacemaking task. And the resultant group contained men who knew the facts and the historical background of such points of dispute as Fiume, the Saar Basin, Shantung. Inasmuch as the United States desired neither new territory nor special trade advantages, these experts could focus on finding the facts, and some glimmering of the truth behind the facts, about each particular problem in the mosaic of peace.

It would seem unfortunate that, before leaving for Europe, Wilson did not tell the American people the reasons why he found it necessary to lead the delegation. Some with foresight, and many later with hindsight, felt that he could and should have taken the American people into his confidence, admitted that he was none too sure of the professions of the Allies, and had therefore determined to go abroad to fight for the right sort of peace. He could have revealed the agreed plan for a prompt preliminary peace, to enable Europe to get promptly to her immense task of relief and reconstruction, and that this would be followed by definitive treaties fixing boundaries, imposing penalties and providing a League to preserve the peace. But on departure he said nothing other than the commonplace.

When Wilson reached Paris on December 14, 1918, the people went into transports of delight, and he steeled himself to maintain his poise. Major Oliver Newman tells of his remarking, that first night, "I don't want to see the devastated regions . . . I don't want to get mad. I want to keep my temper and my reason. I think there ought to be *one* man at the Peace Table who isn't angry, who isn't consumed by hatred and desire for revenge."

It has been said that since the days of Peter the Hermit no man born of woman ever had such hold on human hearts as Wilson in that first month. During the delay in starting the Conference, he visited both Italy and England, where he made an address in Carlisle, his mother's birthplace, saying that he was not important as a man but as a representative of an ideal: Faith in humanity, faith in the moral government of the universe, faith in the power of the spiritual forces of life to triumph over the material powers that be. He told them, "It is moral force as much as physical force that has defeated the efforts to subdue the world."

Just the same, the Peace Conference did not begin on schedule. Some American newspapermen in Paris believed that the Allied chiefs deliberately stalled off the opening session, so that enthusiasm for Wilson could die down before they began to talk terms. The true reason, it seems, was that the war ended so much ahead of expectation that the preliminary spadework could not be done in time. At any event, the first meeting did not come until January 12, 1919, and the first plenary session six days later.

Two worlds came into conflict in Paris. There was the old world, represented by Georges Clemenceau; by Orlando, the dull but greedy Italian Premier; by Lloyd George, the extraordinarily clairvoyant Welshman who had won the war for Britain, but then had precipitated a "khaki election," which he won on the theme of forcing the last farthing from the Hun. These men did not believe in fairies, but looked to the past: There always had been wars and there always would be; after they had made a hard peace, Wilson could have his League. Although each country had a group of League advocates — Cecil for Britain, Bourgeois for France — they did not make the decisions that counted.

Britain wanted trade, commercial advantage, control of the seas. Wilson must pay her price, and abandon freedom of the seas in war, if he expected her on his side in the League argument. France's demands were more directly selfish; this nation of forty millions had one of seventy millions pressing on her western borders. Of course she would take back Alsace and Lorraine, but in addition she wanted to annex the region right up to the Rhine, and to break the rest of the Reich into little bits. She wanted money and materials to repair her devastated regions, from a Germany handcuffed forever. Poor in natural resources, and teeming with under-employed manpower, Italy wanted coal from the Ruhr, food from the Danube basin, a large cash subsidy from the foe, Fiume and other bits of "Italia Irredenta." Then there was Japan. In 1917, Wilson had been forced to join in an Allied expedition to Siberia, because otherwise Japan would have done it alone. Now she wanted to break up China and, at the very minimum, to hold Shantung.

With expectation rather than tradition, America believed in a world of good will rather than one of dog-eat-dog. Wilson represented her philosophy of hope, of belief in the future, one of the major elements that had made America. He came to Europe determined to see that it had a chance.

The conference must solve seven major problems: the Covenant for a League of Nations; French security and the fixing of Germany's eastern and western frontiers; reparations; Italian claims; Japanese claims; the boundaries for the new nations; and the Russian turmoil. It divided into special committees, President Wilson being made Chairman of that on the League.

He found it hard to function as he had in the White House. His role of Chief of State, or Sovereign, was in eclipse when he stepped down to daily intimate discussions with premiers and foreign ministers. Clemenceau termed him a man of *"noble candeur,"* a French form of Simple Simon. He was not used to dealing on equal terms with associates, and often roiled them by his bearing and way of speech. On occasion both Lloyd George and Lord Robert Cecil boiled with rage.

The delay in opening the sessions, and then the tedious spadework of the Committees, took much time; and then the Conference was frozen by interminable debates in which every delegate must make his set speech. At length a Council of Ten was set up to make things move, but even ten were too many for quick action. A Big Four replaced it — Wilson, Clemenceau, Lloyd George and Orlando.

For the first month, the President put most of his evenings on the construction of the detailed plan for the League. But during the day he did not hesitate to oppose a separate Rhenish State, French seizure of the Saar, and other unfair treaty provisions. The League Covenant his committee turned out was, in structure, a reasonably efficient instrument. Just before he departed on a brief visit to America, February 14, 1919, to check on conditions at home — the old Congress would adjourn March 3 — the conference unanimously approved and adopted his proposed Covenant, and agreed to make it an integral part of the Treaty.

As he left, House urged the President to be open and persuasive with the Senate, particularly with Lodge and the Committee on Foreign Relations, to which Wilson assented. When the Colonel continued that he and the delegation could "button up" everything before the President's return through compromises of detail, not principle, he noted that Wilson seemed "startled and even alarmed." But the leave-taking was affectionate.

The President's visit was not a success. The real skill he had showed at Paris in conciliation did not carry through in America. The public needed education on the necessity for a League, but Wilson misjudged its mood, and was too confident. He invited the Senate and House Committees on Foreign Relations to dinner at the White House, and John James Rogers, a Massachusetts Republican Representative, found his charm quite refreshing. But during the evening Lodge would not utter a word, ask a question, or take any part in the discussion, Knox followed the same course, and Borah would not even attend. Wilson's final speech in New York, before leaving for Paris, was unfortunate. The day before, opposing Senators had published a round robin, demanding that peace be made and the League postponed. This provoked Wilson to say he would bring back League and Treaty so intertwined that it would be impossible to separate them. Despite the provocation, this alienated much middle-of-the-road opinion. He would have been wiser to have refrained from proclaiming his justified purpose.

Should Wilson have gone back to Paris? William Allen White termed the return a mistake of the first magnitude. He argued that the Allied leaders at Paris knew of the disaffection in America — more than a third of the Senators had signed the round robin about reservations, to serve notice to Paris. Perhaps Wilson as a persuader in Washington, rather than a crusader abroad, might have been of more net worth to ratification. But the Treaty had not been made, and he went back to see that it was properly done.

Note has been taken of the displeasure with which he received House's recital on his landing at Brest March 13, 1919. Ray Stannard Baker declares House let the President down. "While it is too much to say that there was a direct plot, while Wilson was away, to kill the League, or even cut it out of the Treaty, one can affirm with certainty that there was an intrigue against his plan of a preliminary military and naval peace — which would have indirectly produced the same results."

At any event, Wilson knew that the Senate reservationists had meant business about the Monroe Doctrine. This had been in the people's bloodstream for a century, the phrase was among their household gods, and the country would go along with the Senate in rejecting a covenant which did not exclude any Monroe Doctrine involvement from among the concerns of non-American nations. Ex-President Taft, leading figure in the League to Enforce Peace, canvassed the Republican Senators, and cabled Wilson that three changes must be made in the Treaty for it to win Senate acceptance: the League must keep hands off the Monroe Doctrine; it must exclude our domestic laws and policies, such as immigration and tariff, from League concerns; and must provide for the withdrawal of any member State.

House agreed, as did Lord Cecil; Wilson at first thought concessions would be taken as a sign of weakness, but then determined to get them made. The League of Nations Commission was reconvened and held five sessions between March 22 and April 11, the Conference's most critical period. These amendment pearls were of great price; old French, British and Italian demands were exhumed and new ones presented. Lloyd George and Clemenceau saw the chance to better their bargaining position because of Wilson's dire need. The amendment as to domestic legislation gave no trouble, and withdrawal after two years' notice finally prevailed; but the Monroe Doctrine change brought a crisis.

David Hunter Miller was ready to present the draft amendment to the Commission March 24, but had word to refrain because of high political difficulties. The French were pressing their extreme demands on Rhineland, Saar, Polish corridor and Silesia, reparations to include indemnity, and Wilson was resisting point by point. In the Saar argument, March 28, the Tiger accused him of being a pro-German, and the President asked: "Do you wish me to return home?" Wilson unburdened himself to three of his experts: "I do not know whether I shall see M. Clemenceau again.... In fact, I do not know whether the Peace Conference will continue."

Lloyd George made this the occasion to levy blackmail by objecting to the Monroe Doctrine amendment — seemingly because it localized the scope of the League, but actually in order to club Wilson into agreeing to limit American naval expansion, so that Britain would remain mistress of the seas. Wilson was willing to negotiate ratios on future construction but not to abandon or modify the country's immediate program — even for the Monroe Doctrine amendment.

Between April 3 and April 8, a serious influenza attack put the President to bed. During this time French intransigence over the Rhineland reached such a peak that Lloyd George abandoned his blackmail, and the morning of April 7, Wilson ordered the *George Washington* brought to Brest to take him back to America. House, on the other hand, went with the French; the way he yielded to their reparations program and urged acquiescence as to Rhineland and Saar led Ray Stannard Baker to say that the Colonel "would make peace quickly by giving the greedy ones all they want."

Wilson attended a League Commission session April 10, and offered the Monroe Doctrine amendment to Article X, which, the French stormed, would destroy their security; but on Cecil's suggestion it was adopted, as Article XXI. The next day Bourgeois frankly told an American the French "did not care anything about their amendment . . . but simply that it was a good thing to trade with."

Here was the major crisis of the Conference, from Wilson's standpoint. Clemenceau's lieutenants on the League Commission noted reservations to the new Article XXI, just so as to have a bomb to throw if need arose. The President's call for the *George Washington* showed him of more than half a mind to go home and denounce the European statesmen as evil old men who had sold mankind down the river. Old Hickory might have done so; but Woodrow Wilson, who was more debater than gladiator, thought there was a gambling chance to redeem the peace, and he liked nothing better than venturing his all on a chance.

Safeguarding the Monroe Doctrine through Article XXI would complete the purge which, according to Taft, would insure Senate consent. Suppose he stayed in Paris, yielded a little on territorial and reparations items, would these really matter in comparison with the elixir of the League? Wilson decided that he would neither depart nor surrender. He would make the Tiger and the Welshman pay for every concession, while eventually the League would cleanse the Treaty of sin. It was a momentous decision; despite the fact that Article XXVI — the amending mechanism of the Covenant — was unworkable, a strait jacket rather than his hoped-for "vehicle of life," it might have proved the right one, if only America had entered the League.

Finis had already been written to any hope for a preliminary peace. The French legal expert Fromageot had the military terms ready, soon after Wilson's return from America, and asked the Supreme Council to rule whether they would be for immediate execution by the Germans, or final conditions of peace. Wilson had regarded the military convention as temporary; if it had to go to the Senate, he admitted, it would take months for consent. When this shocked Balfour, the President consulted the American delegation, which agreed "that the preliminary peace was in reality a complete and final declaration of peace which would have to be ratified by all contracting States."

During these tense weeks, Wilson did nothing dramatic to rally his followers across the Atlantic; perhaps he felt that work on the Treaty was the best way. And work he did — "the hardest-working man at the Conference" was the general remark. As in January he had resisted the greedy Hughes of Australia, over outright annexation of the Pacific Islands, so now he stopped France from annexing the Saar, and put her exploitation of its coal — a just reparation — under the League, until a plebiscite fifteen years later. The greedy Poles should have the Corridor, but German-populated Danzig would become a Free City under a League Commissioner, and Silesia be divided after a plebiscite. He turned his face firmly against Italian demands for Fiume, and the withdrawal of Orlando and Sonnino in March did not soften his veto.

Japan's great insistence was that Shantung, which Germany had seized from China and Japan had then captured, be transferred direct to her. The Japanese had already asked and been refused a statement in the Covenant preamble of equality among races. When the Italians left Paris over the question of Fiume, Japan threatened to quit the Conference unless one or the other of her demands were met to save her face. Wilson feared a second secession would kill both Treaty and League and, after forcing Japan's direct promise to get out after five years, yielded the point.

A little later the Italians came back to Paris without having gained Fiume by their dramatic withdrawal late in March. The incident showed the President's effort to apply his experience to his novel problems. His method of leading Congress through focusing public opinion on recalcitrants had worked in America. Italy's insistence on Fiume was stark greed: even the secret Treaty of London which brought her into the war had not promised it, and Clemenceau and Lloyd George privately lauded Wilson's fight. But he had only two weapons of compulsion: return to America or appeal to the people. He chose the latter and appealed to the Italians as a part of the world community of common interest. The effort fell flat, for a reason Hamilton had once pointed out in the *Federalist:* the forces of localism can almost always overpower those of general good. Wilson had even less chance to purge Orlando from Italian power than Franklin Roosevelt had to persuade the Georgia Democrats to retire Walter George. Wilson won momentarily — Italy did not get Fiume by treaty; but the powers did nothing to repair the ensuing rape by D'Annunzio.

To John Maynard Keynes, Fiume as well as the Saar illustrated Wilson's paucity of resource in negotiation. While "he could dig in his toes and refuse to budge," he had no other weapon, and seldom has a statesman of the first rank been "more incompetent in the agilities of the council chamber," or less sensitive to changes in environment. It was killing work, especially as he did not, perhaps could not, use the wealth of informed knowledge of the experts at his disposal, because he didn't have time or patience to hear them. His habit of reading memoranda rather than listening to verbal approximations also hurt him, for a truly great Chief of State must learn to play by ear as well as by note. Both L. G. and the Tiger did so; Wilson fitfully read the score.

The concluding scene represented, in some ways, the greatest triumph of his life — the unanimous adoption by the Conference of the Covenant of the League. The spectacle took place in the Salon des Horologues, in the French Foreign Office. The atmosphere was artificial, from the pot-bellied cupids and leering bacchantes on the walls to the bald-headed old men who sat around the huge table. Wilson rose, read the Covenant with deliberate lack of drama, gave asides that explained certain clauses, and moved its adoption by that plenary session. One by one the delegations responded, and without dissenting voice the League was embedded in the Treaty.

The Germans were not brought to Versailles to receive the Treaty until May 7, 1919, when they took it to Berlin to consider, and did not sign for several weeks. Finally, on June 28, their delegates returned, and the Treaty was signed. As in February, House urged the President, ready to return to Washington, to meet the Senate in a conciliatory spirit. "I have found," the latter replied, "one can never get anything in this life that is worth while without fighting for it." House replied that Anglo-Saxon civilization had been built on compromise. The two men never met again.

Wilson carried back to America his League inseparably intertwined with the Treaty. He expected the Covenant to persuade the acceptance of the Peace Treaty; but the outcome was precisely the reverse. Wilson realized that the Treaty must get a two-thirds Senate vote, but his indignation at the groups which barred his path kept conciliation from guiding his course. The unruly demons of the subconscious often overpower the guards which reason posts over man's conscious mind.

The new Senate had been organized by the Republicans, through a two-vote majority, one of the two being Newberry, of Michigan, who had been elected by dubious means, and later resigned to escape being chased out. But his temporary presence made Lodge chairman of the Committee on Foreign Relations, and set the stage for the Treaty fight.

No longer was Colonel Roosevelt chief among the leaders of the opposition, for he had died in January. Only five days earlier, however, he had written the *New York Tribune:* "For Heaven's sake never allude to Wilson as an idealist. . . . He is a doctrinaire when he can be so with safety to his personal ambition, and he is always utterly and coldly selfish." This did not mean Roosevelt repudiation of the league idea. His last article for the *Kansas City Star,* printed after his death, remarked that "we all of us earnestly desire" a league, but only "wish to be sure that it will help and not hinder the cause of world peace and justice."

But as months passed, an active hatred for Wilson the man came to pervade most Republican politicians, especially in the Senate, where they wanted to hurt him — if possible without hurting world peace, but if necessary letting it pay the price of his sponsorship. And for the first time the President faced audiences which sought to insult him: Irish-American zealots of the Sinn-Fein persuasion, to whom an ounce of Britain outweighed all else; German-Americans, who wouldn't understand Wilson's efforts in Paris to keep their Fatherland from being drawn and quartered; passionate idealists, who shuddered at the Shantung compromise. For each, one issue was enough.

Not long after Wilson reached Washington, he became embittered at the way Senator after Senator deserted the Covenant. He lost the lightness of his Irish blood; a Scottish grimness took command, and a good part of the public concluded that his just determination had been transmuted into petty obstinacy. He did not sense the public's sharp emotional release, the rebound from idealism to "Back to Normalcy," nor did he give due weight to the Treaty's impact on American liberal opinion.

In August he confidently took the cause to the people. As he sped West, the President found his audiences less responsive than formerly, and grew bitter. His health was breaking. California seemed more sympathetic; he started back East with more confidence, but in Pueblo, Colorado, he shed almost a flood of tears. The breakdown had begun; further engagements were canceled, and he was rushed to the White House. In October a stroke affected Wilson's left side.

The Treaty still lay before the Senate awaiting action, but Wilson had practically no contact with the office, duties and powers of the President. Rumors spread that he had gone mad, and the Senate buzzed with scandalous innuendo.

In an institutional sense, this illness was the most significant thing that happened to the Presidency during Wilson's eight years. The Constitution provides that, in case of the President's "inability to discharge the powers and duties of the said office, the same shall devolve on the Vice President . . . and such officer shall act until the disability be removed."

Yet until December 1918, the associates of a live President in government had never faced such a situation. But Wilson left for Paris — amid Republican challenges of the constitutionality of his continuing as President while on a long stay abroad, because, as George W. Wickersham said, he could not "fitly discharge those duties" if out of the country. Wickersham thought they should devolve on the Vice President, but did not know the steps "to set the Vice President in motion." Thomas R. Marshall at once said he would not take over presidential functions on his own motion; he did not know what he would do if Congress adopted a joint resolution directing him; if a court with jurisdiction ordered him, he would.

Ex-President Taft thereupon defended Wilson's course, because "There is no constitutional inhibition, express or implied, to prevent the President's going abroad to discharge a function clearly given him by the Constitution." He could perform all his executive duties from Paris by cable. "Our Constitution is great in its elastic character and in its adapting itself to the changing and varying needs of the unseen future. No other executive is forbidden to leave the country. Kings do it; premiers do it; why should we infer such a restriction when it is not expressed?" Congressional Republicans introduced resolutions providing devolution on Marshall; these were hotly debated but never came to a vote. While in Paris, the President signed many measures, having ruled that the ten-day limit did not begin until the bill was physically in his presence. He accepted McAdoo's resignation as Director General of the Railroad Administration, and named Walker D. Hines as successor; sought appropriations to feed Europe's starving millions; and on his second trip called the new Congress in special session and sent it a message. No real effort was made to interfere with his full control of the office and powers of the President.

The illness brought a renewal of this talk of removal of power to act. By inference, the clause was made to care for situations in which the President could not "take care that the laws be faithfully executed" and perform others of his directly committed duties as Chief of Government. But now he was closely guarded from outside contacts. Mrs. Wilson undertook to bring matters to his attention, as did Admiral Grayson. Both made it a rule never to admit anyone who would upset him, and neither had the political intuition to know when and for whom to make an exception. This was true even in the case of Earl Grey, for whom Wilson had the highest respect, and who had been sent to the United States as a Special Ambassador to inform the President that the British Government would accept the Lodge reservations. After cooling his heels at the British Embassy for three months, he recrossed the Atlantic without ever having been admitted to Wilson's bedside.

For a time, after the first stroke, Wilson was physically unable to sign his name, but Mrs. Wilson and the Admiral "assisted" his faltering fingers. She relates in her memoirs having consulted a famous Philadelphia neurologist, Dr. Francis X. Dercum, as to the state of the President's mental faculties, and was told that he was in full possession of his senses. House is said to have written urging the President to resign. Vice President Thomas R. Marshall was told that it was his duty to act; but, after consideration, declined to take any initiative. It was suggested to Secretary Lansing that he initiate legal proceedings. This would have involved his submitting the situation to the Attorney General, who then would have presented a statement of fact to the Supreme Court, for its determination of the course to be pursued. Attorney General Gregory was never officially consulted.

The Senate's Committee on Foreign Relations undertook to discover whether or not the President was sane. The subcommittee which went to the White House was made up of Albert Fall of New Mexico, a Republican isolationist — later famous for other traits; and Gilbert M. Hitchcock, a loyal pro-Treaty Democrat from Nebraska. The President greeted them with a half hour of spirited, intelligent talk, and they reported that he was completely sane.

But from the practical standpoint, the executive government lacked a co-ordinating tie. The President's Cabinet is an informal and unofficial body without status in Constitution or law, and exists only at the pleasure of the President. The Vice President as such has no administrative or co-ordinating function. Under the law of presidential succession, after the Vice President comes the Secretary of State, the President's senior constitutional adviser. Lansing had never been a familiar of Wilson's, but during the illness, perhaps because of importunities from some other heads of departments, he called some Cabinet meetings for the discussion of administration. As soon as Wilson learned of this, he dictated a curt note dismissing Lansing, and Bainbridge Colby took the helm at the Department of State.

Wilson's health and strength slowly recovered. After about six weeks of crisis, he was able to sign a few bills or documents unaided. But it was a long time before those who guarded his recovery were willing to have unpleasant matters brought to his bedside. Probably Wilson's weakness actually deprived the United States of a chief executive for two or three months.

During this crisis, without White House leadership, the Senate prepared to act on the Treaty. Its members eventually ranged themselves into four groups. At one extreme were the "Isolationists," of whom Borah, Johnson, Knox, and Brandegee were the chief; these wanted to defeat both Treaty and League, and Reed, Shields, and Smith were their Democratic left wing. Next came the self-styled "Reservationists," led by Lodge, who would sacrifice almost anything for the defeat of a Democratic President. Further to the center were the "Mild Reservationists," again chiefly Republicans, but those who greatly desired both Treaty and League, without any important amendments. The fourth group, all Democratic, was of Senators who would take the Treaty as it was; these constituted up to forty-four votes. The Mild Reservationists must go with them to get the two-thirds majority for the Treaty.

Through October 1919, Mild Reservationists and Wilson Democrats joined to turn down all Lodge-inspired amendments, but no word came from the White House to afford a basis for an affirmative Mild Reservationist program. In November, Lodge worked out another set of reservations, and most of the Mild Reservationists went with him on these. One was aimed at the integrity of Article X, the very essence of peace enforcement. From the start, the President had urged the necessity for a collective security for weak nations against strong ones. This reservation declared that the United States would not undertake to safeguard the territorial integrity or the political independence of any other country, or to interfere in controversies between countries, unless Congress especially legislated to do so in each particular case.

Wilson sent word from his sickbed that this was a "knife-thrust at the heart of the Covenant." He wrote Hitchcock that the resolution "does not provide for ratification but rather for nullification of the Treaty. I sincerely hope that the friends and supporters of the Treaty will vote against the Lodge resolution of ratification." And so, November 19, 1919, this cruelly absurd situation developed: a combination of fifty-five pro-League Democrats and anti-League Isolationists voting down the thirty-nine *Reservationists! Lodge's plot had succeeded beyond his wildest initial expectations. Not only had the Treaty been killed, but with such finesse that the public blamed Wilson for its death. On March 19, 1920, there was another ballot, and the Treaty lost by seven votes. Again pro-League Democrats and "bitter-ender" Isolationists had combined to kill it; and this time it was dead beyond resurrection.

Lodge's malice and Wilson's loss of leadership helped dig the grave for the peace, but perhaps the most influential adverse factor was the two-thirds rule for the Senate's consent to a Treaty. On both tests it had received a majority, once within seven votes of the constitutionally required two-thirds. This institutional handicap had plagued the Executive in handling foreign relations from the beginning. The Jay treaty, in 1795, was within a vote of failure; Tyler's treaty annexing Texas was rejected; McKinley's treaty of peace with Spain gained consent only through Bryan's pressure on Democratic Senators, who followed him.

The two-thirds rule later stood like a dragon in the path of our entry into the World Court. The Senate consented in 1926, with five reservations which the League reluctantly accepted. Negotiations dragged until, in 1932, Elihu Root drew up a Protocol defining our rights, obligations and procedures. After long negotiation and debate, the League adopted it, and in 1935 President Franklin Roosevelt submitted it to the Senate with an earnest appeal for its consent.

This set the Isolationists on fire, Father Coughlin made an impassioned appeal for pressure on the Senators, and just a few more than a third voted against it. The "one-third rule," as it should be called, since it allows a group of little more than that size to defeat any measure, likewise blocked "F. D. R.'s" Niagara River Power Treaty; it was not hard to frighten more than a third of the Senators over this "threat" to private power.

The ease with which a third of the Senate can be mobilized against a treaty on a party vote, as was the case with the 1844 Texas rejection, or because of group pressures, as in the instance of League of Nations and World Court, led George W. Wickersham to doubt if any treaty to end a major war can get a two-thirds vote. Undoubtedly the senatorial sword of Damocles explains the increasing employment of Joint Resolutions instead of treaties for important diplomatic accords. The fact that only a majority of each House is required for the passage of a Joint Resolution deprives obstructionist blocs of much of their obstructive force.

This was first shown in the Texas matter. After the Whigs rejected the treaty, Tyler and the annexationists initiated a Joint Resolution which, while delayed by filibustering oratory, won by good margins in both Houses and Tyler signed just before Polk's inauguration. Hawaii came in through the same procedure, under McKinley.

Apparently neither Wilson nor his advisers considered the Joint Resolution procedure in connection with the Versailles Treaty. Which is strange, particularly since three months after he went out of office we ended our formal state of war with Germany by a Joint Resolution of the Congress which Harding signed July 2, 1921. The Treaty of Berlin, signed seven weeks later, did no more than state the conditions Germany accepted in a war already officially closed by our unilateral act.

CHAPTER XIII

Recovery by Proclamation

The history of the Presidency presents no exact counterpart to Franklin D. Roosevelt's first hundred days in the White House.

True, in March 1861 Lincoln confronted secession, but until July he handled its problems without the presence of Congress. In March 1893 Cleveland had to meet a gold panic, but did so by agreeing to the harsh terms of J. Pierpont Morgan. In 1929-1931, Hoover followed the policy of Cleveland and Van Buren, that while the government must support the gold standard, recovery would come from natural economic forces. In contrast, within his first three months in office, Roosevelt halted panic and initiated recovery through a bloodless revolution under all the forms of law!

Such have been the differences in the problems confronting the mind and mood of this incalculable man that, at times, it seems as if we are treating three different presidents. In the first term, he persuaded the American people to pull themselves up by their bootstraps; in the second, he preached a new social gospel; and in the third, he has concentrated upon our military strategy and performance in a globe-girdling war. The three have the common denominator of his qualities and defects, but each demands special treatment.

Franklin Roosevelt, like Jefferson, is an aristocratic country squire who became Democrat by choice. Both inherited traditions of *noblesse oblige;* both had a philosophic belief in the common man and concern for his rights and welfare. Roosevelt too liked people, had the knack of getting along with them, and took to politics from his college days. Some find in his years at Groton and Harvard, and in his relationship with his mother, Mrs. Sara Delano Roosevelt, the formative factors in his talent in persuasion. His law studies at Columbia were less significant, for his law practice became neither livelihood nor spirit of life.

His marriage in 1905 to his fifth cousin Eleanor Roosevelt, niece of the then President, brought a distinct trace of T. R.'s enthusiasms and energies into his life. Note has already been taken that F. D. R. is more unlike than like "Uncle Ted." Some deem him every inch a Delano; the story is told of his mother's having remarked, at a family reunion, about some distant cousin of their immediate strain, "He belongs to the good-looking branch of the family." Franklin Roosevelt liked T. R., but didn't take too much stock in his senior's Progressivism, saying: "Scratch him and you find a Republican." In discussing the Harding-inaugurated policy of having the Vice President at Cabinet meetings, he asked: "What do you think would have happened if McKinley had had to have Uncle Ted at his Cabinets?" Nor did the Oyster Bay branch transfer its support to its Hyde Park cousin. Alice Roosevelt Longworth remarked, during the 1932 campaign: "We have spent all of our lives trying to live up to Father, and now we must spend all the rest of our lives trying to live down to Franklin."

In 1910 Franklin Roosevelt sought election as State Senator in the normally Republican election district embracing Dutchess County. He campaigned with buoyant enthusiasm, the T. R.–Taft feud foreshadowed a change of party, and he surprised his friends (and perhaps himself) by winning the race. His work at Albany served as springboard for his first Washington career.

Like T. R., Franklin Roosevelt leapt at the chance to be Assistant Secretary of the Navy, and his charm, talent and energy developed markedly in his seven years at the task — from 1913 to 1920. He liked Secretary Josephus Daniels, and the two made a good team as America shifted into active belligerency in the first World War. Roosevelt's penchant for the art of military strategy found active employment in perfecting our attack against the U-boat; among the first to press the practicability of a mine barrage from Norway to Scotland, he played a stellar part in its successful execution. Daniels depended on him, and the Navy's efficient procurement, supply and administration during the war was to a considerable degree the result of his endeavors. His association in the "Little Cabinet" and Common Council Club of Wilson's days likewise proved quite useful.

Franklin Roosevelt's candidacy for Vice President in 1920 gave him the chance to get acquainted with the country. His speeches went well, his personality pleased the Democratic chieftains. After the election went against the Democrats, he returned to New York to practise law.

Within a year, he was seized with infantile paralysis, and for more than eighteen months was in the "valley of the shadow." Buoyed by his wife's insistent, inspiring courage, he battled at home through the early crises. In 1924, he began retraining his body by many long visits to Warm Springs, Georgia.

This battle of spirit against matter remade Roosevelt. Probably he could not have survived had he not developed an immense will for power, which has never lessened. Also his experience implanted in him a deep personal sympathy for the sick, suffering and distressed. He could say, with Virgil's Aeneas, "Not myself ignorant of misfortunes, I have learned to succor the unfortunate." Another effect was the banishment of personal fear, for nothing further that could happen to him could be half so bad as the paralysis he had had to fight.

Recovery of health soon brought him real political stature. Governor Al Smith became his close friend, and in 1928 asked that he run for the New York governorship, to help Smith's own presidential chances. The fact that Roosevelt carried and Smith lost New York did not immediately interrupt their friendship, but when the new Governor proved no rubber-stamp, his predecessor began to cool. Soon after Roosevelt set his sights for the White House, Smith joined actively in the effort to head him off.

During the preconvention campaign, low-rating Roosevelt's qualifications was a favorite indoor sport, one important pundit insisting that he was only "a pleasant man who, without any important qualification for the office, would like very much to be President." But Roosevelt's candidacy went forward. James A. Farley and Louis Howe built a nation-wide organization; Roosevelt visited headquarters to thank them particularly. A "Brains Trust" of Raymond Moley, Rex Tugwell, Adolf Berle, Hugh Johnson and Charles Taussig put new faces on old issues; they reported direct to Roosevelt. Democratic statesmen, such as Senator Cordell Hull, were a chief factor. Homer Cummings, of Connecticut, held many conferences in Washington, Daniel C. Roper did good missionary work with the drys. Roosevelt had a majority in the Chicago Convention, but, because of the antique two-thirds rule, the alliance between Smith, the city bosses, and the favorite sons almost caused a deadlock. Then McAdoo, the victim of a similar fight in 1924, helped swing California and Texas to nominate Roosevelt, who flew to Chicago to accept.

Herbert Hoover never had a real chance for re-election; yet no man ever worked harder at the business of being President than "the Great Engineer." His devotion to duty and detail resembled Cleveland's, but these qualities alone do not make a great President; unless the people follow, no man can lead. Moreover, he was unwilling to let the people glimpse him as a human being, because "this is not a showman's job; I will not step out of character." He had personal charm, but the man-in-the-street got the impression of a human machine.

At first he claimed to follow the Madison precept that Congress should make all the policy decisions, and the President only carry out the legislative will. But this theory became more honored in breach than observance.

He was a wizard in administration — as in Russian relief, where he handled some apparently insuperable tasks with a staff of only a hundred and fifty Americans inside that country. Aides still talk of the skill with which he picked executives "just like you pick a friend."

Doubtless, the gods were unjust to Hoover, in letting the world go into an economic tailspin in the late Twenties. His ill-fate resembled Van Buren's, and, until late in 1931, Hoover would probably have indorsed his predecessor's precept: "It is the people's duty to support the Government, not the Government the people." In our earlier depressions, because of this idea, the living generation had gone through the wringer; but Hoover's humanitarianism kept him from complete obedience to this grim doctrine. He begged the great industrialists not to cut wage-rates; then, after it became plain even to him that prosperity was not "just around the corner," he set up Federal agencies to help cushion the adjustment. His constitutional views, however, kept him from more thoroughgoing measures to offset the social distresses of the Great Depression.

Our internal difficulties were intensified by Europe's 1931 currency and credit debacle, which culminated in Britain's going off gold. While Hoover would not follow her example, and clung to gold as fervently as had Cleveland, the resulting gold drain and credit panic finally forced him to emergency action; the new Congress authorized the revival of the Reconstruction Finance Corporation to provide funds for banks, railroads, and farm relief, loans to States for direct relief, and "self-liquidating" construction projects. But his inability to persuade quick action by Congress on other items of his twelve-point recovery program pressed Hoover's nerves to the limit. The coming campaign for re-election brought new insistence that he let the people have some personal glimpses of the President as a harassed human being, but — "I have other things to do when a nation is on fire."

This stiffness, however, was not so determinative of the election outcome as was the general public demand for a change. As Ernest K. Lindley has said, the masses were looking for a Messiah, and while Roosevelt neither looked nor sounded like one, "he was the one sure means of rebuking the party in power."

The period between November 8, 1932 and March 6, 1933 has little resemblance to any other in our presidential history. The shift in power was far more decisive than in Wilson's first election, and the chasm between outgoing and incoming administrations was almost as wide as that between Buchanan's and Lincoln's. Hoover's secretary, Theodore Joslin, insists that his chief "went more than half way," and that had the President-elect joined in the Hoover program, "the misery of the first few months of the Roosevelt Administration would have been avoided." Hoover insisted that a scaling-down of war debts together with international currency stabilization was "imperative of immediate action," while his successor believed recovery must begin at home. President and President-elect did have two resultless meetings. Indeed, there was something fatuous about Hoover's apparent expectation that the nation's newly chosen leader would abandon his own program to kneel before the idols of a defeated and repudiated man.

After the first of these conferences, November 22, 1932, Roosevelt went to Warm Springs, to rest and also to finish picking his Cabinet and drafting his own recovery program. He wanted Cordell Hull in the Department of State, and Carter Glass in the Treasury; the Tennessean was determined not to be anybody's office-boy, and visited Warm Springs reluctantly, but the President-elect persuaded him to accept the first post in the Cabinet. The Virginian demanded a pledge against devaluation, declined when this was not forthcoming; and a New York manufacturer, William H. Woodin, was given that post. Senator McAdoo thought Woodin unqualified, and threatened to oppose his confirmation; so McAdoo's friend Daniel C. Roper was selected for Secretary of Commerce, in the hope that this might mitigate the Senator's wrath. Thomas J. Walsh's choice for Attorney General was generally hailed. For Labor, F. D. R. would bring Miss Frances Perkins, his New York Labor Commissioner. War went to Governor Dern, of Utah, and Navy to Senator Swanson of Virginia. He summoned an old Bull Mooser, Harold Ickes, to the Interior. For Agriculture he picked Henry Wallace, independent Iowa Republican farm editor and eclectic philosopher. Genial Jim Farley was a natural for Postmaster General.

The "Little Cabinet" would be made up of Brains Trusters as well as political war-horses. Felix Frankfurter, brilliant Harvard Law School professor, sent down a host of favorite pupils — "the Hot Dogs," they soon were to be called — and two alumni of Bernard M. Baruch's War Industries Board took important parts in the pre-inauguration program planning. The Warm Springs sessions ended when the President-elect returned to Washington for a second conference with Hoover, on January 20, 1933. But the latter's representations did not change Roosevelt's determination to do his own negotiating with foreign governments.

In February a sudden bank panic transformed depression into disaster. A bad run began on a large Detroit bank, and soon the Michigan Governor declared a statewide bank holiday. Near-by States followed suit, holidays and withdrawal restrictions spread like wildfire, and foreign countries quickened the return of their gold. The country was in a panic when Roosevelt came to Washington to take over the National Government.

He himself refused to be in a panic, declined to cancel the customary Inaugural Parade, and enjoyed it hugely. But while he reviewed the procession, the machinery was in motion for a nationwide bank holiday. There had been exploration on this problem at the time of the last summer's threatened bank crash. Under Secretary of the Treasury Ballantine, Solicitor General Thacher and Assistant Secretary of State Rogers had concluded that such a holiday could be called under a section of the 1917 Trading with the Enemy Act, and rough-drafted a proclamation, which Ballantine took to Raymond Moley two days before Inauguration.

The discussion led Ballantine to feel that the Roosevelt advisers, not anticipating this particular crisis, had made no plan for it, but expected to wait for action until they were in office. "But you can't wait," he exclaimed. "By Monday there won't be a bank open in the whole country." Startled by this, Roosevelt set his folk to work. Ballantine was asked to carry on, and Moley went with Rogers to work on a proclamation.

At the same time, Homer S. Cummings, the new Attorney General, began burrowing for legal authority for the projected bank holiday. One circuit court had held the relevant section of the 1917 Act "probably repealed," but the Supreme Court had not passed on the matter, and he gave an official opinion that the Act was still in force. Originally selected for Governor General of the Philippines, Cummings had been switched to Justice upon Walsh's sudden death. The pressure on him for opinions — curbstone, oral, telephone and written — reached an all-time high during this first six months.

Upon receiving his ruling, the President went ahead on the holiday plan. At one o'clock in the morning of Monday, March 6, 1933, he signed a proclamation that, in view of a national emergency and to prevent the export or hoarding of gold, there would be a three-day bank holiday. At the same time, he summoned Congress to meet March 9. On that day he went before them with a frank statement of the situation, the course he proposed, and the additional powers he needed to prevent catastrophe. "In the event that the Congress shall fail to take these courses," he concluded, "and in the event that the national emergency is still critical, I shall not evade the clear course of duty that will then confront me. I shall ask the Congress for the one remaining instrument to meet the crisis — broad executive power to wage a war against the emergency as great as the power that would be given me if we were in fact invaded by a foreign foe."

The desired emergency banking measures were put through that very day; the Republican minority leader, Snell, urged them because "the house is burning down, and the President of the United States says this is the way to put out the fire."

Before Congress adjourned ninety-nine days later, it had put on the statute books more extraordinary legislation than had been enacted since Reconstruction. In almost every instance, the initiative was Roosevelt's; the bills themselves were in most cases prepared by agents of the National Executive, and often enacted without any change. On its first day, Congress passed the bank-reform legislation; on its last, the National Industrial Recovery Act.

At the time the peaceful change was hailed as "the Roosevelt Revolution." He did not repudiate the label saying in his book *On Our Way* that: "If it is a revolution, it is a peaceful one, achieved without violence, without the overthrow of the purposes of established law and without the denial of just treatment to any individual or class." The very title, New Deal, he traced to the fusion of Theodore Roosevelt's "Square Deal" and Woodrow Wilson's "New Freedom." But like Wilson and Jefferson, in asking Congress for the legislative commitment of powers in which he would have broad latitude of discretion, he never once ignored the form of co-ordinate departmental rank, whatever might have been the fact. In this he demonstrated his skill in the art of democratic leadership.

Equally conspicuous was his care in keeping the people informed. Events moved so fast, his first week, with so many proclamations, executive orders and laws, that on Sunday night, March 12, he was able to talk to the people over a nation-wide radio hook-up — the precursor of his Fireside Chats — explaining to the average citizen just what had actually happened. The effect was tonic. Eight weeks later he reported again, and ever since has relied on direct reports to the people.

The pressure was terrific, Washington seemed a madhouse of helter-skelter activity, but the President showed astonishing strength and endurance. Confident, buoyant, cheerfully experimental, few were proof against him when he turned on his charm. Decisions didn't come through pounding the desk, but as a result of persuasion or amiable insistence. F. D. R. had little trace of his cousin's habit of accent on the imperative, or of Wilson's preference for the elaborate written memo, but preferred to play by ear.

This genius in disorder, with its disregard of the rules of the copybook gods, was among the chief of his assets in the chaotic weeks in which a dozen or more major experiments were shaped. The March calendar of his requests to Congress is indicative: March 9, the bank reorganization bill; March 10, authority to cut governmental operating expenses twenty-five per cent; March 16, "a new and untrod path" to rescue agriculture; March 21, a public works program of over three billions, the establishment of the Civilian Conservation Corps, and relief grants to the States; and March 29, Federal supervision over the sale of securities in interstate commerce.

Under the bank holiday legislation, the government undertook to allow only the "sound" banks among the 17,000 in the country to open; by the middle of April it had licensed all but about 4200 banks, and was strengthening their capital structures. In addition, a limited bank-deposit-guarantee plan added to depositor confidence.

The President had, of course, a program much broader than bank surgery, its chief elements being to raise prices through devaluation, and to reduce the debt burden through cheap money. He began the first in the late spring, through the inflationary amendments to his farm relief bill giving the President discretion to fix the gold content of the currency, within limits. A Wall Street flurry led to the Gold Reserve Act; he cut the dollar gold content by some forty per cent, which so quickened the cheap money policy that, between his inauguration and December 31, 1935, R. F. C. had lent or invested a little more than six billions. Farm debt and credit were vigorously revamped, and the Home Owners' Loan Corporation refinanced over a million mortgaged homes. These basic treatments of America's credit were among the essential piers for recovery.

F. D. R.'s agricultural legislation was quite as revolutionary. By 1932, the nation's farm population was at its peak, but farm cash income was at the lowest it had been for a quarter of a century. After the bank holiday, Roosevelt and his aides began to frame a farm relief bill, to give the farmers a benefit equivalent to the tariff on that part of their crops consumed in the United States, but on a self-financing plan, and without "dumping" abroad. During the campaign George Peek, of Baruch's group, urged a farm recovery plan without drastic crop reduction. But after the election Wallace and Tugwell shifted to acreage control; the Secretary of Agriculture would determine each farmer's cut, and could withhold the "adjustment certificate" unless the farmer kept his word.

The new bill created the Agricultural Adjustment Administration, with so broad a delegation of authority that everything depended on the way it was run. The President said that it was a new and untrod path, but that an unprecedented condition had called for the trial of new means to rescue agriculture; if it did not work "I shall be the first to acknowledge it and advise you." It swept swiftly through the House, but such Senators as Thomas and Wheeler insisted that only devaluing the dollar, buying silver, and issuing greenbacks would help farm prices. When such amendments were tacked on, the inflationists and silver men came across; and May 12, 1933 the bill became a law.

Its critical section was the authority "to provide for reduction in the acreage or reduction in the production for market, or both, of any basic agricultural commodity, through agreements with producers or by other voluntary methods, and to provide for rental or benefit payments in connection therewith."

While farm prices rose for a variety of causes, unquestionably the New Deal's crop control played a highly important part. At first the programs embraced only wheat, cotton, corn and hogs, tobacco, rice, and milk and its products; in 1934, sugar, cattle, rye, flax, barley, peanuts and potatoes were added, and by 1935 almost 3,400,000 individual production-control contracts were in force. Wallace made earnest efforts to effect control through consent, in form at least, and in 1934-1935 conducted referenda among the growers of wheat, cotton, tobacco, corn and hogs on continuing the controls; of the four and a quarter million who voted, seven eighths favored going on with them. It was a matter of dollars and cents rather than principle; since 1932, their income had gone up ninety per cent, or over twice that from all other farm commodities. Through the South and West there was a direct ratio between benefit payments and recovery, whatever might have been the sour memories of plowing cotton under and killing little pigs.

The "Triple-A" processor tax was challenged soon after collection began and the Hoosac Mills Case reached the Supreme Court in the October 1935 term. Stanley Reed, the Solicitor General, argued that its levying was within the National Government's powers under the general welfare clause. But the Court's majority opinion, written by Justice Roberts and announced January 6, 1936, held it clearly unconstitutional. "The Act invades the reserved rights of the States. It is a statutory plan to regulate and control agricultural production, a matter beyond the powers delegated to the Federal Government."

Justice Stone dissented sharply, Brandeis and Cardozo joining, because "Courts are concerned only with the power to enact statutes, not with their wisdom. While unconstitutional exercise of power by the executive and legislative branches of the Government is subject to judicial restraint, the only check upon our own exercise of power is our own sense of restraint." He termed the Roberts opinion a tortured construction of the Constitution, and added: "Language, even of a constitution, may mean what it says. The power to tax and spend includes the power to relieve a nationwide economic maladjustment by conditional gifts of money."

This decision forced a quick substitution, which the President based on a long-range, broad-gauge land-use program: The Federal Government would pay farmers to take poor, or "submarginal," land out of cultivation; some of it would be devoted to soil-building crops; erosion control and reforestation were embraced. The Republicans found the new method in keeping with their 1932 platform, and both parties accepted cash payment to farmers, whether for crop reduction or soil conservation, as a necessity. Despite gaps in its coverage, and creaking in the machinery of control and consent, the farm relief program was one of the big accomplishments of F. D. R.'s first term.

In the summer of 1933, it looked as though Triple-A would be far surpassed by General Hugh Johnson, who also had come to Washington with Baruch's backing. The many millions of unemployed demanded some sort of spread-the-work program. Business believed it must control production, prices, and cutthroat competition, or it couldn't make any money. Organized Labor wanted minimum-wage standards, the abolition of child labor, and universal collective bargaining. Roosevelt resolved to have one bill to combine these purposes; this was the National Industrial Recovery Act, which he signed June 16, 1933.

Business leaped at this chance to control production; Henry I. Harriman, Gerard Swope, Clay Williams and other far-seeing business leaders worked hard on this part of NRA. General Johnson first called on the employers to cut hours and hike wages, to be repaid in the "fair trade practices" provisions in the industry codes. A little later he said they might also incorporate bans against prices under the cost of production, and so nearly every code contained provisions against the chiseler, "loss-leader," and others. He established "advisory boards" for business, labor, and the consumer; but the latter's interests were lost in the rush; in August 1933, Professor William F. Ogburn, the noted sociologist, resigned from the consumers' group in protest.

There were several forward steps, as when cotton textile executives agreed to abolish child labor without constitutional amendment; but codes took time to draft and longer to get working. Johnson lost patience, and, in December 1933, determined on one big push to raise wages and cut hours to get the country going again. He sold the scheme and its "Blue Eagle" to the White House — "the Boss" has a zest for the dramatic. The General's edicts received enthusiastic lip-service, but soon the program began to bog down; our American economy, as complex as it is massive, responds erratically to slogans.

This was shown by the disastrous drive on the consumers' service trades, employing about six million people. Cleaners and dyers were paying help as low as four dollars a week for sixty to seventy hours' work, and racketeering was often resorted to, as in laundries, to stabilize the industry. Johnson put in a code directly fixing their prices, which aroused great consumer opposition. Before long NRA was regarded as the big man's weapon for driving the little fellow out of business.

Any such sentiment meant destruction; unless the people believed in NRA's purposes and methods, they could not be expected to boycott firms without the Blue Eagle. The many code increases of prices looked like gouges. So rapid was the withdrawal of public support, after the fall of 1934, that NRA was almost a living corpse before its juridic burial. At that, much of its thunder was in the index, because most of its provisions for control of minimum prices broke down. Late in the summer of 1934, the pressure got too great for "Old Iron Pants," who resigned without White House objection. His successor, Donald R. Richberg, spoke more softly, but without checking the withdrawal of consent.

A unanimous Court, on May 27, 1935, gave NRA the *coup de grâce* in a case involving the prosecution of one Abraham Schecter, an obscure Brooklyn chicken peddler, for alleged infraction of the wage and hour provision of the code for his industry. Chief Justice Hughes, in the main opinion, exposed the extraordinary character of Congress's delegation to the President of its powers under the commerce clause. In a concurring opinion, Justice Cardozo pointed out that the Act meant that "anything that Congress may do, within the limits of the commerce clause, for the betterment of business, may be done by the President upon the recommendation of a trade association by calling it a code. This is delegation running riot!" But even if Congress had itself enacted the hundreds of codes, he observed, this particular defendant could not be punished, for the commerce clause "does not grant Congress the right to regulate wages and hours of labor in the intrastate actions that make up the defendant's business."

The decision set the President on fire. At his press conference of May 29, 1935, he discussed the implications of a decision he termed more important than any since the Dred Scott case. Waving aside, as correctable, the strictures on delegation running riot, he focused on the declarations about intrastate commerce, in which the Court "has gone back to the old Knight case in 1885 [actually, 1895] which in fact limited any application of interstate commerce to goods in transit — nothing else!" The commerce clause itself must be viewed "in the light of present-day civilization." When it had been written, in 1787, "the country was in the horse-and-buggy age. . . . There were no social questions in those days. . . .

"Does this decision mean that the United States Government has no control over any national economic problem?" he inquired. The next five or ten years must decide whether the country would "relegate to the forty-eight States" all control over economic conditions, or "whether in some way we are going to turn over or restore to . . . the Federal Government the powers which exist in the national Governments of every other nation of the world to enact and administer laws that have a bearing on, and general control over, national economic problems and national social problems. That actually is the biggest question that has come before this country outside of time of war, and it has to be decided."

The relief problem was about as critical as that of the banks, and he moved almost as fast on it. The very day of his bank holiday proclamation, he told a conference of governors he would create a central relief agency to act as a clearinghouse for the relief of the nation.

As Governor he had seen the inadequacy of local assistance, led New York to assume responsibility, and put Harry L. Hopkins in charge of the State emergency relief agency set up. Many other States had followed suit, but they never had enough money to meet their needs, and it became obvious that the Federal Government must shoulder a major share of a load estimated as high as 35,000,000 people. How would it be done? "Dole" was a dirty word; relief through employment was generally adopted to strengthen the morale of the jobless. During the 1932 campaign, he had promised to effect no governmental economies at the expense of the unemployed.

The President had three strings to his relief bow, the most colorful and dramatic the Civilian Conservation Corps, aimed to take boys out of the poolrooms and off the roads. In ninety days some 300,000 were in the camps, and by 1936 over a million youths had been employed. At the same time he set up, under Harry Hopkins, the Federal Emergency Relief Administration, with a $500,000,000 appropriation as a starter — half to go to the States, the rest for direct Federal gifts. The third branch was a Public Works Administration, to provide work and to stimulate the building materials and construction industries.

When he saw that PWA could not get out of the paperwork stage until the next spring, Roosevelt set up the Civil Works Administration as a stopgap. A large number of its projects were bad or stupid — Tory phobias against boondoggling and leaves-raking date from CWA — and the minimum wages, above prevailing rates in the South, caused disturbance; yet by the middle of January 1934 it had 4,250,000 people on its payroll, the pay per worker averaged fifteen dollars, and raised the standard of help. The PWA construction program got going at the turn of the year, and by April 1934 CWA was out of the picture.

Hopkins found it necessary to expand the FERA work program and by the end of that year had almost 2,500,000 on emergency work, in addition to 3,000,000 cases of direct relief. Camps and centers for transients were established. An emergency education program used over 40,000 jobless teachers in nursery, adult and vocational school work for almost 2,000,000 pupils, and Federal aid enabled 100,000 youths to go to college. The 1934 drought brought a special scheme — both work and direct relief for distressed farm families, and purchasing and processing millions of cattle, sheep, and other animals, for feeding relief "clients" over the country.

The nation had a net gain in plant and equipment, the list of buildings and improvements running the gamut from roads and bridges, schools and hospitals, golf courses and grandstands, to 369,000 sanitary privies. The type of employment ran all the way from jobs for steam-shovel men to those for artists and models. Storms of criticism arose against roadside grass-cutting, the "advanced" nature of the art that bedizened the new public buildings, the "communist" and "fellow traveler" influence on camps and youth movements. Perhaps even more important was the resentment of State and local officials and politicians.

Sensing the need for change, early in 1935 F. D. R. presented Congress with a completely revamped plan to take the National Government out of direct relief altogether. The States must shoulder the responsibility for the millions of unemployables, and the Federal Government itself would undertake to give jobs to able-bodied needy unemployed. For these purposes he asked and obtained $4,000,000,000.

This began the WPA phase of relief and re-employment. The planning had been none too good; although these WPA programs gave work to almost 4,000,000 and more people were pushed back on the States than they had the money or organization to handle, 5,500,000 remained on Federal relief. None the less, the new approach was in to stay.

WPA, and especially Harry Hopkins, because of his closeness to the throne, were the targets of continual charges that the relief money went to politicians rather than unemployed. Actually its administrative personnel seldom exceeded 40,000, probably with no more than ten per cent politician spending. Hopkins ran his own show, sometimes quite ruthlessly, and there is considerable testimony to his skill in improvisation in handling emergencies. With all its faults, the Roosevelt relief program was a success. Without it, the other elements of the recovery drive probably would have been ineffective.

The Court's death sentence on NRA quickened Roosevelt's quest for the security of the masses of the people. Within ten weeks of the decision, he submitted and Congress passed the Social Security Act, the keystone of the arch of his program for the future protection of the individual worker. Its foundation was social insurance with government contribution, of the type Bismarck had introduced in Germany half a century before. There were important additions — Federal grants to the States for matched assistance to the blind, dependent or crippled children, maternal and child health and welfare services. Employers and workers both contribute to unemployment funds. Old age security was sought both through old age pensions for the indigent aged, and compulsory old age insurance for the employed, to which employer and worker contributed equally.

In its essence, this measure involved a greater change in the traditional concept of our social institutions than did NRA. The President termed it "a law that will take care of human needs and at the same time provide for the United States an economic structure of vastly greater soundness." Likewise it served as a lift under the wings of the spirit of the people.

Diverse forces were harnessed together to improve the status of labor. From the start, Roosevelt sought to give it greater importance in the national economy and welcomed its political interventions. Section 7-A of NRA's cotton-textile code gave governmental establishment to the workers' equal-bargaining position, through representatives of their own choosing. Little wonder it was hailed as "the Magna Charta of American Labor," and became a White House "must." The abolition of child labor betokened Section 7-A's almost revolutionary nature, affecting almost overnight that which for a decade social reformers had sought in vain through the slow-coach of constitutional amendment.

The White House had provided NRA with machinery for enforcing the labor codes, through a board to mediate or arbitrate controversies under Section 7-A. After the Schecter case decision, Congress adopted the Wagner Act to guarantee labor's collective-bargaining rights and to prohibit certain "unfair labor practices," establishing a new National Labor Relations Board to administer these labor-policy directives. NRA code provisions also afforded the framework for the 1938 Fair Labor Standards Act.

Labor had its own New Deal, with John L. Lewis in command. In the summer of 1933, he re-established the United Mine Workers as the dominating coal-production factor, then opened a campaign for a new type of union, to fit such unorganized mass-production industries as automobiles, aluminum and cement. The industrial union would make a single contract to cover a plant embracing such diverse crafts as pipe-fitting, lathe-tending, welding and test-driving. In 1934, the American Federation of Labor undertook "Federal" unions with a single charter for each plant, but Lewis soon claimed the craft-unions were dealing double in matters of jurisdiction, and intra-Labor fires burned high. Late the next year he set up the Committee for Industrial Organization, containing the most aggressive leadership in the American labor movement.

Roosevelt welcomed this new program, because he believed it the way for labor to get equality of bargaining power in the mass production industries, and perhaps equally because of his need for labor's legions in politics. The New Deal did its best to save organized labor from the consequences of such ill-timed wars with industry as the 1934 cotton-textile strike with its mass-picketings and riots. Aggressive labor leaders, such as Lewis, Sidney Hillman, and David Dubinsky, threw all their weight behind the President's political needs. There were indications that the President believed he was really founding a new farmer-labor radical party, retaining little more of the Democratic inheritance than the city machines and the tradition-guaranteed electoral votes of a solid South that was veering away from him. It would be a personal party, to follow the leader of the bloodless revolution.

"Clever" is the word for Roosevelt's conduct of foreign relations for the first four years of his Presidency — with the brilliance and the changeability it denotes. Only ten years intervene between the London Economic Conference and the Moscow Conference of Foreign Ministers; yet viewed in retrospect the 1933 Roosevelt concept of our international role seems strangely remote in both space and time. One key to the riddle is the human equation — between the variable of the President's moods, and the constant of the will and policy of Secretary Hull.

Despite the fact that F. D. R. had journeyed abroad from early childhood, while a Spanish–American War stay in Puerto Rico represented Hull's pre-1933 foreign travel, the former was a definite nationalist while the latter believed our national self-interest demanded close ties with the rest of the world. After 1920 Roosevelt carried no torch for the League of Nations, but Hull in House and Senate was almost a lone voice in a wilderness of scoffers at foreign trade.

Through the spring of 1933, officers of foreign governments flocked to Washington to talk debts, currency, trade and disarmament. The President sent delegations both to the Disarmament Conference at Geneva, and the later World Economic Conference at London. When Hitler, who had just seized control in Germany, upset the Geneva meeting, F. D. R. appealed to all heads of government that the nations "enter into a definite pact of non-aggression, limit and reduce their armaments, and agree to send no armed force of whatever nature across their frontiers." Then, at Geneva, Norman H. Davis said the United States would join in "negative" or "passive" collaboration with sanctions against an aggressor nation. Our alarmed isolationists immediately charged Roosevelt with playing with dynamite, and he drew back.

The President had also taken an active hand in the preparation of an American plan for the London meeting, and insisted that Hull head the delegation. While it was crossing the ocean Roosevelt decided that the success of the domestic recovery program depended on the raising of values, and "that no human being could, at that moment, determine exactly where even a temporary stabilization point should be fixed for dollar, franc and pound." Therefore he had the Secretary of the Treasury issue, June 15, 1933, a statement that "any agreement on this subject will be reached in Washington, not elsewhere." On July 2, the President cabled Hull that "the sound internal economic system of a nation is a greater factor in its well-being than the price of its currency in changing terms of the currencies of other nations." Hull kept the Conference from immediate final adjournment, but after a short wake it broke up. Both the President's initial essays in Europe had failed.

It was a different story in Latin America. In the fall of 1933, Hull led our delegation to the quinquennial Pan-American Conference. Already we had departed from Manifest Destiny and Dollar Diplomacy — Hoover had withdrawn our Marines from Haiti; and at Montevideo, Hull gave personal attest to the "good neighbor" pledge in Roosevelt's Inaugural by insisting that Carlos Saavedra Lamas, the Argentine Foreign Minister, take the leadership of the Congress. Our determination not to intervene in Latin America to protect property of our citizens was further shown by our signature of a convention that "no State has the right to intervene in the internal or external affairs of another." Revolutionary Cuba constituted the thorniest practical problem, but we sent neither fleet nor troops, and abrogated the Platt Amendment permitting our intervention.

Early in 1936 the President wrote the heads of the twenty American Republics suggesting a conference at Buenos Aires for the consolidation of the peace of the hemisphere. All agreed, Hull again led our delegation, and Roosevelt cruised down on the *Indianapolis* for a spectacular three-day visit. Our hemispheric attitude paid large dividends later when we entered the second World War.

In 1934, Congress was persuaded to delegate to the President the right to make "executive agreements" — not treaties requiring the advice and consent of the Senate — under which existing specific tariff duties could be cut as much as fifty per cent, in return for believed equivalent concessions. The President may have assumed that the Trade Agreement Act would lead only to Yankee horse-trading; certainly George Peek, as his Special Adviser on Foreign Trade, desired nothing more than strictly bilateral bargains. But Hull thought a major revival of world trade indispensable to the preservation of peace; the State Department, therefore, has used the "most-favored-nation clause" to generalize the benefits of each new agreement save that with Cuba, a very special case. F. D. R.'s entourage had little sympathy with Hull's "old-fashioned" belief that in peacetime we must buy if we wanted to sell, Peek made bitter protest, but the mild-mannered Tennessean went ahead. South

American countries and Canada led the way in making agreements with us, and the program achieved such measurable success that, in 1937, Congress lengthened its life.

The next major foreign policy development, the Neutrality Act legislation of August 31, 1935, stemmed out of Mussolini's Ethiopian war, and, backed by isolationists, was accepted in America by interventionists as well. British public opinion had already forced the repudiation of the Hoare-Laval pact, the French Premier's clandestine continuation of his bargain with Il Duce had not become clear, and the League set in motion the creaking machinery of sanctions. Hull distrusted the isolationist purpose, and refused to draft such a bill as they proposed, but the one put on the statute books was supposed to give "passive" or "negative" support to the sanctions hinted two years before. Actually, it made it unlawful to export arms, munitions and implements of war to belligerent countries, and set up an ex-officio National Munitions Control Board. In approving, Roosevelt termed it "an expression of the fixed desire of the Government and the people of the United States to avoid any action which might involve us in war. The purpose is wholly excellent . . . the avoidance of any entanglements which would lead us into conflict."

In his mind, undoubtedly, lurked the expectation that, inasmuch as the Fascists were believed to need great military stores, the armament ban would hurt them but not the Abyssinians. But in reality it proved otherwise, because of the restricted nature of the export prohibitions; in the Senate debate preceding action, Senator Pittman had explicitly stated that neither oil, cotton "or other commodities" were embraced. Mussolini had ample stores of matériel of war, but was short of oil. Britain would not shut him off, because Laval refused to; Laval argued there was no use of France's doing so, because America would sell him any quantity; and so the League never put sanctions in force against oil. Our Act proved passive and negative, in preventing aggression. The Axis dictators concluded that America intended to use no weapon but words.

CHAPTER XIV

Recessional

The four years from NRA's death to Hitler's invasion of Poland is the most inexplicable period of Franklin Roosevelt's Presidency. He has entitled the volume of his private papers for 1935 *The Court Disapproves,* in order exultantly to label the next one *The People Approve.* Undoubtedly his 1936 election majority of eleven million votes constituted a vote of confidence such as no other President since Jackson had received in mid-career. The mystery is why this mandate of the people went largely unused.

As chief political officer of the nation, it is inevitable that each President's public career is appraised politically. From this standpoint, Franklin Roosevelt's first term was a complete success. The results of the mid-term election generally mark the end of the presidential honeymoon, but 1934's balloting strengthened Roosevelt's majorities in both Houses, and increased his prestige. His helping hand to labor, securities control, and T. V. A. experiment had caused the Wall Streets and Park Avenues of America to revile him: "That Man" was destroying free enterprise, private initiative and the American way of life; he was Communist, Fascist, dictator and devil — no charge too far-fetched, no slur too mean. But this was according to bankers, brokers, businessmen and their lawyers, not the rank and file. The Republican politicians unwittingly gave testimony to this effect when they gathered in Cleveland in June 1936 in their National Convention. There was the usual viewing with alarm, but the leaders framed a platform considerably to the left of Hoover, and gave a virtual endorsement of ample Federal funds for the farmer.

Although their nominee, Governor "Alf" Landon of Kansas, had some distinctly progressive tendencies, his advisers fumbled the attack, and caused him to put his foot in it, as in singling out the import of Brazilian babasu nuts as a great wrong to the American farmer. Roosevelt swung into the campaign with an electrifying acceptance speech and by September the trends were unmistakable.

The November victory exceeded even Jim Farley's predictions. The Roosevelt vote of about 27,500,000 was almost 11,000,000 more than Landon's; although the latter received 1,000,000 more votes than Hoover had in 1932, the President's strength increased more than 4,500,000 over his prior total. Only Maine and Vermont prevented an unanimous Electoral College vote. Although George Washington had received every electoral vote in both terms, and Monroe had no opponent in 1820, never had there been such a clean sweep in a contested election as that by F. D. R. in 1936.

Old Hickory had taken his re-election as mandate both to crush nullification and to destroy Nick Biddle's despotic power over the country's money, banking and credit. What use would Franklin Roosevelt make of his vote of confidence? A realistic appraisal of the President's endeavors and accomplishments between March 4, 1933 and the outbreak of the new World War six-and-a-half years later shows that almost every important domestic change began in the first three years — most of them in the first hundred days.

The basic rehabilitation of the country's money, banking and debt structure, the restoration of farm income, and the social security program — Roosevelt's three fundamental achievements — had been put on solid foundations by the time of the election. The strengthening of labor, his fourth great purpose, had sired NRA. The National Labor Board, established in August 1933 under Senator Wagner's chairmanship, was the predecessor of the National Labor Relations Board. NRA machinery for maximum hours and minimum wages reappeared in the 1938 Fair Labor Standards Act. John L. Lewis had begun pushing the industrial union against the craft type in the early thirties, and the seeds for the sit-down strikes, mass picketings and other labor turbulences to unionize the new mass-production industries were sown in the early months of the recovery drive.

The President's public power program, one of his best long-range endeavors, also had been planted when the New Deal was young. The Tennessee Valley Authority had to run the gantlet of the courts, but its broad regional program, with navigation, flood control, afforestation, erosion repair, and so on, went forward despite the legal and political machinations of the private-power interests and the dissensions of the Authority's own board. The holding company act, with its death sentence clause, went on the statute books in the first term.

It is a significant fact that, after the first term, the President effected practically no further basic change in our social and economic institutions. What could have caused this atrophy of the experimental urge?

Perhaps such a slackening is in the nature of things, bright minds get tired even in a Brains Trust, and turn from moving mountains to building molehills. Mobility and bureaucracy are incompatible, for the very mass of our National Government tends to crush experiments into routines; in 1916 the Wilson Administration had a touch of this paralysis.

Yet this could not be accounted the major factor in the new situation. Since 1933, the group close to "the Boss" has undergone continual change; some exhausted their fertility or wore out their welcome, and were slowly pushed to the fringe or quickly sent to Coventry; of the original 1932 Brains Trust, only Tugwell and Berle were in the government ten years later, the one at far remove in Puerto Rico, the other not quite as far away as an Assistant Secretary of State. Of intimate political advisers, only Samuel I. Rosenman and James F. Byrnes have weathered the decade. Captious critics have charged the President with a horror of having any subordinate regarded as a man of power, and with therefore ridding himself of a man whenever he suspects the development of this trait. This ignores the ever-present fact that Harry Hopkins, Byrnes, Frankfurter, Baruch and others have been close to the throne for many years.

Nor have the new recruits necessarily been inferior to the invalided veterans in knowledge, mind or imaginative inventiveness. Tom Corcoran, Ben Cohen, Oscar Cox, Jonathan Daniels, Archibald MacLeish, Robert Sherwood are examples of the variety of traits and talents that have been at hand.

Far more important as a factor is the President himself. To some who think they know the inner man, he remains to this day a country squire, with a real devotion to hard money, rigorous economy in government, and other shibboleths. They point out that F. D. R. did not practise these inner faiths only because of the 1932–1933 emergency, and that in 1936, when he felt the crisis was over, he reverted to balancing the budget, thus precipitating 1937's sharp decline. Such a thesis would help explain the way one of his policies has made faces at another which cancels it, as deficit spending did with the twenty-five per cent cut in Federal salaries in the first term. But it generalizes out of insufficient particulars.

Probably the major causes for the mandate's going unused were, first, the Court fight and Purge, in which many felt the President had looked through a hate darkly, and so did not back his new program; and second, his shift of attention from domestic matters to foreign affairs. From the time of his "Quarantine" speech, late in 1937, F. D. R. concentrated more and more on the danger of another world war.

Franklin Roosevelt's greatest failure was the Court fight. Candidate Roosevelt, in 1932, had termed it a Republican Court, and certainly it was a dangerously divided Court, with four such rock-ribbed conservatives as Van Devanter, Sutherland, Butler and McReynolds; three liberals, in Brandeis, Cardozo and Stone; and two "roving judges" in Chief Justice Hughes and Roberts. In the early New Deal days, some thought the crisis would be over before the Court would reach any cases on it; because of their fear of injunctions, code enforcement was largely by propaganda.

When the Department of Justice sought good test cases, it found bad drafting in many statutes and codes, and held back; the Petroleum Administrator, for example, had jailed one J. W. Smith for violating a code section that actually had been stricken from a preliminary draft and so didn't exist. Orders having the force of law were issued in profusion but were not available to interested parties, which Carl Swisher, in his *American Constitutional Government,* properly terms a "disreputable procedure." Court criticism led to the establishment of the *Federal Register.* In the Hot Oil Cases, the Court held for the first time that a Federal law was unconstitutional because Congress had no right to delegate power to the President without establishing a policy or standard to govern his use of it. The Gold Cases had the narrowest of margins, and McReynolds' dissent that "as for the Constitution, it does not seem too much to say that it is gone," typified the view of four. Only the Ashwander Case, upholding TVA, lightened the gloom on Court approval of social legislation.

In May 1935 Attorney General Cummings wrote the President: "Apparently there are at least four justices who are against any attempt to use the power of the Federal Government for bettering general conditions, except within the narrowest limitations. This is a terrific handicap." The next January he said the real trouble was not the Constitution: "If we had liberal judges, with a lively sense of the importance of the social problems which have now spilled over State lines, there would be no serious difficulties; and the existing constitutional restraint when interpreted by such a Court would be very salutary."

It was not to be wondered at that an active, resourceful, daring President was exasperated by the Rock of Gibraltar Court. For eighteen months before the 1936 election he tried to find a way to get out of this jam. He knew all too well that, even if he won the second term by a big margin, he would be confronted by an irreconcilable Court, and wondered what he could do. It is true that the Court was not an issue in the campaign, except by implication, but in the fall of 1936 he asked Cummings and Solicitor General Reed to survey the situation, and report what could be done to get progressive legislation by the Court. Their report in mid-December showed why the jumble of suggestions would not work.

The day after Christmas, in 1936, Cummings went to the White House to tell the President he had found the solution, and unfolded a general measure of judicial reform, the Supreme Court change to be effected through establishing the Justice's right to retire at seventy on full pay — and at the same time legislating that if he did not, within six months after reaching that age, the President could nominate an additional judge, the Court however not to be increased to more than fifteen members. The scheme was to be a general one covering the whole Federal judiciary; at the time, in Supreme and inferior courts, a total of twenty-nine judges of seventy years or over were affected. The plan also provided for a Court Proctor, to handle the business of the judicial structure, gave attention to the docket congestion, authorized the Attorney General to intervene in any private litigation which raised constitutional questions, applied certain restraints on the issuance of injunctions, and provided for direct appeal from the district to the Supreme Court.

Roosevelt was greatly intrigued with the plan and Cummings made nine or ten drafts of it, which were kept secret. Then on February 4, 1937, a special Cabinet meeting was held, with Vice President Garner, Senators Robinson and Ashurst, Speaker Bankhead, Majority Leader Sam Rayburn and Judiciary Committee Chairman Hatton Sumners also present, at which the plan was announced. The next day the bill went to Capitol Hill.

The storm broke at once; "irreverent hands on the Court and Constitution" were denounced by conservatives everywhere. The Court itself seemed calm, but there came a change in the tenor of its decisions. Roberts shifted his view on a State minimum-wage law, the Court upheld the National Labor Relations Act, and, unanimously, the farm bankruptcy and railroad labor acts. Then Van Devanter broke the conservative phalanx by retiring. These were body blows to the thesis of the necessity for a new Court.

Senator Wheeler of Montana, who became stage manager of the congressional opposition, shrewdly caused more than a month's delay in the opening of Senate Judiciary Committee hearings on the bill. The White House made its own mistakes, which aided the opposition. Tommy Corcoran, James Roosevelt, Joe Keenan and Charles Michelson took charge of the campaign, and determined to "meet the enemy on his own ground" — the Court's decisions — instead of forcing the opposition to attack the bill as a whole. By April the fight had gone sour, and the Senate Judiciary Committee voted to disapprove the bill. Consulted as to tactics, Cummings urged that Joe Robinson be put in charge. The majority leader revamped the bill, increasing the retirement age to seventy-five years, appealed to his senatorial friends on a personal basis, in view of his expectation of appointment to the Court, and reported to the White House that he had the votes. Then, on July 14, 1937, Robinson died and the fight for the bill collapsed.

There were, of course, other causes for its failure. Labor's interest in a Court change had sagged with the Justices' changed decision tenor. The internecine war within labor, together with sit-down strikes, mass-picketing violence and the President's manner about them, had a substantial offsetting effect, as did the developing prosperity, which reduced the crisis-urgency of change. Then again, the President's program of reform had so many objectives, such as the governmental reorganization bill, that Administration efforts were scattered all over the lot. At that, in the view of several shrewd observers, had the initial bill been brought to a vote within two or three weeks of its submission, when the opposition was a minority badly split as to alternatives, it would have passed with a large margin to spare.

The epilogue of this lost battle, oddly enough, was victory in the campaign, and the President exulted, in a statement of August 7, 1939, upon the signature of a Court reform bill, that his final objectives had been reached. The Court personnel did not change between 1932 and 1937, but with the retirement law and death, seven left the bench during the next four years; in 1943, only Stone and Roberts remained of the Court of ten years before. Moreover, from 1937 on, as Swisher declares, the trend of opinions "marked the end of an old era and the beginning of a new one." The Court has moved closer and closer to the Woodrow Wilson view that the Constitution is the nation's "vehicle of life."

The President appointed, in March 1936, a Committee on Administrative Management, whose report set off a congressional battle almost as vigorous as that over the Court bill. An incident at its beginning shows the way he uses memory as one of his most efficient tools of government. At one meeting of the Council Club, in the first Wilson term, there had been a debate between Louis Brownlow and Joseph E. Davies over the way the National Government should be organized, to run efficiently, and Roosevelt had made notes of Brownlow's views. In 1936 he got out his old Navy Department files, found the notes, summoned Brownlow to Washington, and said: "I dug out that memo because the views you expressed in your fight with Joe represent my idea of how government ought to be organized. That's why I have sent for you now."

The Committee's report, which he sent to Congress with his approval in January 1937, called for a larger White House staff; transfer of the Bureau of the Budget from Treasury to the Executive Offices of the President; replacement of the Civil Service Commission by an administrator; concentrating the sprawling mass of a hundred independent agencies under twelve departments, two of which would be new: Social Welfare and Public Works. Also it urged change in the status of the Comptroller General. A further key point was that if the President wished to rearrange administrative agencies, he could report his plan to Congress and, unless within sixty days the two Houses passed a disapproving joint resolution, the new order would go into effect. The sponsors of the reorganization scheme looked on this as a great new governmental device for avoiding congressional filibusters — the Legislature could veto, it did not need to legislate.

Senator Wheeler led the fight against this, as he had against the Court; a hysteria of protest was built up against it, but it finally passed the Senate by a narrow margin. F. D. R. then issued a statement: "It proves that the Senate cannot be purchased by organized telegrams based on direct misrepresentation."

Then, at 1:45 A.M. on April 1, 1938, the President made public an amazing document which, in the form of a letter to a friend (whose name was deleted), sought to repel charges that he planned to become a dictator! Up to that time no American President had felt it necessary formally to deny this imputation. Ringing the changes on the congressional failures to reorganize the government, Roosevelt termed legislative enactment to that end a practical impossibility, and insisted the task must be done by executive order. Just the same, if Congress were to pass a joint resolution disapproving a particular executive order, in most cases he would go along!

This brought no new support for the bill, only wonder why he had felt it so urgent to issue this disclaimer. Later in the month the measure failed, giving F. D. R. his second major legislative defeat.

The next Congress, in January 1939, considered a further reorganization bill, more limited in scope, which finally went on the statute books. It stopped the President from abolishing or creating any department, and many agencies were not to be interfered with. This act shifted the congressional action on an executive plan from joint to concurrent resolution. If within sixty calendar days of its submission, "there has not been passed by the two Houses a concurrent resolution stating in substance that the Congress does not favor the reorganization plan," it would take effect. Roosevelt soon submitted two plans, which Congress affirmatively enacted on July 1, 1939, and then early in 1940 proposed three others. The House disapproved one item, but the Senate did not concur and these plans all went into effect.

There has been little evidence of dictatorship in the President's handling of these reorganizing powers, just as no great increase in the economy of administrative operation has resulted. The surface of the structure was considerably simplified, and experts in public administration hailed the improvement. There is some doubt, nevertheless, whether the reform was fundamental; charts do not tell the whole story; as James F. Byrnes told the Senate, "The nearest earthly approach to immortality is a bureau of the Federal Government." Moreover, the improvement in co-ordination between agencies proved more form than substance. The difficulties in handling new tasks in the "soft war" period were but a prelude to the administrative storm after Pearl Harbor.

The Court plan had not been killed before the new recession, but it exercised a depressing influence on the administrative reorganization measure. To a considerable extent, the sharp subtraction of employment was due to a blundering Federal policy of overhasty hunch.

In 1936–1937 it had looked as if the country were getting into a runaway inflation, the omens causing a variety of efforts to avoid it. This was one reason for the President's move away from a deficit spending policy, and also for a cut in normal operating expenditures. The Federal Reserve took active steps to stiffen credit. As a result of overguessing, the brakes were jammed on too hard, the economic doctors went too far, and the cure proved about as bad as the disease.

A new nose-dive in employment, wages, and income began in the summer of 1937 and was not checked for perhaps a year and a half. The downcurve was even sharper than that in 1929 — as was the comeback, for F. D. R. finally saw the error of judgment and refreshened the spendable income with deficit-financed public works.

The new depression, Court failure and reorganization bill rebuffs built many fires under Franklin Roosevelt's emotions. It is not clear when he made up his mind to punish those Democratic Senators and Representatives who had fought his measures, but as the midterm election year of 1938 opened, he made it plain that such was now a major purpose. Soon people began calling it "the Purge."

In many ways it was an expectable and justifiable presidential determination. The 11,000,000 1936 majority had been to Roosevelt, not to the Democrats who fought him. Surely it made him the great national leader of a new Democratic Party, with new elements and purposes, and he must reorganize his party's hierarchy of command.

Moreover, many of these purported Democrats had imputed dictatorial purposes to him, had denounced him, then had blocked his most important reforms; they weren't real Democrats, and ought not to be in Congress under that name.

If ever the time had come to test out whether the Democratic Party had been born anew, it was 1938. The President soon drew the issue in Georgia, where Senator Walter F. George, honest, able conservative, sought a renomination, and the President publicly opposed him, urging a Federal appointee of his own.

The attack was maladroit, the counter simple and effective. Despite the fact that the President called Georgia his adopted State, its people now looked on him as an outsider trying to dictate in a matter of Georgia's individual concern, and many liberals and progressives went with the conservatives to give Walter George a large vote of confidence. Hamilton's well-known thesis in the *Federalist*, about the power of localism as an antidote to central political control, was proved again. In most of the other efforts to deprive anti-New Dealers of renominations, the outcome was of the same order, the most conspicuous perhaps being that of Senator Millard E. Tydings, of Maryland, whose opposition had been as continuous as that of Harry Byrd.

A few anti-New Deal Congressmen were tripped up — John J. O'Connor, of New York, chairman of the House's Rules Committee, being the most conspicuous — but as much for local as national Rooseveltian reasons. The failure of the Purge showed plainly that F. D. R. had not built a great new political party under the old Jacksonian name. On the contrary, his political future, like his past, would depend on his dazzling, or persuading, blocs of the electorate which had no chemical affinity with one another, and little inclination even to experiment with a mechanical mixture. Once they were out of Roosevelt's House of Magic there was no telling where they would go. Such was the lesson of the primaries, and the fall elections attested to its truth. Republicans and reactionaries made new gains. The 1936 mandate began to look like the one-horse shay.

* * *

Between 1936 and 1939, Roosevelt shifted the focus of his attention from the defeat of his domestic policies to the accelerating dangers of war abroad. Inasmuch as the famous "Quarantine" speech at Chicago, October 5, 1937, came after the Court bill disaster, some have imputed an "any port in a storm" motive to this new field of concentration. They claim that after the 1920 campaign he had said little in defense of the League concept; that in his first three years as President he would run at the first clap of isolationist thunder from any collective-security suggestion he advanced; and it was not until after this major defeat on the home front that he turned abroad — *"Post hoc, propter hoc!"*

This would seem half-truth only. One who knew him well from long before 1920 points out that we must never forget Roosevelt's premier characteristic — first of all he is a politician, and except when blinded by some dislike considers all instant actions in the light of the politically obvious. The country went isolationist in 1920, and after that election, he carried no torch for the League — but neither did anyone else! Justice Clarke left the Supreme Court to crusade for it, but few noted or heeded him; Hughes did little more, and as Secretary of State said our entry into the League wasn't "feasible." The "merchants of death" propaganda gripped a restless generation, and the resultant isolationism had to be reckoned with politically. While Hull refused to draft an isolation embargo bill, F. D. R. held his nose, signed one, and said sweet nothings about it.

The trait in which he puts the most store, in operating politically, is timing; Farley has remarked this as the greatest part of his genius in the first term. The "Quarantine" speech certainly was admirably timed, from the standpoint of the rapid disintegration of the peace of the world. There is some evidence that F. D. R. never lost faith in the League's purpose, but waited until he saw it was politically possible to lead the people away from the false gods.

Japan's seizure of the Chinese province of Manchuria, in 1932, started the path to hell. That critical fall, Secretary of State Stimson believed the liberal Japanese ministry claim that it would stop the outrage, and at first refused to go with the British in punitive measures under League ægis. When he found his error, it was too late. Mussolini improved the example with his piratical pounce on Ethiopia; again, divided counsels declared dividends for banditry. Hitler moved next, to reoccupy the Rhineland militarily in March 1936. Its demilitarization had been at France's 1919 insistence, to keep the wolf from the door; but now she did nothing but stew in a factional debate, her *poilus* did not move. "Might makes right" had now thrice proved supreme. Shortly thereafter, a Fascist-inspired revolution broke out in unhappy Spain, which Fuehrer and Duce used as a training school for their new weapons and Panzer tactics. Again fears, doubts and conflicts of loyalties kept the democracies from helping the Spanish Republic.

These ominous portents were the background for the President's speech at a bridge dedication in Chicago. "The will for peace," he proclaimed, "on the part of peace-loving nations must express itself to the end that nations that may be tempted to violate their agreements and the rights of others will desist from such a course." Then he referred to the outbreak of an "epidemic of world lawlessness," to suggest that, in an epidemic of physical disease, the community had learned to protect itself by instituting "a quarantine of the patients." The inference as to Japan, Italy, and Germany did not need to be made more specific.

The isolationists promptly took the war path against his "dangerous" doctrine, but found no such quick withdrawal on the President's part as in 1933 on his suggestion of our "negative-passive" collaboration in sanctions against aggressors. Now he had much more public opinion behind him as he stood his ground. Deliberate and purposive brutality is not one of our household gods, and indignation at outrage can overcome propaganda and fear.

That winter the Nazi Caesar brandished his mailed fist again, this time through his spoliation of Austria, and soon began to threaten Czechoslovakia, the best of the Hapsburg-succession States. Whiny appeasement ruled Downing Street and Quai d'Orsay, fear of the ogre of Bolshevism led them to refuse Stalin's offer to do his part in collective security, and Chamberlain and Daladier knelt to Hitler at Munich — "Peace for our time"!

This quickstep to Hitler's empire over Central Europe, through surrender or war, had a powerful effect on the attitude of the American people. Few such isolationist leaders as Senator Nye, Colonel Lindbergh, or Father Coughlin changed front, but many followers, to whom isolationism had been neither crusade nor livelihood, moved toward middle ground, and Americans in general began to realize the fatuous nature of the ostrich policy in world affairs. It became more and more obvious that the 1935 Neutrality Act was handcuff, not help, to our need to strengthen the democratic nations. The press began to give more support to Hull's efforts, and then the President's, to get the original measure modified so that the badly crippled democracies could use our industrial facilities to help rearm.

Ambassador Bullitt made a hasty trip home in the fall of 1938, to reveal to the President the French and British lack of military aircraft and manufacturing facilities, and to convey their almost frantic appeal to be enabled to purchase American planes. Roosevelt immediately instructed Secretary Morgenthau to find some way the imperiled democracies could legally contract for combat aircraft, and the energetic Treasury head soon found that where there's a will there's a way, including the towing of the planes across the Canadian border.

War's quickstep changed to the double in the spring of 1939, with the Nazi seizure of the whole Czechoslovakian Republic. The policy of appeasement now stood out in the nakedness of its folly, Britain made an alliance with Poland, France belatedly stirred herself, both Axis and Allies courted the Russians, but in such an apparently double-faced manner that Stalin bought time for Germany. This apparent indignity to the Western Democracies led us to impose what we called a "moral embargo" against shipment of military matériel or machine tools to the Soviet, even though Amtorg, their agent, had already bought and paid for the goods.

During the summer of 1939, Roosevelt and Hull did their utmost to persuade Congress really to liberalize the Embargo Act. The McReynolds amendments authorizing cash-and-carry arms and munitions sales had expired by limitation in May 1939, and the isolationists blocked its revival. Hull wanted the Arms Embargo repealed altogether, but on July 6 a public statement was issued by thirty-four Senators declaring themselves "unalterably opposed" to its repeal or modification, and equally against "any discretion being lodged in the hands of any Chief Executive to determine the aggressor" in any war abroad. A few days later the Senate Foreign Relations Committee voted to defer any change in the statute to the next session.

A group of Senators went to the White House on the evening of July 18 to say that revision was hopelessly frozen. Much concerned, the President remarked that this would gravely hamper our efforts to keep peace.

Thereupon Borah interrupted to tell him that the Senate was a legislative body and "responsible only to the people." F. D. R. said maybe he would take the issue to the people, whereupon the Idaho Isolationist reminded that the Senators could do so too, as with Wilson.

Secretary Hull interjected that he wished the Senator could see the confidential reports crossing his desk every day, but Borah broke in to challenge their authenticity or candor: "I have my own private sources of information, which I consider just as reliable as those of Secretary Hull." He went on to infer that there would be no war. A few days later Hull told the country that the Embargo law "works directly against the interest of the peace-loving nations." On August 31, 1939, Hitler's legions invaded Poland, and World War II had begun.

CHAPTER XV

World Strategist

Seldom has there been such change in the use of our presidential power as that between Hitler's attack on Poland and the end of 1943. Within these fifty-two months each of the six roles of the President has undergone a forced conversion, and the pattern of events has added World Strategist to the list.

During the war's first two years — a period which might be termed America's "soft" war, in distinction to the "hard" war after Pearl Harbor — Roosevelt upset the political precedent against a third term, broke the Isolationists' hold on public sentiment, and put the country squarely back of aid to Britain. He persuaded the Congress — and the country — to adopt a peacetime draft, billions were voted for planes, ships, guns, ammunition and matériel of all sorts, and the nation began its conversion from peace to total defense. Judged by any standard, it was an extraordinary performance, and the fact that the President's new administrative arrangements did not work very well detracts little from the positive record.

Both parties' 1940 presidential nominations were against tradition. The Republicans, meeting at Philadelphia, nominated Wendell L. Willkie, former Democrat from Indiana, who had headed the Commonwealth and Southern in its fight against the Tennessee Valley Authority. Many stories were told of his compelling magnetism, and of the mystery which surrounded the rush of G.O.P. delegates to his banner, but the nominee's dramatic showmanship livened up the campaign.

Mystery likewise surrounded President Roosevelt's third-term intentions. About the middle of the second term, friends of some of his principal lieutenants sought to explore nomination possibilities, only to find the road closed.

From the summer of 1937, close friends felt that the President did not know whether there would be a war before the time for the 1940 nominating convention; but as time went on, he thought it more and more likely and, after Munich, became convinced that it was a ten-to-one bet. His state of mind then, as best can be gathered, was that if the storm he saw in the offing should fail to materialize, he would return to Hyde Park after 1940 — already he had made many of the gestures of a man getting ready to quit office. But Hitler's opening of hostilities made the third term bid a certainty.

Doubtless the President felt there was no Democrat he could feel was sure of election, if he dropped out himself, unless it were Hull, whose age was against him. In addition, the opportunity to lead the nation through a world crisis appealed deeply to his sense of duty as well as personal interest. He had begun to be bored with the housekeeping details of domestic government; administrative management never gave him any lift under the wings. But here was the need for world leadership, a challenge he had no wish to ignore.

For all that, the White House staged no active renomination campaign. The President preserved the appearance of not being a candidate, nor is there evidence of under-cover men going over the country to corral delegates to "draft" him. As a matter of fact, it was not necessary — the practical politicians had not been able to find a substitute nominee in whose victory they felt certain, and they needed the third-term meal ticket, and many who hated Roosevelt personally and politically insisted on his selection. State conventions began instructing that he be "drafted" whether he liked it or not, and the President felt flattered by this testimony to his personal political strength.

By the time the Democratic delegates gathered, at Chicago, F. D. R. could only have escaped renomination by making formal pronouncement that if nominated he would not accept, and if elected he would refuse to serve.

The only approach he made to declination was the message he

sent to Senator Barkley, as Permanent Chairman of the Convention. "The President has never had," Barkley told the delegates the evening of July 16, "and has not today, any desire or purpose to continue in the office of President, to be a candidate for that office, or to be nominated by the Convention for that office. He wishes in all earnestness and sincerity to make it clear that all the delegates to this Convention are free to vote for any candidate."

This did not in the least interfere with his nomination, nor with Roosevelt's interposition in the choice of his running mate. After dropping Garner, for a little the President thought of Senator Byrnes, of South Carolina, but later determined on Secretary Wallace. Although supporters of Paul McNutt went ahead with his candidacy, when Byrnes took a hand the Indianan withdrew, and the delegates chose Wallace as had been ordered.

In accepting the nomination, through a radio address from the White House shortly after midnight July 19, Roosevelt said that no call of party alone would lead him to seek a re-election, but he had asked himself whether he had the right, as Commander in Chief, to call on men and women to serve their country and yet decline to serve, himself, if called upon to do so. "Today all private plans, all private lives, have been in a sense repealed by an overriding public danger"; therefore his conscience would not permit him to turn his back "upon a call to service."

He set the theme of the coming campaign by the declaration that "We face one of the great choices of history. It is not alone a choice of government by the people versus dictatorship. It is not alone a choice of freedom versus slavery. . . . It is the continuance of civilization as we know it versus the ultimate destruction of all that we have held dear." Such was the urgency of public questions that he would "not have the time or the inclination to engage in purely political debate. But I shall never be loath to call the attention of the nation to deliberate or unwitting falsifications of fact."

For the next three months he kept himself out of the actual appeal to the voters, but on October 18 he issued a statement charging "a systematic program of falsification of fact by the opposition. The

President does not believe that it has been an unwitting falsification of fact. He believes it is a deliberate falsification of fact. He has, therefore, decided to tell the American people what these misrepresentations have been, and in what respect they are false."

At Philadelphia, October 23, he denounced the claim "that the President of the United States telephoned to Mussolini and Hitler to sell Czechoslovakia down the river," and its companion of secret commitments to foreign wars. He concluded with the pledge: "We will not participate in foreign wars and we will not send our army, naval or air forces to fight in foreign lands outside of the Americas except in case of attack. It is for peace that I have labored; and it is for peace that I shall labor all the days of my life."

The election outcome was not in grave doubt, but its magnitude surprised even the President, who won 38 States with 449 electoral votes, while Willkie earned 10 States with 82 electoral votes. The popular vote was Roosevelt 27,243,466; Willkie, 22,304,755.

During these months of political decision, the President had been pressing a major change in the country's foreign policy, as represented by the 1935 Neutrality Act. Attention has been called to the intransigence of the Senate Isolationists, as late as July 1939, when Borah said he did not believe war would break out in Europe. When it did, six weeks later, the President and Secretary Hull moved promptly to get out of the strait jacket, and after the most strenuous representations of Administration spokesmen, Capitol Hill began to unfreeze. An official committee of Americans interested in helping the democracies defend themselves began operations in Washington, and in October 1939 brought forward "cash and carry" as a substitute for the existing complete ban on sale of arms and munitions to belligerents. The phrase itself is said to have been coined by Bernard M. Baruch, as a little less odorous than "scuttle and run." In any event, Congress liberalized the statute to permit any belligerent to purchase arms and munitions outright, for cash, and to ship the supplies in other than United States bottoms. Because of Britain's blockade, the practical effect of this change was to keep the

Nazis from our markets, but in form it continued our indifference to whether we sold to aggressor or victim.

Under the circumstances, "cash and carry" could be no other than a transition device, morally dissatisfactory to us and financially crushing upon our democratic customers. Britain mobilized her foreign securities holdings and liquidated them carefully; but by the time of the fall of France, in June, 1940, her till was just about empty, and thereafter it was touch and go whether she could find foreign exchange to continue buying in the United States. So desperate did her cash situation become that in September 1940, while the Battle of Britain remained undetermined, Downing Street sent a trade mission to South America vainly seeking a triangular approach to dollar exchange.

Even before this, however, American opinion began to change, chiefly because of France's sudden collapse and Britain's continued resistance despite being on the brink of defeat. None had been more profoundly moved than the President, who determined that the time had come to transform the New Deal into a National Government. On May 26, 1940, he made a nation-wide broadcast on the imperative need for a more efficient national defense "at this time when the world is threatened by the forces of destruction."

Two days later, he announced the organization of the National Defense Advisory Commission, under the authority of the 1916 National Defense Act. Designed to be a co-ordinating agency for government orders, the President characteristically did not give it a directing head, but named seven persons to fractions of the task: Edward R. Stettinius, Jr., of U. S. Steel, was to handle industrial materials; William S. Knudsen, of General Motors, industrial production; Sidney Hillman of Amalgamated Clothing Workers, labor problems; Chester C. Davis, agriculture; Leon Henderson, of the Securities and Exchange Commission, price stabilization; Ralph Budd, of the Burlington Lines, transportation; and Harriet Elliott, of the University of North Carolina, consumer prices. William H. McReynolds was made Secretary, to be a "clearinghouse." Three of the seven were non-New Dealers and Knudsen was an anti-New

Dealer, so the move was generally hailed as one to broaden the base of government, in order to have all major groups united in the common defense.

Belgium's surrender, the collapse of French resistance, Italy's "stab in the back" and Britain's bloody evacuation through Dunkirk rocked American sentiment to its foundations. The President continued his move toward a National Goverment by appointing stalwart Republicans to head the War and Navy Departments. Henry L. Stimson, who became Secretary of War, had held the same post under William H. Taft, and had been Hoover's Secretary of State. Frank Knox, the new Secretary of the Navy, had been Republican candidate for Vice-President in 1936. Both took office before F. D. R.'s own nomination at Chicago, and the country generally approved the move.

About this same time, leading American supporters of the democratic cause over the world, now sustained by Britain alone, organized the Committee to Defend America, with William Allen White at its head. This group undertook a nation-wide campaign to liberalize the cash-and-carry law, so that Britain could continue to get American material. An Isolation group, the America First Committee, challenged this thesis, and for many months these great antagonists strove to dominate American opinion. Their battle has been likened to an American phase of the world-wide civil war of democracy against anarchy. This is a slight oversimplification, for the America First group claimed to favor the victory of the democracies, and aid to Britain — but only in such a way that America would not be drawn into the conflict; while the Committee to Defend America, although hoping we would not be drawn in, wanted us to help regardless of the incidental danger.

The President shrewdly judged the general feeling to be that about 90 per cent hoped Britain and other democracies would win, and wanted us to aid with supplies, but that as late as September 1940 only about 5 per cent wished us to go to war. This estimate on his part explains many of the otherwise obscure aspects of the destroyer deal and the ensuing lend-lease legislation. With France's collapse, in Churchill's phrase, "the British stood alone" — and were in extremity for guns, ammunition, planes, destroyers and escort vessels. The President greatly wished them to have some of our old World War I stock. The British were willing to make us outright gifts of naval bases in American waters — both Canadian and Caribbean — but F. D. R. thought it much better to seem to have made a *quid pro quo* trade, and insisted on it. Downing Street finally yielded, there was an exchange of notes of executive agreement, and on September 2, 1940, the destroyer-base deal was announced. It was an attest to the shrewdness of his judgment that not even the *Chicago Tribune* attacked the destroyer deal; rather, Colonel Robert McCormick took credit for having initiated the idea of procuring the British bases!

This was the prelude to the lend-lease legislation, perhaps the most novel and flexible device for aiding our Allies developed during the war. Although many contributed to the idea, there can be little doubt that the concept came from the active imagination of Franklin Roosevelt himself. Probably Jean Monnet, idea man of the British Purchasing Commission, Arthur Purvis, his magnetic chief, and Lord Lothian, the British Ambassador, had some hand in shaping details, and Oscar Cox had much to do with the actual draft of the bill. But the President and Secretary Morgenthau actually built the bridge to Britain.

After a few White House press conference trial-balloons, the proposed bill went to the Capitol on January 10, 1941. During the hearings, which occupied the next month, the America First group struggled bitterly but unavailingly against the Committee to Defend America, which had set the stage of public opinion. On February 8, the measure came to a vote in the House and passed, 260 to 165; the Senate debate began nine days later, and after amendments it passed that body March 8, by a vote of 60 to 31. The House concurred in the changes and the President signed the measure, March 11. A note in his *Private Papers* states that "within a few minutes thereafter, Army and Navy war materials were speeding on their way to Great Britain." Telegrams went to arsenals and warehouses to ship the guns and munitions, and the matériel was of real help to the British. Congress soon implemented the act with an appropriation of $7,000,000,000.

By December 1940, the organizational inefficiency of the National Defense Advisory Commission was so manifest that the President set up the first of what was to be an unending chain of new agencies to "co-ordinate" defense production activities. He found authority to do so in the 1939 Reorganization Act's establishment, in the Executive Offices of the President, of an "Office of Emergency Management," which could subdivide itself into whatever emergency agencies circumstances might require. "All I wanted," he told a press conference December 20, "was authority to set it up at any time in the future we needed it. So there it is on the statute books, with very broad powers — real powers." The new agency, entitled the Office for Production Management, repeated the NDAC errors of divided authority and responsibility. Although Knudsen became chairman, Hillman was made co-chairman, and the two kings of Sparta often took a long time to agree. In addition, OPM did not replace NDAC, merely became a new layer of authority on top of it.

The President boldly defended this bad delegation on the ground that among the cardinal principles of organization for defense "is the fact that you cannot, under the Constitution, set up a second President of the United States. In other words, the Constitution states one man is responsible. Now that one man can delegate, surely, but in the delegation he does not delegate away any part of the responsibility from the ultimate responsibility that rests on him."

In a Fireside Chat, December 29, 1940, the President quoted Hitler's recent statements that two worlds stood opposed to each other, that with the democratic world "we cannot ever reconcile ourselves," and "I can beat any other power in the world." This proved to Roosevelt that no man can tame a tiger into a kitten by stroking it, and "there can be no reasoning with an incendiary bomb." Therefore "there is far less chance of the United States getting into war if we do all we can now to support the nations defending themselves against attack by the Axis than if we acquiesce in their defeat, submit tamely to an Axis victory, and then wait our turn to be the object of attack in another war later on."

For these reasons "we are planning our own defense with the utmost urgency, and into its vast scale we must integrate the war needs of Britain." This he termed realistic, practical military policy; "we must be the great arsenal of democracy, for this is an emergency as serious as war itself."

His Budget Message, January 3, 1941, asked for authorizations and appropriations of almost $29,000,000,000, about two thirds of which was for a great defense aid program. "It is not enough," he said, "to defend our national existence. Democracy as a way of life is equally at stake." In the Annual Message, he reported "that the future and safety of our country and of our democracy are overwhelmingly involved in events far beyond our borders." He called for all-inclusive national defense; full support to the resisters of aggression; and no countenance to an aggressor peace. Congress responded to the full.

Aid to Russia, the next major development in our program, came on the President's personal initiative. We had maintained a "moral embargo" against shipping Russia matériel of war, because of her 1939 nonaggression treaty with Germany; and relations had grown quite strained. But two days after Hitler's attack of June 22, 1941, and before any request had come from the Soviet, Roosevelt summoned Under Secretary of State Sumner Welles, examined the new situation, and directed that we send matériel at once, to help Russia carry through the perilous summer.

Goods moved at once, our lend-lease program was stretched, and conferences in the Russian capital in September resulted in the first Moscow Protocol between the Soviet, Britain and ourselves. The President threw his personal weight behind the procurement and dispatch of the items we had promised, helped break through procedural obstructions and service objections, and there ensued a personal correspondence with Premier Stalin which led to increasing confidence between the two governments.

Roosevelt's personal interest shifted more and more from domestic issues to concerns of the war abroad. He made Harry Hopkins Assistant to the President and sent him to London, then to Moscow, to sense the situation and appraise the personalities in high place. In August, the President and Prime Minister Churchill conferred at sea, and agreed on the Atlantic Charter of the Four Freedoms for a democratic world. Not long thereafter, American troops garrisoned Greenland and Iceland, and American naval vessels began furnishing active aid to our ships in European danger zones. Through the summer and fall of 1941, the "arsenal of democracy" furnished an increasing volume of essential supplies to Britain and Russia, and at the same time our own military establishment expanded and equipped itself for a "total defense."

For all that, something basic was wrong with the national situation. Many felt the moral weakness of our thunder in the index. If the cause of democracy were, in truth, as vital to the survival of our way of life as Roosevelt insisted, how could we continue to insist that we furnish goods, not lives, for its defense? Why should millions of Russians and Britons die that we should be free? There was so grave a discrepancy between presidential preachment and national action that many Americans felt sore at heart. Some felt the President was following, rather than leading, public opinion.

During the summer and early fall, the German submarine campaign gave new point to these dissatisfactions. Britain's naval strength, necessarily spread over the seven seas, was now under added strain because of ominous moves by Japan, and proved quite inadequate to check the U-boat. Ship losses reached staggering proportions, not only in Britain's own supply, but on the long new route to Murmansk and Archangel, and to the Persian Gulf, upon which Russia had to depend for Anglo-American aid. The total of British and American building did not replace them. And by October it looked as though Hitler were about to starve Britain and break Russia, because we were on the sidelines.

The omens of early 1917 had reappeared. But still there came no word from the White House that our vital national interest demanded that we get into the shooting war. If ever the fate of democracy trembled in the balance, it was in the last four months of 1941.

Franklin Roosevelt never decided this question; but Japan did by its attack on Pearl Harbor, Sunday morning, December 7, 1941. Among the most interesting of the "ifs" of history is what would have been the outcome of the war if the Japanese militarists had not made their fatal gamble. Suppose, instead of direct attack on us, she had gone after British Hong Kong and Singapore — would we have declared war on her to protect our interests in the Southwest Pacific? At the least, it is subject to doubt.

Our relations with Japan, however, had deteriorated rapidly since July 1941, when she occupied French Indo-China, after the palsied Vichy Government had knelt to her demands. Tokyo was full of saber-rattling, our thin trickle of aid to besieged China was protested, and a military junta took over the government of Japan. In November, she sent a special ambassador to Washington, on the pretense of negotiating a general Pacific peace, at the same time that she was finishing the fitting-out of expeditions to attack us in Hawaii and the Philippines.

Secretary Hull patiently explored each Japanese "proposal." They grew more impossible day by day, during the last two weeks of November.

It chanced that the author of this volume spent the evening of Saturday, December 6 with the Secretary, who said that he had been warning our military leaders that Japan might attack any minute. Within twenty hours news came of the Pearl Harbor holocaust. It should be said, parenthetically, that Japan's "sneak attack" probably will go down in history as the act which saved the democracies of the world from destruction.

During the first twenty-five months of our total war, the United States has undergone a unique conversion, which has touched practically every American institution. One of its most interesting aspects, however, is the variable degree of war's effect on the major fields of national concern. The differences are especially striking between our military mobilization and action; the organization of our economy for production for war; the reactions of our people to war controls and privations, and the policy and execution of our national government. In each, the use of presidential power has played a part.

Neither the leaders nor the people could envisage, at the beginning, the magnitude of the change that must be made, which was nothing less than the transformation of both our economic system and our political structure into radically new types. As Professor Ogburn wrote, in May 1943, "to produce for the motive of winning the war instead of making more profits means a change from the capitalistic State to the social service State" for the duration of the conflict. Winning the war likewise requires a government by executives rather than legislatures and courts. Not only must we have an expanded Executive, "to see that the war tasks are done, but we must have speed and we must have unity," neither of which comport with our traditional democratic ways. "The war State," he continues, "which we are trying to be, is more effective if we give up capitalism and democracy, two of our most cherished institutions, which have been responsible for most of the good things we have in America" — but only for the period of the war, and in order to win. "A modern total war cannot be won by the peacetime State."

Considered by these standards, our military services have come the closest to the needs of the war State and our production for war very close to them. On the other hand, the conduct of government agencies has been spotty and in many ways deficient, particularly in the areas affecting civilian life and public morale. In some fields, Franklin Roosevelt has given brilliant leadership, notably in military strategy in the global war. In several matters on the home front, the defects of his qualities have hurt almost as much as his genius for persuasion has helped the conduct of the war.

Roosevelt's first major military step after Pearl Harbor was the creation of a new organ of combined command. Prime Minister

Churchill came to Washington within a fortnight of our entry, and the two Chiefs of Government soon worked out a procedure for the integration of military planning between the United States and the British Empire, through the Combined Chiefs of Staff. The adjective "Combined" describes a unified staff, committee, Board or other agency in which the Governments of the United States and the United Kingdom have associated together for consultation, planning and action on common problems. In February 1942, the President and the Prime Minister announced the establishment of the Combined Chiefs of Staff Group "to insure complete co-ordination of the war efforts of these two nations, including the production and distribution of their war supplies, and to provide for full British and American collaboration with the United Nations now associated in prosecution of the war against the Axis powers." While on broad strategical questions they would make joint recommendations to the heads of their respective Governments, in minor and immediate matters relating to current operations they would act without delay. Actually it would be "a combined command post for the conduct of all joint operations of the two Governments in the war." Within a few weeks there were gathered, under a single roof, the professional military leadership of the two countries, who continually interchanged their information and views, and made decisions on the war.

Among the toughest problems before the Combined Chiefs has been allocating the "U.S.-U.K." war matériel production among the fighting forces of all the United Nations. The Munitions Assignment Board, which is the agent of the Combined Chiefs in examining the cases of the various claimant nations and arms of service, was also set up early in 1942, to "advise on all assignments, both in quantity and priority . . . in accordance with strategic need." From the start, Harry Hopkins has been its Chairman, and its Executive Officer, Major General James H. Burns, United States Army, bears the reputation of possessing one of the surest judgments in official Washington.

The Combined Chiefs' performance has been noteworthy; informed military leaders declared, as early as July 1942, that already greater unity of command had been achieved between United Nations forces than the Allies ever had in World War I under Marshal Foch. The careful planning and execution of the North African occupation late that year was a case in point.

Roosevelt has taken the keenest interest in the operation of the Combined Chiefs, just as he has in the American service association of Joint Chiefs of Staff to integrate our Army, Navy and Air Forces. From a surface standpoint, it might seem that he has dominated their decisions as Commander in Chief, but this theory does not stand up on analysis.

His restraint is not because he lacks appreciation of the power that exists in that constitutional commitment. On the contrary, he is immensely impressed by it, and once told a confidant that "the Commander in Chief of the Army and Navy of the United States in time of war has the power to do practically any damn thing he wants to do." None the less, he has employed this reservoir with considerable caution.

In September 1942, when he asked Congress to implement the "hold-the-line-against-inflation" program, there is reason to believe that his mind was made up to go forward as Commander in Chief to keep the price level from being broken; but Congress belatedly passed the desired legislation. In a number of instances, chiefly of plants or mines shut down because of labor trouble, he seized them for the Government, as Commander in Chief, and Congress conferred no such statutory powers until long after he had set the military-necessity precedent. But all this is far from indicative of broad employment in civil affairs of the Commander in Chief's authority. Certainly in comparison with Lincoln's use, Roosevelt's is Lilliputian.

It is as a brilliant strategist, not as a dominating commander, that Franklin Roosevelt has most conspicuously focused his abilities in the conduct of the war. F. D. R. has done brilliant things in the higher levels of the direction of the war effort, but as persuader and convincer rather than as commander using the categorical imperative.

Logistics fascinate him, almost as much as the determination of where our combat endeavors will take shape. To oversimplify the nature of his world military interest: it is primarily in determining the *where* of the coming campaigns, and the *how* of getting men, matériel and supplies to the spot; these questions probably take precedence over *who* is to be the troop commander, and precisely *what* sort of campaign technique will be employed.

Not that these latter questions bore the President — far different is the case, according to the reports that seep around. But two influences restrain him from insistent personal interpositions into decisions of chiefly military nature. To begin with, as Commander in Chief and Chief of State, he must make important fundamental decisions of a political character, which are above and beyond the province of the strategist in uniform. In association with Churchill, he must determine the relative importance of the European versus the Pacific theaters of action, in order that the Anglo-Saxon nations may divide the weight of their combined effort between the two overlapping but still separate global wars. How much aid to China? How soon a second front, to share the European war with Stalin? Such determinations are of national policy and, while the military variables need to be appraised and projected by the Marshals and the Kings, only the chief political officer of the nation can make the decision. Once that has been done, he can well afford, as he does, to let the men of outstanding technical skill plan the implementation of these decisions of top consequence.

Almost equally important is the fact that Franklin Roosevelt does not find it hard to confide in trusted subordinates. From the beginning he has shown implicit confidence in the knowledge and wisdom of General George C. Marshall, Chief of Staff of the Army, an officer who has brought experience, aptitude and study to the top level of command. It was fortunate that the President had a principal officer he trusted, and so could avoid Lincoln's frantic search for a real general. Civil chief and military agents have maintained that mutual trust is indispensable to the successful conduct of war by our democracy. Similar relationships have come about between the President and Admiral Ernest J. King, Commander of the Fleet, and General H. H. Arnold, our Air Chief.

As the war went on, F. D. R. became increasingly interested in the higher-level problems of strategy, logistics and supply. Early in 1943 Ernest Lindley predicted that the President would concentrate more and more on world strategy, and leave problems of domestic government in the hands of such an "assistant President" as Ex-Justice Byrnes. The year's events substantially verified the prediction. After sustaining the shock of attack, the United Nations had equipped themselves with men and weapons, to shift from the defensive. Stalin's winter offensive of November 19, 1942, paralleled in time our own beginnings in Guadalcanal and New Guinea, and the great expedition to North Africa. Roosevelt's attention to the global war needs was close and successful.

The year 1943 was one of amazing conferences between the great Allies. The first — between the President, the Prime Minister, Free French leaders, and the top staff minds — took place at captured Casablanca in January, and enabled the projection of the Tunis campaign across the straits into Sicily, and then on to the Italian mainland. Of course such military secrets could not be hinted, but the principle of "Unconditional Surrender" was announced to the public as the sole basis for ending the war. Stalin's much-discussed absence from Casablanca was attributed to the clamant nature of his duties as military Commander in Chief of the Red Army.

The fact that the American and British forces had not opened a second front in Western Europe was thought by some to have been a further reason the Russian chief did not attend. When his chief lieutenant, Molotov, visited the White House in June 1942, the President had pledged that such a front would be opened, and Stalin took this to mean by the end of the year. General Marshall and other American staff heads have held from the beginning, according to report, that there is no substitute for a major offensive in Western Europe, to divide the forces against Stalin, and bring the Nazi war to a close. British experts, more inclined to depend on bombing and sideshows, pointed out the impossibility of mounting and maintaining a major attack on western Europe in the summer of 1942. But for Stalin, the ensuing Moroccan expedition was no substitute for the promised second front, and he bluntly said so in a letter to Henry Cassidy, of the Moscow staff of the Associated Press.

Keeping faith on the second front was among the chief topics at 1943's second great war-planning conference, held at Quebec in the late summer, with Roosevelt, Churchill, Hull, Eden, and the military tops as the principal negotiators.

In September Secretary Hull informed the President that the time had come for direct discussion with Russia, that he intended personally to represent the United States, "whether it is held in Washington, London, Moscow or Chungking," and the Moscow Conference ensued. No commitments had been made in advance, but Hull took with him a detailed plan, which was adopted by the foreign ministers of Russia, China, Britain, and the United States, and proclaimed with Stalin's approval. Such was the achievement of the man from Tennessee that Churchill termed him "that gallant old eagle," and our Senate incorporated the principal points of the Moscow agreement in a resolution pledging America's participation in keeping the peace.

This set the stage for two more dramatic sessions between Chiefs of State. At Cairo, early in December, Roosevelt and Churchill met Chiang Kai-shek for a thorough exploration of the Pacific war. Not only did the leaders plan for combat, but also then announced the steps they would take to render Japan incapable of further menace to world peace. From Cairo, the President and the Prime Minister flew to Teheran, where they met Stalin, who left Russian soil for the first time in a quarter of a century.

It was Roosevelt's first hand-to-hand contact with the monolithic chief of All the Russias but, as he said later, "I got along fine with Stalin." It is reported that Stalin was interested in only three questions: "When will you open the second front in western Europe? How much force will you commit to it? Whom will you put in command?" President and Prime Minister are supposed to have given him definite commitments on each before the sessions adjourned. Their joint announcement indicated that Russia, Britain, and the United States were marching together to total victory. Soon after the President's return to America, he announced the appointment of General Eisenhower to lead the invasion. As the year turns, Russia is sweeping west into old Poland, and a second front is about to be opened by a great Anglo-American force. There could be no finer attest to Franklin Roosevelt's genius as world strategist than the military events of 1943.

On his return to America from these epochal conferences, the President was confronted with multiple revolts at home and must turn his immediate attention to a threatened nation-wide railroad strike for higher pay. Not only did this constitute a grave danger to the national war effort, but it was equally significant as a token of a growing dissatisfaction with executive policy and performance on the home front.

It should be said at the outset that the shortcoming has not been in our production for war. History contains no counterpart of our conversion of an industrial economy from peace to war. In 1940, just about 2 per cent of our national output was of military matériel; three years later, the proportion of a greatly expanded production was close to 50 per cent. Nor was the upward sweep only of dollar volume; the state of the arts had advanced under pressure, as was well illustrated in the building of ships. At the beginning of 1942, our yards had taken an average of 325 days between laying the keel of a vessel and putting it into commission, and a million man-hours were required for the job. As 1943 ended, the average time had been cut to about thirty-three days, while the man-hours were under half a million. Similar production improvements have been achieved in aircraft, tanks, guns, munitions, and a long list of indispensable military needs. In two years' time we have made ourselves a magnificent arsenal for democracy.

To a degree only is the achievement governmental, and here

principally because of the provision of funds both for plant construction, expansion, and conversion, and for the enormous quantities and varieties of end-products sought. It is open to question whether the emergency agencies set up to co-ordinate and control war production have been of vital aid. The War and Navy Departments and Maritime Commission have continued the direct makers of contracts, but under various sorts of collaboration, association, and control, by the supposed great brass brains of the civil agencies. The latters' principal troubles have come not so much from poor organizational form, but from the inexperience, incapacity, or lack of force of the men the President put at the helm, and his frequent reluctance to discharge failures.

Early in 1942, OPM was gently shelved, along with its ally SPAB; Knudsen became a lieutenant general, Hillman returned to his union work, and the War Production Board came upon the stage. Donald M. Nelson, its chairman, had an Executive Order under whose language he could have run the whole domestic war effort. But Executive Orders, like co-ordinators, sometimes sell as low as a dime a dozen. WPB was soon in a battle with the military chiefs over the basic issue of who should determine the quantities of things to be made and the number of men to be available to make them. Eventually the service chiefs won White House approval of their insistence on self-determination of military needs, and WPB became more and more a service agency, riven with factions and clogged by masses of paper work. The original Executive Order allotment of powers atrophied through disuse. The same life-cycle can be discerned in many other war agencies.

This characteristic of form without substance shocks many observant critics. "This Government," observed a thoughtful Briton, "impresses me because of its disorder. We British couldn't get along if our Government had as little order in it as yours has." The observation is not altogether unjust.

At the same time, the lack of order in governmental agencies has not kept us from extraordinary success in making the munitions of war. This is no paradox, but stems out of the fact that the governmental operations often have been two-dimensional, and while excellence on their part would have been of great aid, their lack of it did not vitiate the ability of our mass-production executives to organize for capacity output. WPB'S control of allocation of materials, as between types of end-products, has been vitally necessary, and has increased the war production to some extent. But much of its paperwork has delayed or impeded production. Only in part has the agency justified its existence.

Obviously, the President has the primary responsibility for the ineffective war agency co-ordination, which has arisen because of his imperfect delegation of power to subordinates. His powers are ample enough. The First War Powers Act, signed December 18, 1941, authorized the President "to make such redistribution of functions among executive agencies as he may deem necessary" — surely a broad enough grant. The difficulty is that F. D. R. is just interested in personalities, ideas which are in any sense abstract leave him cold, and he is deficient in any basic sense of order. As a result, he has made inadequate provision of administrative machinery with clear power to reconcile the claims of rival administrators or agencies to power, prestige, enlargement of zone of control. Most of our agencies perform partial tasks which the President sought to co-ordinate through giving one man the right to issue a "directive." In essence, this meant that this officer would instruct or order another officer, of a different department or war agency, but of equal status and authority, to perform a certain act. The issuer of the directive could do so because the President, through an Executive Order, has delegated to him the right to enforce compliance on the part of his equal-status associate. But generally it doesn't work out that way. Each head of agency finds that there is a certain minimum necessity for personal prestige. Men who let themselves be shoved around generally lose, first, acclaim; then confidence; then respect; and eventually such persons hurt rather than help administrative performance. Upon the administrator's maintenance of his public stature may depend job-security for hundreds, perhaps thousands of employees. If his backbone be made of putty, many will seek to stiffen it — "to needle him," in the current argot of Washington bureaucracy.

The President did not lack advisers who could point out the errors to be avoided and the new steps to take. The Bureau of the Budget has developed the technique of governmental administrative management to a high degree, particularly in its insistence upon the development of fields of function to replace institutional overlaps. There has been no lack of perception of developing discords, or of prescription for their avoidance. But Roosevelt has generally been loath to act until the blaze was out in the open, as in the Wallace–Jones battle of the summer of 1943. He has set up agency after agency to amend the situation, beginning with the Office of Economic Stabilization, which he persuaded Justice James F. Byrnes to resign from the Supreme Court to head, and later the Office of War Mobilization, to which he advanced the ex-Justice. Yet the latter has not become an Assistant President to handle domestic matters. Roosevelt still takes personal charge of such problems as how to yield to John L. Lewis's coal strike, and to prevent that of the railroad men. The poor direction of labor relations has had counterparts in the handling of food, gas, prices and civilian morale.

These upsets in executive agency operations have been paralleled by the widening of the gap on Pennsylvania Avenue. This began before the 1942 mid-term election, for most Senators and Representatives, including New Dealers, resent the way they believe Roosevelt has pushed Congress out of its theoretical function of forming national policies. To this institutional loyalty, they add personal resentments because of the way he has short-circuited Congress to go direct to the people with Fireside Chats, although Churchill talks through the House of Commons to the world. Equally exacerbating has been his insistence on handling the labor-relations problem personally as political leader rather than officially as Chief Executive.

The 1942 election was no such repudiation as that of 1918 was to Wilson — the Democrats managed to retain control of both Houses;

but the President distinctly did not, as witness the repassage of the Smith-Connally bill over his veto in June 1943. The prospects of co-operation in the new year are none too promising. A few years ago, the President made a speech to a group of political scientists, in which he said that "democracy is an art." If so, it is one both ends of the Avenue are prone to forget.

The final presidential flourish for 1943 was the burial of the New Deal. Early in December, a visiting columnist elicited a Roosevelt remark that "New Deal" was out as a slogan; "Win the War" should take its place. Actually, this did no more than print the obituary five years after the discovery of the corpus delicti; but Greek fire burned on the editorial pages, and columnists wondered who had planted the story, and why. One termed it a fourth term announcement; another claimed that the President had made a political half-face with the failure of the 1938 "Purge," the term New Deal had been in bad odor ever since, and it was well to drop it for "Win the War." A third saw an abandonment of former principles, in order to get elected again.

This boomerang hurt Roosevelt's pride. At the next White House press conference he made an effort to explain the switch by an elaborately detailed allegory in which "Doc New Deal" had cured the patient of internal maladies. Two years ago, however, there was a very bad accident, the doctor knew nothing about this kind of trouble, and got his partner, an orthopedic surgeon, "Dr. Win-the-War," to take care of the case. At his conclusion, a correspondent shot the obvious question: "Doesn't it all add up to a fourth term declaration?" The President, nettled, shot back: "Oh, now, we are not talking about things like that now. You are getting picayune."

Seldom has the ebb and flow of presidential power been so dramatically exemplified as in this extraordinary situation at the close of 1943. It is as though the American people had given an unexampled vote of confidence to the President in his joined capacities of Commander in Chief and Chief of Foreign Relations, and at the same time had signified lessened confidence — some contend actual lack of confidence — in the same man's role of Chief of Government on the Home Front. In some ways it is almost a geographical division of the leadership of our Chief of State. From the water's edge, he is all-powerful, the trusted spokesman of the people in the struggle for a free world; but within our national boundaries, his primacy has increasing challenge, and his power to persuade grows less and less.

While time will bring continuing reappraisal of Franklin Roosevelt, the present is the time when an understanding of him is of the greatest concern to the living. His mind has length and breadth; whether it possesses depth is a question only time will decree, as with Lincoln. It is quick as a flash: the President perceives a trend of a person's statement sentences before it is put in words. It is a disorderly mind serviced by an amazing memory, and afforded comic relief by passages at arms with the correspondents, and by unpredictable quips, cranks, and wanton wiles. He is no master of logic, but logic is only a tangent to reality, and it is not an important lack.

He is a good hater, and the White House black-list was, perhaps, longer than that of any other President. Yet during the war he has removed many from the list of untouchables, and given them important posts, sometimes with commensurate power.

Roosevelt's likes are as genuine and unpredictable as his hates, as witness Harry Hopkins; he chooses unexpected agents because he likes them, and sometimes they do surprisingly well. He is persuader, rather than commander; clever rather than philosophic; genius at timing more than leader of the people.

All men are to be judged by what they do and the way in which they do it. The statesman must also be judged by what he chooses to do. No man in our times has chosen to do more extraordinary things than Franklin Delano Roosevelt. For generations hence, historians will be appraising the consequences of his acts.

CHAPTER XVI

Retrospect and Prospect

We have found in the school of experience that the use of presidential power constitutes as interesting and perhaps as important a question as exists in the nation today. What light does the record of the first 155 years of the office throw upon the traits and qualities America's Number One Man ought to have?

The requirements for an ideal President are not hard to put on paper. He must be a powerful leader, to speak for the great but usually silent majority of the people. Never for long can the country do without a strong Chief Executive. Generally a strong president makes mistakes, and the people get tired of him, but they must find another to take his place. The worst periods of our history have been when Presidents were weak and Congresses strong.

The President must lead party, Congress and the people, and to do so needs joined talents of persuasion and command. He must come to office with a sense of the general direction in which he wishes to move, but he must avoid being too far ahead of his times, and must refrain from seeking to employ the novel plan or unlooked-for principle. The personal traits most called for by his executive duty is the power to handle men, the ability almost intuitively to recognize the efficient human instrument for his purpose. Furthermore, the President who cannot delegate, and trust when he has delegated, is in a very bad way.

But such a catalogue of traits and talents cannot escape being in the realm of illusion, because no one among the great Presidents whose careers we have surveyed has possessed all of these qualities, and some of them have lacked almost every one mentioned. Therefore let us shift our attention from the unattainable best to the actual good, as shown by experience.

It should be remarked, in passing, that those consulted during the work on this volume have shown little disposition either to add to or to subtract from the list of eight men on whom our attention has focused: Washington, Jefferson, Jackson, Lincoln, Cleveland, Theodore Roosevelt, Wilson and Franklin Roosevelt. Some call attention to the interesting aspects of the White House careers of three strong men who did not become great — Tyler, Polk and Hayes — but do not nominate them for the top group.

The points of resemblance among these eight men would seem more the result of chance than preordination. Perhaps their chief common characteristic, as Professor William F. Ogburn has pointed out to us, is that each had to deal with some great national crisis. The people chose some specifically to introduce a major change into the purpose and policy of the national government: notably Jefferson, Jackson, Lincoln, Wilson, and Franklin Roosevelt. Cleveland came in as a protest against the shabby skullduggery of Reconstruction. In 1788, George Washington was the great rock of patriotic character upon whom the foundations of the new State could be laid. Only Theodore Roosevelt became President without crisis to handle or selection for a change he was to carry through — and he manufactured crises out of causes, to have plenty of storms to ride.

This does not mean that each great national crisis developed a great President. Madison did not grow with the dangers of the War of 1812. Buchanan was paralyzed by Secession, Johnson's brittle courage did not halt Reconstruction's excesses, McKinley succumbed to the warmongers almost without a struggle, and Hoover lacked the qualities to halt the Great Depression. Crises make great Presidents only when organic growth of character can occur in the particular man.

Each of the eight held more than one term, and, with all but Theodore Roosevelt, all were elective terms. This may mean that a bare four years does not provide a sufficient time-span for a holder of the office to prove his title to greatness, though it should be kept in mind that the President's influence begins the moment of his nomination by his party, and in a sense his power covers at the least some four-and-a-half years. One wonders whether Cleveland would today be regarded as a great President had he served only his first term. His examples of heavy-fisted attention to the details of public trust were chiefly of that period. On the other hand, both his great exhibits of expansion of presidential power came in the post-Harrison return. On a first-term basis, probably he would be held a strong man who failed.

Six of the eight have been lawyers — Washington and Theodore Roosevelt the only exceptions — but none of them were great lawyers, and only Lincoln was making his living entirely from legal work at the time he entered the White House. Jackson probably had the best-rounded legal experience, but much preferred war and politics. Franklin Roosevelt kept his law partnership alive after the 1920 campaign, but his chief earned income came from a well-paid insurance post. Why has no really great lawyer ever become a great President?

Without doubt, George Washington lent the greatest personal dignity to the President's role of Chief of State. Not only his individual reserve and impressive mien but his interest in the element of sovereignty in the office led to this result. Next to him was Jackson, with Wilson not far behind. Cleveland had an overweening sense of the majesty of the office of President, but exhibited it chiefly by refusing to make White House hospitality an aid to his political needs.

Jefferson's easy manner caused many to feel that he had no sense of stature as Chief of State; yet whenever his prerogative or position were challenged, he defended them with energy and success. Lincoln's mode was likewise deceptive, yet Seward soon found him no museum piece but keenly conscious of his official primacy and quick to preserve, protect and defend it. Theodore Roosevelt had more assertiveness than dignity. Franklin Roosevelt's genial personality has been a velvet glove for his firm hand as Chief of State.

Which among these eight were first-rate Chiefs of Government, in the sense of Prime Minister rather than King? Again Washington would seem outstanding in this role. The experience he gained in handling the flow of military business as Commander in Chief in the War of American Independence implemented his personal attention to precedent and procedure, and the discrimination between relative importance. He laid the foundations of the new Federal executive departments with a combination of caution and boldness, delegated well, and committed trust with delegation.

Though Jefferson had no such pre-presidential training in public administration, within two years he schooled himself to manipulate the details of the office quite competently. His rare skill in his relationship with the theoretically co-ordinate legislative department brought about team-play until the Embargo crisis. While he did not delegate authority as unreservedly as Washington, that grant to Gallatin was competent and far-sighted.

Woodrow Wilson likewise made himself a first-rate Chief of Government, through as hard a job of conversion as Jefferson's. But his ability was not so much shown in his mastering of the detail of administrative procedure as in the clear-cut nature of the delegations he made and stood behind. Throughout our years in World War I, he made full commitments of authority, and sustained them against hostile criticism.

While Grover Cleveland is generally regarded as a first-rate prime minister, praise may be too lavish. His exposures of fake veteran claims were useful as examples, but his focus on them constituted a misapplication of the time of the President, which is inexpansible. In his second term he avoided this earlier addiction.

Jackson was a better Chief of Government than Lincoln, probably because of the stream of information from the Kitchen Cabinet. Theodore Roosevelt had ample energy to put pressure behind whatever his interests were at the moment, but these were often as short-lived as kaleidoscopic. His Hyde Park cousin shares T. R.'s energy for specific detail, as well as his variability and interruptability of interest, and his unwillingness to make a clear-cut delegation of a complete fraction of presidential power. F. D. R.'s failures as co-ordinator of administration resemble Lincoln's.

Probably Lincoln gave the outstanding presidential performance as Chief of Foreign Relations, for he carried the majority of the people of the Loyal States along with him from the institution of the blockade, soon after Sumter, through the craving of Britain's pardon for the *Trent* blunder, right to the stern demands on Britain over the building of ships for the Confederates. His joined talents as lawyer and leader of opinion proved of the greatest effect.

Next to him has been Franklin Roosevelt, whose skillful leadership of our transition from isolation to war has no counterpart in our annals. F. D. R's genius for timing was best shown in this field; here, too, his facility at persuasion had impressive effect. New transportation facilities have made possible wartime meetings between world leaders, which Wilson could never attain; Roosevelt put them to full use, despite grave personal hazards. The series of meetings of Chiefs of State — Atlantic Charter; Casablanca; Cairo; Teheran — to determine common denominators of war effort and peace purpose, has constituted an extraordinary adaptation of means to ends. Only men of the imaginative urge of Roosevelt and Churchill could have initiated such a collaboration of the heads of the four great free nations of the world. The greatness of President Roosevelt and Secretary Hull in handling our foreign relations will remain memorable.

Jefferson conducted our foreign policy brilliantly for his first six years, as was exampled by the Louisiana Purchase. His effort to gain the fruits of war by measures short of war was shrewdly conceived, and almost succeeded.

Wilson showed rare ability in leading Allied and neutral opinion against the Central Powers. His treaty negotiation at Paris did not deserve all the criticism of the decade of disillusionment. Had we made the League a world reality, today's heartrending struggle might not have occurred. Whatever his ineptitudes in handling the Senate, still Lodge's spleen, the party purpose, and the defect of the Constitution in giving a veto to one over a third of the Senate, cannot escape a major share of responsibility for the failure that ensued.

Cleveland's chief involvements in foreign relations gave him the chance to show his blunt courage, generally for sound national ends, but the manner left much to be desired. Theodore Roosevelt took great credit for such episodes as Santo Domingo, and the Venezuelan blockade, and his course in Panama. But his secret executive agreement with Japan illustrated the danger of his impetuous course.

None of the great Presidents made more use of the power and duty of Commander in Chief than Lincoln, who expanded the command and war powers to provide him with the weapons to fight the war. Although for the first two years his actual military direction was full of blunders, he slowly learned to eschew tactics and back the strategy of a successful General-in-Chief. But he made the most novel and successful use of these powers in controlling civilian affairs outside the actual theater of war. As Commander in Chief he defeated the Copperhead fifth columns, suspended the execution of the writ of habeas corpus, and issued the Emancipation Proclamation.

Neither predecessors nor successors have equaled this employment. Madison fumbled badly in every aspect of his war power. Polk was a first-rate Commander in Chief, hamstrung by Whig generals. Theodore Roosevelt's most dramatic plan to use war power, to take over the Pennsylvania hard-coal mines, remains thunder in his *Autobiography*. In matters of military command, Wilson leaned heavily on Baker, Pershing, March and Bliss. In civil areas he used power sparingly; censorship was voluntary in form, bearing no resemblance to the Civil War suppression of Chicago *Times* or New York *World*. Congress was as far to the right as the President, and no Taney opinion in *ex parte* Merryman stalked Wilson in World War I.

Franklin Roosevelt, as has been seen, makes sparing use of the almost illimitable powers of Commander in Chief, certainly less than Wilson, and amazingly less than Lincoln. In the field of direct military command, he has had the great advantage over his Civil War predecessors of not having been forced to try out a dozen inept military advisers before he found a man he could trust. From the beginning he confided in the wisdom and knowledge of General Marshall, and he soon found in Admiral King the qualities he needed for over-all naval command. This happy chance permitted the President to confine his military decisions to the top level of essentially political determinations, in collaboration with the other Chiefs of State. His knowledge and interest in strategy and logistics led him, of course, to make many inquiries and suggestions as to operating details, but in no known instance to thwart sound tactical dispositions as Lincoln had in McClellan's Peninsular campaign. In essence, Franklin Roosevelt has been a brilliant world strategist rather than an interfering military Commander in Chief.

Nor has he given much evidence of emulating Lincoln in the exercise of war powers out of his constitutional role and independent of congressional commitment. Like Wilson, he went to the legislature for an extraordinary panoply of war powers, and with insignificant exceptions his novel executive acts have been within the canopy of conferment under the first and second war powers acts. Nearly all his proclamations of seizure as Commander in Chief of industrial plants, mines, or railroads resulted from the failure of his labor policy. When he could persuade compliance no longer, he used the form of military seizure to mask the fact of partial retreat from his stand.

Washington did not regard himself as a Chief of Party when he took the oath in April, 1789, but had almost become one before he went out of office eight years later. It must be added he was not very successful at it, as was shown by the schisms in Federalist leadership after 1792. But Jefferson was very much the party leader, perhaps the most adroit and accomplishing one who ever held the nation's first office. His party effectiveness had many facets; the form of persuasion masked the fact of command, and he seemed an "easy boss"; he held the door open for repentant Federalists, and had no long list of proscribed; he nourished the party organization and sustained the party press. In addition, he picked and drilled party whips, to guide his legislative program through the two Houses in an amazingly effortless but resultful way.

Old Hickory's equally conspicuous party leadership was founded on very different personal traits. The people's revolution he captained was quite as extraordinary as Jefferson's in 1800, and his Kitchen Cabinet shrewdly staffed the ensuing struggle to maintain power. Jackson purged his party of nullification and disaffection, but rebuilt his strength to defeat Emperor Nick Biddle and destroy his Bank. Jackson's personal party endured for years after his death.

Lincoln's sobriquet of Master Politician has been given him for other traits than skill in party management. The Republicans made him their candidate in 1860 largely because of the convention struggle between Seward, Cameron, Chase, and a host of favorite sons, and the fact that the choice took place in the rail splitter's home State. Most of the members of his Cabinet deemed themselves of greater stature than this "political accident," and the Republican Radicals on Capitol Hill soon undertook to take party control out of his hands. He shrewdly spiked their guns in such dramatic episodes as the demand for Seward's scalp, and Chase's 1864 nomination bid, but had to turn from party to Union for second-term justification, and Sherman's capture of Atlanta re-elected him. The determined assault that Zach Chandler, Ben Wade, Henry Winter Davis, and their followers made on his restoration program was an earnest of trouble ahead. Lincoln had no such personal political machinery to keep State organizations in line as had served both Jefferson and Jackson. Had he lived, he would surely have been singed by the Reconstruction fires which almost burnt Johnson at the stake.

Cleveland was a protest against party — both against the Republican Senatorial oligarchy and the Democratic city boss machines. In 1892, as in 1884, he was nominated because of the enemies he had made, and in neither term did he learn how to lead his party. Little wonder Bryan took it away from him.

Theodore Roosevelt had a little more success as party leader, although this might have been a different story had Hanna lived. T. R. had a fair amount of skill in arousing public opinion back home against a senator or congressman who opposed him, but in general, the Republican majorities in both Houses responded reluctantly, if at all, to his pressure.

In sharp contrast was Woodrow Wilson, who registered his greatest successes as party leader and spokesman. Trenton schooled him for Washington and he exceeded Jefferson and Jackson in the method and the resultfulness of his employment of this role. Franklin Roosevelt equaled him in the first hundred days, but seldom thereafter.

Wilson was probably the greatest party leader among the Presidents — a fact particularly odd because he did not seem to have the particular traits to tie politicians to him by bonds of deep personal affection and love. He used public opinion to force Democratic recalcitrants back in line, he convinced conservative legislators to follow his lead, he made the Democratic caucus his agent for procuring legislation. It was not until the 1918 election took both Houses away that he lost his magic party touch.

Franklin Roosevelt has had a varied performance as party spokesman. In 1932 he took over the Democratic organization when it was a wreck from the Al Smith campaign. His huge majority came not because of party, but through general public dissatisfaction and distress. The bank crash made him almost a dictator, and solidified his hold on the party machinery to the point where he could get almost anything he insisted on. He used the Jeffersonian formula of team-play in talking to Congress, and in the 1933 Annual Message spoke of "building a strong and permanent tie" between the legislative and executive branches of the Government, under "the impulse of common purpose."

This lasted through the 1936 campaign, but was shattered by Court fight, reorganization bill, and Purge. Since 1938 there has been little more White House talk of any strong and permanent tie. . . . The President's hold on the voting public has been such that the party insisted on electing him to a third term, but this was not so much because of party leadership as because he could carry local tickets into office better than any other man.

In one respect, his service as Chief of Party has been quite deficient. Through twelve years of party primacy, Franklin Roosevelt has not encouraged the building of a party, as contrasted to a personal, organization; neither has he developed a new generation of growing party leaders to carry on his work when his own race is run. "What other Democrat is there except Mr. Roosevelt?" a columnist recently asked. "The party is Mr. Roosevelt and nothing else."

In time of crisis, perhaps the most important of the roles of our Number One Man is to lead public opinion. He might be termed the nation's Chief Morale Officer. This makes it pretty certain that, in any high crisis such as war or business depression, he will be caught on the horns of a dilemma which can almost be reduced to this formula: Since the President has sources of information superior to those of the mass of the people, he is presumed to know what is coming. Therefore if he knows, and fails to act, he is a knave; if he does not know, he is a fool.

Much of this "either-or" damnation was applied to Hoover in the 1929 depression, and similarly to Franklin Roosevelt for his failure to prevent that of 1937. This sort of criticism makes no allowance for the fact that if he knows and tells all that he knows, he will deepen the depression. Similarly, in connection with the present war, if Franklin Roosevelt knew its imminence and failed to act, critics would apply the first proposition; and if he did not know, the second. Such oversimplifications illustrate one reason why a President has such a hard time maintaining his leadership of public opinion.

Lincoln probably performed this essential function better than any other of the Presidents, with Franklin Roosevelt as the nearest competitor. Both have been sensitive to the climate of opinion, and keenly aware of the shifting public moods. Lincoln talked of not changing horses while crossing a stream, but never hesitated to shift his dependence of support from one to another group, his insistence being that he must keep a majority of Northern opinion supporting the Union cause. The chief difference, perhaps, between his basic method and that of F. D. R. is that Lincoln was willing to be a little in front and to lead opinion, while Roosevelt often seems to want the public to lead him. This is why he has found "timing" of the utmost importance. Be that as it may, the fact remains that Lincoln's careful but courageous leadership increased the unity of the Loyal States as the war proceeded, and was his greatest achievement in saving the Union.

Wilson's efforts, until late October 1918, were attended with amazing success. His speeches, letters and statements on domestic policy were models of clarity and conviction, while his handling of war issues after we entered World War I was almost an all-time high of effective persuasion. Jackson knew how to quicken the pulse of the common people, as the Bank fight demonstrated. Jefferson manipulated public opinion with considerable skill through his messages, but much more by suggestion to the party press. When he was confronted with the unpopularity of the Embargo he could find no way to offset it, and made no appeal to the people that had stabilizing effect. Theodore Roosevelt put great stock in the press as a corrective for G.O.P. opposition, and developed the launching of trial-balloons to a fine point. Cleveland had no skill at all in press relations, but depended on his messages and an occasional letter to get strength for his policies. Of the eight great Presidents, his handling of the formation of public opinion was the least successful.

One turns to the future with a feeling that the past gives some guidance to what perhaps we may expect. If the record has any core of meaning, it is that the way any individual in the high office will use his presidential power is altogether unpredictable. The employment depends upon the interaction of constants and variables, and of the two the constants seem less and less significant in comparison with the shift in nature and magnitude of the elements which shape the office at any point of time. In truth, change is the only sure constant in presidential power.

This should be a most comforting characteristic, instead of one to view with foreboding. Immeasurable as have been the alterations in America's social and economic institutions in the last quarter of a century, even greater ones can be envisaged in the span looming ahead. We have run the gamut of a war we thought we won, a few years of bitter faithlessness and false prosperity, then economic ruin and unimaginable distress. We recovered in part, only to be engulfed in a world-wide civil war in which our cherished institutions were at stake. These volcanic eruptions of the conflicts of force within Man's nature show no sign of cessation. The pressures of conversion from peace to war, in all likelihood, will dwarf in comparison with the perils of the counter-revolution from war to peace.

Irrespective of the individuals who occupy the White House during these kaleidoscopic years to come, it can be confidently predicted that the President of the United States will employ old powers in new ways, or discover new sources of power, if he even begins to cope with the crises which will continue to arise. It is of the essence that a President in a time of crisis find and employ power adequate to cope with the emergency. Weak men in the nation's high office will fumble as Buchanan. Strong men in time of crisis will continue to make great Presidents.

THE END

Bibliographical Note

The material on the use of presidential power is so large in volume and variety that I have not undertaken to present a comprehensive bibliography upon the subject. Several are already available, such as those prepared and revised by the bibliographical staff of the Library of Congress. The casual student will find in the notes to Professor Edward S. Corwin's *The President: Office and Powers* (New York, 1940) citations of sources which afford a useful guide to historical and juridical literature of the Presidency's institutional development. Likewise he might well consult the works cited in E. Pendleton Herring's *Presidential Leadership* (New York, 1940); Harold Laski's *The American Presidency* (New York, 1940); and Wilfred E. Binkley's *The Powers of the President* (Garden City, New York, 1937).

My own interest has focused more on the way the various incumbents used the powers and prerogatives of the position, and how they altered its nature. As a result, I have given no elaborate treatment of constitutional contentions or court debates over the office, but have concerned myself chiefly with how the office changed with the personalities who held it and the crises they had to meet. My reading has covered more than a thousand volumes, a number of which have been continually consulted, but most of them only incidentally.

A foundation, of course, is the official record, as given by James D. Richardson's many-volumed *Messages and Papers of the President* (Washington, 1897–1899), brought up to date with subsequent official publications. Then the collected letters and papers of the Presidents are invaluable in the sidelights they throw on background and motive of various policies and moods. The diaries of John Quincy Adams, James K. Polk, and Rutherford B. Hayes, and the personal apologia of Benjamin Harrison, Cleveland, Theodore Roosevelt, Taft and Franklin Roosevelt, throw great light on crises, conduct and self-justifications.

The works I found most useful in the Constitutional Convention creation of the office were Max Farrand, *Records of the Federal Convention* (3 vols., New Haven, 1911), a great treasury of fact and interpretation; Charles Warren's *The Supreme Court in United States History* (2 vols., New York, 1926); Burton Alva Konkle's writings on James Wilson; Corwin's 1940 volume already cited; the volume on *Pennsylvania in the Constitutional Convention,* by John Bach McMaster and F. D. Stone (Philadelphia, 1888), and the *Federalist.*

The two volumes on George Washington by Nathaniel Wright Stephenson and W. H. Dunn (New York, 1940) proved an illuminating guide to his presidential operation.

Jeffersoniana is voluminous in the extreme, including a "Cyclopedia" in which one can find apposite text to sustain any thesis. Francis W. Hirst, in his *Life and Letters of Thomas Jefferson* (New York, 1926), seems to have gotten at the nature of that extraordinary genius a little more understandingly than most of the other interpretive biographers, particularly as to the presidential years. Henry Adams' amazing series on *The History of the United States* (1889-1894) affords a strange combination of scholarly research and whimsical, often bad-tempered deduction, which makes it as interesting to read his brilliantly cynical prose as it is dangerous to adopt his conclusions. The literature on the Louisiana Purchase is enormous, some of it, like Everett S. Brown's *The Constitutional History of the Louisiana Purchase, 1803-1812* (Berkeley, California, 1920), is quite rewarding. Louis Martin Sears, on *Jefferson and the Embargo* (Durham, North Carolina, 1927) is first-rate.

No works on Jackson have been more helpful than those by Marquis James: *Andrew Jackson: the Border Captain;* and the later *Andrew Jackson, the Portrait of a President* (Indianapolis, 1933 and 1937). He knew his man perhaps more intimately than any other biographer of Old Hickory, even the contemporaries, and judged him sympathetically as to the entirety but sharply as to specific faults. Martin Van Buren's *Autobiography* (Washington, 1920) throws shadow as well as light on the Little Magician's relations with his chief. John S. Barrett's research and conclusions, in his *Andrew Jackson* (New ed., New York, 1931), have been helpful. The years between Jackson and Lincoln are pictured in detail in my own volume, *The Eve of Conflict: Stephen A. Douglas and the Needless War* (Boston, 1934), which has a compendious bibliography of sources.

The most useful work on Lincoln as President has been done by James G. Randall, in his *Constitutional Problems under Lincoln* (New York, 1926). Clarence A. Berdahl's dissertation on *War Powers of the Executive in the United States* (Urbana, Illinois, 1920) proved illuminating. My own research for *Conflict: the American Civil War* (New York, 1941) and *Abraham Lincoln and the Fifth Column* (New York, 1942) naturally had a shaping effect on the two chapters on Lincoln in the present volume. The general picture of the White House under fire from Johnson through Arthur is drawn out of another of my books, *The Age of Hate: Andrew Johnson and the Radicals* (New York, 1930), supplemented by H. J. Eckenrode's first-rate *Rutherford B. Hayes* (New York, 1930), Allan Nevins' *Hamilton Fish* (New York, 1936), and the standard histories of Oberholtzer, Channing and Rhodes.

Allan Nevins' *Grover Cleveland, a Study in Courage* (New York, 1933), together with the volume of Cleveland letters he edited that same year, are illuminating. George F. Parker's *Recollections of Grover Cleveland* (New York, 1911) is interesting and generally dependable. Denis Tilden Lynch, in his *Grover Cleveland, a Man Four-Square* (New York, 1932), has written vividly and often with sure understanding. But the best source on the Trustee concept and practice is Cleveland's own words, in public papers and his later Princeton lectures, *Presidential Problems* (New York, 1904).

Theodore Roosevelt's *Autobiography* (New York, 1913) combines naïve self-revelation and skillful justification of novel and impulsive action. It should be used in connection with Oscar King Davis's *Released for Publication* (New York, 1925), Joseph Bucklin Bishop's *Theodore Roosevelt and His Times* (2 vols., New York, 1920), and Mark Sullivan's sure-footed volumes on *Our Times* (New York, v.d.). Herbert Croly's *Marcus Alonzo Hanna* (New York, 1912) is the best treatment of the boss who became a statesman.

Woodrow Wilson's pre-presidential writings are essential to an understanding of his course of action in the White House and the Crillon, particularly *Congressional Government* (Boston, 1885), *Constitutional Government* (New York, 1908), *The State* (New York, 1895); and *The New Freedom* (New York, 1913). The biographies about him run the gamut from adulation to diatribe. In some ways William E. Dodd showed a deep understanding in his book, *Woodrow Wilson and His Work* (New York, 1921); William Allen White, in his *Woodrow*

Wilson, the Man, His Times and His Task (Boston, 1924), focused on defects that made Wilson the architect of his own misfortune. Ray Stannard Baker's monumental series reflects a better-balanced picture. Arthur D. Howden Smith's *Mr. House of Texas* (New York, 1940) portrays the latter's consequence to the utmost limits, to which Mrs. Wilson's *My Memoir* (New York, 1939) is a badly needed corrective. David J. Houston's *Eight Years with Wilson's Cabinet* (New York, 1926) has some good characterization.

On Versailles itself, John Maynard Keynes's spirited polemic *Economic Consequences of the Peace* (London, 1919) makes strange reading today, except as fascinating caricature. Allan Nevins' *Henry White* (New York, 1930) gives needed correction to the dogma of Wilson as a blinded Samson. Paul Birdsall's *Versailles Twenty Years After* (New York, 1941) is an admirably researched and rejudged appraisal.

The literature on Franklin Roosevelt is voluminous and confusing, as is bound to be the case when time lacks for perspective. Ernest K. Lindley's early volumes — *Franklin D. Roosevelt: a Career in Progressive Democracy* (Indianapolis, 1931); *The Roosevelt Revolution, First Phase,* (New York, 1934); *Roosevelt in Mid-Channel* (New York, 1937) — afford the most friendly picture of the candidate for the nomination, the conductor of the Roosevelt revolution of the first term, and to an extent the explanation of the disastrous defeats of 1937–1938. One after another of the discarded lieutenants have opened the floodgates of wrath, as George N. Peek and Samuel Crowther, *Why Quit Our Own?* (New York, 1936); Raymond Moley, *After Seven Years* (New York, 1939). "Genial Jim" Farley, in his *Behind the Ballots* (New York, 1938) did not go so far, but pulled the curtain back a little way. Carl Swisher's treatment of the Court fight and the Reorganization bill defeats in his *American Constitutional Government* (Boston, 1943) afford first-rate appraisals of these second-term troubles.

The present President's own private publications on the period throw considerable light on some of his words and deeds, notably, *On Our Way* (New York, 1934), and the ensuing series of *The Public Papers and Addresses of Franklin D. Roosevelt* (8 vols., New York, v.d.). While not all-inclusive, the omissions are often quite as illuminating as the insertions and explanatory notes.

The chief field of information on F. D. R.'s moods and techniques, however, is in the voluminous newspaper and periodical literature concerning him, together with the quasi-official books that have been issued by favored authors to show the rightness of his course. No one can map or estimate the accuracy or interpretive skill of this enormous hodgepodge of fact and fancy. In twenty years, perhaps, the grain will have begun to be winnowed from the chaff.

Index

ADAMS, CHARLES FRANCIS, Lincoln's Minister to Great Britain, 126–127; prevents recognition of Confederacy, 127
Adams, Henry, quoted on democracy, 34–35
Adams, John (2d Pres. of U. S.), his concern over his position as Vice President, 27–28; opinion of Washington's authority, 38; re-elected, 43; his term as President, 50–51; his judgment of John Marshall, 58; 24, 25, 32, 96, 207
Adams, John Quincy (6th Pres. of U. S.), opposes control of appointments in Louisiana Territory by the President, 63; Secretary of State, opposes joint action with England against European interference in the Americas, 78; elected President by the House, 79–80; thought Jackson surrendered to the nullifiers, 92; denounces Mexican War, 100; 54, 74, 84
Adams, Samuel, complains of lack of Bill of Rights, 32
Adamson eight-hour law, 217–218
Agricultural Adjustment Administration declared unconstitutional, 261, 262
Akerman, Amos Tappan, appointed Attorney General by Grant, asked to resign, 149
Aldrich, Nelson Wilmarth, Senator from Rhode Island, 187, 204
Altgeld, John Peter, Governor of Illinois, demands withdrawal of U. S. troops in Chicago railroad strike, 167, 168
American Federation of Labor, 269
American Tobacco Co., ordered dissolved by Supreme Court, 193
Anderson, Maj. Robert, ordered to defend himself at Sumter if attacked, 104; his concentration of forces disavowed, 105
Andrew, John Albion, war Governor of Massachusetts, 128
Annual Message of the President on the state of the Union, 38; Jefferson's, 56–57; F. D. R.'s of 1941, 296
Antitrust suits, 192–193, 196

Appomattox Court House, end of Civil War, 107, 139
Arkansas, Military Governor in control, 120–121
Arms Embargo, Secretary Hull seeks its repeal, 287
Army Reorganization Act, 142
Arnold, Gen. Henry H., Air Chief, 303
Arthur, Chester Alan (21st Pres. of U. S.), a reform President, 97; refused to accept a second term, 101; removed as Collector of Customs in New York, 151; becomes President on Garfield's assassination, 152–153
Article I of the Constitution, xiii
Article II of the Constitution, xii–xiii, 109, 147
Article X of the League Covenant, under attack in Senate, 248–249; XXI, to safeguard the Monroe Doctrine, 240–241; XXVI, 241
Articles of Impeachment against President Johnson prepared, 144
Ashurst, Henry Fountain, Senator from Arizona, hears plan of Court reform, 278
Ashwander Case, upholds TVA, 277
Atlanta, fall of, 114; captured by Sherman, 130, 219
Atlantic Charter, 297, 315
Aurora, Republican journal of Philadelphia, attack on Washington, and his retort, 48

BABCOCK, ORVILLE E., President Grant's secretary, involved in Whisky Ring scandal, 148–149; negotiates treaty of annexation with Santo Domingo, 149–150
Bailey, Joseph Weldon, Senator from Texas, 225
Baker, Newton Diehl, Secretary of War in Wilson's Cabinet, selects Gen. Pershing for Commander in Chief of the American Expeditionary Force, 212; 219, 316

Baker, Ray Stannard, 239–240
Balfour, Arthur James, at Peace Conference, 241
Ballantine, Arthur Atwood, Under Secretary of the Treasury, in bank holiday, 257
Baltimore riots, 114
Bancroft, George, American historian, his judgment of Polk, 101
Bank holidays, 257–258
Bank of the United States, established, with Nicholas Biddle as Government director, 79; fought by President Jackson, 83, 86–87; Jackson vetoes recharter, 88; removes Government deposits, 89; 90, 129, 318, 321
Bankhead, William Brockman, Speaker of the House, hears plan of Court reform, 278
Barbary State depredations on Mediterranean commerce, 40
Barkley, Alben William, 290
Baruch, Bernard Mannes, heads War Industries Board, 231; his "cash and carry" plan eases Embargo Act, 291; 257, 260, 262, 275
Bayard, Thomas Francis, Ambassador to Great Britain, in Venezuela boundary dispute, 171
Belmont, August, 204
Bemis, Prof. Samuel Flagg, 46
Benedict, Elias Cornelius, friend of President Cleveland, 156–157
Benton, Thomas Hart, has resolution against Jackson expunged from Senate journal, 89; on Jackson's hanging threat, 91; Congress asked to make him lieutenant general in Mexican War, opposed by Calhoun, 100
Berle, Adolf Augustus, one of F. D. R.'s "Brains trust," 254, 275
Bernstorff, Johann Heinrich, Count von, German Ambassador at Washington, is handed his passports, 228, 229
Biddle, Nicholas, made government director of second Bank of the United States, 79; opposes Jackson, 86–88; loses out in the election, 89; 95, 274, 318
Big Business, its evils criticized by Cleveland, 163; hatred of Theodore Roosevelt, 204
Bill of Rights, its lack complained of by Jefferson and Sam Adams, 32; justification for ignoring it, 111
Birdsall, Paul, his *Versailles Twenty Years After*, 234

Bismarck, Otto Edward Leopold, Prince von, 261
Bissell, Wilson Shannon, Cleveland's law partner in Buffalo, 158
Black, Jeremiah Sullivan, Attorney General, his interpretation of the Constitution on secession, 103
Blackstone, Sir William, English jurist, his *Commentaries* cited, 13
Blaine, James Gillespie, Republican leader, 137; Mulligan letters brought to light in his campaign against Cleveland, 155–156; 150, 206
Blair, Francis Preston, of Jackson's Kitchen Cabinet, 82; his efforts at negotiating peace with Jefferson Davis, 135
Blair, Montgomery, dropped from Lincoln's Cabinet, 130
Blennerhassett (Harman) "conspiracy," 59
Bliss, Tasker Howard, in World War I, 218, 230; at Peace Conference, 234; 316
Blockade, under Law of Nations, 110; cuts off Europe's supply of cotton from Southern States, 127–128, 315; by Britain, in World War I, 215, 227
Bolingbroke (Henry St. John), Lord, his essay *The Idea of a Patriot King* cited, 14
Borah, William Edgar, refuses Wilson's invitation to White House dinner, 238; "Isolationist" on Paris Treaty, 248; his challenge to Hull, 287
Bourgeois, Léon Victor Auguste, at Peace Conference, 236, 240
Bourgin, Frank, 56
Boutwell, George Sewel, one of the Managers in impeachment of Johnson, 146
Bragg, Gen. Braxton, his saying of Cleveland, "We love him for the enemies he has made," electrifies Democratic National Convention, 156; 114
"Brains trust," none at hand to advise Cleveland, 165; F. D. R.'s, 254, 275
Brandegee, Frank Bosworth, Senator from Connecticut, "Isolationist" on Paris Treaty, 248
Brandeis, Justice Louis Dembitz, in processor tax case, 262; 276
Breckinridge, Henry, 208
Bristow, Benjamin Helm, replaces W. A. Richardson as Grant's Secretary of the Treasury, 148; resigns as result of Whisky Ring scandal, 149

Brown, Jacob, at Battle of Lundy's Lane, 77
Brown, John, as to his responsibility for Civil War, 102
Brownlow, Louis, 208, 280
Bryan, William Jennings, gets control of party away from Cleveland, 164; Cross of Gold crusade, 176; responsible for Wilson's nomination for President, 204, 225; in Wilson's second campaign, 217; resigns as Secretary of State, 227; his help in McKinley's treaty with Spain, 249; 209, 319
Bryce, James, on the Constitutional Convention, 13
Buchanan, James (15th Pres. of U. S.), his conduct of the Presidency before secession, 102–103; reorganizes his Cabinet, 104; receives Commissioners from South Carolina, 105; agrees to send help to Sumter, 106; a target for Radical Republicans, 108; 5, 136, 256, 312, 322
Budd, Ralph, of the Burlington Lines, named on Advisory Commission, 292
Buena Vista, battle of, 100
Buffalo (N. Y.) ring rule cleaned up by Cleveland, 154
Bull Moose Party, 216
Bullitt, William Christian, on lack of military aircraft in Britain, France, 286
Bunau-Varilla, Philippe Jean, succeeds de Lesseps in Panama Canal Co., 186
Burchard, Rev. Samuel Dickinson, his "Rum, Romanism and Rebellion" speech in the Cleveland-Blaine campaign, 156
Bureau of the Budget, 280, 308
Bureau of Corporations, 193
Burleson, Albert Sidney, Postmaster General in Wilson's Cabinet, 208, 222, 229
Burns, Maj. Gen. James Henry, Executive Officer of Munitions Assignment Board, 300
Burnside, Gen. Ambrose Everett, the tragedy of Fredericksburg, 113; the Vallandigham case, 117, 139
Burr, Aaron, near election as President, 25; prevented by Hamilton's hatred, 53; trial for treason, 59; charges "Presidential persecution," 60
Burroughs, John, American naturalist, 189
Butler, Nicholas Murray, 234
Butler, Pierce, Supreme Court justice, 276

Butt, Archibald, friend of Presidents, 195
Byrd, Harry Flood, 283
Byrnes, James Francis, considered as running mate for F. D. R., 290; resigns from Supreme Court to head war agencies, 308; 303, 275, 282

CABINET, system established by Washington, 29; his appointments, 30–32; Lincoln's, 126
Cairo, meeting of F. D. R., Churchill and Chiang Kai-shek, 304–305
Caldwell, Prof. Lynton Keith, 55
Calhoun, John Caldwell, seeks Presidency, 79; his wife in social war, 82; takes up doctrine of nullification, 90; resigns as Vice President, enters Senate and makes deal with Clay for compromise tariff bill, 93; opposes lieutenant generalship for Senator Benton, 100; stirs up slavery question, 101; 74, 75
California, struggle in Congress over its admission as free or slave, 97, 101; its acquisition accomplished by Polk, 101; gold rush, 184
Cameron, James Donald, sought third term for Grant, 152; 318
Canada, attempt at its conquest by U. S. a failure, 76–77
Canning, George, British Prime Minister, proposes joint action against European interference in Americas, 78
Cannon, Joseph Gurney, 187; 204
Cardozo, Justice Benjamin Nathan, in processor tax case, 262; 276
Carmack, Edward Ward, Senator from Tennessee, 173
Carranza, Venustiano, 215
Cass, Lewis, resigns as Secretary of State, 104; 184–185
Cassidy, Henry, of the Moscow staff of the Associated Press, 304
Caucus system, used by Jefferson to enforce discipline, 63
Cecil, Edgar Algernon Robert, Lord, at Peace Conference, 236, 239–240
Chamberlain, George Earle, condemns Wilson's war efforts, 210–220
Chamberlain, Neville, at Munich with Hitler, 286
Chandler, Zachariah, 111, 122, 128, 137, 318
Chase, Salmon Portland, opinion of Lincoln, 107; letter drives him from presidential race, 129; resigns from Cabinet but is retained by Lincoln, 133; pre-

[331]

sides at Johnson's impeachment trial, 144; 126, 136, 318
Cherokee Nation, its treaty rights upheld by Supreme Court, but ignored by Georgia, 86
Chicago Times, suppressed by order of Gen. Burnside, 117, 316
Chicago Tribune, approved destroyer deal with Britain, 294; 132
Chickamauga, redemption of, 113
Chief of Government, President's constitutional duty and powers as, 3–4; Washington's achievements, 29–30; Lincoln's indifference, 107
Chief of State, President's prerogatives as, 3; Jackson's concept embraced by Lincoln, 107
Churchill, Winston Spencer, British Prime Minister, seeks war supplies from U. S., 294; confers with F. D. R. at sea over Atlantic Charter of the Four Freedoms, 297; comes to Washington for military planning between Britain and U. S., 299–300; meets with Chiang Kai-shek and Stalin, 304–305; talks to world through House of Commons, 308
Civil Service Commission, Cleveland's support, 159; to be replaced by an administrator, 280
Civil Service reform, its first impetus, 152–153
Civil War, problem of getting power to fight, 108 *et seq.;* 180
CWA, 266
CCC, 260, 265–266
Clark, Champ (James Beauchamp), beaten for Democratic nomination for President by two-thirds rule, 204
Clarke, John Hessin, leaves Supreme Court, 284
Clay, Henry, made Speaker of the House, 75; seeks Presidency, 79; Secretary of State under J. Q. Adams, 80; nominated for President by National Republicans, defeated by Jackson, 88; makes deal with Calhoun and passes compromise tariff bill, 93; becomes party leader on Harrison's death, 96; his part in the Compromise of 1850, 97; 84–87, 92, 206
Clayton Act, to modernize Sherman Antitrust Act, 210, 219
Clayton-Bulwer treaty, 184
Clemenceau, Georges Eugène Benjamin, at Peace Conference, 236–237, 239–243; 212

Cleveland, Stephen Grover (22d and 24th Pres. of U. S.), his removals from office, 83; position of the Presidency in his first term, 137; his rise to the office, 154; as Governor of New York, 155; his record as President, 156–164; his second term, 165; "Silver Letter," 166; Chicago railroad strike, 167–170; Venezuela boundary case, 170–172; receives visit from McKinley, 174; Theodore Roosevelt's opinion of him as politician, 177; on arbitration commission in coal mine strike, but operators reject him, 180; the 1893 gold panic, 251; his lack of skill in press relations, 321; 95, 153, 178–179, 199, 254–255, 312–314, 316, 318–319
Clinton, De Witt, 76
Clinton, George, 10
Coal strikes, 179–181, 196, 308, 316
Cockburn, Admiral Sir George, captures Washington, 77
Cockrell, Francis Marion, in clash with Cleveland over nominations, 160
Cohen, Benjamin Victor, 276
Colby, Bainbridge, made Secretary of State in place of Lansing, 248
Colombia, 185–186
Commander in Chief of Army and Navy, President's power as such, 3, 22; attention given by Washington, 39; Indian troubles, 40; Jefferson's aversion to a standing army, 72; Lincoln's problems over Civil War, 107, 108; Theodore Roosevelt sends fleet around the world, 181–182; Wilson's conduct of World War, 225, 226; F. D. R. as World Strategist, 288, 317
Committee for Industrial Organization, 269
Committee system in Congress, 37, 56
Committee to Defend America, headed by William Allen White, 293–294
Compromise of 1850, 97, 102
Confederate States of America, title decided on by seceded States at Montgomery convention, 102; British and French recognition feared, but prevented by Lincoln and Adams, 107, 127; ended, 135; 133
Confederation, its ills diagnosed by Madison, 12; ends existence of its Congress, 24; its army holdover, 40; 15, 27, 30–31, 33, 35, 46
Congress, its lack of power under the Confederation, 6; Madison's plan, 12; ends its existence, 24; First Congress

of the U. S. assembles, 26–27; establishes State, Treasury and War Departments, 31; committee system of transacting business instituted, 37; passes Non-Importation Act, 64; declares war against Britain, 76; struggle over admission of California, 97; its part in the Civil War, 110–111; Joint Committee on the Conduct of the War, 129; Wilson's complaint about the committee system, 199; under complete dominance of Wilson, 206; declares war on Germany, 229; resentment over treatment by F. D. R., 308; 142, 171, 172, 311

Conkling, Roscoe, political boss of New York, 97, 137, 147; denounces Garfield as dictator and resigns from Senate, 152

Constitution, powers it confers on the presidential office, 3; adopted by the Constitutional Convention, 5; "Separation of Powers," 12–13; its completion and final adoption, 21–22; ratified by States, 24; its application, 30 *passim;* Thirteenth Amendment, 120, 135

Constitutional Convention, creates the Presidency and adopts the Constitution, 5–6, 8; delegates, 10; presided over by Washington, 7, 17; adopts plan of a single Executive, 17; changes name to President, with Vice President, and provides term of office and method of election, 19–21; South Carolina's, 102

Cooke, Morris Llewellyn, 214, 220–221

Coolidge, (John) Calvin (30th Pres. of U. S.), his conduct as President, 5; teamwork with Mellon compared, 71; his Presidency a symbol of stock market prosperity, 97; 157

Copperheads, in Lincoln's Administration, 316

Corcoran, Thomas Gardner, in Court reform campaign, 279; 276

Cornwallis, Lord Charles, surrender, 28

Cortelyou, George Bruce, a Republican appointed to office by Cleveland, 156–157; 190

Corwin, Prof. Edward Samuel, 12, 139

Cotton-textile code, 268

Council of State, to assist the President, proposed in Constitutional Convention, but turned down, 19

Courier and Inquirer (N. Y.), financed by Nicholas Biddle with funds from the Bank of the United States, 87

Court reform, attempted by F. D. R., fails, 276–279, 282, 320

Covenant of the League of Nations, unanimously adopted, 243; before the U. S. Senate, 245; Article X under attack, 248–249; Article XXI, to safeguard Monroe Doctrine, 240–241; Article XXVI, 241; 237–238, 241, 244

Cox, Oscar Sydney, in lend-lease preliminaries, 294; 276

Crane, Charles Richard, 211

Crawford, William Harris, Senator from Georgia, 76; Secretary of the Treasury under Monroe, seeks Presidency, but is knocked out by a stroke of paralysis, 79–80

Crittenden compromise, 106

Croker, Richard, confers with Cleveland, 165; sneers at "ingrate in politics," 203

Cromwell, William Nelson, arranges purchase of the assets of the French Panama Canal Co., 186

Crop control, effect on farm prices, 261

Crowder, Gen. Enoch Herbert, 210

Cumberland Road Bill, vetoed by Monroe, 79

Cummings, Homer Stillé, in the F. D. R. campaign, 254; succeeds Walsh as Attorney General, 257–258; criticism of Supreme Court, 277; offers plan for reform of Court, 278

Curtin, Andrew Gregg, Governor of Pennsylvania, 128

Cushing, Caleb, Attorney General in Pierce's Cabinet, opinion on enforcing Fugitive Slave Act, 169

Czechoslovakia, seized by Hitler, 285–286; 291

Czolgosz, Leon, shoots McKinley, 175

DALADIER, EDOUARD, at Munich with Hitler, 286

Daniels, Jonathan, 276

Daniels, Josephus, Secretary of the Navy in Wilson's Cabinet, 252–253

Davenport, Homer Calvin, his cartoons of Mark Hanna, 175

Davies, Joseph Edward, debates on efficient government, 280; 208

Davis, Chester Charles, named on Advisory Commission, 292

Davis, David, Supreme Court justice, 110; wrote majority view in *ex parte Milligan,* 139

Davis, Henry Winter, enraged over pocket-veto by Lincoln, 122; 318
Davis, Jefferson, his hope in secret agents, saboteurs, fifth column societies, 133–134; refuses proposals for peace, 135
Davis, Norman Hezekiah, at Geneva Disarmament Conference, 270
Davis, Oscar King, friend of Theodore Roosevelt, 177
Day, Charles, 214
Debs, Eugene Victor, leader in Chicago railroad strike, 167–170
Debts of the Confederation, payment recommended by Hamilton, 33–34
Democratic Party, 79, 102
Dennett, Tyler, historian, discovers records of Theodore Roosevelt's secret relations with Japan in Russo-Japanese War, 183
Department of Foreign Affairs, in the new U. S. Government, retitled Department of State, with Jefferson as incumbent, 31–32
Department of Justice, seeking test cases, 276–277
Depression of 1837, 95; new one in 1937 checked by F. D. R., 282
Dercum, Dr. Francis Xavier, passes on Wilson's mental faculties, 247
Dern, George Henry, Secretary of War in Theodore Roosevelt's Cabinet, 256
Dewey, George, American admiral, takes battle fleet to Venezuelan coast, 183
Díaz, Porfirio, 214
Dickinson, John, American statesman, 8
Dix, Gen. John Adams, his arrest ordered by Gov. Seymour for suppression of New York newspapers, 118
Dodd, William Edward, describes plot to set up Theodore Roosevelt as divider of power with the President, 220; 226
Dominican Republic, its customhouses seized by Theodore Roosevelt, 182
Donelson, Andrew Jackson, Jackson's private secretary, 82
Donelson, its capture by Grant claimed by Halleck, 113, 121
Douglas, Stephen Arnold, his part in the Compromise of 1850, 97; battle with Buchanan over "Popular Sovereignty," 102
Dred Scott case cited, 264
Duane, William John, Secretary of the Treasury, removed by Jackson, and replaced by Taney, 89
Dubinsky, David, labor leader, 269
Dunning, Prof. William Archibald, 109

EATON, JOHN HENRY, Secretary of War in Jackson's first Cabinet, 81–82
Eckenrode, Hamilton James, biographer of Hayes, 152
Eisenhower, Gen. Dwight David, appointed to lead invasion, 305
Electoral College, method of electing President and Vice President and manner of appointment, 19, 71; Roosevelt-Landon contest, 274
Eliot, Charles William, President of Harvard, 158
Elliott, Harriet, named on Advisory Commission, 292
Ellsworth, Oliver, examines Constitution for President's title, 27–28; on President's right of removal, 37
Emancipation Proclamation, 109, 118–120; a military necessity, 133; 127
Embargo, brought forward by Jefferson, 65; blow to British labor, 67; Castlereagh on, 68; Gallatin declares force needed for enforcement, 69; repealed, 70–71, 223; 64, 72, 75, 314
Embargo Act, its liberalization sought by F. D. R. and Secretary Hull, 286–287
Eustis, William, Secretary of War in Madison's Cabinet, 76
Evarts, William Maxwell, of counsel for Johnson in the impeachment proceedings, 145; Secretary of State in Hayes's Cabinet, 150
Executive, a problem in the Constitutional Convention, 15–18; later termed "the President," his term of office, method of election and style of address agreed on, 19–21
Executive agreement, as used by Grant, a precedent for Theodore Roosevelt, 150; its use by F. D. R., 271

FAIR LABOR STANDARDS ACT, 268, 274
Fall, Albert Bacon, 247
Farley, James Aloysius, his part in electing F. D. R. President, 254; Postmaster General in the Cabinet, 256; in 1936 campaign, 274
Farm bankruptcy act upheld by Supreme Court, 278
Federal Emergency Relief Administration, 266
Federal Government, and "Dual Federalism," 12; employment of armed force by, 22
Federal Register, established because of Court criticism, 277

Federal Reserve, stiffens credit to avoid inflation, 282; Banks created by Wilson, 210; 166
Federalist, Hamilton's writing, 9; his comment on the Louisiana Purchase, 61–62; 242, 283
Federalists, appointed to office by Washington, 36; opposition to party and Hamilton, 43; many retain offices under Jefferson, 53–54; adopt Burr's cause, 59; New Englanders oppose Louisiana Purchase, 62; sweep fall elections in New England, 69; make last ditch fight against war, 75; party disappears, 78; 12, 24–25, 32, 51–52, 70, 84, 222, 318
Field, Stephen John, Supreme Court justice, attacked by Judge Terry, 169
"Fifty-four forty or fight," slogan on which Polk was elected President, 99
Fillmore, Millard (13th Pres. of U. S.), attains Presidency through death of Zachary Taylor, 96–97; Clayton-Bulwer treaty negotiated in his Administration, 184; 102
Fireside Chats, 259, 295, 308
First Congress of the U. S., assembles in New York, inaugurates Washington as President, 26–27; establishes State, Treasury, War Departments, 31; 145
Fish, Hamilton, Secretary of State under Grant, prosecutes American claims against Britain for losses through Confederate raiders, 149
Fishbourne, Benjamin, 35–36
Fiske, John, his story of fears of Bible burning by Jefferson's order, 53
Flood, Henry Delaware, at Baltimore Democratic National Convention, 204
Floyd, John Buchanan, Secretary of War in Buchanan's Cabinet, dismissed, 106
Folk, Joseph Wingate, 208
Foraker, Joseph Benson, Senator from Ohio, 187
Foreign relations, President's responsibilities, 3; problem in Washington's Administration, 43–44; Jefferson's activity as Chief of, 72; Lincoln's success in, 107, 315; T. R.'s record, 182
Frankfurter, Felix, 257, 275
Franklin, Benjamin, at the Constitutional Convention, 7–8, 10; his plan of a nonprofit Executive, 16; quiets bitter debate in the Convention, 17; 22
Free silver fight, in Cleveland's second term, 165–166
Frémont, Gen. John Charles, issues order freeing slaves in Missouri, is removed by Lincoln, 118–119; his candidacy for President ridiculed by Lincoln's reference to Adullam's Cave, 130
French Revolution, 32, 44
Frick, Henry Clay, 191
Fromageot, M., French legal expert at Peace Conference, 241
Fry, James Barnet, Provost Marshal General in Civil War, 210
Fugitive Slave Act, 169
Fuller, Melville Weston, appointed Chief Justice by Cleveland, declines Cabinet appointment, 159

GALLATIN, ALBERT, Secretary of the Treasury in Jefferson's Cabinet, 55–56; proposes internal improvements, 57; feuds with Secretary of the Navy Smith, 64; prefers war to the Embargo, 65–66; enforces the Act, 66; value of his teamwork with Jefferson, 71; 63, 70, 72, 314
Garfield, James Abram (20th Pres. of U. S.), assassinated, 152; 97
Garland, Augustus Hill, 140
Garner, John Nance, Vice President, hears plan of Court reform, 278; dropped as running mate for F. D. R., 290
Gary, Elbert Henry, of Steel Trust, 191
Genet, Edmond Charles, appointed by French National Assembly as representative in the U. S., 44; recalled on demand of Cabinet, 45–46
George, Walter Franklin, Senator from Georgia, 243; F. D. R.'s opposition to him futile, 283
Georgia, 86
Gerry, Elbridge, at the Constitutional Convention, 16
Gilmore, James Roberts, plans for peace, 134–135
Gist, William Henry, Governor of South Carolina, recommends quitting the Union, 102
Gladstone, William Ewart, 199
Glass, Carter, 256
Goethals, George Washington, reforms War Department, 221
Gold Reserve Act, cuts dollar gold content, 260
Gold standard, 251, 255
Government reforms, proposed by F. D. R., fail of passage, others enacted, 280–282
Grant, Gen. Ulysses Simpson (18th Pres. of U. S.), Whisky Ring cases, 60; his

[335]

capture of Donelson claimed by Halleck, 113; made Commanding General, 114; his bloody march on Richmond, 134; named Secretary of War *ad interim,* but quits, 143–144; asks repeal of Tenure of Office Acts when President, 146–147; record of his Administration, 147–148; accepts gift of team and equipage from Whisky Ring, 148–149; is refused third term, 152; 4, 5, 73, 125, 137

Great Depression, 163, 251, 255, 257, 312, 320

Greeley, Horace, thunders in *Tribune* for immediate emancipation, 118; his attempt at peace negotiation fails, 134

Green, Duff, of Jackson's Kitchen Cabinet, 82

Gregory, Thomas Watt, Attorney General in Wilson's Cabinet, decides railroads can be taken over, 230

Gresham, Walter Quintin, Secretary of State in Cleveland's Cabinet, dies, 171

Grey, Edward, Earl, Special Ambassador of Britain to U. S., 246–247

Grier, Robert Cooper, Supreme Court justice, 110

Groesbeck, William Slocomb, of counsel for Johnson in the impeachment proceedings, 145

Grundy, Felix, 74, 75

Guiteau, Charles Jules, assassin of President Garfield, 152

HABEAS CORPUS, writ of, suspended by Lincoln, 109, 114, 133

Haig, Sir Douglas, 212

Halleck, Gen. Henry Wager, his translation of Jomini's *The Art of War* impressed Lincoln, who made him General in Chief, 113; claimed credit for capture of Donelson, 113

Hamilton, Alexander, at the Constitutional Convention, 7–8, 12; his writing in the *Federalist,* 9; persuades New York to sign Constitution, 9, 24; his opinion of the common people, 10, 29; on Committee on Style, 21; in Washington's Cabinet as Secretary of the Treasury, 29, 31; recommends payment of Confederation's debts, 33–34; proposes establishment of a National Bank, 34; feud with Jefferson, 43; denounces John Adams, 51; hatred of Burr prevents election as President, 53; 17, 25, 40, 42, 45–47, 52, 54, 61, 226, 242, 283

Hamilton, Paul, Secretary of the Navy in Madison's Cabinet, 76

Hamlin, Hannibal, 130

Hancock, John, Governor of Massachusetts, 39

Hanna, Marcus Alonzo, permits nomination of Theodore Roosevelt for Vice President, 175; his labor views, 176; battle with Roosevelt for control of party, 187; 157, 188, 226

Harding, Warren Gamaliel (29th Pres. of U. S.), his Administration compared with Grant's, 147; signs joint resolution ending war with Germany, 250; 5, 97

Harper's Weekly, 202

Harriman, Henry Ingraham, 263

Harrison, Benjamin (23d Pres. of U. S.), his opinion of trusts, 191; 164, 313

Harrison, William Henry (9th Pres. of U. S.), elected by the Whigs, dies three weeks after inauguration, 96

Hartford Convention, lays basis for a New England revolution, 69

Harvey, George (Brinton McClellan), editor of *Harper's Weekly* and the *North American Review,* maneuvers Woodrow Wilson into Governorship of New Jersey, 202; his break with Wilson, 203

Hawley-Smoot tariff, 204

Hay, John, Lincoln's secretary, 126

Hayes, Rutherford Birchard (19th Pres. of U. S.), declined a second term, 101; entered White House under cloud of "the Crime of '76," 150; conduct as President, 150–153; railroad strike of 1877, 169; 137

Hayne, Robert Young, 91

Hays, William Harrison (Will), 220, 222

Henderson, Leon, named on Advisory Commission, 292

Henry, Patrick, sought as successor to Washington, 48; 24

Herron, George Davis, special agent in World War, 232

Hill, Lt. Ambrose Powell, 114

Hill, Gen. Daniel Harvey, 114

Hill, David Bennett, Governor of New York, 165

Hill, Isaac, Jackson's Kitchen Cabinet, 82

Hillman, Sidney, labor leader, 269; named on Advisory Commission, 292; returns to his union affairs, 306

Hines, Walker Downer, succeeds McAdoo as Director General of Railroad Administration, 246

Hirst, Francis Wrigley, quoted on Madison and Jefferson, 74
Hitchcock, Gilbert Monell, on committee to learn if Wilson was sane, 247; letter from President on Lodge resolution, 249
Holding company act, and its death sentence clause, 275
Holmes, Oliver Wendell, Supreme Court justice, in Northern Securities case, 192–193
Holt, Joseph, plans to send help to Sumter, 106
Home Owners' Loan Corporation, refinances mortgaged homes, 166, 260
Hood, Gen. John Bell, 114
Hooker, Gen. Joseph, his muddling in Civil War, 113; 124, 129
Hoosac Mills Case, 262
Hoover, Herbert Clark (30th Pres. of U. S.), the Great Depression, 163, 251, 255; his hard work as President, 254; meetings with President-elect F. D. R., 256; 293, 312, 320
Hopkins, Harry L., in charge of emergency relief, 265–266; target for accusations, 267; made assistant to President, 297; chief of Munitions Assignment Board, 300; 226, 275, 310
Hot Oil Cases, 277
House, Edward Mandell, enigma of his influence on Wilson, 224–226; sought to prevent his going to the Peace Conference, 234; urged Wilson to meet Senate in conciliatory spirit, 243–244; 157, 217, 235, 239–240
Houston, David Franklin, his judgment of President Wilson, 213–214
Houston, Samuel, President of Texas Republic, helps annexation to U. S., 98
Howe, Louis, his part in the election of F. D. R., 254
Huerta, Victoriano de la, leads Mexican revolution, 214–215
Hughes, Charles Evans, Governor of New York, 195; defeated by Wilson for Presidency, 216–217; discusses U. S. entry into League of Nations, 284; 222, 276
Hughes, William Morris, Australian representative at Peace Conference, 242
Hull, Cordell, and the income tax measure, 218; in F. D. R. campaign, 254; made Secretary of State, 256; heads delegation to London Economic Conference, 270; heads delegation to Pan-American Conference, 271; refuses to draft isolation embargo bill, 284; seeks repeal of Arms Embargo, is challenged by Borah, 287; warns that Japan might attack any minute, 298; goes to Moscow for conference, 304; his handling of foreign relations, 315; 269, 286, 291
Hunter, Gen. David, his freeing of slaves voided by Lincoln, 119

Ickes, Harold Le Clair, Secretary of the Interior in F. D. R.'s Cabinet, 256
Indemnity, for slaves seized in Revolutionary War, 46–47
Indian troubles, 40–41; sale of their lands, 189–190
Indiana treason trials, 133, 138
Inflation, efforts to avoid it, 282; F. D. R.'s "hold-the-line" program, 301
"Isolationists" in Senate, on Paris Treaty, 248; help kill treaty, 249; help kill Root's Protocol on World Court, 250; 288, 291

Jackson, Andrew (7th Pres. of U. S.), comes to office through political revolution, 73; conqueror of the Greeks and hero of Battle of New Orleans, 74, 77; nominated by Tennessee General Assembly, beaten in House election by J. Q. Adams, 80; elected President by a landslide, 81; his wife, Rachel, 82; champions Peggy O'Neale, 82; "spoils system" credited to him by propaganda, 83; his fight against the Bank of the United States, 84, 86–89; against nullification, 84, 86; re-elected over Clay, 88; triumphs over Bank, 89, 318, 321; retort to South Carolina's ordinance of nullification and secession, 91; Proclamation against the State's action, 92; his interest in the annexation of Texas, 98–99; Farewell Address, 108; 5, 79, 90, 93, 95, 126, 128, 135, 137, 154, 174, 190, 206, 209, 216, 226, 312–314
Jaquess, James Frazier, sees Jefferson Davis with plans for peace, 134–135
Jay, John, appointed Chief Justice by Washington, 30; goes to London as peace envoy, 46; treaty ratified, 47, 249; declines reappointment, 58; 32
Jefferson, Thomas (3d Pres. of U. S.), influence as party leader, 4; poor public speaker, 11; almost beaten by Burr

for President, 25; his judgment of Washington quoted, 25-26; in Washington's Cabinet as Secretary of State, 29, 31-32; opposes National Bank, 34; offers resignation over feud with Hamilton, 43; seeks neutrality in war between France and Britain, 44-45; his First Inaugural as President, 50; his manual of rules for the Senate, 51; condemns Sedition Act, 58; Burr trial, 59-60; purchases Louisiana Territory from Napoleon, 61-64, 187, 315; Embargo repealed, 65-71; his fears of a strong army responsible for unpreparedness in 1812 War, 77; 5, 40, 42, 46-48, 52-57, 72, 78, 80, 90, 94-96, 164, 194, 197, 207-209, 223, 251, 259, 312-314, 317-318

Johnson, Andrew (17th Pres. of U. S.), his succession to Presidency on Lincoln's assassination, 97; Military Governor of Tennessee, 121, 130; nominated on ticket with Lincoln by National Union Convention, 130; his effort to carry on Lincoln's restoration policy, 137; issues proclamation restoring North Carolina to the Union, 138; exercise of the pardoning power, 140; his "swing around the circle," 142; attempt to oust Stanton leads to the impeachment, 121, 137, 140, 143, 144; it fails of conviction by one vote, 144-145; 37, 95, 140, 150, 152, 155, 313

Johnson, Hiram Warren, Senator from California, ignored in Hughes campaign, 216-217; "Isolationist" on Paris Treaty, 248; 222

Johnson, Gen. Hugh Samuel, one of F. D. R.'s "Brains trust," 254; in charge of National Industrial Recovery Act, 262-263; resigns, 264

Johnson, Richard Mentor, protests veto of Maysville road bill by Jackson, 85; 75

Johnson, William Samuel, on Committee on Style of Constitutional Convention, 21

Johnston, Gen. Joseph Eggleston, 114

Joint Committee on Conduct of the War, in Civil War, 129; attempt at revival in World War, 218

Joint Resolution in Congress, a means of avoiding a two-thirds majority of the Senate, 99, 250

Journal of Commerce (N. Y.), suppressed by Lincoln, 117; victim of a hoax, 118

Kansas City Star, prints Theodore Roosevelt's desire for a league, 244

Katsura, Count Taro, signs "Memorandum" with Taft, representing President Roosevelt, 183

Keenan, Joseph, in Court reform campaign, 279

Kendall, Amos, of Jackson's Kitchen Cabinet, 82

Kentucky-Virginia Resolutions, 79, 90

Key, David McKendree, Postmaster General in Hayes's Cabinet, 151

Keynes, John Maynard, 243

Knox, Frank, made Secretary of the Navy in F. D. R.'s Cabinet, 293

Knox, Gen. Henry, Secretary of War in Washington's Cabinet, 31-32; 40

Knox, Philander Chase, as Attorney General under Theodore Roosevelt, prosecutes trusts successfully, 192; at dinner at White House with Wilson, 238; "Isolationist" on Paris Treaty, 248

Knudsen, William S., named on Advisory Commission, 292; appointed lieutenant colonel, 306

Ku-Klux Klan of Southern whites, 148

LANCASHIRE, its starving textile workers and the blockade, 128

Land, Franklin Knight, 211

Land speculation in Prairie States, 95

Landon, Alfred Moss, defeated by F. D. R., 274

Lansing, John, delegate to Congress from New York, 10

Lansing, Robert, Secretary of State in Wilson's Cabinet, 217; sought to prevent Wilson from going to the Peace Conference, 234; calls Cabinet meetings, is dismissed by Wilson, 247-248

League of Nations, what kept the U. S. out, 224; 236, 250, 284, 315

League to Enforce Peace, 239; 227

Lee, Richard Henry, proposes title for the President, 27

Lee, Gen. Robert Edward, crosses Potomac, 113; maxim on "Duty," 157; 114

Lend-lease, and the destroyer deal, 293; legislation enacted, 294; program extended, 296

Lesseps, Ferdinand de, builder of Suez Canal, begins work on Panama Canal, his company goes bankrupt, 185

Leupp, Francis Ellington, Indian Commissioner, 189

Lewis, John Llewellyn, re-establishes dominance of United Mine Workers' Union, 268; 269, 274, 308

Lewis, William Berkeley, of Jackson's Kitchen Cabinet, 82

Lincoln, Abraham (16th Pres. of U. S.), his strength in the Constitution, 3; his fumble in war, 4; election assured by break-up of the Democratic Party, 102–103; problems over Civil War, 107–108; suspends writ of habeas corpus, 109, 114, 133; his exercise of war powers, 109–115; Emancipation Proclamation, 109, 118–120; Vallandigham case, 116–117; his retort to Seward's assumption of Premiership, 124; success in foreign relations, 126–127; as propagandist, 131, 133; his "On to Richmond" order and General Order No. One, 132; assassination gives Presidency to Andrew Johnson, 97, 121, 131; a retrospect, 136; Wilson quoted on his spirit, 198; 5, 84, 95, 106, 125, 128–130, 137, 138, 140, 141, 154, 164, 190, 197, 213, 217, 219, 221, 227, 230, 251, 256, 301–302, 312–318, 321

Lindley, Ernest Kidder, prediction on F. D. R., 303; 255

Livingston, Robert R, his part in Louisiana Purchase, 61, 87; 92

Lodge, Henry Cabot, Wilson's bitter personal enemy, 234; at White House dinner with Wilson, 238; begins fight against Paris Treaty, 244; leader of "Reservationists" against Treaty in Senate, 248; 175, 316

Logan, John Alexander, sought third term for Grant, 152

London Economic Conference, 269

Long, Breckinridge, 208

Longstreet, Gen. James, 114

Longworth, Alice Roosevelt, her quip on F. D. R., 252

Lothian, Lord, British Ambassador to U. S., in lend-lease negotiations, 294

Louisiana, military governor in control, 120–121; Federal troops withdrawn, 151

Louisiana Purchase, territory bought from France, 57; opposed by New England Federalists, 62; appointment of all officers of the Territory in President's hands, 63; 61, 87, 187, 315

Love, Thomas Bell, 225

Ludendorff, Gen. Erich von, 229, 232

Lundy's Lane, Battle of, 77

Lusitania sinking, Bryan's note, 217; American lives lost, 227

Lyons, Richard Bickerton Pemell, Lord, British Minister in Washington, 127

MACLAY, WILLIAM, on the title of the President, 27; on powers of the President, 36–38; description of Washington, 39; insists on military force to aid tax collectors, 41

MacLeish, Archibald, 276

Madison, James (4th Pres. of U. S.), as Commander in Chief in a major war, 4; at the Constitutional Convention, 7–10; "best-informed man in debate," 11; his plan for Congress, 12; on fixing the extent of the Executive's authority, 16; agrees on neutrality in war between France and Britain, 45; service under Jefferson, 53; Secretary of State in his Cabinet, 55; his part in the Louisiana Purchase, 61; succeeds Jefferson in Presidency, 70; his conduct of the War of 1812, 76–77; re-elected, 78; 18, 21, 42–43, 47, 54, 64, 68, 72, 74, 85, 87, 145, 312, 316

Mansfield (William Murray), Lord, English jurist, 8

Marbury, William, claims property right in office, in *Marbury* vs. *Madison*, 58

Marbury vs. *Madison,* Chief Justice Marshall decides against the Government, then throws case out, 58–59

March, Peyton Conway, in World War I, 218; 316

March to the Sea (Sherman's), 114

Marroquin, José Manuel, dictator of Colombia, 185–186

Marshall, Gen. George Catlett, F. D. R.'s confidence in him, 302, 317; on the question of a second front, 303

Marshall, John, as possible successor to Washington, 48; succeeds John Jay as Chief Justice, 58; his action in *Marbury* vs. *Madison*, 58–59; Jackson's opposition to his decisions, 84; decision on Cherokee Nation treaty rights ignored by Georgia, 86

Marshall, Thomas Riley, Vice President of the U. S., 217; question of functions while President is abroad, 246

Martine, James Edgar, Senator from New Jersey, 203

Maryland, in conflict with Virginia over use of Potomac River and Chesapeake Bay, 6

[339]

Mason, George, at the Constitutional Convention, 10; proposes seven-year term for the Executive, 16
Mason, James Murray, Confederate diplomat taken from the *Trent,* 127
Massachusetts, suppresses civil war, 6; signs Constitution, 24
Max, Prince of Baden, agrees to Fourteen Points, 232
Maximilian, and his Mexican adventure, 127, 135
Maysville road bill, picked for veto by Jackson, 85
McAdoo, William Gibbs, made Director General of Railroad Administration, 230; resigns, 246; helps swing California for F. D. R.'s nomination, 254; opposed Woodin for Treasury post, 256
McClellan, Gen. George Brinton, in Civil War, 112–113; his procrastination upsets Lincoln, 118; fails to capture Richmond, 119; "slows," 132; 124, 317
McCormick, Col. Robert Rutherford, assumes credit for initiating the trade of naval bases with Britain, 294
McCormick, Vance Criswell, in Wilson's campaign, 217; 214
McKinley, William (25th Pres. of U. S.), as Commander in Chief in a major war, 4, 51; averse to Spanish-American War, 174; treaty with Spain, 249; assassinated by an anarchist, 175–176; 157, 188, 222, 226, 234, 252, 313
McNutt, Paul Vories, 290
McPherson, John Rhoderic, Senator from New Jersey, 160
McReynolds, James Clark, Supreme Court justice, 276–277
McReynolds, Samuel Davis, his amendments for cash-and-carry arms and munitions expire, 287
McReynolds, William Henry, made secretary of Advisory Commission, 292
Medill, Joseph, editor of the *Chicago Tribune,* 132
Mellon, Andrew William, and Coolidge as a team compared, 71
Merriam, Charles Edward, on plot described by Prof. Dodd, 220; 256
Merryman, John, 114, 316
Mexico, Government prepares to fight U. S. annexation of Texas, 98; President Díaz flees revolution, 214; revolutionists clash with U. S., Vera Cruz occupied, 213, 215

Michelson, Charles, in Court reform campaign, 279
"Midnight judges," appointed by John Adams, but turned out by repeal of the judiciary act, 58
"Mild Reservationists" in Senate, on Paris Treaty, 248
Military Reconstruction Acts, their effect on Johnson's command of the Army of Occupation, 140
Mill, John Stuart, 199
Miller, David Hunter, at Peace Conference, 240
Miller, Samuel Francis, Supreme Court justice, 110
Milligan, Lambdin P., conviction of treason overturned by Supreme Court, 138–139
Mills, Ogden Livingston, 220
Minimum-wage law of State upheld by Supreme Court, 278
Missionary Ridge, 113, 133
Mississippi, loss of her cotton market, 68
Mitchell, John, head of miners' union in coal strike, 179–180
Moley, Raymond, one of F. D. R.'s "Brains trust," 254; prepares proclamation for bank holiday, 257
Molotov, Vyacheslav, assured of opening of second front, 303
Monnet, Jean, of the British Purchasing Commission, 294
Monroe, James (5th Pres. of U. S.), his part in Louisiana Purchase, 61; author of the Doctrine, 74; Secretary of State in Madison's Cabinet, 75; succeeds Madison, announces his Doctrine, 78; 54, 61, 84–85, 87, 274
Monroe Doctrine, in Venezuela boundary dispute, 171–172; its principles in the World War, 228; fought over at Peace Conference, 239–241
Montesquieu, Charles Louis de, his *Spirit of the Laws* quoted, 13–14
Montgomery convention of seceded States, adopts title of Confederate States of America, 102
Moody, William Henry, 190
Morgan, John Pierpont, in the 1893 gold panic, 251
Morgan, John Tyler, Senator from Alabama, 185
Morgenthau, Henry, Secretary of the Treasury, 286, 294
Morris, Gouverneur, at the Constitutional Convention, 8; in Continental Congress, and Minister to France, 9; favors

[340]

election of Executive by the people, 18; on Committee on Style, 21; inaugurates system of doing business by committees, 37; succeeds Jefferson as Minister to France, 44; his view of Louisiana Purchase, 62; 12, 20, 22

Morris, Robert, at the Constitutional Convention, 8

Morton, Oliver Hazard Perry Throck, his attitude toward Lincoln, 128; controls Senate, 137, 147

Moscow Conference of Foreign Ministers, 269, 304

Moscow Protocol, 296

"Mugwumps," independent voters for Cleveland, 156

Mulligan letters, in the Cleveland-Blaine campaign, 155–156

Munitions Assignment Board, 300

Murphy, Charles Francis, 204

Mussolini, Benito, his Ethiopian war, 272, 285; 291

My Memoir, by Mrs. Woodrow Wilson, 226

Myers vs. United States, a case of removal from office by Wilson, 147

NAPOLEON, influences that led to his sale of Louisiana to the U. S., 61; haste to forestall his change of mind, 62; renews war with Britain, 64; invades the Spanish peninsula, 67; 65, 68, 187

Napoleon (Louis) III, his Mexican adventure with Maximilian, 127; 128

Nashville (U. S. gunboat), in Panama "revolution," 186

National Assembly of France, appoints Genet as representative in U. S., 44

National Bank, proposed by Hamilton, and established, 34; causes schism in Cabinet, 35

National debt, its reduction, 57; Jackson's desire for using the Treasury surplus in wiping it out, 84

National Defense Advisory Commission organized, 292, 295

National Industrial Recovery Act, 258, 263; declared unconstitutional by Supreme Court, 264

National Labor Relations Act, upheld by Supreme Court, 278

National Labor Relations Board, successor of National Labor Board, 268, 274

National Munitions Control Board, ex officio, 272

National Republican Party, its expansionist program, 79; part of its members form Whig Party, 83; nominates Clay for President, 88; 87

Navy, six ships provided for, 40; Jefferson's dislike of large one, 56; fleet sent round world by President Theodore Roosevelt, 181–182, 190, 196

Neagle, David, U. S. Marshal, kills Judge Terry, 169

Nelson, Donald Marr, chairman of the War Production Board, 306

New Deal, title traced to fusion of Theodore Roosevelt's "Square Deal" and Wilson's "New Freedom," 259; attempt to purge Antis, 283; replaced by "Win the War" slogan, 309; 275–276, 292

New Jersey, threatens New York with commercial embargo, 6

New York Times, 132

New York World, its distribution forbidden in Gen. Burnside's area, publication suppressed by Lincoln, 117, 316; victim of a hoax, 118

Newberry, Truman Handy, elected to Senate by dubious means, resigns, 244

Newman, Oliver Peck, 208; meets Wilson at Peace Conference, 235

Newton, Sir Isaac, mentioned, 25

Niagara River Power Treaty, defeated in Senate by two-thirds rule, 250

Nichols, Wilson Cary, 68

Nicolay, John George, one of Lincoln's secretaries, 126

Norris, George, 214

North American Review, 202

North Carolina, reverses rejection and signs Constitution, 24, 35; opposes the Embargo, 68; proclamation for its restoration to the Union, 138

Northern Securities Co., attacked by Theodore Roosevelt, 188; Supreme Court reverses itself and orders its dissolution, 192

NRA, 263–264, 267–268, 274

Nullification, confronting Jackson, 84; his purpose to defeat South Carolina's effort, 86; taken up by Calhoun, 99; Jackson's proclamation against it, 92

Nye, James Warren, Isolationist leader in Senate, 286

O'BRIEN, ROBERT LINCOLN, 156

O'Connor, John Joseph, victim of F. D. R.'s purge, 282

Office of Economic Stabilization, 308

"Office of Emergency Management,"

[341]

called "Office for Production Management," 295
Office of War Mobilization, 308
Ogburn, Prof. William Fielding, resigns from consumers' group in NRA, 263; on resemblances among Presidents, 312; 299
Olney, Richard, Attorney General in Cleveland's Cabinet, advises calling out troops in Chicago railroad strike, 167; made Secretary of State on Gresham's death, takes up Venezuela boundary dispute, 171
O'Neale, Peggy, wife of Jackson's Secretary of War, an embarrassment to his Administration, 82
Orders in Council, of the British Government, 47; Jefferson seeks their relaxation, 64–65; 75–76
Ordinance of Nullification, passed by South Carolina convention, 91; Jackson issues Proclamation against the authors, 92
Oregon, long voyage around Cape Horn hastens action on Panama Canal, 185
Oregon boundary dispute, 101
Osgood, Samuel, Postmaster General in Washington's Cabinet, 31

PAGE, WALTER HINES, characterization of Theodore Roosevelt, 173
Panama, Theodore Roosevelt's direct action, 179, 316; "revolution" encouraged by him, 182; Republic born and recognized by U. S., 186–187; 196
Panama Canal, 184–187, 189
Pan-American Conference, 271
Panic, of '73, recovery from, accomplished by Secretary of the Treasury Sherman, 150–151; in Cleveland's second term, 165
Pardons, constitutionality upheld by Supreme Court, 140; Cleveland's method of dealing with them, 157
Parker, Judge Alton Brooks, defeated for Presidency by Theodore Roosevelt, 187, 202
Party, political, as unofficial electoral college, 4
Party chief, President's position as, 4; Jefferson as, 4; Roosevelt studies Jefferson on, 72; Lincoln challenged as, 107; Wilson as, 319
Paterson, William, his New Jersey Plan at the Constitutional Convention, 12
Patronage, as handled by Cleveland, 158; his battle with Senate, 160

Payne-Aldrich tariff, 204
Peace of Ghent signed, 77
Peace Conference of Paris, 233–243
Pearl Harbor, attacked by Japan, 125, 282, 288, 298–299
Peek, George, urges farm recovery plan, 260; Special Adviser on Foreign Trade, 271
Pemberton, Gen. John Clifford, 114
Pennsylvania, its view of the Constitution, 23; signs, 24; goes Republican in 1808 election, 69
Penrose, Boies, Republican boss of Pennsylvania, 220
Pension bills vetoed by Cleveland, 157, 189
Perkins, Miss Frances, Secretary of Labor in F. D. R.'s Cabinet, 256
Perry, Commodore Oliver Hazard, his fight on Lake Erie, 77
Pershing, Gen. John Joseph, selected to command American Expeditionary Force, 212; his attitude in World War I, 230; 316
Personal appearances of Presidents before Congress, 207
Petroleum Administration, punishes violation of code that didn't exist, 277
Pickering, Timothy, treasonable correspondence with Britain, 69
Pierce, Franklin (14th Pres. of U. S.), 102, 169
Pierce, William, delegate to the Constitutional Convention, quoted on James Wilson, 8
Pinckney, Charles, at the Constitutional Convention, 8; his work on the Constitution, 9, 12; seconds plan for a single Executive, 15; objects to electoral college scheme of electing President, 20; opposes Article II, 21–22
Pittman, Key, Senator from Nevada, 272
Platt, Thomas Collier, makes Theodore Roosevelt Governor of New York, 174; forces his nomination as Vice President, 175
Platt Amendment, 271
Poinsett, Joel Roberts, against South Carolina's nullification, 92–93
Poland, invaded by Hitler, 273, 288
Polk, James Knox (11th Pres. of U. S.), his conduct of Mexican War, 4; elected on slogan "Fifty-four forty or fight," 99; Mexican War, 100; as Commander in Chief, 316; dies three months after leaving office, 101
Pomeroy, Samuel Clarke, his letter on

Chase drives Treasury head out of race for Presidency, 129
Post, Louis Freeland, 208
President, office of, powers under the Constitution, 3, 35–36; six aspects of service in, 3–4; created by the Constitutional Convention, 5; term, method of election and style of address agreed on, 19–21; Jefferson's interpretation of, 57–60; Jackson's expansion of, 86; at low ebb, 95; weak contributions by Fillmore and Pierce, 102; powers exercised by Lincoln in war, 108–115, 120–122, 131; Cleveland's use of, 172; broadened by Theodore Roosevelt, 178–179; Wilson's committee on the nature of, 214; its ebb and flow in F. D. R.'s regime, 309–311
Press conferences at the White House, 131, 211
Price Current, a new paper in Philadelphia, 69
Proclamation, issued by Jackson against the nullifiers of South Carolina, 92, 94; by Lincoln for troops and a blockade of Southern ports, 109–110; Emancipation, 109, 118–120
Progressive Party, 205; 216–217
Public opinion, President as leader of, 4; Tyler's failure as Chief, 96; Lincoln's ability as Chief, 131–133, 135–136; as handled by Cleveland, 163; as worked by Wilson, 211
Public Works Administration, 266
"Purge, the," 276, 282–283, 320
Purvis, Arthur, chief of the British Purchasing Commission, 294

"Quarantine" speech by F. D. R., 276, 284–285
Quay, Matthew Stanley, Republican boss of Pennsylvania, 181
Quebec, war-planning conference, 304

Race riots, as propaganda for Radical Republicans, 142
Radical Republicans, their challenge to Johnson, 37, 97; get control of both houses, 107; deride Emancipation Proclamation, 120; rage at Lincoln, 140–141; Managers in impeachment proceedings, 146; control of Grant, 147–148; their spread of hatred, 149–152; 122, 129–130, 137, 138, 141
Railroad strikes, 65, 167–168, 169, 305, 308
Railroads, taken over by Government in World War, 230
Randall, Prof. James Garfield, 108, 111
Randolph, Edmund, at the Constitutional Convention, 8, 10; presents the Virginia Plan, 11, 14; denounces plan of a single Executive, 15; appointed Attorney General by Washington, 31; issues proclamation of "neutrality" in war between France and Britain, 45; 42
Randolph, John, of Roanoke, dislike of Madison, 64
Rayburn, Sam Taliaferro, Majority Leader of the House, hears plan of Court reform, 278
Raymond, Henry Jarvis, editor of the *New York Times,* 132
Reconstruction, question of its effects had Lincoln lived, 140; Wade-Davis bill, 120, 140; 142, 169, 185, 258, 312
Reconstruction Finance Corporation, 166; revived in Hoover's Administration, 255; 260
Reed, James, "Isolationist" on Paris Treaty in Senate, 248
Reed, Stanley Forman, Solicitor General in processor tax case, 262; reports on Court survey, 277–278
Removal of executive officers, power of, 36–37
Reorganization Act of 1939, 295, 320
Representatives, to elect President, lacking electoral majority, 21; at inauguration of Washington, 28; 19
Republican Party, *see* National Republican Party
Republicans, pressure on Jefferson for offices, 54
"Reservationists" in Senate, on Paris Treaty, 248; help kill Treaty, 249
Rhode Island, remains out of the Federal fold, 24, 38; support of Federal Government sought through Washington's appointments, 35; ratifies Constitution, 39
Richardson, William Adams, appointed Secretary of the Treasury by Grant, replaced by Benjamin Bristow, 148
Richmond, saved through Lincoln's blunder, 113; ready for peace by negotiation, 133
River Queen, Lincoln and Seward hold conference aboard with Southern Commissioners, 135
Roberts, Justice Owen Josephus, in proc-

[343]

essor tax case, 262; shifts view in minimum wage law, 278; 276, 279

Robinson, Joseph Taylor, Senator from Arkansas, hears plan of Court reform, 278; put in charge of the bill, but dies, and the plan collapses, 279

Rogers, James, newspaperman, 189

Rogers, James Grafton, Assistant Secretary of State, 257

Rogers, John James, at White House dinner with Wilson, 238

Rogers, Prof. Lindsay, quoted on Wilson, 206, 210

Rogers, Walter Stowell, draws plan for White House press conferences for Wilson, 211; discusses plot described by Prof. Dodd, 220; arranges worldwide distribution of 14-point speech, 231–232

Roosevelt, Franklin Delano (32d Pres. of U. S.), his conduct of a planetary war, 4; studies Jefferson in party leadership, 72; incurs party hatred, 114; member of "Common Council Club," 208–209; his skill in leading Congress, 210; submits Root's Protocol on World Court to Senate and it is rejected by two-thirds rule, 249–250; activities of his three terms, 251; as Assistant Secretary of the Navy, 252; marriage, 252; attacked by infantile paralysis, 253; his "Brains trust," 254, 275; his Cabinet, 256; orders bank holiday, 257–260; farm relief, 261–262; signs National Industrial Recovery Act, 263; declared unconstitutional by Supreme Court, 265; conduct of foreign relations, 269–272; re-election, 274; Court fight, 276–279; fails to accomplish government reforms, 280–282; seeks to purge anti-New Dealers, 283; "Quarantine" speech, 284–285; with Hull seeks liberalization of Embargo Act, 286–287; as World Strategist, 288, 317; elected for third term, 290–291; names Republicans to his Cabinet, 293; personal correspondence with Stalin, 296; creation of combined command, 299–300; action in labor troubles, 301; his trust in subordinates, 302–303; meeting with Chiang Kai-shek and Stalin, 304–305; his authority under the War Powers Act, 307; labor relations, 308; replaces New Deal with the slogan "Win the War," 309; his likes and hates, 310; a near-dictator, 319; his most important role Number One Man, 320; 5, 84, 107–108, 128, 173, 190, 226, 243, 256, 266–268, 273, 289, 292, 294–295, 312–315

Roosevelt, Theodore (26th Pres. of U. S.), press conferences, 131; his use of the executive agreement, 150; activities as President, and the "Ananias Club," 173, 188; in Spanish-American War, 174; elected Vice President, succeeds to Presidency on McKinley's assassination, 175; characterization of McKinley, 176; ability as a politician, 177; called himself "steward of the people," 178; his *Autobiography*, 178, 190; sends U. S. Fleet around the world, 181–182, 190, 196; his conduct in foreign relations, 182–183; wins Nobel Prize for promoting peace, 184; Panama Canal negotiations, 185–187; as a phrasemaker, 188; love of outdoors, 189; his appointees, 190; prosecution of trusts, 191–192; his line of distinction between good and bad corporations, 193–194; attitude toward third term, 194; in conflict with Taft over party leadership, 204; his delegates bolt party convention and form Progressive Party, defeated by Wilson, 205; declines nomination of Bull Moose Party, 216; hatred of Wilson, 219; wild to get into World War, 230; declares Wilson has no authority to speak for American people, 233; faith in press as corrective, 321; his death, 294; 97, 211, 220, 222, 252, 259, 312–314, 316, 319

Root, Elihu, his creation of a General Staff for the Army, 195; Protocol on World Court accepted by League of Nations, rejected by U. S. Senate, 249–250; 190, 234

Roper, Daniel Calhoun, in the Roosevelt campaign, 254; made Secretary of Commerce, 256

Rosenman, Samuel Irving, 275

Rush, Richard, 76

Russia, war declared by Germany, 215, 224; withdraws from the conflict, 219

Russo-Japanese War, attitude of Theodore Roosevelt, and record of his relations in the affair, 182–183; 184

Ryan, Thomas Fortune, 204

SANTO DOMINGO, treaty of annexation with U. S. fails of ratification, 149–150; 196, 316

Schecter, Abraham, chicken peddler, his prosecution results in declaring NRA unconstitutional, 264, 268

Schofield, Gen. John McAllister, becomes Secretary of War when Stanton relinquishes the office, 145; put in charge of coal miners' strike, 180–181

Schurz, Carl, Secretary of the Interior in Hayes's Cabinet, 151

Scott, Gen. Winfield, at Battle of Lundy's Lane, 77; in command of warship at Charleston against the nullifiers, 92; in Mexican War, 100; offers his "Views" of the secession situation, but they are ignored, 103; protects the capital during Lincoln's inauguration, 106; recommendation of Halleck, 113

Secession, threat of South Carolina, 91; Attorney General Black's interpretation of the Constitution on the question, 103; and Buchanan, 312

Sedition Act, nullified by Jefferson, 58

Selective Service Act, passage procured by Wilson, 210

Senate, committee proposes title for the President, 27; its first rebuff to the President, 37–38; in battle with Cleveland over patronage, 160

Senators, their scheme of electing President dangerous, 21; at inauguration of Washington, 28; 19, 238–239

Sevier, John, 74

Seward, William Henry, on the President's duty, 104; signs order suppressing two New York newspapers, 118; informed of the Emancipation Proclamation, 119; assumes rights of Premier, 123–124; in *Trent* affair, 127; resigns but is retained by Lincoln, 133; 313, 318

Seymour, Horatio, Governor of New York, protest on Vallandigham case, 116; orders arrest of Gen. Dix for suppression of New York newspapers, 118

Sherman, John, Secretary of the Treasury in Hayes's Cabinet, 150; his antitrust act, 191

Sherman, Roger, at the Constitutional Convention, 8, 10; opposes a single Executive, 15–16; his "Connecticut Compromise" passes, 17; explains purpose of electors, 19–20; 22

Sherman, Gen. William Tecumseh, cited, 4; his march to the sea, 114; captures Atlanta, 130, 219

Sherman Antitrust Act, invoked against Northern Securities Co., 191; its first test, against the Sugar Trust, renders act null, 192; modernized by Wilson, 210; 193

Sherwood, Robert Emmet, 276

Shields, John Knight, "Isolationist" on Paris Treaty in Senate, 248

Silver, Government buying called for in agricultural bill, 261

Simmons, Furnifold McLendel, Senator from North Carolina, 208

Sit-down strikes, 274

Slavery, and Lincoln's view, 118

Slidell, John, Confederate diplomat taken from the *Trent,* 127

Smith, Adam, English economist, 199

Smith, Alfred Emanuel, Governor of New York, his efforts to head off F. D. R. from the Presidency, 253–254; 319

Smith, Arthur Douglas Howden, biographer of Col. House, 225

Smith, Ellison DuRant, "Isolationist" on Paris Treaty in Senate, 240

Smith, James, Senator from New Jersey, agrees to nomination of Wilson for Governor, 202

Smith, J. W., jailed for violating a code that didn't exist, 277

Smith, Robert, Secretary of the Navy in Jefferson's Cabinet, feuds with Gallatin, 64

Smith-Connally bill, repassed over F. D. R.'s veto, 308–309

Smoot, Reed, Senator from Utah, 97

Snell, Bertrand Hollis, Republican minority leader, backs F. D. R.'s efforts for bank holiday, 258

Social Security Act, 267–268

South Carolina, efforts over nullification fought by Jackson, 86, 90; his Proclamation against the State, 92; convention repeals its tariff nullification, 93; secedes from Union, 102, 104; suffers bayonet rule under Reconstruction, 148; Federal troops withdrawn, 151; 68

Spanish-American War, responsible for Theodore Roosevelt's becoming President, 174; 199, 270

"Spoils system," improperly credited to Jackson as originator, 83

Stalin, Joseph, his offer at co-operation refused by Britain and France, 285–286; personal correspondence with F. D. R., 296; winter campaign of

1942, 303; meets with F. D. R. and Churchill, 304–305; 302
Stanton, Edwin McMasters, Secretary of War in Lincoln's Cabinet, persuades President to sign an order suppressing the *New York World* and *Journal of Commerce*, 117–118; declared Tenure of Office Act unconstitutional, 143; his resignation asked for and refused, and results in Johnson's impeachment, 143–144; flees office on failure of impeachment court to convict, 145; 125, 126, 140
Stearns, Frank Waterman, friend of Coolidge, 157
Stettinius, Edward Riley, Assistant Secretary of War in Wilson's Cabinet, 221
Stettinius, Edward Riley, Jr., named on Advisory Commission, 292
Stevens, Thaddeus, assailed Lincoln, 128; proclaimed status of the President, 141–142; 147
Stimson, Henry Lewis, his early faith in Japan misplaced, 284–285; made Secretary of War, 293
Stone, Justice Harlan Fiske, in processor tax case, 262; 276, 279
Strikes, Chicago railroads, 167–168; railroad strike of 1877, 169; coal miners, 179–181, 196, 308, 316; sit-down, 272
Sullivan, Mark, compares the Roosevelts, 173–174; *Our Times* quoted on challenge to T. R., 180
Sumner, Charles, his co-operation with Lincoln, 126
Sumners, Hatton William, hears plan of Court reform, 278
Sumter, 105, 109, 123, 315
Supreme Court, upholds treaty rights of Cherokees, ignored by Jackson and Georgia, 86; upholds validity of charter of the Bank of the United States, 88; approves Lincoln's use of war powers without benefit of Congress, 110; decisions in *ex parte Milligan* and *ex parte McArdle*, 138–139; Eugene Debs and Chicago railroad strike, 168–170; trust decisions, 191–193; "Triple-A" processor tax declared unconstitutional, 262; NRA declared unconstitutional, 264; reform bill offered by F. D. R., 276–279; changes in personnel, 279
Sutherland, George, Supreme Court justice, 276
Swanson, Claude Augustus, Secretary of the Navy in Theodore Roosevelt's Cabinet, 256
Swartwout, Samuel, embezzlement as Collector of Customs, 83
Swayne, Noah Haynes, Supreme Court justice, 110
Swisher, Carl Brent, his *American Constitutional Government*, 277; 279
Swope, Gerard, in NRA, 263

TAFT, WILLIAM HOWARD (27th Pres. of U. S.), as Chief Justice, writes majority opinion in *Myers* vs. *U. S.*, 147; negotiates "Memorandum" with Count Katsura in Japan, 183–184; elected President, 195; Governor General of the Philippines and Chief Justice, 203; conflicts with Roosevelt over party leadership, 204; defeated by split in party, 205; attempt at tariff reform, 209–210; defends Wilson's going abroad, 246; 190, 211, 216, 222, 227, 234, 239, 241, 293
Taft-Katsura Agreement, revealed after Roosevelt's death, 184
Tammany, in disrepute, 155, 163; sends delegation to National Convention for David B. Hill, 165; 203
Taney, Roger Brooke, his elevation to Chief Justice by Jackson, 81; as Attorney General declared the Supreme Court had no authority over Congress in U. S. Bank case, 88; replaced Duane as Secretary of the Treasury, 89; grants writ of habeas corpus which was ignored, 114–115
Tariff, advocated by the Whigs, 84; "of Abominations," 90; favored by Calhoun, 90; new bill passed, 91; reduction accomplished by Polk, 101; Cleveland's little knowledge of it, 156; Wilson tariff bill battled in Senate, 160
Taussig, Charles William, one of F. D. R.'s "Brains trust," 254
Taylor, John, Senator from Virginia, 77
Taylor, Zachary (12th Pres. of U. S.), in Mexican War, 100; dies of cholera morbus, and Fillmore becomes President, 97, 101–102; 73
Tennessee, Andrew Johnson appointed Military Governor, 120–121
Tennessee Coal & Iron Co., stock bought by United States Steel Corp., 191
Tennessee Valley Authority, upheld by Supreme Court in Ashwander case, 277; fought by Commonwealth & Southern, 288; 273, 275

Tenure of Office Act, to undermine Johnson's power, 37, 142; its provisions and aims, 142–144; breaches rights of President, 145; repealed, 161
Terry, Judge David Smith, killed in attack on Justice Field, 169
Texas Republic, annexed by Tyler, 98–99
Thacher, Thomas Day, Solicitor General, on bank holiday, 257
Thomas, Gen. George Henry, 125
Thomas, (John William) Elmer, insists on devaluing dollar, buying silver, 261
Thomas, Lorenzo, appointed interim Secretary of War, 144
Thompson, Huston, 208–209
Tilden, Samuel Jones, 150
Tillman, Benjamin Ryan, in conflict with Theodore Roosevelt, 187
Title of President, forms proposed, 27
Tompkins, Daniel D., Governor of New York, 69
Treasury, its surplus, and appropriations by Congress, 84; its independence accomplished by Polk, 101
Treaties, their negotiation, 3; John Jay's, ratified, 47, 249; Cherokee Nation's nullified by Georgia, 86; effect of two-thirds rule, 249; Versailles, defeated, 249; Tyler's, annexing Texas, 249–250; Niagara River Power, defeated, 250
Trent affair, 127, 315
Tribune (N. Y.), 118, 134, 244
"Triple-A" processor tax declared unconstitutional by Supreme Court, 262
Trumbull, Lyman, assails Lincoln, 128
Trusts, Theodore Roosevelt's attitude toward them, 191; Harrison's opinion of them, 191; Supreme Court decisions, 191–193
Tugwell, Rexford Guy, one of F. D. R.'s "Brains trust," 254; plans acreage control, 261; 275
Tumulty, Joseph Patrick, 222
Turner, Frederick Jackson, on the effect of the Louisiana Purchase on the Constitution, 61
Tweed, William Marcy (Boss), New York politician, 148
Two-thirds rule, imposed on 1832 Democratic National Convention by Jackson, 99; beats Champ Clark out of nomination for President, 204; in the Senate defeats the Paris Treaty, prevents entry of U. S. into World Court, 249
Tydings, Millard Evelyn, Senator from Maryland, beats attempt at purge, 283
Tyler, John (10th Pres. of U. S.), elected Vice President with William Henry Harrison, becomes President through his death, 96; his annexation of Texas, 98–99; treaty of annexation beaten by two-thirds rule, but passed by Joint Resolution, 249–250; 152

UNDERWOOD, OSCAR WILDER, Senator from Alabama, 208
"Unconditional Surrender," announced as basis for ending World War II, 303
United States vs. *E. C. Knight*, decided against Government by Supreme Court, 192

VALLANDIGHAM, CLEMENT LAIRD, Ohio Copperhead, sent over to Confederacy, 116; trial for treason, 133; 139
Van Buren, Martin (8th Pres. of U. S.), compared to Talleyrand, joins Jackson, 80; made his Secretary of State, 81–82; picks Maysville road bill for Jackson to veto, 85; follows Jackson in Presidency, 95; beaten for another term by Polk, 99; the 1837 panic, 163, 251; 92, 96, 226, 255
Van Devanter, Willis, Supreme Court justice, 276; retires, 278
Venezuela, boundary dispute won over Britain, 165, 172; Kaiser sends fleet to seize principal ports, 182–183; 316
Vera Cruz, American occupation, 213, 215; 224
Versailles, Court of, Jefferson as Minister to France, 31; Treaty of, in World War, 234; signed, 243; beaten in U. S. Senate, 245, 250
Vest, George Graham, Senator from Missouri, in clash with Cleveland over nominations, 160
Veto, Howard White on Jefferson's use of, 64; pocket-veto by Lincoln, 120, 140; Cleveland's record, 157; F. D. R.'s, 308–309
Vice President, office of, created by Constitutional Convention, and method of election, 19; holders of office who became President, 96; their lack of strength, 98
Virginia, in conflict with Maryland over use of Potomac River and Chesapeake Bay, 6; signs Constitution, 24
Virginia Plan, laid before the Constitutional Convention by Edmund Randolph, 11, 14

WADE, BENJAMIN FRANKLIN, enraged over pocket-veto by Lincoln, 122; to become President if Johnson were expelled by impeachment court, 144; 128, 137, 318
Wade-Davis reconstruction bill of 1864, pocket-vetoed by Lincoln, 120, 140
Wagner, Robert Ferdinand, Senator from New York, 274
Wagner Act, 269
Walker, Robert James, 128
Wallace, Henry Agard, Secretary of Agriculture in F. D. R. Cabinet, 256; his acreage control plan, 260–261; running mate for F. D. R. in third term, 290; battle with Jesse Jones, 308
Walsh, Thomas James, Attorney General in F. D. R.'s Cabinet, 256; death, 257
War of 1812, 64, 85, 312
War Industries Board, 231, 257
War Powers Act, 307
War Production Board, 306–307
Warren, Charles, historian of the Supreme Court, 59
Washington, Booker Taliaferro, 188
Washington, George, takes oath as first President of the U. S., 3; presided over Constitutional Convention, 7–9, 22; inaugurated, 27–28; establishes a Cabinet, 29, 32; method of making appointments, 35–36; power of removal, 36–37; as Chief of Public Opinion, 38; takes command of militia in Whisky Rebellion, 41–42; re-elected for second term, 43; sends John Jay to London to get peace treaty, 46; his Farewell Address, 47; reactions on his retirement, 48–49; suffers party hatred, 114; Life by Woodrow Wilson, 200; 10, 17, 20, 23–26, 34, 39, 51–52, 54, 71–72, 95, 164, 198, 207, 223, 226, 274, 312–314, 317
Wayne, "Mad Anthony," 41
Webster, Daniel, his part in the Compromise of 1850, 97; 84, 92
Weems, Mason Locke (Parson), 200
Welles, Gideon, Secretary of the Navy in Lincoln's Cabinet, informed of the Emancipation Proclamation, 119; 126
Welles, Sumner, Under Secretary of State, sends matériel to Russia, 296
Wheeler, Burton Kendall, insists on devaluing dollar and buying silver, 261; delays hearings on Court reform bill, 278–279; leads fight against government reforms, 280

Whig Party, splits off from Republicans, 79, 83–84, 89; elects William Henry Harrison President, 96; ignores Fillmore as leader, 97; denounces Mexican War, 100; 101, 222
Whisky, Rebellion in Pennsylvania, 41–42; tax, repealed, 57; Ring, 60, 148–149
White, Henry, with Wilson at Peace Conference, 234
White, Howard, on Jefferson's use of veto, 64
White, William Allen, on plot described by Prof. Dodd, 220; his opinion of Wilson's attendance at Peace Conference, 234, 238; heads Committee to Defend America, 293; 228
White House Correspondents' Association, born of the press conferences with Wilson, 211
Whiting, William, his *War Powers Under the Constitution*, 111
Wickersham, George Woodward, on powers and duties of President while he is abroad, 245; doubts treaties can get through Senate because of two-thirds rule, 250; 234
Wilkes, Capt. Charles, his removal of Mason and Slidell from *Trent* disapproved, 127
Wilkinson, Gen. James, in Burr treason trial, 60
Williams, Clay, in NRA, 263
Willkie, Wendell Lewis, nominated for President by Republicans, 288; defeated by F. D. R., 291
Wilmot Proviso, 100
Wilson, Henry, Republican leader, 137
Wilson, James, at Constitutional Convention, 6, 9; becomes Agent General for King of France, 8; offers plan of a single Executive, 15–16; chairman of "Committee on Detail," 17; favors electoral college method of electing President and Vice President, 20–21; persuades Pennsylvania to sign Constitution, 24; 25
Wilson, (Thomas) Woodrow (28th Pres. of U. S.), as Commander in Chief in a major war, 4; studied Jefferson as party leader, 72; abandons press conferences, 131, 211; his removal of a postmaster upheld by Supreme Court, 147; likened to Lincoln and Jefferson, 197; quoted on the spirit of Lincoln, 198; sneered at as the "scholar in politics," 198; his *Congressional*

Government quoted, 199; marries Ellen Axson, 199–200; his *Constitutional Government* quoted, 200–201; as president of Princeton, 201; elected Governor of New Jersey through maneuvers of George Harvey, 202; breaks with him, 202, 203; defeats both Taft and Roosevelt for President, 205; his dominance of Congress, 206; appears in person before that body to urge measures, 207; method of leading Congress, 208–209; confidence in his appointees, 212; his "one-track mind," 213; the New Freedom, 214; Mexican revolution and occupation of Vera Cruz, 215; World War I and re-election to a second term, 216 *et seq.;* hailed as "most powerful ruler in the world," 223; his conduct of the war, 225, 226, 230–233; felicity as phrasemaker, 227; attends Peace Conference, 234–244, 315; attacked by stroke, 245–248; Paris Treaty killed, 249–250; greatest party leader among Presidents, 319; 5, 71, 107, 125, 128, 154, 157, 210, 228–229, 256, 259, 308, 312–317, 321

Wilson, William Lyne, battle over his tariff bill in Senate, 160; considered by Cleveland as Assistant President, 165–166

Wilson, Mrs. Woodrow, in *My Memoir* quotes her husband on Col. House's compromises, 226; 246–247

Wirt, William, government counsel in Burr treason trial, 60

Wood, Leonard, refused a command in World War I, 230

Woodin, William Hartman, Secretary of the Treasury in F. D. R.'s Cabinet, 256

Woolley, Robert Wickliffe, 208, 222; in Wilson campaign, 217

World Court, defeated in Senate by two-thirds rule, 249–250

World War I, its start, 215–216; Joint Resolution in Congress ends U. S. part, 250; 128, 131, 224, 252, 294, 301, 314, 316, 321

World War II, begins, 287; 271, 274

WPA, 267